IRAQ

A POLITICAL HISTORY
FROM INDEPENDENCE
TO OCCUPATION

IRAQ

A POLITICAL HISTORY
FROM INDEPENDENCE
TO OCCUPATION

Adeed Dawisha

PRINCETON UNIVERSITY PRESS

PRINCETON AND OXFORD

Copyright © 2009 by Princeton University Press
Published by Princeton University Press, 41 William Street,
Princeton, New Jersey 08540
In the United Kingdom: Princeton University Press, 6 Oxford Street,
Woodstock, Oxfordshire OX20 1TW

All Rights Reserved

ISBN: 978-0-691-13957-9

Library of Congress Control Number: 2008940035

British Library Cataloging-in-Publication Data is available

This book has been composed in Adobe Garamond

Printed on acid-free paper ∞

press.princeton.edu

Printed in the United States of America

10   9   8   7   6   5   4   3   2   1

For Karen

CONTENTS

ACKNOWLEDGMENTS

The research for this book was facilitated by the generous support of a number of institutions. The Carnegie Foundation of New York selected me as a Carnegie Scholar for the academic year 2004–2005. Freed from teaching and administrative duties, I was able to devote myself fully to the project. Indeed, during that year, the bulk of the research for the book was done. A travel grant from Miami University's Philip and Elaina Hampton Fund for Faculty International Initiatives allowed me to undertake two trips to Lebanon to work in the extensive archives of the Jafet Library of the American University of Beirut (AUB). I am grateful to AUB's President, Professor John Waterbury, his office, and the staff of the library for facilitating my work in that great institution. I spent many "dusty" hours in the Department of Special Collections, situated in the basement of the library, consulting Iraqi archives that extended all the way back to the early 1920s. I was also able to secure a grant for the summer of 2006 from the American Academic Research Institute in Iraq (TAARII), which allowed me to write Chapters Four, Five and Six, and thus complete the analysis of the monarchical period.

I also wish to thank members of my graduate class in 2005 and 2006 who contributed to my own understanding of the conceptual bases of the book. David Rashid, a young undergraduate, offered to help with research for the book during the spring semester of 2006. In thirty years of research and writing, I had never used research assistants, but David was insistent and I took him on, and he did not disappoint.

In some parts of the manuscript I have drawn on material that I had published earlier in issues of the *Middle East Journal* and the *Journal of Democracy.* I am grateful to the editors and publishers of these journals for granting me permission to reprint segments of my articles in this book.

IRAQ

A POLITICAL HISTORY
FROM INDEPENDENCE
TO OCCUPATION

Introduction

This book examines the political development of Iraq from the inception of the state in 1921 to the post-2003 years of political and societal turmoil. Its premise is that from the very beginning of the state the Iraqi project in fact devolved into three undertakings: the consolidation of the state and its governing institutions, the legitimization of the state through the framing of democratic structures, and the creation of an overarching, and thus unifying, national identity. The book is different from other studies of Iraq's political history,[1] in that it traces the development of each of the three projects of governance, democracy, and national identity separately, while at the same time highlighting the way they impacted and shaped one another.

The idea for this book took shape in the post-2003 period as I searched for answers and tried to make sense of the quagmire into which Iraq seemed to be sinking. A few months into the American occupation of the country, there were signs of a promising future: the end of a brutal tyranny, plans for a liberal constitution, hope for economic rejuvenation, and the possibility of a democratic Iraq that would become the beacon for fundamental political transformations in other Arab states, mired as they were (and still are) in authoritarian cultures and practices.

There were disquieting signs, too. The new masters, strangely unschooled in the complexities of the land over which they now held dominion, seemed unable to understand the nuances of the country they were supposed to administer. The Department of Defense had focused its energies and resources on winning the war against Saddam Husayn's army, but once that task was brilliantly accomplished in April 2003 the administrators of the victorious power dealt ineptly with ensuing post-war problems. Indeed, they contributed to these problems by implementing a number of imprudent policies. One such policy was the disbanding of the Iraqi armed forces, which left a dangerous security void that was quickly filled by enemies of the new political order.

There can be little doubt that in the initial crucial months after toppling Saddam valuable time was wasted by the American administration in Iraq. While the civilian and military administrators dithered and meandered, Ba'thist diehards and disaffected officers, who had been in total disarray at the end of the military campaign, found time to organize against the new order. To the surprise of those who had followed the deliberate build up toward the war, the United States seemed to lack a comprehensive plan for the development and reconstruction of the country which the administration had promised, and indeed had intended, to embark immediately upon.[2] As the American effort began to stall, and the promise of a rejuvenated Iraq began to fade in the face of administrative ineptitude and indigenous violence, even those Iraqis who initially had welcomed the forcible removal of Saddam's procrustean dictatorship would soon begin to eye the American endeavor with mounting frustration. Later on, a few years of futility would turn frustration into outright hostility.

The hope that handing over sovereignty to the Iraqis in the summer of 2004 would steer the country back onto the path of purposeful governance and peaceful political development would soon dissipate as successive governments, first appointed by the Americans, later elected by the Iraqis, would fail in the most rudimentary functions of governance. Indeed, five years into the new era, the living conditions of Iraqis had sunk into an abyss of misery and malcontent.[3] And this would be compounded by the inability of the state to provide security for its citizens. To Max Weber, who defines the state as possessing "a monopoly over the legitimate use of physical force,"[4] security is paramount. The state should be able to project power throughout its geographic domain, and if a threat to its dominance should arise, the state should have the capacity to subdue it. The post-2003 Iraqi state, however, was simply unable to meet these criteria. Neither in facing the Sunni insurgents, nor in confronting the various Shi'ite militias, were state security forces a match for their belligerent local adversaries. Five years after the collapse of Saddam's political order the state was still unable to extend essential services and provide a secure environment for its citizens, with the result that in the perceptions of Iraqis, state institutions would recede almost into irrelevance.

But the predicament of post-2003 Iraq could not be confined only to the seeming failure of the state in discharging its basic responsibilities. Concomitant with the efforts by the Americans and their Iraqi allies to establish and cement the authority of the state, the results of which were middling at best, were two other projects: maintaining an internally cohesive social order and thereby sustaining an overarching national identity, as well as creating durable democratic institutions. As for the former, there were disturbing signs early in the occupation of a visible and vociferous rise of ethnosectarian loyalties as the primary elements of identity. The communal divide would soon become violent, spreading in scope with the passage of time, and the conflict would shift from a confrontation between the American forces and the "Resistance" to intracommunal violence in which Sunnis and Shi'ites shed the blood of one another with seemingly carefree abandon. This inevitably would lead to the flight of over 2 million Iraqis to neighboring countries, and perhaps a million or so others displaced inside the country, as internal cross-migration accelerated in response to either targeted attacks and threats, or people's propensity to be with their own folk in situations of pervasive violence and fear. What ensued was a country largely divided along ethnosectarian lines. Even the capital city, Baghdad, which had always been viewed and portrayed as the archetypal melting pot of Iraq's various communities, became, five years into the new era, a perceptibly divided city with its eastern neighborhoods predominantly Shi'ite, and its western areas mainly Sunni.

Nor would the third American project of creating resilient democratic attitudes and institutions meet with more palpable success. Sabotaged by ethnosectarian loyalties that were to lead to rigid political cleavages, democracy would become hostage to narrow particularistic concerns. In the wake of the December 2005 general elections, which created so much hope and optimism, by drawing four out of five eligible Iraqis to the voting booths, over 90 percent of parliamentary seats ended up being distributed among parties and coalitions that were all defined by ethnic and sectarian identities. Indeed the party with the largest number of seats, the Shi'ite United Iraqi Alliance (UIA) was formed at the urging of, and had as its mentor, Grand Ayatollah 'Ali al-Sistani.

It came as no surprise therefore that the members of the national assembly, reflecting voter preferences, would succumb to highly partisan political behavior that focused on promoting narrow interests at the expense of the public good. Legislative achievements were notable for their stunning mediocrity. Unbridled recriminations abounded, but bills or initiatives of consequence for the country were hardly discussed, let alone acted upon. Indeed, as governmental ineptitude and societal fracture grew with time, the assembly members, the supposedly quintessential agents of the democratic ideal, likewise would distance themselves from the country's pressing needs and problems, responding to no urgency beyond the demands of their own political lethargy.

As America's footprints sank deeper in the treacherous quicksand of Iraq's discords and tensions, it was obvious that the seeming failure of the American project in Iraq was not just a failure of state institutions, but one also of molding a unified Iraqi identity and of fashioning robust representative institutions. The primary culprit, it seemed, was the prevalence of an entrenched ethnosectarian mindset that would disrupt institutional stability and turn democracy into an extension of the interests of competing local groups. In such an environment, doubts would be raised about the ability of the United States and its Iraqi allies to hold Iraq together in a fashion that would resemble the country that had existed for over eight decades.[5]

But was the American endeavor really so unique, indeed so alien, to Iraq that it was bound to fail? In fact, there is a compelling argument to be made that the probability of communal conflict was pretty high given the nature of Iraqi society and the Iraqi state. While American and subsequent Iraqi policies might have contributed to, even accelerated, ethnosectarian entrenchments, they did not create them. The fragility of the social order was structural to the land of Mesopotamia, and was a function of the complex relationship between the state and its institutions on the one hand and indigenous social units espousing complex identities on the other hand.

The narrative of a socially fractured Iraq and the way the state tried to deal with this seemingly structural problem did not arise after April 2003. The story is as old as the history of the Iraqi state itself, born from the forcible amalgamation of three Ottoman provinces after the collapse of the Istanbul-based multi-national Ottoman Empire in the wake of World War I. This was hardly unique to the case of Iraq; the post-World War I exercise of state-creation in the Middle East reflected the general reorganization of British and French imperial interests in the area.[6] States were thus created not necessarily in response to the national demands of indigenous populations, but to satisfy the political and economic interests of the imperial powers. The resultant artificial creations were faced not only with the task of governing, an already difficult undertaking, but also with fusing multiple, and more often than not conflictual, indigenous identities and interests.

There can be little doubt that a major obstacle to stability was the country's manifold identities, which were complex as well as competing. From the early beginnings of the Iraqi state, the ruling elite and their British patrons recognized the potentially fissiparous nature of Iraqi society, divided as it was among Sunnis, Shi'ites and Kurds, and exacerbated by a pronounced urban-rural divide. A number of strategies were adopted to narrow the various societal dislocations: embracing an all-encompassing nationalism, advocating secularism, and endeavoring to build national institutions (schools and colleges, the army, the bureaucracy, etc.) to overcome fissiparous communal loyalties. The project to create a national identity, to sculpt a "nation" out of the different and disparate communities, became a critical undertaking as essential to the future of Iraq as building state institutions and creating an effective and credible process of governance.

The British and the newly crowned king also recognized early on in the monarchical period (1921–1958) that a key route to amalgamating the country's disparate groups into a coherent whole was through the construction of civic institutions. Concepts such as the rule of law, civil liberties, competitive elections, the guaranteeing of minority and other communal rights, et cetera would be incorporated into the body politic through constitutional design, with the hope that the different groups would be brought willingly into the political bargain. Thus, very soon after the state was born in 1921, the governing elite (which included the British during the mandate period, 1921–1932) agreed to hold elections for a constituent assembly that would, among other tasks, turn the infant country into a democratic, constitutional monarchy.

The problem, however, was that the two projects of building strong central governing structures, so vital for a socially fractured society, and of creating representative institutions that would legitimize the political order, but by definition would constrain governmental action, were bound to clash. Thus, members of the governing elite, while recognizing the benefits of democracy for the legitimacy of the political order, were also hardly enamored with the prospect of ceding power in a truly meaningful way. As we shall see, throughout the monarchy and into the first few years of the republican period, an almost schizophrenic attitude toward democracy existed among Iraq's rulers. This is clearly discernible in the country's uneven march toward democratic ideals and practices, in which democracy would go through an extended period of harassment, and then suddenly allowed to function, only to be harassed yet again. Even so, governance in the monarchical period was imbued with enough civility and self-restraint to allow it to tolerate oppositional views and activities, if not consistently throughout the time of the monarchy, then at least for significant periods within it.

The ethnosectarian societal structure and the idea of democracy were thus in no way unique to post-2003 Iraq; they presented similar problems and opportunities to the ruling elites in the more than eight decades that predated April 2003. The critical difference lay in the realm of political institutions. In the more than eight decades of monarchical and republican rule, government, parliament, political parties, civic organizations, et cetera never advertised themselves as anything but national institutions with national agendas. The motives for this stand may not have been particularly palatable to the ideological puritan. These were not the kind of intentions heartily applauded by the committed followers of secular nationalism. There was always the suspicion that beyond their constant and passionate proclamations of fidelity to the nationalist cause, the ruling elite, the bulk of which belonged to the Sunni minority, recognized their unquestionable need for a national project in order to defray the inevitable resentment of the other groups, especially the majority Shi'ites. Be that as it may, until 2003, Iraq's successive rulers presented themselves and advertised their policies as nothing but nationally oriented, even when at times reality fell short of the stated ideal.

In contrast, ethnosectarian factors were to become the main determinants of institutional structures and policy preferences in the post-2003 period. Governmental and bureaucratic positions were apportioned in accordance with ethnic and sectarian criteria, and this was publicly lauded and lionized as the only way forward for the country. Societal segmentation was also evident in the structure and purpose of political parties, and in the singularly partisan deliberations of the national assembly. In such a milieu, ethnosectarianism would be embedded in the body politic of the country, and would reside at the forefront of peoples' consciousness. There is no more compelling explanation as to why the Iraqi state remained resilient for over 80 years and why it unraveled so quickly after 2003.

Whatever the differences and similarities in the pre- and post-2003 Iraq, the one thing that emerges clearly from a discussion of Iraqi politics and history is that the Iraqi project was essentially three separate, yet interrelated, functional projects, each of which was pursued through a specific agenda, but all of which would have one common goal—the sustenance of an Iraqi nation-state. The task for Iraq's political elite throughout the country's political development was the building of state governing structures, creating a national identity, and fostering democratic institutions that would legitimize the state and its governing elite and help promote national consolidation.

The concluding chapter of this book tries to make sense of a simple yet pertinent query: is Iraq withering away? This of course does not necessarily mean the demise of Iraq as a legally constituted sovereign state, or its ultimate dismemberment. The question is whether there will be an Iraq that would resemble the country as it existed from 1921 to 2003, a sovereign, seemingly unified member of the international community. As I pondered this puzzle, it seemed to me that the most useful and effective way to make sense of the post-2003 apparent waning of the country—the failures of state institutions, the frailty of democratic attitudes and commitments, and the fragility of a coherent national identity—is through a systematic understanding of the same three projects as they were first undertaken by the British and the Iraqi ruling elites in 1921, and then developed during the life span of the country right through to the tumultuous happenings of the post-2003 era.

CHAPTER TWO

Consolidating the Monarchical State, 1921–1936

From conception to birth, the period of gestation for the Iraqi state was just under eleven months. While debates and policy conflicts within British policy-making circles over the future of Mesopotamia had raged for much longer, the arrival in October 1920 of Sir Percy Cox as the new High Commissioner of Iraq, tasked with ending direct British military rule and establishing an indigenous government, signaled British determined intent to create a state in the land of Mesopotamia. The form of the political system, namely a constitutional monarchy, took shape at the Cairo Conference in the spring of 1921, and the process was finally crowned with the enthronement of King Faysal on August 23, 1921.

The task of directing the ship of state devolved to a governing elite that consisted of the British, the King, and a group of senior politicians, most of whom had been Faysal's political companions and had served under him during the Arab rebellion against the Ottomans and later in the short-lived Arab government in Syria. Thus, the creation and later consolidation of the Iraqi state was essentially an elite project. Bearing in mind Harold Lasswell's contention that politics is mainly about who gets what, why, and how,[1] competition among the group that constituted the political elite was inevitable. As we shall see later in this chapter, the effort to accumulate power, as well as to deny it to the other, was responsible for much of the tension between the King and the British High Commissioner. Political maneuvering, conflict, and sometimes deadlock characterized this period, and it involved bringing other players into the power game, such as members of the cabinet, opposition leaders, even tribal sheikhs.

Intra-elite competition did not, however, rise above the primary goal of consolidating the state and its institutions, an objective agreed upon by all parties. Given that the state had been assembled by the British from three disparate Ottoman provinces, with two of these provinces, Mosul in the north and Basra in the south, containing people that were hardly sanguine about the dominance of the center with its minority Sunni population, it was hardly surprising that the path toward consolidation would follow the one treaded by Europe centuries earlier. Charles Tilly's account of state consolidation in Europe rests on a premise that posits the waging of war as central to the process. Tilly argues that in the early and high middle ages, power was disbursed and shared among many feudal lords who paid no more than lip service to monarchs. But monarchs gradually monopolized the coercive instruments of power increasingly at the expense of the Lords, so that by the 17th century, monarchs were able to govern their realms through dominant and disciplined armed forces, police, and local magnates.[2] Throughout the years covered by this chapter, British forces and later on the Iraqi army constantly engaged recalcitrant tribal leaders in the Kurdish north and Shi'ite south. That the dominant Sunni elite in the center were unable to fully integrate the south and especially the north into the main body politic, as French and British monarchs were able to do three centuries earlier, could not have been but a contributing element to the demise of the monarchy in 1958, and to the turbulent and violent post-monarchical eras.

Members of the ruling elite were also cognizant of the need to bring the people into the political bargain through economic benefits, extension of services, and some form of participation in the political process. The literature on state consolidation suggests that coercion alone might not be able to sustain state endurance over the long haul. Again, the history of state development in Europe is a case in point, where, according to Tilly, the use of force was followed by a process of bargaining with the populations that eventually led to "the expansion of popular consultation in the form of elections, plebiscites, and legislatures."[3] This is confirmed by Michael Mann who maintains that force is only one of three components of state power. The other two are economics and ideology.[4] Acceptance by the populace of state governing structures is a more powerful guarantee of stability and survival. It is in this context that Max Weber defines the state as "a human community that successfully claims the monopoly of the *legitimate* use of physical force within a given territory"[5] (my italics). Legitimacy here is defined in terms of the acceptance by the people of the state and its government. Governance therefore predicates not only on the ability of the governing elite to exercise force and project power, but also on the consent of the governed. And indeed, the ruling elite in Iraq were sensitive to the need to bring in elements of the population outside the elite structure into the political process. From the very beginning the British insisted on, and the King and the other senior politicians agreed to, a monarchical political system that would be constrained by constitutional guarantees. Yet, as we shall see, these guarantees would be purposely limited by constitutional powers and privileges accorded to the executive authority, which would be subject more readily to British influence than a large and more cumbersome institution of peoples' representatives.

Early Debates over Statehood

Initially, when the British army finally defeated the Turks and entered Baghdad in March 1917, the British government saw no reason to veer away from its age-old colonial policy of direct rule. Even though an official governmental memo emphasized the preference of His Majesty's Government for an Arab administration in Baghdad that would carry out the burdens of governing the three ex-Ottoman provinces of Baghdad, Mosul, and Basra under British guidance, Iraq in fact had come under the direct political control of the British. The country was divided into administrative districts, each of which was manned by British personnel, with the local population almost entirely excluded from political power and decisions that impacted their own lives.

The advocates of the "colonial" position argued that the indigenous population was on the whole too backward for self-rule. The concept of the "state" as a set of institutions exercising political authority over a population within a specified territory was alien to the majority of the inhabitants. Primordial loyalty on the whole was accorded to religion and to the head of the clan or tribe. There were, of course, among the literate classes men who concerned themselves with political affairs and issues that transcended their immediate milieu. They well knew what a state meant, and they agitated for an independent Iraqi state. They were to later constitute an active and vociferous opposition group to British tutelage. Even so, these constituted a distinct minority of a much larger societal sector that, for over five centuries of Ottoman rule, had resided on the political margins of a vast entity, in which the "state" and "government" meant little more than distant and unfathomable individuals and institutions.

The rationale for Iraqi un-preparedness for statehood, a variant of the "White Man Burden" argument, was to quickly be overtaken by events. In the wake of World War I, a new value system, tirelessly advanced by the United States, spurned European colonialism, preaching instead concepts of self-determination. President Woodrow Wilson went into the Paris Peace Conference of 1919 armed with his celebrated fourteen points that included "self-determination for the peoples of recently collapsed empires" and the founding of a League of Nations. The conclusion of the peace conference saw the creation of the mandate system, a compromise between annexation and direct control on the one hand and total independence on the other hand. Under the mandate system, political power would devolve to the indigenous people of fallen empires under the supervision and protection of specific great powers. And this process would be overseen by the League of Nations' Permanent Mandates Commission.

Wilson's liberal ideas found a ready echo among the informed classes in Iraq's major cities, particularly Baghdad. These "nationalists" exploited Wilson's ideas to fuel the simmering anti-British resentment that resided particularly among the southern mid-Euphrates tribes, their sheikhs, and their Shi'ite religious leaders. But neither the resolutions of the Paris Peace Conference, nor indigenous agitation for independence would sway the unbending British Acting Civil Commissioner in Iraq, Captain Arnold T. Wilson, who believed fervently that colonial rule was the only practical policy option for Iraq. To Captain Wilson, those agitating for self-rule in Iraq were a self-interested malcontent clique trying to rob Iraq of the best administration for its current condition, namely, British direct rule.[6] When Gertrude Bell, the Colonial Office Representative in Iraq, who later during the early years of the Iraqi monarchy would be depicted as the "uncrowned queen of Iraq,"[7] wrote a memorandum advocating the creation of an Arab government, Captain Wilson attached his own memo belittling Bell's conclusions.[8] Wilson thought that any deviation from colonial rule would lead to the loss of Iraq, an eventuality that would constitute a major blow to British interests. His General Staff in Baghdad issued a report citing Iraq's critical importance to the British Empire:

> The future power of the world is oil. . . . The Mosul province and the banks of the mid-Euphrates promise to afford oil in great quantities. . . . With a railway and pipeline in the Mediterranean, which is forecast within the next ten years, the position of England as a naval power in the Mediterranean could be doubly assured, and our dependence on the Suez Canal, which is a vulnerable point in our line of communication with the East, would be considerably lessened.[9]

Captain Wilson and his staff in Iraq persisted in frustrating Whitehall's efforts to implement in some form the resolutions of the Paris Peace Conference, and in his dispatches to London he consistently dismissed Iraqi resistance to British rule as merely the work of a few inconsequential extremists.

In early June 1920, a major revolt against the British began in the mid-Euphrates area in Iraq's Shi'ite south. The heavily armed and surprisingly determined tribes scored a number of early and significant successes, so that by August, much of the south of the country (but not the port city of Basra) had slipped out of British control. However, once reinforcements of the British army began to arrive, the course of the insurrection was reversed and by late October, the British were again completely in control of the country. The insurrection's main political casualty was Captain Wilson and his unbending colonialist policies.

The Genesis of the State

In early October, the more malleable and pragmatic Sir Percy Cox arrived in Iraq to assume the responsibilities of High Commissioner. He set out to implement the policies dictated by the new international norms exemplified by President Woodrow Wilson's fourteen points and the strictures of the League of Nations. Whitehall confirmed its commitment "to the creation and support of an independent Arab state in [Iraq]. . .to rendering assistance as may be required [and] to the support of a. . .constitutional monarchy. . . ."[10] Immediately upon his arrival in Baghdad, Cox gathered the city's dignitaries and announced that he had come "by order of His Majesty's Government to enter into councel with the people of Iraq for the purpose of setting up an Arab Government under the supervision of Great Britain."[11] In a matter of less than three years British expectations of their future role in Iraq had shifted radically from direct political control to indirect influence over an indigenous governing structure.

What that meant was a more complex set of assumptions about governance than the straightforward concept of direct colonial rule. The British had to construct a state in which government would be drawn from the country's own inhabitants, yet the British would retain enough political authority to check unacceptable policies and decisions by the indigenous government. Inherent in the formulation was a dilemma that was to bedevil British-Iraqi relations for years to come. In order to make sure that Britain's political interests would be preserved, a strong government, acceptable to its people and able to provide security and prosperity needed to be put in place. Yet, inevitably at times the British would have to rein in this supposedly "strong" government when there was a conflict of interests. As we shall see, in the first decade of Iraqi statehood the King and his government were put time and time again in the untenable situation of trying to gain popular legitimacy by pursuing independent policies, only to see the credibility of the government undermined through strong armed British interference.

A further dilemma for the British concerned the issue of constitutionalism and representation. One need not be a cynic and suggest that British advocacy of a constitutional monarchy and parliamentary democracy was mere lip service. As an old and distinguished democracy itself Britain no doubt genuinely desired to create states in its own image, hence the insistence on a constitutional monarchy. Stephen Hemsley Longrigg, a British official and a keen observer of Iraqi politics of the time, contends that there was no alternative to "representative, parliamentary democracy. . . . Neither to the British, nor to any Western observer did it occur in 1920 not to install the forms of government both familiar at home and seemingly demanded in Iraq."[12] But it is also true that regardless of Britain's own proclivities, the post-World War I political environment, with its emphasis on self-determination further constrained British freedom of maneuverability on the question of representation and constitutionalism. Britain's predicament was how to reconcile its repeated assertions on its preference for democracy with its need to preserve its interests through a centralizing political authority, over which it would retain significant influence. Again, as we shall see, with time this dilemma would end up devaluing the political process to the detriment of all the institutions concerned—the British, the King, his government, and Parliament.

Setting up a constitutional monarchy proved to be a trickier proposition for the British than at first imagined. Their choice of Faysal, the third son of Sharif Husayn of Hejaz, was not met with the unanimous approval that they had hoped and worked for. Many Iraqis, especially in the predominantly Shi'ite south and Kurdish north, were not particularly enamored with the idea of a non-Iraqi Sunni sovereign. Indeed, even in Baghdad, approval was not given lightly. The first Iraqi premier under the British administration, 'Abd al-Rahman al-Gailani, confided to Gertrude Bell that even with his intense hatred of the Turks, he would much rather have them rule Iraq than the Hejazis. He explained that apart from their Sunni faith, there was precious little that bound the Hejazis to Iraq.[13] Moreover, Iraq was hardly devoid of legitimate indigenous candidates who had resisted Ottoman rule prior to World War I and who had long-standing constituencies and power bases.[14] Recognizing, however, the country's communal plurality, where no local candidate would command universal support, the British stuck with the idea of an outsider with no direct connections to any of Iraq's diverse communities.

Faysal, himself, came from aristocratic Arab lineage, and already had an established reputation. He had fought the Turks, entered Damascus at the head of a victorious Bedouin army, and became the King of Syria. Expelled from Syria by the French, he had continued to espouse and work for the independence of Arab lands. Faysal thus had the kind of credentials that could command the support of tribes and urbanites alike. The British, on their part, felt that Faysal would have learned a valuable lesson from his relations with the French during his short tenure in Syria, and thus would be more amenable to British demands and dictates. In the words of Winston Churchill, Britain's Colonial Secretary, Faysal offered hope for the "best and cheapest solution."[15]

On his arrival in Iraq, Faysal met with hardly the enthusiastic reception that he had expected. He had hoped to be warmly embraced by the people; instead he felt reticence, even hostility.[16] In Basra, where he had first arrived on June 23, 1921, the inhabitants had their own preferred candidate, Sayyid Taleb al-Naqib, and there were currents among them that advocated autonomy. As his train moved north toward Baghdad, he encountered the lower Euphrates tribes and the Shi'ite 'Ulama of Najaf and Karbala who were not enthused by the prospect of a Sunni Sharifian from Hejaz ruling over them. Only in Baghdad were the British able to organize a relatively vibrant welcoming reception.

Immediately, the British set out to legitimize Faysal's rule. Eschewing direct elections, which they feared might produce an unanticipated outcome, they devised instead a caucus system to be administered in the various provinces of Iraq, where local administrators would have greater leverage over the result. In this system, administrators of a province, city, or district would invite the notables, leaders, and prominent individuals of a specific locale to a meeting in which the administrator would extol the virtues of Faysal's candidacy, then ask if there were any objectors. When the attendees responded with the expected "No," they were asked to sign an already prepared declaration accepting Faysal's candidacy. As planned, the overall results validated the choice of Faysal as King, but not without a few surprises. The two Kurdish provinces of Kirkuk and Sulaymaniya voted against Faysal, and while the other provinces voted in favor, a number produced divided votes, some attaching provisos demanding true sovereignty and the prompt convening of a Constituent Assembly. In a number of southern provinces, however, the tribes, wary of the Hejazi prince and his Sunni Sharifian companions, did acquiesce to Faysal's ascendancy to the throne, but made it conditional on the continuation of the British mandate. Regardless of whether this sentiment was genuinely expressed, or whether it was, as the Iraqi sociologist the late 'Ali al-Wardi suggested, the product of British manipulation,[17] Faysal's happiness at the result must have been tempered by the unevenness of the responses, particularly as these were not supposed to happen since the election and its results were produced under what was thought to be "controlled conditions."

STATE INSTITUTIONS

The state that emerged after the Constitution was written and passed by the Constituent Assembly in 1924 was a monarchy in which the Head of State was given wide latitude in policy-making powers even though the system was designed to be constitutional and parliamentary. So while the Constitution, known as the Organic Law, declared sovereignty to belong to the nation, it added that this sovereignty was entrusted by the people to the King. Even such a pillar of the monarchical regime as Tawfiq al-Suwaydi, would criticize this provision for granting to the King a right that should belong to Parliament, the institution that is supposed to represent the interests of the people. Al-Suwaydi unequivocally contended that "if sovereignty [was] to be entrusted, it should be entrusted to the people not the King."[18] Yet, monarchical power vis-à-vis the Parliament, as enshrined in the Constitution, was broad, preponderant, and decisive:

> [The King] confirmed laws, ordered their promulgation and supervised their execution. He could also proclaim martial law. . . . He issued orders for the holding of general elections and for the convocation of Parliament. He . . . prorogued and dissolved [Parliament]. When Parliament was not in session, the King issued ordinances. . .for the maintenance of public order and expenditure of public money not provided by the budget. These ordinances had the force of law. . . . The King [selected] the Prime Minister. . .[and] according to the Second Amendment Law of 1943, the King was empowered to dismiss the Prime Minister. . . .[19]

Indeed, the Constitution conferred on the council of ministers (cabinet) little independent policy-making powers, essentially making the cabinet an advisory body to the King. Throughout this period, the Monarch was an active participant in the decision-making process,[20] which did put in serious question the claim of a constitutional monarchy.

Even though the relationship between the King and his cabinet was constitutionally tilted in favor of the former, the center of power tended to shift depending on the strength, charisma, and commitment of the primary players. Faysal, an undoubtedly assertive and highly respected monarch, endeavored to make sure that the prime minister and his cabinet would always submit to the Royal will, and would not act independently of the King's views, wishes, and requirements. Thus, even someone such as the shrewd, self-assured and forceful Nuri al-Sa'id, whom Faysal relied upon to push through the contested and highly unpopular Anglo-Iraqi 1930 treaty, would be dismissed in 1932 because the King felt that Nuri's power base was expanding beyond acceptable limits. In the words of the British Ambassador, Nuri's dismissal reflected a tendency of Faysal "to change the bowling whenever a member of his team [had] taken enough wickets to distract public attention from the captain of the side."[21]

Faysal's son, Ghazi, possessed none of his father's attributes, and the levers of power tilted toward the council of ministers during his short reign. The trend continued with Regent, later Crown Prince, 'Abd al-Ilah, who governed in the name of the young and weak Faysal II. 'Abd al-Ilah interfered constantly in the policy process, but he had little political acumen and was totally lacking in charisma. Thus, while Nuri's wings had been authoritatively clipped in 1932, his influence and power grew rapidly after the death of Faysal I, so that he gradually came to dominate the Iraqi political landscape to such an extent that the last two decades of the monarchical period are usually referred to as "Ahd Nuri" (Nuri's era).

The broad constitutional powers given to the King were a function of the British desire to narrow the parameters of policy-making in order to safeguard their interests: controlling one man was easier and more efficient than controlling an entire parliamentary institution. In the words of the British High Commissioner, Henry Dobbs, there was "real danger that irresponsible extremist majority may. . .seek to paralyze state activities. . . . It [was] therefore essential to have provision for enabling the Executive to carry on."[22] To the British, of course, the "Executive" meant not only the King, but also the British High Commissioner, which under the mandate system, acted literally as a parallel executive authority.

Nor did Faysal object to these wide-ranging powers. He was an outsider, whose indigenous support, he well knew, was uncertain. He thus recognized early on that he could not fall back on "personal popularity" or "charismatic pull" to formulate and implement tough and unpopular policies that were necessary for the development and progress of the state. So while Faysal had agreed to a parliamentary and constitutional democracy, he also sought powers that would elevate the Executive above the other institutions of the state. Faysal was not inclined to have his power undermined by Parliament when he knew that during the mandate period, which took up literally the bulk of his reign, a duality of power and responsibilities already existed with the British.

This parallel power structure was not confined to the top policy-making levels, but extended to the entire governmental and administrative structure. Cabinet ministers as well as provincial governors, district executives, and city mayors, were assigned British "advisors" whose views were expected to be taken "into careful consideration" by the Iraqi officials. Before making any decision, a Minister would have discussed the matter with his advisor, and advisors regularly attended cabinet meetings.[23] As the mandate power until 1932, Britain asserted its right as a seasoned world power to "assist" the indigenous political elites who were new to the complexities of governance in running the affairs of the infant state.

The Iraqi population, however, especially the urban educated and nationalist crowd, saw this "assistance" through a less benevolent prism. They conceived of it as a blatant maneuver for political control. The term "mandate" was never accepted by Iraqi nationalists, who equated it with colonization and imperialism, and agitated ferociously against it, whether in Parliament, or in newspapers, or in organized mass demonstrations. Statehood, Iraqis argued, was meaningless when every governmental and administrative decision was subject to intervention by British personnel. In Iraqi circles, this was dubbed the "abnormal situation". Interestingly, even the British seemed to agree with the characterization. The following passage is from a 1928 official British report on the administration of Iraq:

> The abnormal situation is the result of the fact that Iraq is sovereign yet under British mandate, so according to the constitution, Iraqi ministers are responsible to Parliament, yet they are under the influence of their English advisors. . . . The Iraqi government controls and administers the railways and the Basrah Port, yet it does not own them. It can institute martial law, but only with the approval of the English military. It has an army which it cannot move without consultation with the High Commissioner. . . . Foreign nationals are granted special privileges in Iraq without Iraqis having similar privileges abroad.[24]

Faysal's wide powers vis-à-vis the other institutions, particularly that of Parliament, thus need to be seen within the context of a country that was subject to competing pressures and interests. Chief among these was the paramount position of the British and their determination not to allow anything to erode this position, while fierce Iraqi resentment raged, especially among the influential urban nationalist circles, against British prominence in the political life of Iraq.

Dilemmas of Rule

From the very beginning of his rule, Faysal had to try and resolve, or at a minimum walk a very thin line among contradictory choices. First, as has been indicated, there was the very wide gulf between British interests and Iraqi nationalist aspirations. Faysal could not escape the reality of his investiture. Put plainly, he was chosen by the British, and he would become King through their influence and effort, even manipulation. Until his death in 1933, the British continued to be the major political and military force in the country. The High Commissioner was a towering political figure the King could not ignore. Yet, to be perceived as weak toward the British, or worse still as an agent of their interests in Iraq, would undercut seriously his legitimacy among the politically active, vociferous, and increasingly influential Iraqi nationalists.

Faysal's dealings with the British and the Iraqi nationalists were akin almost to a high-wire act. At times, he confronted the British when he thought they had gone too far. A sample of this occurred even before his enthronement, when Britain's Colonial Office insisted that in the coronation speech Faysal should clearly declare that ultimate political authority in Iraq rested with the High Commissioner. Faysal objected vehemently, arguing that he could not agree to a stipulation that would irreparably undermine the dignity of the Crown and his own standing among the people. Sir Percy Cox, the British High Commissioner, was persuaded by Faysal's adamancy, and in turn was able to persuade the Colonial Office to drop the subject.[25] But given the political realities of the time he simply could not be as resolute in all instances. Instead, he would vacillate between the British and the nationalists' positions, arriving, he would hope, at a compromise that might not fully satisfy both, but would at least not completely alienate each of the two parties.

One such dilemma occurred immediately after his coronation. To Iraqis, the Minister of the Interior, responsible for internal security and administrative appointments for the provinces, was perceived as the most powerful cabinet portfolio after the Prime Minister.[26] In order to show his people, especially the nationalists, that he was his own man, the King wanted someone untainted by known sympathies for, or relationships with, the British. Sir Percy Cox, on the other hand, needed someone he could trust to lead a ministry in charge of internal security. A deadlock ensued for over three weeks until the candidacy of an obscure officer, with unknown political tendencies, was put forward and gratefully accepted by the two fatigued parties.

The British would characterize the King's stubbornness, and his reluctance, sometimes even refusal, to grant them their wishes as playing into the hands of the nationalists. Dispatches to London consistently spoke of a King misled by nationalist "extremists" or of Faysal and the nationalists as secret bedfellows. The former, more charitable, opinion was held by Gertrude Bell, but other British officials propagated the latter, more serious, accusation. Henry Dobbs, the successor to Percy Cox as High Commissioner, sent a dispatch to London in August 1923, accusing Faysal of "actively encouraging the election of extremists to the Constituent Assembly."[27] The British clearly felt that not only their, but the King's own, interests would be jeopardized by his tilt to the "extremists."

That, however, was decidedly a partial view. As indicated earlier, Faysal consistently endeavored to respond in a way that would not irreparably alienate the two polar forces, the British on the one hand and his Iraqi constituency on the other. In his dealings with both, he always had the authority of his office in mind. The tug of war over the first Anglo-Iraqi treaty was a case in point. His Majesty's Government had proposed a treaty in late 1921 to replace the mandatory document, but to Iraqi nationalists the proposed treaty seemed but a camouflage for the mandate system. Ratification of the treaty stalled for over eight months as the King and Iraq's Council of Ministers, responding to nationalist and religious demands to abolish the British mandate over Iraq, sought a clear abrogation of the mandate in the new treaty. Tensions escalated throughout the first half of 1922, and disturbances were reported in some Iraqi cities and in the tribal areas of the mid-Euphrates. Relations between the King and High Commissioner reached breaking point, with Faysal, exploiting Iraqi unhappiness with the proposed treaty, warning Cox of an impending revolt, for which British policy would be wholly to blame.[28] Cox responded with a harshly worded reply, but with the impending first anniversary of Faysal's investiture on August 23, 1922, he was advised not to send the strong response. On their part, the two nationalist political parties, *al-Nahdha* and *al-Watani* decided to organize a large anti-treaty protest on the first anniversary of the King's enthronement.

On the appointed day, August 23, the opposition parties, seemingly in collusion with the Chamberlain of The Royal Court, Fahmi al-Muddarris,[29] timed their 10,000-strong demonstration to coincide with the arrival of Cox to the Palace to congratulate the King. Slogans against the treaty and against the British in general were shouted by the multitude as the High Commissioner made his way to the courtyard of the Palace. Seething with anger, Cox wrote the King demanding an apology, the immediate firing of Muddarris, and the arrest of seven leaders of the protest. The King, trying to placate the High Commissioner, sent back that very day an effusive apology and dismissed his Chamberlain, but was silent on the arrests. The following day, the King developed acute appendicitis which required immediate surgery, but the indignant Cox stormed into the palace just before the surgery and demanded that the King sign the arrest warrant there and then. On this issue, however, the King stood his ground, refusing to sign the warrants. Taking advantage of the King's incapacity, Cox assumed the responsibility of arresting and deporting the seven nationalist leaders, as well as forcing the sons of the two most senior Shi'ite clerics to leave Iraq for Iran.[30] On his recovery, the King realized that he might have gone too far in siding with the nationalists and resisting British dictates, so he agreed to sign a letter drafted by the Office of the High Commissioner, in which he expressed his gratitude to "His Excellency" for adopting "the necessary measures . . . in order to maintain public interests and preserve order and peace. . . ."[31] Not long after, Faysal received the news that he hoped would placate the nationalists: Britain's Secretary of State for the colonies, Winston Churchill promised to do all he could to facilitate the admission of Iraq to the League of Nations.

As the British were inclined to see the nationalists as rabble rousers who represented an insignificant constituency, Faysal also turned to the tribes to achieve outcomes that he sought but felt would not be supported by the British. As early as 1922, Faysal working through his Sharifian administrators, secretly cultivated the support of tribal sheikhs known for their hostility to the British to balance those who were allies of the mandate power. Thus, anti-mandate disturbances that occurred that year among some mid-Euphrates tribes were generally believed to have erupted through at least some collusion by the King that included financial incentives coming directly from the palace. Again, in his negotiations with the British over the 1927 treaty, the King secretly induced the same tribal leaders to agitate against the treaty and to demand full British withdrawal. For their pains, and to exhibit the value of Royal pleasure, some outstanding land cases were settled in the sheikhs' favor.[32] Obviously, the King was not above using less than scrupulous tactics to strengthen his bargaining position vis-à-vis the British. Indeed, the Acting High Commissioner and his Counselor in Baghdad were so incensed with the King over his "intransigence" during the 1927 negotiations that they had at some point even talked about the possibility of expelling him.[33]

In fact, these episodes illustrate the dilemmas of both the British and the King. To reiterate, the British desired strong state governing institutions to curb the activities of anti-British nationalists and religious leaders. That necessitated a strong central authority that was allied to them. The King on the other hand, while needing British support, also recognized that his own credibility, and thereby ability to rule effectively, depended on indigenous support as well. The King knew that he suffered from a "credibility gap" as an outsider, and as such he recognized that support from consequential elements of society, be they the emergent middle classes, religious leaders, or tribal elements, would not be forthcoming unless he presented himself as a patriot, concerned first and foremost with Iraqi, not British, interests. And that, as he well knew, meant inevitable clashes with the High Commissioner, which in some instances would entail putting his foot down and holding fast to his position, and at other times eventually relenting and backing down. Indeed, this ended up being a win-win situation for the King: he either got what he wanted, or when he would concede to the High Commissioner, he was perceived by the population as having put up a good fight on behalf of the nation against very difficult odds. Either way, his credibility would be enhanced, his legitimacy cemented, and his hold over the reins of power consolidated.

By the same logic of institutionalizing the Hashemite monarchy in Iraq, and implanting the authority of his office in the consciousness of the people, Faysal did not shirk from siding with the British against the opposition if he felt that the opposition had stepped beyond acceptable bounds. He was especially resolute if the opposition resisted or dragged their feet on a particular policy which he happened to support. In other words, while he was at pains to demonstrate that he was a true patriot, he also was not going to be, or be seen as, a mere instrument in the hands of the nationalists.

An early illustration of Faysal's willingness to side with the British and take on the opposition forces if he thought that they were acting against the national interest as he perceived it can be gleaned from the intense conflict that preceded the elections to the Constituent Assembly in 1924. The Council of Ministers had passed the treaty but, with Faysal's prompting and against the declared wishes of Cox, had added the proviso that the treaty needed to be approved by the Constituent Assembly. From this sprang the need for elections, and partly in preparation for that, the King appointed a new prime minister, 'Abd al-Muhsin al-Sa'dun, a man known for his toughness and fortitude. In the spring of 1923, Sir Percy Cox returned from London with a new protocol lowering the life span of the treaty from twenty to four years. The British shift of policy resulted partly from Iraqi efforts and partly from London's unhappiness with the huge expenditure incurred by the British forces in Iraq. The King, however, presented the new protocol to the Iraqi people as a seminal concession by the mandatory power extracted by the King through his devotion and commitment to Iraqi interests and resilience in defending those interests.[34] Thinking that all obstacles delaying the ratification of the treaty were now eliminated, the King, his prime minister, and the British began preparing for what they thought would be a smooth election for a Constituent Assembly.

Their hopes, however, were soon to be dashed when the senior Shi'ite clergy produced fetwas (religious edicts) opposing the treaty and any elections meant to legitimize the treaty. Emissaries from the King to the most senior Shi'ite cleric, Sheikh Mahdi al-Khalisi, who was a most determined and vitriolic critic of the treaty specifically and the British role in Iraq generally, were brusquely rebuffed and accused of apostasy.[35] The cleric made no secret of his belief that the King was "a man who had sold himself to the devil, and had become a toy in the hands of the English," and in one instance, he declared in front of a large audience: "I am discarding Faysal," and then raising his hand, he took off a ring from his finger adding, "just like this."[36] This intimation of Royal subservience to clerical authority was hardly camouflaged to go unnoticed.

The King naturally took this as a challenge to his and his government's authority. It was obvious that for the infant state to survive, its most hallowed institution, the Executive Branch of its government, had to impose its authority on all Iraqis. It was imperative that Khalisi be dealt with, but the King and even the British were concerned that the cleric's status among the Shi'ites and the southern tribes would incite a large and unmanageable rebellion. Prime Minister Sa'dun, on the other hand, insisted that the government could not be seen to be a hostage to the will or whim of a man, or group of men, representing sub-state institutions. Exploiting Khalisi's Persian roots, the government moved swiftly to modify Iraqi law to allow it to expel foreigners who were deemed to be a threat to public safety. A few weeks later while the King was traveling in the south of Iraq, Sa'dun cabled the King of his intention to arrest Khalisi and expel him. Faysal cabled back his ascent, urging his minister to "adopt a resolute plan" in order to "preserve security and the dignity of the government."[37] Khalisi was duly arrested and deported to Iran, and would remain there until his death. When other clerics in the Shi'ite holy cities of Najaf and Karbala protested the arrest and declared that they too would leave Iraq, hoping to incite an insurrection of sorts, the government obliged them by escorting those with Iranian nationality to the border with Iran, but keeping the holders of Iraqi nationality in Iraq under police surveillance. Faced with the government's resolute stance, support for the clerics' cause among the commoners quickly vanished.

It would not take long for the clerics who left for Iran to realize their error. Their departure had incited very few scattered and inconsequential protests that were nipped in the bud by the security forces. Now that their property, positions, and followers were at the mercy of competing Ulama, they proceeded to petition the government to allow them to return to Iraq. The King and his ministers in Baghdad would not relent until the clerics signed a public statement which declared that they "would not interfere in political matters," that the King was the one "responsible for the nation's needs and politics," and that they would pledge their "support for the Hashemite monarchy in accordance with their Islamic beliefs."[38] That they did was, according to a number of analysts, an historical moment signifying the end of clerical political leadership.[39] The state, barely eighteen months old, had won a significant battle with one of the most powerful and authoritative institutions in Iraq.

A few years later, the King again would stand firm against bitter opposition from Iraqi nationalists to push through a project that he and the British wanted implemented. In September 1929, the new Labor government in Britain signaled its intention to enter into a new treaty with Iraq that would pave the way for Iraq's membership of the League of Nations in 1932. As proposed by the British, the treaty would give the Iraqis total control of their security and defense, hitherto held by the British. The Iraqis, however, would allow the British to move their forces in Iraq and use Iraqi amenities in the event of war, and to establish two British air force bases in the middle and south of the country. Additionally, equipping and advising the Iraqi army would be undertaken only by the British.

King Faysal was adamant in supporting the treaty, seeing the benefit of joining the League of Nations far outweighing any concessions to the British.[40] Anticipating intense public opposition,[41] he appointed the steely Nuri al-Sa'id to the premiership with the task of pushing the treaty through a possibly recalcitrant Parliament. Nuri duly dissolved Parliament, held new elections, which were strictly controlled, thus ensuring a compliant Parliament, and closed down the more strident anti-treaty newspapers. Even so, opposition to the treaty did not abate; in fact it intensified. Demonstrations filled the streets, anti-treaty pamphlets were printed and clandestinely distributed, and the opposition took every opportunity to voice their hostility to the new accord. Indeed, some members of the opposition took their complaints about the treaty to the Secretary-General of the League of Nations, insisting that the treaty "does not grant Iraq true independence; rather it allows Britain to exploit the country in accordance with its imperialist designs."[42] But the King and Nuri gave not an inch, and the treaty was duly ratified by the quiescent Parliament in November 1930. Public opposition again fell victim to the resolute power of state governing institutions. Two years later, as the date for Iraq's entry into the League of Nations approached, the King conferred on Nuri Iraq's highest honor, the Rafidayn Medal.[43]

THE STATE AND THE KURDS

As we shall see in the chapter on identity, the Kurds, who constitute fewer than 20 percent of the country's population, are of a different ethnic stock to the rest of the Iraqis. They speak dialects of Kurdish, a different language from Arabic, the official language of the state. The Kurds' abiding national aspiration has always been for a state of their own, which would only add to the already difficult relationship they had with the central authorities in Baghdad.

Successive Iraqi governments, therefore, had to deal with numerous Kurdish insurrections that demanded either outright separation or, at a minimum, cultural and sometimes economic autonomy. The Baghdad authorities consistently adopted a hard line stance toward Kurdish demands for fear of losing the oil that was located in the northern cities of Mosul and Kirkuk, both of which the Kurds claimed to lie within their geographic domain. An International Commission of Inquiry, which was created by the League of Nations, went to Mosul in 1925, and reported that five-eighths of the territory's population was Kurdish. While in effect substantiating Kurdish claims, the Commission nevertheless recommended that Mosul remain as part of the State of Iraq.[44] In the second half of the 20th century the Kurds would propagate Kirkuk as the capital of Kurdistan, even though demographically it had been dominated by Turkomen.[45] Iraqi authorities, however, were in no way inclined even to meet Kurdish demands halfway. They saw any compromise as the beginning of a perilous path at the end of which lay Kurdish secession. Another concern for the Baghdad government was the possible spill-over effect that a successful separatist movement would have on the Shi'ite population in the south. The end result of all this was that Kurdish areas were never really integrated politically or culturally into the Iraqi state.

Even before the birth of the Iraqi state in 1921, the British would have a taste of Kurdish penchant for political independence. When the British decided to appoint Sheikh Mahmud Barzinji, a local Kurdish leader, as governor of the Kurdish-speaking province of Sulaymaniya, the Sheikh repaid the kindness of His Majesty's Government by proclaiming himself "King of Kurdistan," and declaring a revolt against British rule. He repeated this a number of times during the 1920s, and every time Britain's Royal Air Force (RAF) would bomb his forces and put down the insurrection.[46] Finally in 1930, Sheikh Mahmud led widespread demonstrations that got so out of hand that troops had to be brought in. Mahmud was forced to surrender and was placed under house arrest for more than 20 years.[47] Throughout the first decade of the Iraqi state, the British and the Iraqi authorities expended large resources on the Kurdish problem, as the Kurds proved to be more than a passing irritant for the British administration in Iraq and the infant Iraqi state.

It was not as though the Iraqi ruling elite, populated as it was by Arabist Sunni politicians, was particularly partial to Kurdish demands or aspirations. Encouraged by seeming British indifference, the government in Baghdad would indeed issue public statements that were sensitive to Kurdish demands, but then rarely act on them. In December 1922, an Anglo-Iraqi joint declaration recognized the rights of the Kurds to establish an autonomous political structure within Iraq, and in the following year, the Iraqi government announced that Kurdish would be used in Kurdish areas and Kurds would fill official positions in the Kurdish provinces. However, in 1924, Baghdad overlooked any promises it made regarding Kurdish autonomy, and instructed its officials to conduct elections in the Kurdish areas for Iraq's Constituent Assembly. Through this maneuver, Phebe Marr tells us, "Kurds were . . . brought under the sovereignty of the new Iraqi state by fiat."[48] And indeed, when the 1930 Anglo-Iraqi treaty was concluded, not one clause of the document dealt with, or even mentioned, the Kurds. Responding to the enraged reaction of the Kurds, and trying to allay the concerns of the League of Nations, whose International Commission of Inquiry a few years earlier had endorsed the demands of the Kurds to adopt Kurdish as their official language, the Iraqi authorities in Baghdad promulgated the "Local Language Law," which was meant to sustain Kurdish as the spoken and written language in the Kurdish region.[49] The problem was that when it came to implementation, governmental efforts were either non-existent or at best half-hearted.

The Kurds' abiding problem was that, contrary to the Shi'ites, there was almost no political constituency in Iraq that cared at all about Kurdish political or cultural rights. On the contrary, the King, the Sunni politicians and notables, and even the opposition parties cast a wary and suspicious eye at the Kurds and their perceived proclivity for separatism.[50] On the whole, the British were more sensitive to Kurdish political and cultural demands than the Arab government and population in Iraq. However, they well understood the economic importance of the Kurdish provinces to the stability and prosperity of the country that they had created. The British, therefore, perceived the Kurds as a disintegrative force, determinedly unwilling to partake in the building of a unified Iraqi community. Stephen Hemsley Longrigg, a senior British official, thought that "Kurdish claims were . . . frankly separatist." He then characterized Kurdish unhappiness with their subjugation to "an Arab government" as a "profoundly unsatisfactory and even a menacing element" in Iraq's national life.[51] As Iraqi independence approached with the country's entry into the League of Nations in 1932, the political ambiguity of the Kurdish situation provoked widespread unrest that was deemed destabilizing enough for the RAF to yet again conduct bombing campaigns in Kurdish areas.

This pattern of Kurdish demands for cultural and political assertion and autonomy that is met with indifference by the ruling elite in Baghdad, which in turn ignites a violent response that ends up being crushed by the army supported by the RAF, persisted throughout this period of Iraq's political development. From the very beginning of the Iraqi state, and carrying into the first decade and a half of its life, there existed a sense of almost irrevocable fracture between the state, whose institutions, as we shall see in more detail in Chapter Four, were being increasingly molded by an exclusivist Arab ideology, and the ethnically distinct Kurds, whose isolation from the Arab majority was reinforced by the inaccessibility of the mountainous terrain they inhabited.

The State and the Shi'ites

While divisions between the Sunni community, whose members permeated authoritative state institutions, and the majority Shi'ite population never acquired the rigidity of the Arab Kurdish divide, the two Arabic-speaking groups nevertheless eyed each other with much mistrust that at times expanded into outright hostility that erupted into violence. For the government, the relationship of the state with the Shi'ite population, clergy and commoners alike, became a recurring public policy issue throughout the first decade and a half of statehood. The Shi'ite domain in the south of Iraq was essentially tribal, with a hybrid authority structure of tribal sheikhs and senior clerics, known as *mujtahids*. Even before the arrival of Faysal, Sir Percy Cox realized that any pretense to statehood must predicate on an acceptance by the population that state power was paramount and state institutions constituted the authoritative instruments of policy. In other words, the state could not tolerate a competitive power structure based on the Shi'ite tribal/clerical domain. In the negotiations with the Shi'ite tribes over amnesty terms for the tribal sheikhs who led the 1920 insurrection against the British, Cox used recently appointed government officials and agents to negotiate directly with the tribes, refusing resolutely to acknowledge any mediating role for clerical leaders known as mujtahids. In this he purposely elevated state law and jurisdiction over the age-old clerical power to adjudicate disputes.

In order to de-couple the tribes from the clerical establishment, the Iraqi government continued the British policy of making the "paramount sheikhs responsible for law and order and the collection of revenues in their districts, and to tie them to the [state] through grants and privileges."[52] The separate legal code for the tribes, known as The Tribal Criminal and Civil Disputes Regulations, which had been introduced by the British in 1918, was confirmed by King Faysal and made part of Iraqi law in 1924. The code was based on a perception of an Iraqi society culturally divided between a modernizing urban population and a traditional rural community. Regardless of the debates on the motives and wisdom of such a division,[53] the tribal regulations undoubtedly cemented the position of the sheikhs, allowing them to deal directly with state institutions and personnel, thus eschewing the intervening role desired and demanded by the clergy. Motivated by self-interest, tribal sheikhs were less inclined to unquestioningly abide by clerical anti-governmental pronouncements and proclamations.

This, however, did not mean the demise of Shi'ite clerical power in the south of Iraq. Traditions were too entrenched to disappear overnight, and the sway the leading mujtahids still held over the flock was well recognized and accepted by Faysal and his administration. Shortly after Faysal's investiture, Sheikh Mahdi al-Khalisi, the leading Shi'ite cleric, demanded the appointment of a man of an Indian nationality for the mayorship of Samara', a Sunni city that housed one of the most revered Shi'ite shrines. The King was wary about rejecting Khalisi's nomination, but was equally disinclined to appoint a non-Iraqi to the position. So he sought the intervention of 'Ali al-Bazargan, an influential urban Shi'ite politician, who was able to come up with an Iraqi candidate acceptable to the cleric. Clearly relieved, the King told the interlocutor, "God bless you 'Ali, you saved me." When Bazargan took the nominee's name to the Minister of the Interior, the Minister confirmed: "It was not only the King whom you saved; you saved all of us."[54]

As for the tribes, what emerged was a rough balance between pro-clerical and pro-British tribes, and this was well-illustrated early in Faysal's reign. When the Saudi Ikhwan mounted a raid into Iraq's Euphrates area in the spring of 1922, in which over 700 Iraqi villagers were killed, the mujtahids called a conference in the holy city of Karbala, in which a number of tribal leaders gave pledges to fight the Ikhwan under orders of the mujtahids. But other tribal leaders, after consulting with Sir Percy Cox, who preferred state diplomacy, boycotted the conference, and even denounced its proclamations and recommendations.[55] The strongest clerical-tribal bonds would emerge when the state enacted laws that tribes resisted. In these instances, religious proclamations by the clergy in support of the tribal positions undoubtedly undermined the state's capacity to enforce such laws peacefully and within the law. Instead, the state would revert to physical coercion, a practice that, as we shall see later, was used more than once with singular ferocity during the turbulent 1930s.

The disconnect between the state and the Shiʿites was the residue of historical circumstance. Under Ottoman Sunni rule, the Iraqi Shiʿites were barely tolerated, and as long as they remained relatively peaceful and paid some taxes, the state generally treated them with benign neglect. On their part, much of the Shiʿite population limited their contact with state institutions to a bare minimum. They developed their own set of laws, based on religious norms and tribal custom, and they shunned Turkish schools, preferring their own *Jaʿfari maddrassas* (Shiʿite religious schools). Many had sought and eventually acquired Persian citizenship in order to avoid serving in the Ottoman army. Inevitably, when the state was formed in 1921, the role that the Shiʿite population would play in the governance of their country erupted into a major public policy debate.

Recognizing the demographic weight of the Shiʿite population, King Faysal reached out to the community's clerical and tribal leadership from the very beginning of his monarchy. He also realized the paramount importance of incorporating the Shiʿites into the state's political structure. But he came against three main hurdles. In the first place, there were few educated and trained Shiʿites who would be able to fill governmental posts. Secondly, because of clerical prohibition, most Shiʿites were reluctant to enter public service that was dominated by Sunnis and led by non-Muslims (i.e., the Christian British), and thirdly, the Sunni ruling elite exhibited no less disdain of the Shiʿites than that held by their Ottoman co-religionists before them.[56] Even before Faysal's ascendancy to the throne, the first council of ministers which was formed under Sir Percy Cox was predominantly Sunni. It did have one Jewish member, but not a single Shiʿite. It took Cox almost five months of constant pressure to make the senior ministers accede to his demands to appoint a Shiʿite among their rank. In the broader political domain, the administrative positions in the provinces of Iraq continued to go to Sunnis even in those provinces with overwhelming Shiʿite majorities.[57] The Sunni response of course pointed to the lack of qualified Shiʿites, whose educated cadres were the product of on the whole Shiʿite *maddrassas* that taught religion and the Arabic language, but dealt hardly at all with the various pedagogical elements of a modern secular curriculum.

On taking office, Faysal felt that Shi'ite relative educational unpreparedness should not be allowed to become a fissiparous agent that might lead to national dislocation. He thus made every effort to prod the Sunni establishment to include Shi'ites, and was not prepared to be stumped into inaction by the argument of Shi'ite inferior educational attainment. Once when the newly appointed Dean of the Law College refused to accept a high school certificate issued by a *maddrassa*, insisting instead that the students take an entrance exam, Faysal intervened and forced the Dean to change his mind.[58] And when the Director of Education, Sati' al-Husri, protested to the King, Faysal explained that the country "faced a problem. The Shi'ites were getting restless because so few posts went to them." Recognizing that the reason was the dearth of Shi'ite degree or certificate holders, the King wondered whether something could be done to compensate for the educational deficit "of the Ja'fari young men."[59] Since most of these Shi'ite young men had spent their youth in *maddrassas* and were too old to attend high school on a full-time basis, Husri suggested the creation of an evening high school that would allow day workers to complete their high school requirements in preparation for entry into governmental agencies or higher education. The King embraced the idea immediately, and the school was promptly established.

Such royal interventions were meant to show that the state embraced all sectors of Iraqi society. But well-meaning as these gestures undoubtedly were, state institutions and organizations were run entirely by Sunnis, aided until 1932 by British advisors. For purposes relating to his own legitimation, as well as that of the state that he headed, it was imperative for Faysal to incorporate the majority Shi'ites into the political and administrative system, and to be seen as the sovereign of all Iraqis, regardless of their communal affiliations. Yet, due to the paucity of qualified Shi'ites, a predicament compounded by Sunni prejudicial attitudes, the process was slow and clearly disappointing to those Shi'ites who wanted to partake in the affairs of state.

Not that these willing souls constituted a majority among the Shi'ites. Throughout this period, the bulk of the community, tribal and susceptible to the pronouncements of the religious hierarchy, continued to be suspicious of the state, its institutions, and agents. Such was their mistrust of the Sunni-dominated state institutions that the Shi'ites on a number of occasions expressed a wish "to return to the days of absolute British control [rather] than be under the heel of an entirely Sunni administration."[60] Sentiments such as these reflected not only sectarian distance, but also the gradual loss of tribal autonomy as a result of the steady ascendancy of the state's coercive powers.

THE STATE AND THE TRIBES

Shi'ite tendency to keep their distance from state institutions and to follow the community's age-old norms and practices was manifested most dramatically in tribal behavior. The insurrection of 1920 was based mainly in the mid and lower Euphrates tribal areas in the south of Iraq. That insurrection was a major catalyst in the British decision to speed up the creation of an Arab government in Iraq. While the revolt was fanned by anti-foreign sentiment, it was also a manifestation of the uneasy relationship between the tribes and central authority. That milieu of mistrust and general wariness between government and the tribes continued right through the first decade and a half of the monarchical period.

In the mandate period, 1921–1932, the state was too weak to confront, let alone discipline, the tribes. More than seven years after the creation of the state, with the Iraqi army still weak and undersupplied, while the tribes were armed to the teeth, the British High Commissioner would write to London that the withdrawal of British forces would hasten the demise of the Iraqi state.[61] Faysal was not incognizant of the state's vulnerability in the face of a tribal eruption. Just before his death in 1933, he wrote in a confidential memorandum that the government was "far and away weaker than the people,—there were . . . in the country at large more than 100,000 rifles whereas the government possessed only 15,000."[62] That meant that any suppression of the tribes would have had to be undertaken by British forces, with the inevitable result of a disastrous loss of legitimacy for the country's ruling elite. Moreover, in his struggle for paramountcy with the British, the King sought the support of anti-British tribes to balance those known for their closeness to the British. It was hardly surprising that Faysal would expend much effort in cementing his relationship with these tribal leaders, trying as far as he could to act on their demands, petitions, and grievances, and to enhance their economic position through land settlement regulations that favored tribal chiefs. He supported, even encouraged, the Constituent Assembly in 1924 to endorse a specifically tribal legal system in which disputes within and between tribes were settled by the tribes themselves, effectively giving Iraq two parallel legal systems. During the Faysal years, 1921–1933, the state tolerated, even indulged, the tribes, and in return, apart from small and isolated incidents, the tribal domain desisted from challenging the authority of the state and its institutions, remaining on the whole peaceful and obliging.

King Faysal died suddenly on September 8, 1933. He was succeeded by his only son Ghazi, who at 21 lacked all of his father's attributes: intellect, acumen, and of course, experience in public affairs. The moderating influence and wise counsel that had resided in the palace was lost to the politicians and administrators who would run the country's affairs. Very soon after Faysal's death the state would clash with the tribes over the issue of conscription. The idea of universal military conscription had been the object of intense debate from the very beginning of the Iraqi state. The defense establishment, backed by Baghdad's politicians, had advocated it strongly, citing the absolute centrality of a strong army to a functioning state, with compulsory conscription acting as a unifying national agent. The British had been cool to the idea, unconvinced of Iraq's need for a large army. But now that the country had gained full sovereignty through membership of the League of Nations, British capacity to control policy had been considerably curtailed. Iraq's political leaders, however, had another nemesis far more resistant to the idea than the British. Tribal sheikhs ferociously challenged the notion of universal conscription as they feared not only the loss of their able-bodied men, but also the prospect of these men returning to the tribal domain having been infested with subversive new ideas of national egalitarianism and social justice. Faysal had supported conscription but had counseled caution and dialogue.[63] This moderating influence disappeared with his death, and four months after, in January 1934, Parliament enacted a universal conscription law.

Tribal rage was compounded when at the end of the year the newly appointed prime minister, 'Ali Jawdat al-Ayubi, went to great lengths in rigging a general election that brought his friends and supporters into Parliament. The illegalities were so blatant that the Senate, the other parliamentary chamber, refused to deal with the Chamber of Deputies. The election produced a considerable decline in the number of tribal representatives. Indeed, the Shi'ite community as a whole was poorly represented. A number of Baghdad politicians belonging to the opposition *al-Ikha'* Party, whose own parliamentary numbers had dramatically fallen, made common cause with tribal leaders of the mid-Euphrates region, inciting them to revolt and promising support. Tribal sheikhs met clandestinely with a number of prominent Iraqi politicians, particularly Hikmat Sulayman, Rashid 'Ali al-Gaylani, and Yasin al-Hashimi, all members of *al-Ikha'* Party, in which various anti-government plans and strategies were discussed, and all parties swore on the Qur'an to remain united in their commitment to topple the government. Indeed Sulayman became the conduit between the tribes of the mid and lower Euphrates and those of the Diyala province.[64] Not surprisingly, tribal lawlessness in the mid-Euphrates increased perceptibly, and a massive petition was presented to the young King. Faced with a seeming imminent tribal revolt, al-Ayubi resigned. However, Ayubi's successor, Jamil al-Midfa'i was hardly any more acceptable to the restive tribes. Although he tried energetically to reach out to the "opposition" by sending ministers to meet with tribal sheikhs and appealing to the Baghdad politicians, particularly members of *al-Ikha'*, to enter into talks with the government, it was to no avail. If anything, the tribal situation in the mid-Euphrates deteriorated, and mini-insurrections erupted in a number of areas. Troops were sent, but the military effort was half-hearted, and the Chief of Staff counseled against a military solution.[65] Faced with the same implacable enemy of its predecessor, the Midfa'i cabinet had little choice but to tender its resignation. It had remained in office a paltry thirteen days. This time, the King asked Yasin al-Hashimi, the leader of *al-Ikha'* and a friend of the disaffected tribal leaders, to form the government.

The tribal leaders who had risen against the government considered Midfa'i's resignation a great triumph. They arranged a large procession of tribesmen who entered Baghdad in March 1935 and roamed the streets of the capital city brandishing their rifles behind their leaders who went straight to Hashimi's offices to congratulate him. But that was hardly the purpose of the theatrics. Soon, they would demand their pound of flesh: greater political influence and more land rights, which could only be extracted at the expense of other tribes that did not happen to support the mini-coup.[66] The grounds were laid for further tribal upheaval.

Rebellions, fuelled by land tenure disputes and the conscription law, erupted in the summer of 1935 and quickly spread to a number of cities of the mid-Euphrates region.[67] This time, as we shall see later in this chapter, the government responded with new resolve and dispatched the army and its infant air force to the troubled areas. The armed forces were able to quell various eruptions in the following twelve months with purposeful savagery.

In the period spanning the summers of 1935 and 1936, the government had to contend with, and ultimately defeat with the force of arms, seven tribal insurrections, five of which occurred in the mid-Euphrates area, and two erupted in the north, one by the Kurds and one by the Yezidis in Sinjar between Mosul and the Turkish border.[68] But 1936 proved to be the year that saw the twilight of tribal power. For the first time since the creation of the state in 1921, the tribes had been made to taste the full venom of the state's displeasure. The rebellions had failed at a great cost of life and possessions to the tribes, their leaders, and their members. The tribes continued to enjoy legal separateness, and were able to continue to exert influence over the policy-making process through the presence of their leaders in Parliament and their alliances with the Baghdad politicians. But their ability, through the use, or the threat, of force, to challenge the central political authority as they had done intermittently since the creation of the Iraqi state, was now gone for good. The catalyst for this consequential change in the power relationship was the country's young, but increasingly effective, armed forces.

The Armed Forces

The majority of Faysal's lieutenants who accompanied him to Iraq were Ottoman-trained Iraqi officers in his Hejazi army that had entered Syria victoriously and later declared an Arab government in 1920. As military officers, they agitated for the creation and expansion of an indigenous Iraqi army. There was, of course, the sense that an army was essential to preserving the integrity of the new country. Of all the other institutions, it was perhaps the most visible and psychologically most relevant manifestation of the country's existence and endurance. Perhaps also, the army was seen by Faysal's companions, all Sunnis from middle- and lower-middle-class families, as an eventual coercive guarantee against the established families and clans of the Shi'ite majority. Consequently, the army grew under British tutelage to 7,500 men by 1925. Against the advocacy of the Iraqis, the British saw no reason for the army to grow beyond this number, and indeed it remained at that level until the end of the mandate period and Iraq's admission into the League of Nations in 1932. Within one year of Iraqi independence, the army's number jumped to 11,500 men and by 1936, it had reached 20,300.[69] The air force, which was non-existent before 1932, had grown in 1936 to four squadrons numbering seventy-two airplanes.[70] Correspondingly the number of British forces fell, from thirty-three infantry battalions in 1921 to only one by 1928 and vanished completely before the end of the decade.[71] While by 1936 Iraq's armed forces might not have been strong enough to defend the country against the likes of Turkey or Iran, it certainly had become more than capable of taking on competing armed sectors of Iraqi society, thus not only asserting the integrity of the state, but also, and possibly more importantly, psychologically imprinting the power of the state onto the consciousness of indigenous fissiparous forces. In 1932 the first such effort to subdue indigenous dissident groups occurred.

The Assyrians, who had migrated from Anatolia and were settled by the British in villages in the north of Iraq after World War I, felt especially threatened by the prospect of the end of the mandate period. Numbering in population just 20,000 to 30,000, and favored by the British, the community had rocky relations with neighboring Kurdish and Arabic-speaking villages. Their mistrust of the Iraqi government was more than reciprocated by Baghdad, as the Assyrians formed the bulk of the British trained and officered military force called the Levies. Used by the British to subdue Kurdish rebellions, they had earned the enmity of the Kurds, and their status as a sector of the British military forces earned them no friends among the country's Arab population or among Iraq's officer corps. With Iraqi independence looming, the Assyrians foresaw a threatened future in the Iraqi state, and they demanded autonomous status, which raised fears in Iraqi government circles of plots to divide Iraq.

The increasingly volatile situation reached a climax in the summer of 1933 when a confrontation between armed Assyrians and a unit of the Iraqi army resulted in far more casualties among the Iraqi soldiers than from the Assyrian side.[72] News of the clash created an atmosphere of anti-Assyrian hysteria in Baghdad, which seemed to be encouraged and abetted by the ruling elite themselves. The army thus was given broad latitude to deal with the "Assyrian menace."[73] It did not help the Assyrians that the commanding officer of the Iraqi army in the north was General Bakr Sidqi, a Kurd who detested the Assyrians. In less than a month, hundreds of Assyrians, most of them unarmed civilians, were massacred by Iraqi troops and Kurdish irregulars. It is unclear as to the extent of Sidqi's culpability in this human carnage, but such was the panic in Baghdad that he was hailed a national hero. The newly independent state had successfully met what it had projected as, even manipulated into, the first challenge to its capacity to impose law and order in the country.

In the mid-Euphrates tribal rebellions during 1935–1936, however, the state was confronted with a challenge to its authority far more formidable than anything the few Assyrians could muster. As we have seen, unrest began in the tribal areas early in 1935 as a result of tribal complaints about land tenure, but also because of general Shi'ite grievances about their exclusion from the policy-making process, which were intensified by their inability to veto, or reverse, the much abhorred conscription law. Reports of tribal unrest, of tribesmen challenging security forces in their towns and burning bridges in anticipation of army moves prompted the government to ask for a military assessment. These, after all, were not a few hundred fighters that the Assyrians produced; tribal alliances could muster upward of 20,000 well-armed tribesmen. The report of the Chief of Staff confirmed these fears: victory could in no way be guaranteed, the number of available troops was small, logistics in the southern marshes were difficult, transportation systems were inadequate, and soldiers, many of whom belonged to the rebel tribes, could not be trusted.[74] Indecision among cabinet members led to the dispatch of troops too few to be effective, and which simply bolstered rebel confidence. The state was to succumb as the government fell and the youthful King Ghazi was made to appoint a prime minister known to have been the rebels' choice. If the Assyrian episode highlighted the state's capacity to project power, the tribal rebellion in the spring of 1935 sowed renewed doubts about state authority among Iraqis.

Soon, however, these doubts were laid to rest. Further tribal insurrections in the summer and fall of 1935 were met with increasing resolve by the government and army. Having cut the railway line, seized a government office, and fought the police successfully, the tribes now were confronted by an Iraqi army vastly different in performance from the one that engaged them half-heartedly a few months earlier. Under the command of the ruthless Bakr Sidqi, the troops bombarded rebel tribesmen mercilessly. What created real panic among the tribes was the first appearance of Iraq's infant Royal Air Force, which bombed the villages from the air. Hundreds of tribesmen were killed; rebel leaders were captured, publicly humiliated, and court marshaled with some receiving the death sentence. But independent in spirit, and still unconvinced of the government's resolve, the tribes rose again in 1936. This time they resolutely engaged army units killing ninety men and downing two aircrafts. But Sidqi and his troops prevailed, meting out savage punishment. Homes were destroyed, innocent villagers imprisoned, and scores of men were hanged on the spot in public, with their corpses left hanging for all to see and ponder the unforgiving power of the state.[75]

Tribal rebellion became a thing of the past after 1936. For those who had presided over the development and progress of the fragile state over the first decade and a half of Iraq's history, the army had served the purpose of its hasty creation in the early days of statehood. The country's armed forces had triumphantly subdued powerful sub-state groups bearing centrifugal tendencies. Having kept the state from falling apart, the army became the most critical and consequential institution in the state. The successful military engagements against the Assyrians and the Euphrates tribes catapulted the military into becoming the arbiter of power in Iraq. It would not take long for the military to become the custodian of power.

CHAPTER THREE

Framing Democracy with a Certain Indifference, 1921–1936

While the form of democracy may differ from one state to another, and while democratic institutions may vary among countries, the one constant is the meaning of democracy: "rule by the people." As early as the 4th century BC, Aristotle held the view that "supreme power ought to be lodged with the many, rather than with the . . . few."[1] He went on to say that regardless of how virtuous a ruler may be, a political order based on "good laws" is preferable to one ruled by a "good man."[2] Aristotle, however, was no naïve idealist; he was well aware of the difficulties inherent in the rule of the many, even for the more manageable Greek city-states. It is this tension between the obvious desirability of the ideal and the complex road trodden to achieve the ideal that has informed contemporary analyses of democracy and the process of democratization.

Twentieth century writings on the meaning of democracy have increasingly drifted away from defining the essence of the ideal in terms of virtue and general good, focusing instead on the "institutional arrangements [by] which individuals acquire the power to decide by means of a competitive struggle for people's vote."[3] Building on this "procedural" definition,[4] as well as exploring the substance of governmental decisions, Robert Dahl identifies eight minimal conditions for a functioning democracy: freedom to form and join organizations, freedom of expression, the right to vote, eligibility for public office, the right of political leaders to compete for support and votes, availability of alternative sources of information, free and fair elections, and institutions for making government policies depend on votes and other expressions of preference.[5] What Dahl does here is to look not only at the procedures for democratic participation, but also at the constraints placed on governmental decision-making by democratic institutions.

What needs to be clarified is that these are "minimal" conditions for mature democracies that tend to reside mainly in the Northern Hemisphere. If these "minimal" conditions were to be applied to the developing world, the analyst would be hard put to identify a single democracy, with the possible exception of India. This dilemma is certainly true in the case of Iraq. As we shall see, democratic institutions were indeed introduced and functioned with varying degrees of effectiveness in this early period of Iraq's development, and indeed through much of the monarchical period. But at no time were all of Dahl's conditions satisfied. And as such, we can correctly conclude that when set against the rigorous standards of mature Western democracies, monarchical Iraq fell short, indeed way short, of the Western democratic ideal. But as Lawrence Whitehead reminds us the wide range of historical, cultural, and social contexts do matter when trying to assess the applicability of democracy.[6] Thus, setting the bar so rigidly high misses crucial variations in the degrees of freedom that are found across space and time, and minimizes useful comparisons among different historical periods within and between countries. For instance, not taking account of the degrees of freedom would lead to the conclusion that the monarchical period was no different from the era of Saddam Husayn. Such a conclusion is both spurious and patently false.

There can be little doubt that the ruling elite throughout the life of the monarchy dominated the policy-making process, but Parliament and the political parties were by no means without the capacity to influence politics. That in and of itself was a singular achievement given that Iraq in 1921 lacked almost all of the social requisites of democracy first formulated by Seymour Martin Lipset.[7] Iraq was poor, non-urban, and utterly unindustrialized. The country's middle class, usually depicted as the social engine for the push toward democratization,[8] was minuscule. While homogenous societies are seen as better equipped for the transition to democracy,[9] Iraq, as we shall see, suffered from serious ethnic and sectarian fissures. Finally, a high level of education, which "is far more significant than income or occupation,"[10] was almost non-existent in a population where illiteracy stood at 95 percent.[11] Still, with all these drawbacks, and with an Executive that was accorded wide-ranging constitutional powers, which it exercised resolutely, democratic institutions, particularly the political parties and the press, cannot be said to have had no impact on the political process.

EARLY DEVELOPMENTS

In the 19th century, the concept of democracy was absent from the intellectual horizons of the vast majority of the inhabitants of the three Ottoman provinces in Mesopotamia, which later were to constitute the modern state of Iraq. The social fabric of society was dominated by traditional and rigid forms of hierarchical authority, which allowed little scope for dissent. The Ottoman Sultan 'Abd al-Hamid II (1876–1909), given to obsessive paranoia, used his legions of secret police and informants, and made cause with traditional leaders, to ensure people's compliance, and to stifle the slightest possibility of any critique of his avowedly absolutist rule. To most of the people who lived in Baghdad, Basra, or Mosul, their only political gesture occurred during Friday prayers when in unison they would call for Allah's blessings on the despot in Istanbul.

The resultant lack of political consciousness engendered a deep-seated disdain for politics; an attitude that situated the public space outside the concerns of the people, even those who were city dwellers. The late Iraqi sociologist, 'Ali al-Wardi, tells us that the people's attitude was encapsulated in the typical response "politics is not *shughli* (my concern); I want *shughl* (a job) that feeds me."[12] Furthermore, other common sayings among the people of the time suggest an attitude of unquestioning deference to the rulers: "Wise are the rulers;" "God is always with the Sultan'" and "kiss the hand that you cannot sever."[13] These and other similar sayings betray an almost ingrained subservience to the rulers and/or distancing one self from the political domain.

Some change came in the first decade of the 20th century when constitutional and parliamentary ideas stimulated by the constitutional movements in Tehran in 1906 and Istanbul in 1908 began to make their way into cities such as Baghdad, Mosul, Basra, Najaf, and Karbala impacting the political consciousness of the small, yet increasingly active, literate class.

The Young Turk revolution in 1908 curbed the Sultan's absolutism and paved the way for elections to the Ottoman Parliament. The Committee for Union and Progress (CUP) promised and enacted liberal reforms that created not just new political currents, but also a new environment of intellectual ferment. Clubs and societies that hitherto would have been forcibly forbidden were born and their numbers increased rapidly. Political parties, even ones in opposition to the CUP such as the Moderate Liberal Party and the Coalition Party, were formed. To Iraqis the first provincial elections to the Ottoman Chamber of Deputies in 1908 constituted a novel, even disturbing, phenomenon. The illiterate 95 percent of the population which resided on the margins of political society viewed the elections with much bemusement and not a little suspicion. Rumors abounded that the elections were a governmental trick to levy more taxes or worse to force people into the Ottoman army. It was inconceivable to these people, who had lived and worked under the dictates of absolutist rule, that holders of power would voluntarily ask for their opinions and input.

The more politically aware sector of society quickly grasped the utility of the elections. In addition to notions of political representation, the elections constituted a means for enhancing their own influence and stature in their respective communities through greater proximity to those who held the main levers of power.[14] Regardless of motives and concerns, the process of electing and being elected did suggest to many a different path to governance from the absolutism of Sultan ʿAbd al-Hamid.

The election was conducted fairly and the elected delegates included a Shiʿite and a Jew, an occurrence that was literally unthinkable in the Hamidian era.[15] Four years later, the next election was more energetically contested and "Iraqis witnessed for the first time [the phenomenon] of party competition among the candidates."[16] In that election a number of candidates, especially from the southern cities of Basra and ʿAmara, who had vociferously opposed CUP policies and practices won parliamentary seats.

The same winds of liberal change, albeit from a different direction, were having a considerable impact on the Shiʿite holy cities of Najaf and Karbala. The 1906 Persian constitutional revolution created a split (and with that a fierce debate) among clerics and their respective followers in Iraq's two holy cities between those who wanted to follow the example of the Persian constitutionalists and those who continued to advocate monarchical absolutism. It was only natural that prior to 1908, the advocates of absolutism in the holy Shi'ite cities held sway over the masses, their cause aided by Sultan Hamid's despotic political structure. But the tide turned after 1908 when the political climate became friendlier to the constitutionalists. In 1909, a Baghdad newspaper published a report titled, "The Free vs. the Supporters of Retrogression," chronicling the proceedings of a public meeting in the Shi'ite holy city of Karbala, in which the invited speaker blamed the violent death of the venerated Imam Husayn in AD 680 on the evils of absolutism. He then went on to argue that the vagaries of absolutist rule were singularly foreign to the principles of justice and equality among all of God's children that are embodied in the teachings of Islam. The paper then pointedly declared that while the speaker had been heckled by a few reactionary advocates of absolutism, his point of view in fact was shared by the majority of those attending the event.[17]

This in no way should suggest an intellectual transformation among the majority of Iraqis toward liberal values. The bulk of the population, illiterate and oblivious to the esoteric debates, would be appalled by such "ungodly" ideas of equality before the Law of men and women and of Muslim, Christian, and Jew. Furthermore, many clerics continued to be hostile to the encroaching liberalism. They were even opposed, some vehemently, to the reading of newspapers and magazines by the literate class, which they considered to be at best a waste of time better spent studying religious texts, and at worst an importation of ideas subversive to the Islamic way of life.[18] Still, while by no means universally accepted, the constitutional movements did etch a different political and intellectual path in the consciousness of the literate and politically aware segments of society.

The period of liberalism and political opening did not last very long, as the CUP was soon to turn to authoritarianism and to an avowed policy of forcing Turkification on the Arabic-speaking provinces. Consequently, political activities in the three provinces were curtailed and these were channeled increasingly into secret anti-Ottoman parties and societies.

Soon, however, World War I would bring the British into Iraq to restimulate liberal and constitutionalist impulses. The British publicly promised that their goal was not to conquer but to liberate the Iraqis from Ottoman colonial and repressive rule. To the bulk of the population, such sentiments sounded more than a little strange. Accustomed to living for centuries under imperial dominion, Iraqis were further baffled by Britain's declaration that a referendum would be held to decide the form of government desired by the indigenous population. One tribal sheikh told a British official: "[Y]ou, the rulers, asking us to tell you our choice of government. . .is a strange request; something we had not heard before. Why should I be involved in this process? If you were to appoint as governor a Christian or a Jew or an Ethiopian slave, that for me would be my government."[19] It was seemingly incomprehensible to most Iraqis that the greatest conquering empire of the time, possessed of unparalleled power and the highest culture, should ask its conquered, and by definition lesser, subjects to determine their own political future.

In fact, as we have seen, that attitude was very much shared by the Acting High Commissioner in Iraq, Colonel A. T. Wilson, who felt that these newly liberated people would be best served by living under direct British rule. Not withstanding the few nationalists, contemptuously dismissed as agitators by Wilson, who demanded independence, the bulk of the population, Wilson would argue incessantly, were nowhere near ready to assume the heavy burden of statehood. He thus set out to engineer the kind of referendum results that were commensurate with his own vision. In his hands, the referendum turned into *"madhabit"* (declarations) by groups of sheikhs and land-owning dignitaries, whose economic interests were served by continued British presence,[20] and who, according to Wilson, would speak on behalf of their illiterate tribesmen and followers.

When the "referendum" was concluded, the majority of *madhabit* emphatically supported British presence. A typical declaration, manifestly deferential, was the one submitted by the people of Karbala, even though religious leaders earlier had issued a *fetwa* (a religious edict) against non-Muslim government:[21]

> In accordance with the order from our just government of Great Britain, may its justice persist, to choose a rule for Iraq. . .we obeyed the order and decided that for the general benefit of all, we resolve to be under the tutelage of our compassionate and magnanimous government of Great Britain at least for the time being until Iraq advances. [And in any case], *the decision is in the hands of those who have the right to decide.*[22] [Italics added]

On the other hand, no amount of pressure and persuasion would dissuade the politically informed Muslim representatives of Baghdad from declaring themselves against British rule, opting instead for an Arab Muslim king limited by a legislative council situated in Baghdad.[23] In his dispatches to the Colonial Office, Wilson belittled the Baghdad declaration as the work of "amateur politicians in Baghdad."[24] He made sure to extract declarations from other Baghdadi groups that defended Britain's political control, and to forward these to London. Philip Ireland, a close observer of Iraqi political development during that period, concludes that while on the whole the Iraqi population was probably in favor of continued British occupation, the picture was not as one-sided as that presented by Wilson to London. Ireland concedes that "the instructions issued by the Acting Civil Commissioner, the method of selecting those who signed the declarations, the personal interviews [that were] conducted and the safeguards adopted so that none but favorable views might be registered, precluded a 'genuine expression of local opinion in Iraq from ever finding its way to H.M. Government, unless the local opinion were satisfactory to the Civil Administration itself."[25] There was of course no shortage of urban and tribal Iraqi notables, who in their effort to win favor with those who were currently the custodians of power, would make the kind of supportive declarations desired by the British.

The referendum exhibited the contradictions inherent in Britain's policy to Iraq. On the one hand, Britain had expressly committed itself to the notion of self-determination. London had declared more than once its desire to see Iraqis choose a representative government. Yet the British also well-understood Wilson's plea for an effective political and security structure in Iraq. And Wilson argued with passion and more than a little justification that such an outcome was possible only under British rule. Furthermore, given the strategic asset of the land of Mesopotamia to the British, H.M. Government was naturally concerned about the prospect of a freely elected nationalist Arab Muslim group assuming the reins of power in the area.

Among the politically informed and active Iraqis, such ambiguities (which would plague British attitudes and policies throughout the mandate period) only confirmed British perfidy; that Britain's true intent was not to grant the inhabitants of the ex-Ottoman provinces the right to sovereignty and self-determination. Consequently, in the post-referendum period membership of anti-British secret societies increased. Composed mainly of urban young men, sometimes in alliance with Muslim clerics and tribal leaders, these clandestine organizations agitated against the British presence through covert recruitment, secret meetings, distribution of subversive leaflets, and occasionally through resort to violence.

The British, for their part, were determined to meet dissent resolutely. Thus, in one notorious instance, a secret anti-British group based in Najaf executed an armed attack against the British headquarters in the city, and succeeded in killing the British military governor. What concerned the British was that the assault was a collaboration between the Najafis and members of contiguous tribes. The British therefore retaliated instantly and mercilessly. They first surrounded the city, cutting off water and food for forty days. Then they launched a massive attack in which scores of rebels were killed. More than a hundred others were captured, of whom thirty were hanged, and many of the city's notables were either imprisoned or expelled.[26]

The groups and political societies that agitated against Britain's presence might have differed on methods and tactics, but they tended to agree on the central goal of creating an independent Iraqi state governed by a constitutional monarchy.[27] For example, in its memorandum to the League of Nations, al-'Ahd al-'Iraqi Organization demanded "a civil constitutional monarchical government" for Iraq. Article two of the constitution of another such organization, Haras al-Istiqlal, demanded a king for Iraq whom they suggested could be one of the sons of Sharif Husayn of Hejaz with the proviso that he should be a "democratic constitutional monarch."[28] The proliferation of these secret societies was attested to by a 1919 British police report which stated that "every Muslim Arab of education in Baghdad was a member of a society, with branches in all the important towns in Mesopotamia [whose goals were] the expulsion of the British and the establishment of Arab rule."[29] The insistence of these societies and organizations on constitutionalism and democratic rule was having an echo in London, but they did not impress Colonel Wilson. In a June 1920 memorandum to the Colonial Office, he advised in the strongest terms: "We must be prepared, regardless of the League of Nations, to go very slowly with constitutional and democratic institutions, the application of which to Eastern countries has been attempted of late years with such a little degree of success."[30] Conflicted, British policy was wavering again, but this time a decisive resolution was forced on it through the eruption of the 1920 insurrection.

Known to Iraqis as the Great Uprising of 1920, the insurrection, as we have seen, began among the Shi'ite tribes of the mid-Euphrates in June and quickly spread to the tribal areas of the lower Euphrates, so that within a month much of the south of Iraq outside a few urban centers was ablaze. Soon after, tribes to the north and west of Baghdad also rose up. It took the British four months to subdue the uprising; a period of intense fighting, punctuated by defeats and reverses, with a huge cost in men and material.[31]

Told by Iraqis, much of the recorded history of the uprising focused on the military operations of the tribes against the British army, and on the political rivalries that plagued, and eventually weakened, the rebellion. But in the midst of the narrative on military engagements there are also accounts of attitudinal changes, of new vocabulary that would have been the domain of the *effendiya*, the literate urban classes, seeping through to the commoners—words such as "independence" and "freedom" that a year or two earlier would have been shunned by the common people as irrelevant to their daily concerns had now become part of their lexicon.[32] Memoirs and histories of the 1920 uprising also recount incidents of political organization and nascent efforts at creating representative institutions.

For short periods, the Iraqis were able to expel the British from some southern towns and cities. Faced with the resultant political vacuum, the inhabitants more often than not established, through a consultative process, civil organizations approximating to temporary governments to maintain law and order as well as provide essential services. This included policing streets and neighborhoods, collecting taxes, organizing health services, rationing water, creating judicial courts, and establishing local governments.[33] One Iraqi eyewitness and participant in the local government in Karbala maintains that much of this administrative structure, fashioned by the Iraqis, was in fact kept in place by the British after they retook the rebellious towns and cities.[34]

In Najaf, the other Shi'ite holy city, which constituted the moral center and ideational heart of the revolt, the inhabitants went a step further in establishing their temporary government. In an eyewitness account:

The Najafis agreed on the necessity of creating executive and legislative councils. A committee of [notables] was formed which decided on an executive council consisting of the leaders of the four main districts of the city. The committee further decided that each of these four districts was to elect two members to sit on the legislative council. Elections were duly held [on August 25, 1920]. Boxes were positioned at the entrance of all city markets for people to place their votes. The votes were counted and the winners [were announced].[35]

Even though Najaf had been touched by the Ottoman and Persian constitutional movements a decade or so earlier, still this election was a remarkable feat as the impulse emerged spontaneously from the people themselves, in a period which pre-dated the establishment of the state, and in a city where tribal norms prevailed and clerics dominated political life.

CONSTITUTIONAL PROCESSES AND DEBATES

The British were able to finally defeat the insurrection, but the cost had been so high that any fanciful notions of direct rule were quickly abandoned. The new High Commissioner, Sir Percy Cox, was tasked with creating a state under Arab rule. The British decided on a monarchy and Faysal, the third son of the Sharif of Mecca, was offered the crown.

Immediately, the British and the presumptive king embarked on a campaign of persuasion to endow a veneer of legitimacy onto the future Iraqi monarchy: Faysal needed to be seen indigenously and be presented abroad as a man chosen by the people. Instructions went to local authorities in the various provinces to hold a series of caucuses to debate and vote on the ascension of Faysal to the throne. Soon, however, this turned into the same kind of process that was used in the referendum, where a series of *madhabits* (declarations) endorsing Faysal were sought. The process, as we saw in the last chapter, was meticulously designed to ensure a unanimous "yes" vote in favor of Faysal,[36] while at a minimum creating an impression of grassroots participation. The British thus had great expectations that Faysal's candidacy would be approved easily and unanimously. And indeed most of the provinces voted for their future king, some even demanding the continuation of Britain's oversight. But there were some unpleasant surprises for the British. The two overwhelmingly Kurdish provinces of Kirkuk and Sulaymaniya actually voted against, Mosul insisted on adding stipulations for the safeguarding of minority political and cultural rights, Basra delayed the process, initially insisting on a loose federal system, and Baghdad, where much of nationalist activity was concentrated, demanded an "independent, constitutional and parliamentary democracy, tied to no outside power."[37] Baghdad went further by requiring "the convening of a national assembly within three months of Faysal's coronation."[38] The posturing of the largest city in the proposed monarchy was not something Sir Percy Cox had anticipated given the amount of effort the British had put into a process expected to seamlessly produce the desired affirmative results.

From then on, there developed an uneasy, at times openly hostile, relationship between the nationalists, who demanded true parliamentary democracy and the High Commissioner and other British personnel who were not averse to granting some political freedoms, as long as these did not undermine British political dominance. This gathering conflict reached a breaking point a year after the investiture of Faysal. The same members of the Baghdad caucus who had insisted on the monarchy's constitutionality dispatched a memorandum to the King castigating him for delaying the establishment of a "legislative assembly to which the government would be responsible, in accordance with established stipulations of constitutional government."[39] They also added that no treaty with Britain should be negotiated before the assembly "is elected in complete freedom."[40] While it could be easily argued that such a memorandum fell within accepted parameters of democratic discourse, the High Commissioner perceived it as a dangerous, even insulting, act of political agitation by a small and unrepresentative minority. He thus moved against the leaders of the group, expelling a number of them out of Iraq.

The anger at the actions of the High Commissioner was felt beyond the educated and professional classes. The clerics who had unequivocally demanded of Faysal a constitutional and parliamentary rule,[41] now produced *fetwas* prohibiting participation in the elections for the proposed Iraqi Constituent Assembly, unless the government and the British responded to the peoples' legitimate demands, which included rescinding existing emergency laws, asserting the freedom of the press and the right to assembly, allowing the formation of political parties, and repatriating the political leaders that were expelled by the British.[42]

In a way, this episode was a microcosm of Britain's dilemma in Iraq that would continue throughout the mandate period, 1921–1932. While notions of independence and freedom had begun to penetrate Iraqi consciousness, there was still a huge divide between the nationalist and democratic aspirations of the few literate and vociferous urban elites and the majority of Iraqis who were still indifferent to the radical ideas of political change and democratic transformation. Barely a year earlier, Sir Percy Cox had asked a group of tribal sheikhs from the south what kind of governance they would prefer for their future independent country. Their response was indicative of the political proclivities of the majority of Iraqis. It was brief and to the point: "Allah is our ruler, Muhammad is our prophet, and Cox is our governor."[43] In a demographic landscape still dominated by rural populations and tribal values, Cox could be excused for dismissing the Baghdad nationalists and democrats as a radical minority hardly representative of the population as a whole.

This dilemma fed into the contradictions inherent in Britain's own policies, torn as it was between a commitment to representative government and a need to assert the right of a dominant empire to control the destiny of a people whose political maturity was still in its infancy. Thus, while the Colonial Office would declare that Britain was committed to a "constitutional monarchy" and had undertaken to make this happen, Cox would give himself the power to officially control any executive decisions made by the Iraqi Cabinet.[44] As we have already seen, the pull of these two contradictory impulses bedeviled the relations of the British with the indigenous political elite throughout the mandate period. In terms of democratic development, it was manifested in the turbulent short life span of the country's Constituent Assembly, Iraq's first elected Parliament.

PARLIAMENTARY DEVELOPMENTS

During the first decade of the infant state, Britain endeavored to regulate its relations with Iraqi governments through a series of treaties, all of which were intended to safeguard and legitimize British hegemony. The first treaty was accepted by the Cabinet in 1922, but was subject to approval by a constituent assembly. Recognizing how hostile Iraqis had become to any notions of "mandatory" jurisdiction over them, Britain formulated the 1922 treaty essentially to substitute for the detested term. In reality, however, the Anglo-Iraqi treaty bestowed on British officials broad supervisory functions over the country's political and administrative apparatus, and made the country militarily and financially dependent on Britain.

Opposition to the treaty and to the government's treatment of the opposition, which was spearheaded by nationalist elements and the Shi'ite clergy delayed the two-tiered elections to the National Assembly until late 1923. It was finally concluded in February 1924. The elected deputies gathered in Baghdad on March 27, 1924 to hear King Faysal open the long-delayed Constituent Assembly.

The King had eloquent words for parliamentary democracy. He extolled the virtues of freedom, reminding the parliamentarians that Islamic laws were based on "consultation," and urged them to ratify the draft constitution and set the electoral procedures for Parliament.[45] But neither the constitution nor the electoral law was the first item for discussion. Bending to British demands, the first item that the Assembly was tasked to discuss and pass was the Anglo-Iraqi treaty. The British felt confident that the treaty would pass quickly, since out of the 100 elected deputies no more than fifteen had voiced anti-treaty opinions.[46] Three weeks before the Assembly was to convene, the *Baghdad Times*, the mouthpiece of the British establishment, wrote:

> In the opinion of competent judges the complex passing of the Anglo-Iraqi Treaty is no longer in doubt. It is estimated that there will be at least 60 strong partisans of the Treaty and a considerable proportion of the remaining 40 will also vote for it, if the Assembly is properly guided.[47]

Very soon, however, what the British had thought to be "a docile and amenable [assembly] proved an illusion."[48] To the nationalist contingent in the Assembly, the treaty simply enshrined the mandatory relationship through a different mechanism. The members of the Assembly, having listened to the King's unqualified praise for democracy and freedom, resolved to take him, his government, and the High Commissioner to task.

The treaty's swift passage which the British had hoped for, indeed expected, turned into more than two months of heated and openly hostile debate. The British probably got an early inkling of this when immediately after the Royal opening of the Assembly, one of the nationalist deputies, Naji al-Suwaydi, suggested that the treaty be presented first to the people so that the deputies could act according to the nation's "wishes and aspirations."[49] This, the Assembly and British knew, was tantamount to the rejection of the treaty and it set the political mood for the passionate and vehement assault on the treaty. Al-Suwaydi and other educated and articulate deputies who harbored strong nationalist sentiments very quickly began to sway opinion within the Assembly, particularly among key tribal sheikhs, against the treaty on the grounds that it limited Iraq's independence and imposed on it an excessive financial burden.

As opposition to the treaty within the Assembly solidified, becoming increasingly strident, so did anti-British passions on the street of Baghdad and other Iraqi cities. Demonstrations against the treaty grew more frequent and more virulent. This in turn had a radicalizing impact on the Assembly's deputies, particularly on a number of elected tribal leaders who had been counted on to endorse the treaty. Whether these tribal leaders rationally gauged the intense unpopularity of the treaty among the public, or whether they themselves were carried by the same emotional fever that was sweeping the country, they did shift their allegiance, turning into vociferous advocates of either rejecting the treaty altogether or at a minimum amending the more unpalatable provisions. Using age-old tribal poetic lexicon, based on notions of honor and manhood, they would assail the treaty as an instrument for the slavery of Iraqis, something that would never be allowed by the proud tribesmen who, a mere four years earlier, had sacrificed themselves for the honor of their country.[50] By early June, the debate in the Assembly had become dominated by raucous anti-British rhetoric. One deputy described the treaty, its articles, and appendices, as a "deadly blow to our independence, meant to negate our very being,"[51] while another charged that anyone who accepts the treaty would be "committing treason which means the loss of religion, honor and freedom."[52] This prompted a prominent tribal leader to threaten another 1920-style insurrection if Britain continued to insist that the treaty would not be amended.[53]

The British, becoming ever more disturbed by the mounting stridency in the tone of the opposition, hinted that any further delay in the ratification of the treaty would have a negative impact on the fate of the northern province of Mosul, which at that time was a point of contention between Iraq and Turkey.[54] There were, to be sure, deputies who advised acceptance, regardless of how grudging this might be. After all, as Nuri al-Sa'id reminded his more obdurate colleagues, Iraq was a small country that lacked an army and modern armaments. It needed the protection of the imperial power at least for the time being. Antagonizing Britain now was not a path trodden by wise men.[55] But such counsel would fall on ears deafened by the clamor to reject or radically revise the treaty.

By June 9, it was evident to the King that the atmosphere in the Assembly was such that any earlier hopes for the passage of the treaty were quickly diminishing. That put him in a delicate, indeed awkward, position being pulled as he was between the demands of the British to which he knew he had to adhere and the vigorous opposition of his "peoples' representatives" to which he needed to be seen to be sympathetic. He thus invited a number of the deputies to the palace and implored them not to overplay their hand. In measured tones, the King said: "I am not telling you to accept or to reject the treaty. You should do what you think is best for the country. But if you decide to reject the treaty, you must not leave [me] hanging between heaven and earth. You will have to come up with another solution."[56] The Royal request prompted a debate in the Assembly on an immediate vote on the treaty, but those voices hoping for a positive outcome were soon drowned by passionate appeals against the treaty, and the debate once more stalled, so that the President of the Assembly had little choice but to postpone proceedings.

It was then that Sir Henry Dobbs, Cox's successor as British High Commissioner, who tended to see any opposition to the British in the Assembly as the work of rabble rousers,[57] resolved to act decisively to stem the gathering anti-treaty tide. On the morning of June 10, more than two months after the convocation of the Assembly, Sir Henry drove to the Palace and delivered a final warning that the treaty had to be ratified by midnight of the same day, or else the King had to use his constitutional prerogative and prorogue the Assembly. Faced with the threat of dissolution, members of the government and the security forces scrambled that evening and rounded up 69 of the 100 deputies, some literally forced out of their beds, and made them vote on the treaty. Even then only 37 voted for the treaty, with 24 against and 8 abstaining.[58] Britain had finally won the day. They subverted the democratic process through the blatant use of political coercion. And throughout the following decade, they kept interfering in the workings of the Parliament, suppressing resolutions and amendments and threatening the dissolution of the institution.[59] Still, during the short life of the Constituent Assembly, parliamentarians, having quickly grasped the functions of the institution and their own responsibilities, had mounted a valiant defense of what they perceived to be the country's best interests.

The Constituent Assembly was an auspicious beginning of parliamentary life in Iraq. The relative freedom in which debates were conducted and, until the intervention of the High Commissioner, the neutrality of the government, augured well for the expansion of Parliament's role in Iraq's political life.[60] But taking their cue from the British, successive Iraqi governments single-mindedly worked to weaken Parliament by making it subservient to the Cabinet and the Prime Minister.

A number of constitutional and institutional factors allowed the government to achieve that goal, and do it rather easily. To begin with, as we have seen in the last chapter, the Constitution granted the Executive, particularly the King, enough powers to make it the dominant policy-making institution. With regards to the Parliament, the King could adjourn, prorogue, or dissolve the institution, and when the Assembly was not sitting, the King had the constitutional right to issue ordinances, with the concurrence of the Cabinet, having the force of law. Reflecting this pattern of granting extensive constitutional rights and privileges to the King, Part III of the Constitution would state: "Legislative power is vested in Parliament and the King."[61] This intrusion into the raison d'être of Parliament naturally weakened the institution, making it beholden to the Executive.[62] No wonder that one parliamentarian would be moved to declare that the constitutional system made the King "the sole custodian of power."[63] In the context of broader executive-legislative relations, successive cabinets, unhappy with the specter of opposition, persistently threatened Parliament with dissolution, and time and again obtained Royal injunctions to achieve that goal.[64] Constrained by its constitutional fragility, Parliament had little appetite to determinedly and effectively challenge, let alone reverse, governmental policies. In fact, Parliament did not pass a single vote of no confidence in any Cabinet throughout the entire life span of the monarchy.

Another factor that contributed to parliamentary weakness was the country's electoral law that gave the government great facility to interfere in the electoral process. The electoral law had been passed by the Constituent Assembly after the ratification of the Treaty and the approval of the Constitution. It provided for a two-tiered, indirect electoral system. A general election, consisting of primary voters, would yield a set of secondary electors who would then elect the parliamentary deputies. This system provided the Royal Court and the government with smaller, more manageable number of electors. Moreover, the government literally was given two opportunities to interfere in the process; what they might miss in the first round, they could rectify in the second. More often than not in collusion with the British Residency, governments actively rigged elections. This was particularly the case in the elections that preceded the ratification of treaties with Britain. Determined that the treaties would pass with as little opposition as could be arranged, the British would put pressure on the King to ensure the election of candidates to the Chamber of Deputies that the British considered well-disposed to their policies.[65] This manipulation of the electoral process invariably produced ready-made governmental majorities:

> Confidential orders [from] the government to provincial officials proved sufficient to secure the election of its candidates whether they were residents of the district or even known there. Thus in 1925, all but four of the government candidates were returned. . . . In 1928 all the deputies returned from Basra, 'Amara, Diyala, Dulaim, Hilla and Arbil Liwas (provinces) were government nominees. Of the thirteen Baghdad deputies, all but five were government candidates. In these two elections, as well as in that of 1930, a number of Opposition candidates were conscientiously included by the government on the principle advocated by the King that talented members of the Opposition would

raise more difficulties outside Parliament. . . . Thus in 1928, half of the twenty-two Opposition members returned to the Chamber had been previously given the government coupon.[66]

This account is supported by an official member of the British Residency who agrees that the list of elected deputies tended to correspond closely to that of government-sponsored candidates that would have been conveyed to provincial officials prior to the election.[67] Indeed, one tribal deputy, seemingly suffering an attack of conscience, felt compelled to announce in the Chamber in the wake of the 1928 elections that he was there representing the province of Kut, yet being from the province of Diyala, he in fact did not know a single soul from Kut.[68] Naji al-Suwaydi, the vigorous opposition figure, but still a pillar of the monarchical political order, in a newspaper interview in 1936, lambasted successive Iraqi governments for "selecting the deputies without bothering even to wait for the election."[69] The result, according to another observer, was "deputies with short hands and severed tongues."[70] Not withstanding the hyperbole, there can be little doubt that constant governmental manipulation of the electoral process undermined Parliament's autonomy, stunting its ability to legislate independently of the Executive.

Contributing to this process of parliamentary decline was the uneven quality of the deputies themselves. More than one third of the members of the Constituent Assembly were tribal leaders, many of them hardly literate. Thus, for the most part, they were oblivious to, and uncomprehending of, parliamentary procedures.[71] In the debates over the electoral law in the Constituent Assembly, the problem of illiteracy was indeed broached by a few educated deputies who, on the whole, tended to emanate from the cities. To them, the notion of someone participating in the legislation of laws that he in fact would not be able to read, let alone comprehend, was galling.[72] They, however, found little support in the Assembly as many of the deputies recognized that the tribes constituted an important segment of Iraqi society. Hence, they could not be excluded from political representation through the introduction of some form of an educational, or even a simple literacy, standard. Moreover, there was still a strong residue of respect and admiration for the tribesmen who had risen against the British in 1920 and had paid with their lives. The result was that not only was there heavy tribal representation, but the deputies from tribal areas became the backbone of what came to be called the "government list," and were notorious for doing the government's bidding in the Chamber.

In spite of all of these shortcomings, the work of the Parliament during the first decade of its life was not without its fair share of achievements. While it was unable to consistently check ministerial dominance, it did serve on a number of occasions as a brake to ministerial initiatives, slowing down imperfect legislation and unearthing irregularities, thus forcing ministerial reassessments.[73] Not even the most senior and consequential governmental figure could escape the lashing tongues of the opposition, which generally compensated for its lack of quantitative weight with sustained, yet well thought out, assaults on the government and its policies. Interestingly, these biting criticisms were in general listened to attentively by government figures and thoroughly replied to. A case in point was the debate over the 1930 Anglo-Iraqi Treaty. The Iraqi government, under intense pressure from the British, had accepted the new treaty as a necessary prelude to Britain's acquiescence to Iraq's entry into the League of Nations. In the parliamentary debate, members of the opposition, such as Yasin al-Hashimi, Rashid 'Ali al-Gayalani, and Sadeq al-Bassam, assailed the treaty in strong and uncompromising, yet measured, tones.[74] Their condemnation of the treaty strongly implied a censure of the King and his Prime Minister, Nuri al-Sa'id. In his response, Nuri was no less fervent and no less civil. His defense of the treaty was couched in pragmatism. This was not the ideal treaty, he readily conceded. He even agreed with a number of the opposition's criticisms, pointing out that had Iraq been a sovereign country and not under the British mandate, he would not have advised the King to sign the treaty. But under the circumstances, he insisted, this was the best that the country could hope for.[75] The deputies did end up ratifying the treaty by a 69–13 margin, and the senate confirmed the ratification with an 11–5 vote. Not unexpectedly, the government had its way; still the debate was poignant and hard-hitting, and its daily proceedings were followed fervently by the literate public.

Occasionally, Parliament scored more tangible successes: modifying a governmental bill, forcing the government to adopt some of its ideas, and making a minister think twice before submitting a policy proposal. On more than one occasion, Parliament was instrumental in the downfall of governments.[76] In 1925, Prime Minister Yasin al-Hashimi tendered his government's resignation because he felt that he no longer commanded the confidence of the Parliament. A year later, Parliament elected a member of the opposition as its president against the express wishes of Prime Minister 'Abd al-Muhsin al-Sa'dun, who took this as a political snub and resigned.

Beyond such and other tangible results, Parliament also impacted the population in critical intangible ways. It was a propitious learning experience for many of the country's rising political class. Stephen Longrigg, a member of the British Residency, tells us that "even a semi-nominated Chamber contained enough of intelligence, experience, and public spirit to be a valuable deliberative and critical body."[77] Imperfect as it was, Parliament still allowed for discontent to be voiced from within the political system, thus limiting the possibilities of violent eruptions.

POLITICAL PARTIES

The constitutional document, known as the Basic Law, that was ratified by the Constituent Assembly in 1924 was modeled on the British political system, and as such provided for many of the civil liberties that would be found in Britain. Foremost among these were the rights of free expression, publication, assembly, and the forming and joining of political parties within the law.

Indeed, political parties existed before the creation of the state, but these were underground organizations agitating for Iraqi independence, particularly as Britain's declaration in 1917 that it had come as a liberator of Iraq had not panned out a full two years later. In 1919, two secret organizations, *al-'Ahd* and *Haras al-Istiqlal*, taking advantage of the public's frustration with British recalcitrance on Iraqi independence, undertook a variety of activities, from anti-British propaganda to incitement of tribes to contacts with other Arab political organizations, for the purpose of igniting and cementing a nationalist, anti-colonial, sentiment. It is not clear how successful in achieving their goal these two organizations were, but they might have played a role in the insurrection of 1920.[78] Regardless, they did provide an institutional precedent, as well as a number of seasoned political activists, for the political parties that were to be formed legally after the birth of the Iraqi state.

Almost a year after the ascension of Faysal to the throne, a group of men, most of whom had been active against the British, finally had their request to form a political party accepted by the Ministry of Interior. *Hizb al-Watani al-'Iraqi* was duly born on August 3, 1922. Two weeks later, another party called *Hizb al-Nahdha al-'Iraqiya* entered the political arena. With their anti-British views, these two parties immediately adorned the mantle of the opposition. Dominated by educated and politically active Shi'ite men, these two parties did not differ much on ideology or political platform, and easily could have merged into one party. But the competition for spiritual and ideational leadership within the Shi'ite community between the two most senior clerics, Muhamed al-Sadr and Mahdi al-Khalisi, splintered the community, giving rise to two sets of political allegiances that were manifested in the creation of the two political parties.[79] In response to the declared radicalism of the two opposition parties, the British and the King encouraged supporters to form a government party called *al-Hizb al-Hurr al-'Iraqi*. But in this initial and formative period of institutional development, it was the two anti-British parties that dominated the political theater, and it did not take them long to make their presence felt. Within days of their birth, they organized a joint demonstration in front of the Palace, and handed in a memorandum demanding a representative government that would be responsible to a legislative council and an end to British interference.[80] As we have seen, this drew the wrath of the then High Commissioner, Sir Percy Cox, who made sure to expel almost the entire leadership of the two parties. The absence of opposition seems to have made the governmental party irrelevant, and within a year it folded.

Nahdha reappeared on the political scene in 1924 and *al-Watani* in 1928, both being members of the opposition, but by then in weakened form with almost no parliamentary representation. They nevertheless continued to vigorously oppose the British, raising their opposition to unprecedented levels during the charged debates over the Anglo-Iraqi treaty of 1930. Their voice might not have been heard in Parliament, but their radical ideas were propagated in public meetings and through their newspapers, and as such had a distinct impact on debates within the Parliament. By then other parties had been formed, such as the government parties *al-Taqadum*, formed by Prime Minister 'Abd al-Muhsin al-Sa'dun, and *al-'Ahd*, formed by Prime Minister Nuri al-Sa'id in 1930. *Al-Sha'ab*, formed in 1925 and *al-Ikha' al-Watani*, created in 1930, were parties that opposed the government mainly in regard to Anglo-Iraqi relations, particularly over the two treaties of 1927 and 1930. Unlike the earlier opposition parties, the membership of *al-Sha'ab* and *al-Ikha'* was broader, constituting a more balanced representation of the country's sects and ethnicities.

The opposition parties mounted spirited campaigns questioning various details of the treaties not just in Parliament, but again also publicly through their own newspapers, and other independent, yet politically sympathetic, outlets.[81] On occasions, even governmental parties joined with the opposition in Parliament. In one instance, Prime Minister 'Abd al-Muhsin al-Sa'dun saw fit to negotiate certain financial and security articles in the 1927 treaty which he deemed to be too restrictive. When the British would not compromise, his party joined the opposition in rejecting the said articles, and that led to the fall of his government. What ensued was a prolonged governmental crisis, in which over a period of more than three months the King was unable to find a candidate willing to form a Cabinet.[82] It is of course true that with regard to the various Anglo-Iraqi treaties, the British and the King invariably were to eventually have their way. But the opposition parties, through parliamentary debates and in their ability to arouse public feelings, made the road to the treaties a rocky one.

By the mid 1930s, most of these parties had vanished from the political scene. One possible reason was that after Iraq signed the 25-year treaty with Britain in 1930 and after it had acquired international recognition of its sovereignty when the country was accepted into the League of Nations in 1932, the raison d'être of the opposition parties, which had centered mainly on their anti-British stance, was much diminished, hence they "died natural deaths."[83] That left the government parties lacking an "other" for the purpose of maintaining their own political identity and cohesion, and they too disappeared quickly from the political scene.

Another reason for the disappearance of the parties was their tendency to coalesce around a very small number of people, and in some cases just one politically dominant individual. No wonder therefore, that the life span of the parties seemed to be linked to the political fortunes of their leaders. This was particularly true of the government parties, such as *al-Taqadum* and *al-'Ahd*, which began their lives for no other purpose than to ensure parliamentary majorities for prime ministers al-Sa'dun and al-Sa'id, respectively, and instantly departed the political scene once their leaders resigned the premiership. The opposition parties hardly behaved differently, even those with extensive popular backing, such as *al-Watani*, whose support base, according to one seasoned observer, claimed "the merchant, landowner and businessman alongside the laborer, peasant and peddler."[84] Even so, the party did have one dominant figure and moving spirit in the person of Ja'far Abu al-Timman, and when he decided to "give up political life in November 1933," the party disbanded less than six months later.[85] Similarly, the other opposition party with a national mass following, *al-Sha'ab*, effectively ceased to exist as a political force very soon after its founder and central figure, Yasin al-Hashimi, became Minister of Finance in 1926.

Any analysis of the institutional development of political parties in the country's first decade and a half clearly shows that these parties had neither the institutional strength nor the ideational direction and purpose of their more established and sophisticated Western counterparts. Nevertheless, political parties in Iraq did contribute to the emergence and sustenance of a relatively liberal political environment that allowed opposition to important policies to be propagated and heard both by the public at large and by the Palace and the government. By the mid 1930s, the notion of *ahzab al-mu'aradha* (opposition parties) had entered people's political consciousness and their everyday lexicon.

THE PRESS

Newspapers were essential vehicles in disseminating the ideas and programs of the opposition parties. By manipulating the electoral process, Iraq's governments, aided and egged on by the Palace and the British, were able to keep the impact of opposition parties inside Parliament to manageable proportions. But those parties had access to another outlet, their newspapers, to publicize their political and socioeconomic visions, vociferate their criticisms and demands of the governments, and lay out for the people a case for an alternative political path. Articles and editorials critical of governmental policies and personalities were a staple of Iraq's media output from the very beginning of the monarchical period. In fact, as early as the outset of the 20th century, the press would play a major role in shifting the attitudes of the literate segment of the population away from unquestioning acceptance of absolutism as a political and religious duty.

While papers existed before the 1908 Constitutionalist Movement, they were few and mainly official mouthpieces that printed governmental directives and announcements. At times, however, they were allowed to carry topics that were meant to enlighten a predominantly backward and conservative population, and sometimes (though rarely) even entertain controversial issues, such as female education.[86] The 1908 Constitution which relaxed censorship precipitated a media revolution. Within three years no less than sixty-nine newspapers and journals had been published in Baghdad, Basra, and Mosul.[87] Most of these papers, however, were poorly produced and amateurishly written, consisting more often than not of personal attacks that were devoid of political and social value. It was hardly surprising that many of these papers ended up vanishing as abruptly as they had appeared. The newspapers that ended up having a longer life span were the ones that saw themselves as communicators of people's concerns, as well as their frustrations with the authorities. Such papers had no qualms about forcefully censuring the Ottoman authorities over such issues as the perceived neglect of the Arabic speaking parts of the empire and the persistence in favoring Turkish over Arabic which, according to one paper, "would cause all Arabs to unite against [the Ottoman authorities.]"[88] A British official surveying the political scene in Baghdad in 1912 was moved to declare that he was "much struck of late by the increasing freedom with which . . . anti Turkish sentiments were expressed here."[89] While the number of newspapers dwindled after the initial euphoria of the liberal opening, those that remained made up in the quality of their opinion and analysis what the reader had lost in the sheer quantity of choice.

When the British arrived in Iraq during World War I, they promised a tolerant disposition to oppositional views and criticisms. A Christian power replacing Muslim imperial authority in an Islamic country, Britain sought the support of at least the literate segment of Iraqi society by trying to retract the long arm of the state. It is in this context that the British declaration of their intent not to occupy Iraq but to liberate it from Ottoman tyranny would best be understood. A primary beneficiary of this enhanced atmosphere of liberalism was the press, which was allowed greater leeway in the breadth of topics covered and in the depth and zeal with which these subjects were broached. This was attested to by a "nationalist" journalist who would concede that the press fared much better in that period of direct British control than it did later on in the era of Iraqi independence.[90] And indeed, in the run-up period to Faysal's candidacy, newspapers became the main debating forums, opening up their pages to wide spectrums of opinion. It was not uncommon that a newspaper would report a supportive statement to be followed a few days later by a host of unflattering responses and opinions.[91]

This tradition of questioning and criticizing carried through into the monarchical period. During the first decade of the monarchy, which was dominated by concern over the mandate and the extent of British powers in Iraq, the press "presented an articulate opposition to British control, characterized by telling criticisms both of British policies and of their prejudices in dealing with Iraqis."[92] When Britain claimed that it could not divest herself of her status as a mandate power because of her obligation to the League of Nations, an opposition paper retorted: "Suppose the League asked Great Britain to put her fleet at its disposal, would Great Britain agree as she has agreed to the yoke of the mandate [over Iraq?]"[93] Almost a decade later, similarly harsh criticisms were leveled at the 1930 Anglo-Iraqi treaty. To one nationalist paper, the treaty's clauses were "fetters mercilessly placed around the necks of the Iraqis to condemn them to servitude for a quarter of a century longer."[94] Britain and its perceived imperious presence in Iraq was the main focus, indeed the raison d'être, of the majority of the nationalist and oppositional papers.

One of the few papers that consciously linked British power with the country's socioeconomic ills was the daily *al-Ahali* (the People), which was the mouthpiece of a group of middle-class intellectuals who advocated political independence and social-democratic principles. Not a political party per se, *Jama'at al-Ahali* (the Ahali Group) was more a conglomerate of progressive young men drawn from all sectors of Iraqi society, a number of them educated abroad, with varying ideological proclivities, who were united in their commitment to the political and socioeconomic progress of the country, and in their belief that the interests of the people should be placed above all other interests. Vigorous and committed to the ideals of *al-Sha'biya*, populism, they formed the political grouping in the early 1930s, and for the next few years, the group's activities hovered on the margins of clandestine politics. Their newspaper, *al-Ahali* (and because of censorship its various incarnations), became one of the most respected and widely read newspapers in monarchical Iraq.

The group's goals and principles, which were articulated candidly and forcefully in the opinion page of the newspaper, were to have a democratic Iraq independent of the British, to reduce the socioeconomic disparities among the country's population, to expand free public education and health services, and to reform personal status laws in accordance with modern practices.[95] However, *al-Ahali* would argue that because there was an unholy alliance between the British and the indigenous exploitative class socioeconomic reform could not properly take place while the British remained the hegemonic power in Iraq. The paper continued to draw out this relationship. For example, one editorial attacked the government for not undertaking any reform because it was constituted from, and supported by, men who, through the aid of imperialism, exploited the people.[96] Because of its stinging attacks on various governments, particularly that of the increasingly dictatorial Yasin al-Hashimi (March 1935–October 1936), the paper was constantly harassed by security forces and repeatedly closed down.[97] The *Ahali* group would immediately publish another newspaper, carrying a variant on the name, and would carry on where its predecessor left off.[98] Indeed, after every closure, it seems, rather than temper its strident tone, the paper would in fact lash out at the government with even more venom.

The *al-Ahali* newspaper (and its various incarnations) was somewhat of an aberration, because it lasted for over three decades, which was in stark contrast to other papers that were mouthpieces of political parties and groups, whose life spans were generally short. Between 1919 and 1933, sixty-one papers were published in Iraq,[99] many of them were voices of the opposition and most of them folded a year or two after publication.[100] At times, this happened as a result of governmental harassment. But in other instances, the papers stopped publication simply because the parties they represented ceased to exist.

The path that the press trod between 1921 and 1936 was similar to that trodden by Parliament and the political parties, the other institutions of democracy. Their impact was hampered by consistent and resolute governmental interference, by a British response that at best was indifferent and at worst hostile, and by a certain political immaturity among the flag bearers of democracy in Iraq who, on the whole, eschewed organizational imperatives in favor of coalescing around a few dominant leaders. Thus, while opposition was forcefully voiced, particularly in regard to British dominance, it was more often than not associated with individuals, rather than with broadly based, ideationally coherent, political coalitions, which made it easier for the Palace and the Cabinet, as well as the British, to either disregard it, or muzzle it altogether.

While those acting on behalf of the state did their utmost to limit the impact of democratic institutions on the political process, and while they were aided in their quest by some structural deficiencies in the institutions themselves, these institutions, the Parliament, political parties and press, at a minimum succeeded in advancing the spirit of dissent and the idea of opposition among the people of Iraq, particularly the urban middle class. In many ways, therefore, the hesitant development of democratic practices mirrored the uneven development of state institutions in the years between the creation of the Iraqi monarchical state in 1921 and the execution in 1936 of Iraq's (indeed the Arab world's) inaugural military coup.

CHAPTER FOUR

The Uncertain Nation, 1921–1936

If the process of constructing and managing governmental and democratic institutions proved hardly a smooth and easy endeavor, then creating a nation out of Iraq's disparate communities was to be just as, if not more of, difficult a task. After all, the borders of the country were agreed on in the Cairo Conference of March 1921, a mere three months before Faysal's arrival in Iraq, and not solidified until the 1926 Brussels agreement. In fact, the shape of the new country, which entailed the amalgamation of the three ex-Ottoman *vilayets* (provinces), Mosul, Baghdad, and Basra, into the new state of Iraq, might not have come to fruition had it not been for the dogged and tireless efforts of Gertrude Bell during the Cairo conference.[1] Faysal's new country was thus an artificial creation; the off-spring of the reorganization of British interests in the Middle East. Yet in order to make the project viable, the ruling elite recognized the importance of amalgamating the disparate peoples that were now housed within the borders of the state into at least a semblance of a unified and functioning nation.

Nation is an elusive concept that evades precise definition. "I am driven to the conclusion," Hugh Seton-Watson tells us, "that no 'scientific definition' of a nation can be devised. . . . All that I can find to say is that a nation exists when a significant number of people in a community consider themselves to be a nation."[2] It thus seems that at its most basic, nation is a form of identity. Individuals identify with their nation in the same way that they might identify with other forms of collective identity, such as religion, race, tribe, and ethnicity. And indeed, belonging to an Iraqi nation need not nullify other forms of sub-national identities. Thus, it is perfectly natural for an Iraqi man to also identify himself as a Sunni (his sect) and a Dulaimi (his tribe). The crucial question, however, is to which of these identities is he most attached and loyal? To speak of an Iraqi nation means that all other forms of belonging, including the sectarian and tribal, should be subordinate to the supreme sense of attachment and loyalty to an Iraqi nation.

From its Latin origin, *natio*, which the Romans contemptuously used to depict foreigners of lesser social status than Roman citizens, to its grandiose use in Europe after the 17th century as the ultimate object of people's loyalty, the intellectual development of the concept of the nation mirrored the political contours of European history.[3] By the middle of the 19th century, these ideas clustered into two main intellectual strands:[4] a German conception that saw nations as cultural creations, their beginnings implanted in a remote, even immemorial, past, and a French/English formulation that conceived of the nation as a purposeful construction of the state, or at least of determined political segments within it.[5] Ernest Gellner is a firm exponent of the latter position: "Nations as a natural, God-given way of classifying men are a myth. . . . Nationalism . . . sometimes takes pre-existing cultures, and turns them into nations, sometimes invents them . . . that is a reality."[6] Even a cursory glimpse into Iraqi history would tell us that the German conception of an immemorial Iraqi nation is in no way sustainable. As we shall see later in this chapter, one of the most urgent and important tasks that was undertaken by the new Iraqi state was to mold disparate communities, divided by ethnicity, sect and tribe, lacking social and cultural connections, into one viable nation.

In this sense, therefore, Iraq follows the pattern expounded by French and English thinkers of the 18th and 19th centuries. One can see Iraqi national developments reflected in the words of the 19th century French historian and philosopher, Ernest Renan, who saw the role of the French monarchs as indispensable to the creation of the French nation. In his celebrated essay, "What Is a Nation?" Renan relates that the French nation was created by "the King of France, partly through his tyranny, partly through his justice."[7] This proposition is certainly applicable to the case of Iraq. From the very beginning of the state, King Faysal worried over the country's communal divisions and tried valiantly to merge these into a coherent Iraqi nation, intervening constantly, for example, to bring Shiʿite youth into Iraq's body politic, and encouraging a national secular curriculum to replace existing religious and particularistic teachings. Nor did he shirk from resorting to physical force in subduing separatist political and cultural tendencies.

But this was no easy task for the King and his government. The state that the British assembled in 1921 had major fissures between Arab and Kurd, Sunni and Shi'ite. These fault lines overlapped with, and indeed were cemented by, the cultural and economic disparities that existed between the urban and rural areas. Of the rural population, much of which was abjectly poor and illiterate, 65 percent was Shi'ite and only 16 percent was Arab Sunni.[8] These communal divisions would prove to be some of the most obstinate hurdles to social and political integration in Iraq during the first decade and a half of the country's life, and even beyond.

THE COMMUNAL DIVIDE

In the south, the Basra *vilayet* was predominantly Shi'ite with extensive human and material connections to Persia on the country's eastern border. Baghdad and the central part of Iraq was populated primarily by Sunnis who shared their sect with the Ottoman rulers and Iraq's Arab neighbors. Mosul and the north contained substantial non-Arab populations, mainly Kurdish, and to a lesser extent Turkomen. Added to this demographic mix were smaller but influential communities of Jews and Christians, who were on the whole city dwellers, except for the Christian Assyrians and Chaldeans who lived in villages north of the city of Mosul.

The new state would experience its fair share of communal violence, and as usual minorities would suffer: Assyrians at the hands of Kurds and Arabs, later Jews at the hands of other Iraqis, and later still Turkomen at the hands of Kurds. While the magnitude of these conflicts, and the human tragedies engendered by their periodic eruptions, must not be minimized, it still remains the case that the most significant demographic dislocation in Iraq was between Arabs and Kurds who were separated on ethnic lines, and between Sunnis and Shi'ites who divided along sectarian affiliations.

Of the two divides, the case of Kurd against Arab was the thornier issue. Constituting around 18 percent of the Iraqi population, and speaking an Indo-European language, the Kurds possess a fully developed sense of nationhood that has been frustrated by the various states and their governments in which the Kurds constituted significant minorities. This sense of nationhood furthermore was acknowledged by the outside world. The 1920 Treaty of Sèvres, signed by the Allied Powers and the Ottoman government, called for the establishment of an autonomous Kurdish political entity in the "areas lying east of the Euphrates, south of . . . Armenia and north of . . . Syria and Mesopotamia." The Treaty further provided that if within one year of the implementation of the treaty, "the majority of the Kurdish population in these areas desire independence," then subject to a recommendation from the Council of the League of Nations, Turkey should agree to "renounce all rights and title over these areas."[9] Kurdish aspirations were, however, frustrated by the emergence of Mustafa Kemal in Turkey, who would not ratify the treaty and who proceeded to establish effective military control over the Kurds of eastern Turkey.

Throughout the 19th century, the Kurds in Iraq had been able to lead a relatively autonomous existence. They were able to achieve this because the rugged and grueling mountainous terrain, as well as their economic self-sufficiency, reduced contact with, and dependence on, outsiders, to say nothing of the ferociousness with which the Kurds have been willing to defend their territory.[10] When the Ottomans made an effort to assert their authority over the more inaccessible parts of their empire, they precipitated major uprisings in the Kurdish areas in 1837–1852 and 1880–1881. Up until the collapse of their empire, the Ottomans could hardly claim to have had their authority accepted in the Kurdish areas in what are now northern Iraq and southeastern Turkey. No wonder, therefore, that throughout the more than eight decades that began with the creation of the Iraqi state and ended with the forcible removal of Saddam Husayn and his regime, the "Kurdish problem" remained the most enduring and difficult predicament of successive Iraqi governments. The attitudinal distance entailed in the ethnic divide between Arab and Kurd was too powerful a stumbling block. Consequently, overtures from the essentially Arab government in Baghdad were always half-hearted, and deep down the Kurds always desired a state of their own, having been constantly aware, and made aware, of their ethnic uniqueness in a predominantly Arab milieu. It is in this context that someone such as Bakr Sidqi, Iraq's military hero and strongman in the mid-1930s, would confide to the German chargé d'affaires in Baghdad that, being the son of a Kurdish father, the dream of a sovereign Kurdish state would always "reside in his heart."[11]

The Sunni-Shi'ite divide is different in the sense that it is essentially a conflict between Arab and Arab. Shi'ism emerged as a result of the dispute within the early Muslim community over the succession to the Prophet Muhammad. The Sunnis, who formed the majority, believed that God's guidance passed from the Prophet to the Muslim community as a whole, basing their belief on a saying by the Prophet: "My community will not agree on an error."[12] The Sunnis, thus, accepted the progression of Islamic history from the Prophet to all his successors (the Khalifas) "who have held office, regardless of the method of selection, so long as they were able to make their claims effective."[13] The Shi'ites, however, believe that succession to the Prophet should have devolved onto his cousin and son-in-law, 'Ali, and subsequently to all his heirs. They go further by endowing a kind of religious infallibility onto 'Ali and all his descendants, who are recognized as the Imams of the Shi'ite community. The twelfth Imam disappeared in the ninth century, and Shi'ites believe that he went into concealment, to appear later as the Mahdi, when he would restore peace and justice to the world.

While in Iraq and Iran the Shi'ites constitute a majority, in the world of Islam as a whole, it is the Sunnis who form the overwhelming majority. As is generally the case with minorities, the Shi'ites have been persecuted throughout Islamic history. Hence a deep-seated bond exists among Shi'ites in general, leading in the case of Iraqi Shi'ites to a strong affinity with their Iranian co-religionists. This kinship was strengthened over time by the existence in Iraq of the two holiest cities in Shi'ite Islam, Najaf and Karbala, which attracted Iranian pilgrims throughout the ages, constituting something akin to an open flow of humanity. As strong as these sectarian ties are, the ethnic divide between Arab and Persian proved a more powerful impulse. Iraqi Shi'ites thus exhibited little enthusiasm for political links with Iran or for a separate state of their own. This was true not only over the formative years of the state, but throughout the 20th century.

As Arabic is their mother tongue, and as they share the same ethnic characteristics of the Iraqi Sunnis, Iraqi Shi'ites demanded no more than a restructuring of the political and socioeconomic balance which since Ottoman days had been heavily in favor of the minority Sunnis. In fact,

Ottoman authorities followed pronounced policies aimed at marginalizing the Shi'ite community. In assessing the condition of the Shi'ites under Istanbul's dominion, the prominent Iraqi politician and intellectual, Kamel al-Chaderji writes: "No Shi'ite was accepted in the military college or in the bureaucracy, except on very rare occasions. There were all kinds of hurdles preventing Shi'ites from even entering high schools. The state did not think of the Shi'ite community as part of it, and the Shi'ites did not consider themselves to be part of the state."[14] Trying to rectify this historical injustice, the Shi'ites, more than once, specifically in 1927, 1932, and 1935, drew up manifestos articulating their demands of the Sunni-dominated Iraqi government. These included greater Shi'ite participation in government, parliament, and civil service; the teaching of Shi'ite jurisprudence in the Law school, changes in the taxation system in the rural Shi'ite south; and government investment in health and education in Shi'ite areas.[15] Perceiving the government's response as slow and half-hearted, the Shi'ites mounted anti-government eruptions and insurrections. But these were usually manifestations of the community's desire to improve its sociopolitical status in the country; at no time did the Shi'ites articulate a yearning to extricate themselves from the Iraqi state.

Still in terms of national consolidation, the Shi'ites, most of whom in the formative years of the state belonged to the tribal confederations of the south, mistrusted the urban Sunni elite who ruled the country.[16] The result was a relatively enduring perception during this period that the Iraqi nation and the Iraqi state were essentially Sunni projects. 'Ali al-Wardi relates an incident in the early days of the Iraqi state during 'Ashura', the anniversary of the defeat and martyrdom of the Shi'ite Imam Husayn in Karbala in AD 680 at the hands of the Ummayads of Damascus, the citadel of Sunni Islam. In the first year of his reign, King Faysal and a number of his ministers and policy-makers, including Sati' al-Husri, the virulently Arab nationalist Director General of Education, were invited to attend the re-enactment of the battle which was performed annually in the Shi'ite neighborhood of Kadhmiya in Baghdad. The King and his mostly Sunni entourage accepted gratefully, seeing the event as an opportunity to showcase the new symbol of a unified Iraq, the newly designed national flag. Unfortunately an embarrassing problem for the V.I.P. attendees soon developed when all attempts by the horseman carrying the new

Iraqi flag to move toward Imam Husayn's ranks were frustrated as he and his flag were determinedly nudged toward the vicinity of those acting the roles of the Syrian Ummayads, thus becoming a target of the biting denunciations and curses of the Shi'ite mourners. When all efforts by Iraqi officials to move the flag onto to the Shi'ite (i.e., Iraqi) side failed, the flag was discreetly withdrawn.[17] While efforts were made, particularly by King Faysal, to bring the Shi'ites into the affairs of the state, the Shi'ite community remained on the margins of the national project, and were on the whole incidental to it.

Iraq's communal fissures, particularly between Shi'ites and Sunnis and Arabs and Kurds, were exacerbated by a pervasive tribal structure that posed numerous problems for national consolidation. Beyond the Bedouin's innate discomfort with authority, his attitude to the idea of a nation was bound to be informed by the fragmented, even conflictual, milieu in which he lived and functioned, a milieu vastly different to that of the nation which entailed a unity of purpose and a common esprit de corps. According to Hanna Batatu, Iraq's monarch had "a social meaning diametrically opposed to that of the tribal shaykh. . . . The shaykh represented the principle of the fragmented or multiple community (many tribes), the monarch the ideal of an integrated community (one Iraqi people, one Arab nation). Or to express the relationship differently, the shaykh was the defender of the divisive tribal *urf* (customs law), the monarch the exponent of the unifying national law."[18] What is interesting is the enduring nature of tribal ties and outlook. Bassam Tibi in his analysis of the modern Middle East tells us that "neither in the imperial nor in the territorial state were tribes transformed into a homogenous polity; tribal ties have always been the basic element of group reference, despite the fact that they were suppressed and rhetorically renounced. This happened in the past within the framework of a universal Islamic *Umma* and in the present with reference to the secular idea of the nation."[19] And in Iraq these values extended beyond the rural areas to the cities. 'Ali al-Wardi maintains that as late as the 1960s, modernization in the cities was superficial, that deep down many city dwellers were Bedouin at heart, and that the trappings of modernity, such as Western clothing, were mere camouflage for deeply ingrained tribal values.[20] Thus, in addition to the ethnic and sectarian divides, tribal dominance, and the pervasiveness of tribal values, undermined, or at best slowed down, the effort by the political elite to fashion a universal national identity to which citizens felt a sense of belonging and attachment.

A major problem was that the political and cultural elites in Baghdad who were trying to construct a national identity and instill a sense of nationhood into the population were primarily Sunni who on the whole seemed suspicious of Shi'ite commitment to the national project. For instance, a book by a Syrian Sunni, which was titled *al-'Uruba fi al-Mizan* (Arabism in the Balance) and which was published in 1933, equated the Iraqi Shi'ite population with the Sassanid Persians, lamented the Shi'ites' indifference to Arab nationalism, and accused Shi'ite teachers of being more loyal to Iran than to Iraq. This engendered widespread acts of sedition, including attacks on security forces. The disturbances were quelled only after an appeal by the highest Shi'ite cleric, and after the author was put on trial and briefly imprisoned.[21] Such incidents only added to Shi'ite alienation from, and frustration with, the dominant Sunni class to the extent that on a number of occasions, Shi'ites expressed a wish "to return to the days of absolute British control [rather] than be under the heel of an entirely Sunni administration."[22] One such occasion occurred in 1927 during another observance of 'Ashura'. A clash between the security forces and a procession of Shi'ite flagellants precipitated a riot in Baghdad's Shi'ite neighborhood of Kadhmiya in which civilians, policemen, and soldiers were killed. The Acting British High Commissioner put the blame on Sunnis whom he claimed had conspired to stir up strife during 'Ashura'. To that a Shi'ite leader responded: "What we want is British control, to save us from Sunni domination. . . ."[23] While the Shi'ites did not demand political separation from the state, neither was there an attitudinal proximity between them and the Sunnis during this period.

For those tasked with imbuing Iraqis with a sense of nationhood, the ethnic, sectarian, and tribal diversity of the new country must have seemed too great an impediment to be surmounted. As late as 1933, more than a decade after the creation of the Iraqi state, King Faysal would acknowledge in a memo circulated to a number of senior Iraqi politicians the immense difficulties entailed in fashioning a nation out of the disparate groups that inhabited the country:

Iraq is one of those countries that lack religious, communal and cultural unity, and as such it is divided upon itself; its power dispersed. . . . The Arab Sunni government rules over a Kurdish population, the bulk of which is ignorant, that is led by people with personal ambitions who use the [Kurds'] ethnic difference to advocate secession. [The government also rules over] an uneducated Shi'ite majority that shares the same ethnicity with the government, but which was persecuted by Turkish (Sunni) rule . . . that [divided] the Arab population between the two sects. [This led] to the perception, which I have heard thousands of times, that taxes and death are the Shi'ites' lot in life, while public positions are reserved for the Sunnis. . . . In addition, there is the tribal mindset, plus the influence exercised by the sheikhs over the tribesmen, and the fear that [this influence] would wane in the face of enhanced governmental authority. . . .

All these schisms, ambitions and particularisms . . . undermine the peace and stability of the country, and only through material and judicious power could these dislocations disappear over time, and a true nationalism could replace religious and sectarian fanaticism. . . .

[But] in conclusion, and I say this with a heart full of sadness, there is in Iraq still no unified Iraqi nation. [Instead], there are various human groups, devoid of any patriotic ideal, imbued with religious traditions and absurdities, connected by no common tie, giving ear to evil, prone to anarchy, always on the ready to rise against any government. Out of these masses we want to fashion a people which we would train, educate and refine. But because the creation and fashioning of a nation is such a difficult endeavor in these circumstances, the immenseness of the effort to achieve these goals can only be imagined.[24]

COMMUNAL BRIDGES

It is clear from Faysal's words that, approaching the end of his reign, the King was truly troubled by what he saw as a Herculean task ahead. To Faysal, creating a nation out of the country's disparate groups was proving to be far more arduous an undertaking than constructing and administering functioning state institutions. Faysal could see the visible trappings of statehood—government, bureaucracy, army, police, schools, et cetera, but he seemed less than sanguine about the prospects of putting together and securing the underpinnings of nationhood.

The custodians of the national project, the men tasked by Faysal to perform the seemingly impossible, might have thought the King's words unduly dark and pessimistic. Otherwise, they would not have accepted the undertaking and, as we shall see later, pursued it with such vigor. These men, after all, were unwavering believers in the power of nationalism, and true to the optimism demanded by their fervent faith in their creed, they would have argued that the fault lines between communities were not as unyielding as was painted by their sovereign.

Prior to World War I, a nationalist network was emerging that brought together anti-Istanbul elements from Baghdad and Basra. Moreover, some of these nationalists established contacts with similar minded men in Egypt and Syria.[25] Thus, even in those early days there existed a rudimentary nationalist sentiment which opened up political horizons that lay outside immediate locales. The connection between "Shi'ite" Basra and "Sunni" Baghdad was especially pertinent. In 1912, Sayyid Talib, Basra's influential leader, demanded the independence of Iraq, meaning specifically Baghdad and Basra. His call was celebrated by the many young nationalists in Baghdad. Indeed the year before, the Baghdadi nationalists had established the National Scientific Club, whose name belied its political anti-Turkish character and purpose. The founders of the club immediately asked Sayyid Talib to be its president. Talib telegraphed from Basra his agreement, promising to continue to offer his life "for the advancement of my beloved country."[26] The club brought together Sunni and Shi'ite intellectuals and political activists, and when, at the end of 1913 the Ottoman authorities pursued the club's Baghdadi leaders, they fled to Basra, seeking and receiving the protection of Sayyid Talib.[27] While this hardly constituted a fully fledged nationalist movement, it nevertheless exhibited a certain ideational proximity among an elite group of politically aware men of different sectarian attachments living in various parts of Iraq.

The British military conquest of Iraq, predicating on such advertised concepts as independence and liberation, further encouraged this nationalist spirit. After all, the proclamation uttered by the victorious British General Sir Stanley Maud in 1917, "our armies have not come into your cities and lands as conquerors, or enemies, but as liberators,"[28] gave hope to the possibility of a future independent state for the land of Mesopotamia. This was reinforced a year later by a joint British-French declaration stating that their purpose in fighting the Ottomans was primarily "to liberate the Arab peoples from the Turkish yoke."[29] However, the reluctance of the British administrators in Iraq to act on these promises and translate them into real policy became one of the causes of the "1920 Revolution," which as we saw earlier centered on the Shi'ite South, but received widespread support from, the Sunni population in Baghdad and other parts of Iraq.

While the concern articulated by King Faysal of the deep-rooted divide between Sunnis and Shi'ites had legitimate bases, the 1920 revolution showed clearly that in the face of perceived universal threat this communal fissure was purposely and purposefully narrowed. It is difficult to pinpoint the event that facilitated the revolt, but early in the year Grand Ayatollah Muhammad Taqi al-Shirazi, issued a famous *fetwa* that banned Muslims from choosing or electing those who resided outside the faith to rule over Muslims. This literally de-legitimized British rule, making it almost a religious duty to rebel against the British.[30] Other Shi'ite clerics followed with their own edicts supporting that of the Grand Ayatollah. These *fetwas* were to fuel the flames of discontent already felt by disaffected tribesmen, who were primarily Shi'ites, but with a few Sunnis among them, as well as urban nationalists, mostly Sunnis but with a minority Shi'ite presence. Such diverse groups naturally had differing motives and interests, but they were all united in their determination to see the end of British rule.[31]

Anti-British sentiment gathered momentum throughout the first half of 1920. It was fanned by religious events that invariably turned into political demonstrations. This was not a new phenomenon. What was new was the increasing tendency of Sunnis and Shi'ites to attend these events and celebrate them together, symbolizing a unity of purpose against the outsider. This was something that Iraq had rarely seen before. Thus, during the holy month of Ramadan, a large procession would leave the Baghdad Shi'ite neighborhood of Kadhmiya and go to the Sunni neighborhood of A'dhamiya, which lay on the opposite side of the Tigris river, where the senior clerics of the two communities would embrace to signal their unity in Islam, and the two communities would pray together. The following week, the same would happen, this time in reverse direction. And when the anniversaries of the deaths of Imam 'Ali and later Husayn occurred (the former dying as a result of the Sunni-Shi'ite schism in early Islam, the latter perishing at the hands of the Sunni Ummayads), Sunni delegations participated in the wakes, emulating their Shi'ite counterparts in wailing and beating their chests.[32] There can be little doubt that the main spur for the growing empathy between the hitherto distant sects was the presence of the hegemonic non-Muslim British. It did not escape the attention of someone as perceptive as Gertrude Bell. "The extremists have adopted a plan that is difficult to counter," she wrote to her father in June 1920. "It is the uniting of Shi'ites and Sunnis, that is the unity of Islam. [Prayers] are held sometimes in Shi'ite mosques, sometimes in Sunni mosques, and are attended by both sects. In reality, these meetings are political, not religious . . . and they all evolve around the idea of enmity to the infidels."[33]

The actual insurrection erupted and was maintained primarily in the Shi'ite mid and lower Euphrates part of Iraq. But it received much support from urban Sunni elements. That support was on the whole moral in nature, consisting of fiery mosque speeches and pamphlets extolling the revolution. Moreover, a number of Sunni ex-Ottoman officers lent their expertise to the rebels south of Baghdad. There were also a few acts of sedition: some of Baghdad's youth sabotaged a section of the railway north of the city, and later burned a British transportation depot. Beyond the urban centers, the rebellion did spill over into Sunni tribal domains, particularly to the north and northwest of Baghdad, which compelled British forces to withdraw from Ramadi and Ba'quba, while Fallujah was cut off from Baghdad for months.[34] While the contribution of the Sunni population to the 1920 uprising should not be overstated, as the heart of the rebellion and the bulk of the operations were centered in the Shi'ite area, the insurrection itself and the events that preceded it, showed that a higher cause or a perceived common enemy could overcome the historical differences that divided the two communities.

If the common enemy in 1920 was the British occupier, in early 1922 it was the warlike "Ikhwan" hordes of Nejd in the Arabian Peninsula. Driven by their fanatically held ultra-puritanical version of Sunni doctrine and their intense hostility to the Hashemites, they mounted a major raid into Iraq's Shi'ite domain in March 1922 in which several hundred tribesmen were killed. Senior Shi'ite clerics decided to hold a conference in

Karbala to discuss ways to counter any future incursions by the Ikhwan. While the call to attend was made specifically to Shiʿite tribal chiefs and urban notables, invitations were issued also to a number of Sunni clerics and prominent civilians, who met in Baghdad in a large gathering. The consensus of the meeting was that Iraq's Sunnis should stand shoulder to shoulder with their Shiʿite brethren against the Ikhwan's ultra-puritanical form of Sunni Islam. A *fetwa* was issued and signed by a number of senior Sunni clerics which legitimized taking up arms against the intruders from Nejd. A Sunni delegation from Baghdad was elected to attend the conference in Karbala. A similar delegation of Sunnis was dispatched from Mosul, and a number of notables and tribal chiefs from Tikrit in Iraq's Sunni heartland signed a declaration pledging themselves and their money to any resolution produced by the conference.[35] The conference produced little more than pledges to fight the Ikhwan under the banner of the King, but the Sunni-Shiʿite rapport was of much greater significance for those tasked with creating a unified national identity. Here was a situation where Iraqi Sunnis pledged to fight alongside their Shiʿite countrymen against their Sunni co-religionists from across the border in Nejd. The hopeful sculptors of the nation would argue that, as in the events of the 1920 insurrection, the coming together of Sunni and Shiʿite in the face of Ikhwan belligerency in 1922 was if not a solid, then at least an encouraging, basis upon which to construct a robust national identity.

The National Idea and Its Custodians

If the British were tasked with assembling the Iraqi state, then the responsibility for creating and nourishing a national identity fell on the King and his coterie of close companions and confidants. Faysal, after all, had had prior experience in leading an Arab administration during his brief tenure as King of Syria, in which efforts at dismantling Turkish cultural influence were begun, and in certain areas, such as Arabizing the school systems, met with considerable success. The man who spearheaded the undertaking in Syria was Faysal's Minister of Education, Satiʿ al-Husri, who followed his mentor to Iraq to become the country's Director General of Education.[36] From that position Husri exerted profound influence on the educational and cultural orientations of the country, particularly in its crucial formative years. He disseminated his ideas on nationalism and nation-building through purposeful educational policy, such as shaping school and college curriculums and appointing like-minded educators, many of whom he imported from other Arab lands.

Husri was an exemplary Arab nationalist, whose notion of nationhood transcended the boundaries of Iraq to include all the Arabic-speaking lands. To him, it was this universal and unitary vision that defined the Arab nation. Predetermined and eternal, this Arab nation, Husri maintained, rested on the unity of its linguistic community and the coherence of its continuous history. As such, Husri was an unbending believer in the German idea of cultural nationalism. As we have seen, the primary premise of cultural nationalism maintains that nations are organic beings, founded immemorially on passions implanted by history. A nation is not a political creation, since it resides in the very being of its people, imposing on them a homogeneity and uniformity that separates them from other human groups. Central to this endeavor is the spoken and written word. Language is at the heart of national formation, since it is the medium through which national consciousness spreads.[37] Husri thus would vehemently argue that people who spoke Arabic as their mother tongue were Arabs, the very people who recognized the common thread of their long and distinguished history.

But what of Iraqi nationalism? Why should nationhood not be framed within the narrower, possibly more manageable, context of Iraq rather than the larger and more amorphous Arab framework? A number of reasons explain the emphasis on Arab, rather than a specifically Iraqi, nationalism. First, there can be little doubt that those who were entrusted with formulating and directing cultural policy in Iraq were themselves genuinely and deeply committed to the concept of the in-separateness of the Arab nation. And they were backed by a King and his Sharifian companions who themselves had fought not only for the independence of the Arab lands from the Ottoman empire, but also for the creation of a unified Arab kingdom under Faysal's father, Sharif Husayn of Hejaz. The ideological milieu in which Iraq's ruling elite conducted their affairs was unquestionably Arabist in its disposition.

Secondly, the majority of the Arab nationalist political elite in Iraq were Sunnis. The Sunni presence was felt not just throughout Iraq's political establishment, but also in the educational system and among the officer corps of the country's armed forces. Yet, the Arab Sunnis were a decided demographic minority in Iraq, constituting a mere 20 percent of the population. It is thus hardly surprising that the Sunni minority would gravitate toward the Arab world where Sunni Islam was the predominant sect. If the Shi'ites and Kurds would register legitimate concern over the loss of their status in an expanded Arab nation, then by the same token it would be natural that the Sunni community would be the most welcoming of the idea.

Thirdly, in spite of the divergences in the attitudes to Arabism among Iraq's communities, the Sunni political elite, their faith in Arab nationalism unshaken, felt that they could gradually mold not just the Shi'ites, but other Iraqi religions and sects, into the broader Arab project. They would achieve this by insisting on the secular nature of the Arab nation. Husri would remind everyone time and time again that Arabs had existed long before Islam,[38] and by implication, long before the original fissure in Islam between Sunni and Shi'ite.

There was, of course, the already alluded to problem (as perceived by the Sunnis) of the strong affinity that existed between the Iraqi Shi'ites and their co-religionists in Iran, which had been reinforced by an Ottoman Sunni administration whose attitude toward the Shiites oscillated between active hostility and contemptuous neglect. Many of Iraq's Sunni elites felt that the proximity of Iraqi Shi'ites to those of Iran was too close for comfort. Because of the holy cities of Najaf and Karbala, thousands of Iranians visited, some living in Iraq in what was almost an open border. Moreover, many of the Shi'ite Grand Ayatollahs had come from Iran, studied in the theological seminaries of Najaf or Karbala, and rose to positions of leadership among Iraq's Shi'ites. The feeling among the Sunni elite was that Arab Shi'ism was being contaminated by Persian influence,[39] and for the Arab project to succeed, this nefarious influence needed to be expunged. And it was around this period that an old derogatory term, *shu'ubi*, was resurrected to describe any proximity to Persian Iran.[40] As we shall see later, Husri and his disciples would work through the educational system to establish the predominance of Arabist values and attitudes over *shu'ubi* proclivities. Nevertheless, they would take heart from the occasional coming together of the two communities in the face of outsiders (as happened in the 1920 insurrection and the Karbala conference of 1922). And in any case, they would argue that the Shi'ites shared the same ethnic characteristics of the Sunnis and spoke the same language, which in their formulation, happened to constitute the central and most consequential element of nation-building.

While Husri and the other custodians of the nationalist idea had no time for those who pointed to Iraqi "particularism" in arguing against the "Arab nation" construct, they did encourage pride in, and loyalty to, Iraq. To Husri and his companions and disciples, the two positions did not have to be mutually exclusive. On the contrary, they tried to mold Iraqi patriotism into Arab nationalism. All the notions of love of country, a feeling of community, a sense of togetherness, could be nurtured within the political boundaries of Iraq as well as the ideational parameters of the Arab nation. The goal, according to one Iraqi analyst, was to "melt the various (Iraqi) groups into the crucible of one country (*watan*) before moving on to achieve the Arab nationalist (*qawmi*) aspiration."[41] Husri and the other nationalists, therefore, depicted the building of, and loyalty to, Iraq as going hand in hand with, indeed as inseparable from, the Arab nationalist march. In a history textbook for high school students published in 1946, King Faysal was portrayed as a man who first and foremost was devoted to building the Iraqi nation-state, while never losing sight of the broader Arab nationalist project.[42]

Indeed, those entrusted with the nationalist project went even further: they endeavored to symbolize and portray Iraq as the centerpiece of any Arab nationalist undertaking. One of Husri's successors as Director-General of Education, Sami Shawkat, would liken Iraq's situation in the late 1930s to that of Prussia's leadership in the unification of Germany in 1871. "Prussia sixty years ago used to dream about uniting the German people," Shawkat said in a speech to members of the nationalist *al-Muthana* Club. "What is to prevent Iraq from dreaming about uniting the Arab lands now that it has achieved its dream of becoming independent."[43] Such hopes of Arab unification seemed to be well invested in Iraq. The nationalists would look back to the past and proudly point to the dazzling civilization that flourished in Baghdad under the 'Abbasid dynasty at a time when the West languished in the darkness of the medieval ages. By the middle of the 9th century, scholars working in the large library of Baghdad's *Bayt al-Hikma* (Hall of Wisdom) had translated and commented on the main works of the Greek philosophers. In the Hall of Science, which had a complete library and laboratory, medicine, astronomy, and mathematics flourished. Much of the philosophic and scientific work done in 9th century Baghdad was in later centuries translated by Europeans and used in their universities. The custodians of the nationalist project in Iraq would ask: Who else among the other Arabs could match such a pedigree?

As for the present, Iraq in the 1920s and 1930s was, as Husri and the others would remind Iraqis, one of only four countries with a measure of independence, at least in matters of domestic policy. The other three were Yemen, Saudi Arabia, and Egypt. The first two were dismissed as too backward and tribal to lead an Arab renaissance, while the culturally advanced Egypt was too xenophobic, ever ready to reject its Arab heritage, and hence unwilling and incapable of assuming the leadership of the Arab world. It was thus not a coincidence, the nationalists would remind their audience, that with Husri and his disciples, Iraq had become the intellectual headquarters of the nationalist undertaking.

EDUCATION: THE ROUTE TO NATION-BUILDING

Determined to leave their imprint on the country's ideological compass, Husri and his associates turned to education. In this, he was merely treading the path of earlier generations of nationalist thinkers and activists. For the great European nationalists of the 18th and 19th centuries education had been the primary medium by which a sense of nationhood would be instilled in the hearts and minds of the state's citizenry. To Rousseau, for example, it was the "test of education to give to each human being a national form, and so direct his opinions and tastes, that he should be a patriot by inclination, by passion, by necessity. On first opening his eyes, a child must see his country, and until he dies must see nothing else."[44] It was the leaders of the French Revolution who acted upon Rousseau's ideas. They instituted a comprehensive state system of education, the primary purpose of which was to create patriotic citizenry.[45] In schools, the teaching of patriotic history replaced the classics, the arts were geared to arousing national passion, and French was aggressively taught as the only national language at the expense of the native idioms formerly taught among the country's various ethno-linguistic groups. Higher education received the same treatment,[46] where Latin and classical authors gave way to French and French writers.

What clearly emerges from this discussion of the European experience is that for the nationalist the purpose of education is not so much to transmit knowledge, but to mold the individual's identity into that of the state and the nation it represents; not to make people and citizens better informed, but to make them more determined nationalists. One thus can readily agree with Ernest Gellner's contention that for the ruling and political elite, the state's monopoly over education was "more important, more central than [its] monopoly of legitimate violence."[47] The lessons from the history of nation-building in Europe were not lost on Husri and his cohorts.

In the period prior to the birth of the Iraqi state in 1921, education, such as it was, was hardly the state's abiding concern. Jews and Christians had their own parochial schools, and the few literate Shi'ites, on the whole, had attended religious institutions. State-established schools were meager in number and deficient in educational standards.[48] Husri set out to establish a state-controlled educational system with a standardized curriculum that would be taught in all schools.

If the primary goal of the educational system was nation-building, then it was hardly surprising that the teaching of history would take pride of place in the nationalist enterprise. How else would tales of the glory, achievement, and heroism of a people's ancestors be told, and indeed retold. Real, exaggerated, even invented, such renderings become the "evidence" of the excellence of the nation's "immemorial" past. "A heroic past, great men, glory," writes Ernest Renan, "is the social capital upon which to build a national ideology."[49] But this is not the history that is found in works of painstakingly detached scholarship. The history that the nationalist seeks is not an academic discipline; rather, it is a political tool to be exploited and manipulated for national aims.

To this purpose, Husri imported young Arab intellectuals, primarily from Palestine and Syria, whom he knew to be committed and vocal Arab nationalists. They were employed as teachers of history, language, and social studies in Iraqi secondary schools. This group of committed nationalists would become the purveyors of Husri's pedagogical mission: if the object of the exercise is to wage a struggle for independence and political rejuvenation, Husri would argue, then that can only begin by searching for revelation from history, for "faith in the future of the nation derives its strength from a belief in the brilliance of the past."[50] The relevant term here is "brilliance"; history books were not to dwell on the embarrassments of the past, but stress and embellish, even mythologize episodes of accomplishments and success. Thus one history book, written in 1931 and taught in Iraqi secondary (high) schools, was little more than a panegyric of Arab contribution to human progress throughout history, and particularly under the Baghdad-based 'Abbasid dynasty, yet the five centuries of Ottoman domination of Iraq were dismissed in a few pages.[51] If this history was at best "guided" if not "doctored" that in no way disturbed Husri. After all, he had issued a directive to teachers of history in Iraq's elementary schools in 1922 reminding them that the ultimate objective of historical studies was "the strengthening of patriotic and nationalistic feelings in the hearts of the students."[52] This wholesale effort to inculcate nationalist values was, to say the least, a tough undertaking, but one that Husri believed in and embarked on with a passion.

The success of the enterprise predicated on the existence of a homogenized curriculum that is directed from Baghdad and taught uniformly in all Iraqi schools. That is why Husri was virulent in his opposition to parochial schools, objecting to any subsidies to them unless they came under the auspices of the Ministry of Education. In order to get them to use his curriculum, he advocated instituting a government-administered national examination. Even though he came into conflict with the British advisors and the Shi'ite clerical establishment, he persisted in seeing these schools as promoting parochial values that would inevitably undermine the nation-building project.

Husri would even veto projects that seemed to fall within the parameters of his educational vision. In order to meet his demands for the expansion of public education, it was suggested that teacher-training colleges should be opened in several Iraqi provinces. But Husri rejected the proposal arguing that this would lead to a weakening of the national identity. If such colleges were to open, say, in the cities of Mosul and Hilla, he contended, they would be dominated respectively by Christians and Shi'ites. The solution, therefore, was to have such colleges placed in the capital where students from all parts of the country can attend together to develop a spirit of community, of national, rather than parochial, identity.[53] Husri's rationale might sound odd, even nefarious, but to Husri it was merely an affirmation of his commitment to do anything he could to make sure that sectarian and regional loyalties, so powerful in Iraq, were subsumed within a broader sense of national belonging that would evolve around the concept of a collective and distinctive Arab identity.

There was a sense of the autocrat in Husri in the way he approached nation-building in Iraq. This was fueled by an abiding fear, even phobia, of sectarianism, particularly among the Shi'ites, about whose relations with their Persian co-religionists Husri harbored much suspicion. At times this was taken to absurd limits. Once he fired the Shi'ite poet Muhammad Mahdi al-Jawahiri from his teaching job for singing the praises of an Iranian summer resort, which Husri considered to be *shu'ubi*, exhibiting an affection, perhaps even loyalty, to Iran. In his memoirs, al-Jawahiri, a celebrated Arab intellectual and a universally beloved poet, writes that he also had praised the beauty of resorts in Lebanon, Syria, and Palestine. "Would that qualify as *shu'ubi* too?", he asks caustically.[54]

This tunnel vision translated into an educational and ideological elitism that eventually constrained the expansion of education.[55] Thus, over the entire period of the mandate, much of which education was under Husri's direction, no more than 800 high school students graduated,[56] and as late as 1932 the expenditure on education was still under 8 percent of the state budget.[57] Admittedly, the Shi'ites resisted enrolling into public schools, but even so, Husri's elitist policies, designed to produce the right kind of graduate, undoubtedly played a role in the narrowness of the educational base.

Policy Outcomes

Husri's elitism was motivated principally by a concern that by spreading itself too thin, the government would lose control over provincial schools. This would mean ceding ideational direction to persons who might not share the ideological proclivities of the political elite in Baghdad. Only those vetted by Husri and his associates would be allowed to carry the educational mission, and given Iraq's meager demographic resources, the quality available to Husri was limited. Even with the importation of Arab, non-Iraqi teachers, the numbers could not sustain the spread of nationalist-directed education into the provinces. That was why Husri would insist on concentrating education, especially above the intermediate, middle school, level, in the large urban centers. And when these centers produced well-qualified teachers (who by definition also would be ideologically palatable to the political elite in Baghdad), then the government would embark on spreading the educational mantra to the provinces. Interestingly enough, while Husri and the British clashed on many issues, they were of one mind on this issue.

Regardless of the efficacy of the theory, what this policy meant in practice was the cementation of urban Sunni predominance in the political and cultural spheres. The policy was radically changed when the Shi'ite Muhammad Fadhil al-Jamali became the Director-General of Education in 1933. Through his education at the American University of Beirut, Jamali had become an ardent Arab nationalist, and thus had come to his position with impeccable ideological credentials. Jamali nevertheless strongly disagreed with Husri's elitist policies, working tirelessly over the next decade or so to spread secular and nationalist education into Shi'ite areas. Phebe Marr contends that Jamali's influence was "second only to Husri."[58] There can be little doubt that his policies played a critical role in eventually assimilating Shi'ite youth into Iraq's body politics.

Jamali began by establishing directorates of education in the provinces, and these were tasked with bringing up the levels of primary school instruction in rural areas to the standards enjoyed by urban schools. The goal was to allow provincial graduates to enter secondary schools. He also made sure that students from Shi'ite provinces were able to enter the

Higher Teachers Training College in Baghdad, even sometimes at the expense of better qualified urban Sunni and Christian students. And he facilitated the acceptance of provincial students, particularly Shi'ites, into the foreign mission program. He also opened a secondary school in the Shi'ite holy city of Najaf, staffing it with high quality teachers.[59] Jamali consistently rejected accusations of favoring Shi'ites, claiming that his policy was aimed at spreading education to all Iraqi provinces, and indeed his policies did accelerate the expansion of education in Iraq, so that for example the number of secondary school students increased from just over 2,000 in 1930 to almost 14,000 in 1940, and by the latter year, every province had a secondary school.[60] Even so, it is clear that the greatest beneficiaries of his anti-elitist educational policies were the Shi'ites from the southern provinces. The point here is that although Jamali was a Shi'ite, he was no less nationalist than Husri. Under his stewardship, therefore, education continued to be structured around a uniform curriculum, which was directed from Baghdad, and which consciously propagated secular nationalist themes and ideas. Jamali's policies were to bear fruit in the post-World War II period as ever greater numbers of Shi'ites were incorporated not just into an expanding Iraqi nation, but also into the mainstream of the Arab nationalist idea.

The other main communal group in Iraq, the Kurds, remained exogenous to the nationalist project. They had been brought into the political process by offers of minor Cabinet positions and representation in the national assembly, as well as token membership in the army's officer corps. Occasionally, the King would venture to the northern provinces to meet with his subjects and promise them political reconciliation.[61] But these efforts were infrequent, half-hearted, and always lacked the commitment of real resources. In any case, even if the King were genuine about bringing the Kurds into the national bargain, he would be pedaling against a very stiff head wind. The Sunni political elite, as we have seen, were virulently Arabist, and if there was an effort to bring into the center groups from the margins, it would be aimed not at the culturally distant Kurds, but at the Arabic-speaking, ethnically similar Shi'ites, and even Christians.

The thrust of the ideational battle waged by that nationalist generation excluded the Kurds, and this led to almost purposeful neglect of their concerns and demands. When the 1930 treaty with Britain was negotiated by Nuri al-Sa'id, he was content to omit any reference to the special position of the Kurds in an Arab Iraq, which prompted Kurdish leaders to demand the separation of Kurdistan under British protection. Nuri and his government, trying to allay the concerns of the League of Nations, responded by making equivocal gestures to Kurdish cultural autonomy. Even so, when the time came for these gestures to be translated into practical policy, the process fell far short of the League's expectation.[62] No amount of Kurdish appeals to revisit their demands for cultural and administrative autonomy would dissuade the Baghdad government from its uncompromising policy position, which increasingly reverted to the use of force.[63]

Apart from a few gestures here and there, the political and cultural elite in Baghdad did not care to respond constructively or in a spirit of true reconciliation to the demands and concerns of a non-Arab community that happened to constitute almost one fifth of Iraq's population. No wonder then that the abiding feature of the relationship between the Arabist government in Baghdad and the Kurdish population in the north was one of resentment, suspicion, and violence. It was as though the ruling elite in Iraq had decided that the ethnic divide between Arab and Kurd was so deep and intractable that reconciliation and compromise would constitute more difficult policy options than the use of force. As the late Majid Khadduri explains, "the short-sightedness of the Iraqi government in handling Kurdish affairs was reflected by their merely crushing [Kurdish] revolts by force."[64] In this spirit of un-compromise, violent eruptions characterized the relations between the Iraqi government and the country's Kurdish population. Five major Kurdish uprisings against Baghdad spanned the period 1921–1936.[65] The natural tension that would be expected to exist between two ethnically separated groups, and that could have been lessened by adopting conciliatory political and cultural policies, was in fact exacerbated into an ever deepening fissure by the relentless pursuit of exclusionary Arab nationalist symbols and values by the political and cultural elite in Baghdad.

The longer the Kurds remained on the cultural periphery, the more difficult it was for them to enter, and be integrated into, the state's institutions. Throughout this period, the Kurds continued to be woefully underrepresented in the country's political and administrative institutions, lagging behind not just the dominant Arab Sunnis, but also the Shi'ites. The inability, indeed unwillingness, of the state to seriously tackle the Kurdish problem in the early years persisted in years to come, where, as we shall see in later chapters, mounting Kurdish estrangement from Arab Iraq was never genuinely addressed, let alone rectified.

While most state institutions seemed to be less unwelcoming of the Shi'ites than of the Kurds, in one of these institutions, neither the Shi'ites nor the Kurds fared well. When the Iraqi army was established in 1921, the officer corps was immediately filled by Iraqi ex-Ottoman officers, the vast majority of whom were Sunnis, who had joined the Arab revolt against the Ottomans, serving with Faysal's army that entered and occupied Damascus in 1918. There were a few ex-Ottoman, non-Arab Sunni officers, particularly Kurds (the most notable, as we have seen, was Bakr Sidqi), who joined the ranks of the newly formed Iraqi army. These few officers were in fact the exception to the rule, and their numbers in the army in no way and at no time represented their demographic weight in the country.[66] As the army grew, so did the ethnosectarian divisions within it, where the overwhelming majority of the officers were Sunnis, whereas the rank and file was populated on the whole by Shi'ites and a few Kurds. The military college, which was established in 1921, exacerbated this imbalance. The educational requirements to enter the college meant that most of those who were accepted would be Arab Sunnis. Moreover, the Sunni political elite, cognizant of its minority status in the population, was inclined to fill the ranks of the most sensitive state sector, the military-security establishment, with its own people. By 1936, a few Kurds and Shi'ites, and even fewer Christians, had graduated from the college, and the overwhelming numbers both in the college and among the officer corps generally belonged to the Sunnis.[67] 'Abd al-Karim al-Uzri, a Shi'ite and a scion of the monarchical regime who occupied a number of important cabinet portfolios, laments in his memoirs that "the military college did not represent the Iraqi population with its various groups and regions." Rather it favored "one group (the Arab Sunnis) at the expense of the other groups, a situation that created a defect in the country's political equilibrium."[68]

One outcome of this imbalance was the ease with which the army became politicized. Nationalist advocacy did not stop with the schools but was extended into the military establishment, so that by the second half of the 1930s the bulk of the upper and middle ranks of the officer corps of the Iraqi armed forces were Sunnis who were imbued with the Arab nationalist spirit. These officers increasingly saw their mission not just to defend the integrity of their country against outside aggression, but also to be the custodians of the nationalist idea inside Iraq itself. This meant not only the rise of xenophobic proclivities against fringe groups within Iraq, but also a growing tendency to meddle in the domestic political affairs of the country; a tendency that was fed by the continuous resort to military force in subduing uprisings in the north and south of the country, and that ultimately and inevitably would pave the way for the military coup of 1936, the first such usurpation of political power in the Arab world.

CHAPTER FIVE

Turbulence in Governance, 1936–1958

On October 29, 1936, planes from the infant Royal Iraqi Air Force circled over Baghdad then dropped leaflets demanding the ouster of nationalist Prime Minister Yasin al-Hashimi, who had taken to characterizing himself as the Bismarck of Iraq. Army units began an advance on Baghdad and another wave of planes dropped bombs in the vicinity of governmental buildings. It did not take long for Hashimi to tender his resignation to the young King Ghazi, and along with other senior members of the government, including Nuri al-Sa'id, hurriedly left Iraq. The King duly asked the army's candidate, Hikmat Sulayman, to form the next Cabinet. By imposing its will on the political leadership, the army, under the leadership of the notorious, yet at the time popular, Kurdish general Bakr Sidqi had executed a successful military coup, which was to become the precursor for a spate of military coups that bedeviled not only Iraq, but most of the Arab world, over the following four decades. Indeed, it is no exaggeration to say that in the 1936 military coup could be found the seeds of the momentous events that were to usher the end of the monarchical period in July 1958.

COUPS AND AUTHORITARIAN RULE, 1936–1945

While the 1936 Bakr Sidqi military coup is usually associated with the name of the general who led the assault on Baghdad, and in whose name the demand for a change of government was made, it was influential civilian politicians associated with the *Ahali* group, with its broad support base, that provided the intellectual impetus, justification, and even the initial organization. The group, propagating a "populist" doctrine, predictably found itself at odds with Hashimi's personalized authoritarianism. Yet, the most determined of the *Ahali* politicians was Hikmat Sulayman, whose objection to Hashimi had more to do with personal animosity and political ambition than with a polar ideological vision.[1] To gain strategic support from within the group, Sulayman sought out the blessing of the respected and popular Shi'ite politician, Ja'far Abu al-Timman,[2] who was then the acknowledged leader of *al-Ahali*. As the group tilted toward the necessity of removing Hashimi, it also came to realize that force would be needed to oust "Iraq's Bismarck"—the kind of overpowering punch that can be delivered only by the army. A number of clandestine meetings followed, with Sulayman acting as the conduit between the group and Sidqi. Indeed, even Kamel al-Chaderji, probably the most committed democrat in the *Ahali* group, gave his blessings to the forcible removal of the Hashimi government.[3] The group in fact wrote the coup's communiqué that demanded a government that would "represent the people under the leadership of Hikmat Sulayman,"[4] and the letter was taken to King Ghazi by Sulayman himself. When the new government was formed, the *Ahali* politicians and supporters occupied a number of prominent portfolios.

For both the young King and the *Ahali* group, short-term gains and an exaggerated sense of their own influence and popularity blinded them to the perilous long-term consequences of the army's entry into the political sphere. Ghazi, lacking his father's wisdom and foresight, resented the overbearing presence of the older politicians, most of whom had served in his father's army that fought the Ottomans in World War I and later had accompanied him first to Syria and then to Iraq. Hashimi on his side had thought the young monarch to be irresponsible, and tried to curb his powers, making him more of a symbol than an actual policy-maker. Bitter at what he perceived to be his attempted marginalization, Ghazi confided in some of the young and ambitious army officers, whose company he much preferred anyway, his displeasure and frustration with Hashimi, even inciting them to conspire against the government.[5] Little did he know then that he had helped sow the seeds for the later destruction of the monarchy and the murder of his own son.

The *Ahali* group conspired with the military in the ouster of Hashimi because its members harbored the age-old illusion that civilians using the powers of governance could tame those with a monopoly over the instruments of coercion, when the latter had just used those very instruments to usurp power. Prior to the coup, General Bakr Sidqi had calmed the fears of the *Ahali* leaders by promising to "return the army to the barracks after the coup and leave governance to the civilians."[6] Driven by intense hostility to Hashimi and comforted by their perceived popularity among the urban middle class, the *Ahali* leaders were more than ready to accept Sidqi at his word.

Armed with a "populist" agenda, members of the *Ahali* group, now dominating the government under the premiership of Hikmat Sulayman, promised to follow a reformist public policy dedicated to bypassing "the established alliance of Sunni politicians and rural landlords, redistributing power and privilege and developing a broader-based constituency among the middle and lower classes."[7] They soon began to work on a program meant to curb the power of the tribal leaders by reconsidering, even annulling, laws that were passed in the early 1930s that greatly restricted the rights of the peasants. Forming themselves into *Jama'at al-Islah al-Sha'bi* (National Reform Group), they additionally advocated the creation of trade unions, expansion of public education to the lower classes, and distribution of uncultivated lands to landless peasants. They pledged their fidelity to democracy, especially freedom of the press, which had been anything but a priority of the ousted regime.[8] In foreign relations, the new government seemed to reverse the Arabist orientations of its predecessor by pursuing stronger ties with Iraq's immediate non-Arab neighbors, Turkey and Iran.

The new government very soon found itself facing a number of enemies. Nationalist army officers were suspicious of a government, none of whose three main leaders was either Sunni or had articulated strong Arab sentiments. The Sunni army officers, committed Arab nationalists, came to gradually perceive the new leaders to be lukewarm at best on Arab matters and concerns. In internal affairs, tribal leaders were bound to resist the determined socioeconomic reformism of the Cabinet. Rebellions soon erupted in the mid-Euphrates region, necessitating the diversion of sorely needed resources, and creating fissures within the government.

Ironically, the government's most debilitating enemy turned out to be Bakr Sidqi himself. He consistently frustrated governmental policies either by interfering in the policy process or by taking actions without even consulting the responsible ministers.[9] Sidqi made a habit of attending ministerial meetings, and he soon formed the "Higher Defense Council" which essentially operated as a parallel policy-making institution.[10] The situation came to a head during the tribal uprisings in the south of the country. Sidqi and Sulayman decided to crush the rebellion. The air force was dispatched to bomb tribal villages, killing scores of men, women, and children around the city of Samawa, and when the corpses arrived in the holy cities of Najaf and Karbala for burial major demonstrations erupted culminating in attacks against government and police buildings. As tension spread throughout the south, Ja'far Abu al-Timman, himself a Shi'ite, tendered his resignation along with Chaderji and two other ministers. They chastised Prime Minister Sulayman, and by implication Sidqi, for "spilling the blood of our citizens,"[11] and doing it without the approval of the Cabinet.

Whether the Cabinet was really kept in the dark seems to be a matter of historical dispute. Taha al-Hashimi, the ex-Chief of Staff, contends in his memoirs that the Cabinet met to discuss the tribal problems and agreed on a vigorous response.[12] Similarly, the historian 'Abd al-Razzaq al-Hasani relates a conversation with Hikmat Sulayman that suggested that Abu al-Timman and Chaderji had despaired of the southern tribes and had talked of using force against them.[13] And the prominent tribal leader, Muhsin Abu Tibikh, categorically says that the Cabinet gave the order for the attack on the tribes.[14] On the opposite side of the argument, the historian Majid Khadduri maintains that the decision to carry out military action was never brought to the Cabinet for approval.[15] In light of the conflicting accounts, the letter of resignation submitted by the four ministers, which was not contradicted by the Prime Minister at the time, clearly maintains that the Cabinet had not approved the operations against the tribes. What the other accounts point to are meetings and conversations in which the possibility, even advisability, of force was broached. This is different from an official Cabinet meeting in which all the ministers collectively approve the action. And that, according to the letter of resignation, did not happen. That the Cabinet was sidelined while the army undertook a major operation against a segment of the Iraqi population was the final repudiation of the *Ahali's* aspiration for governmental independence in carrying out political and social reforms.

The resignation of those civilians who initially had formed the political pillar of the coup resulted in a more rapid slide toward military authoritarianism. Indeed, Sidqi's penchant for political control and arbitrary decisions was felt even by Prime Minister Sulayman himself, who was the General's most ardent supporter in the Cabinet. In one instance, the prime minister was reduced to asking the foreign minister of Turkey, who was in Baghdad after signing the Sa'dabad Security Pact among Turkey, Iraq, Iran, and Afghanistan, to broach the subject of the army's interference in politics with Sidqi. In a meeting at Sidqi's house, Turkey's Foreign Minister extolled the virtues of the Turkish defense forces for its self-imposed distance from the political sphere, adding that only harm would ensue if army officers were to become involved in political matters and decisions. Sidqi remained silent, fully absorbed in his guest's treatise, yet clearly, even contemptuously, unmoved.[16] After all, Sidqi possessed the instruments of coercion, and regardless of what constitutional rights the Prime Minister thought he might have had, real power was Sidqi's to wield.

Sidqi's reign lasted less than a year, ending with his assassination in August 1937. Fleeting as it was, this period of military dominance in politics had a major impact on the future development of state institutions, particularly on the notion of civilian control. The military now had developed a taste for power and was loath to relinquish it. When, after Sidqi's death, Prime Minister Sulayman insisted that he and his Cabinet would remain in office, Arab nationalist officers, who were instrumental in Sidqi's violent removal from power, threatened to remove him by force, and fearing an array of unpleasant options ranging from death to a possible civil war, Sulayman duly resigned. A mere ten months after he and the *Ahali* group had come to power with such great hopes for real reform, Hikmat Sulayman was forced out of office by the very army that he had courted, and which had brought him and his colleagues to power.

The new military leaders pledged to keep out of politics—a patently worthless promise now that they had become the new arbiters of power. So it was simply a matter of time before they would find the new prime minister, Jamil al-Midfa'i, and his Cabinet wanting on some governmental action or policy. Personal interests and ideational dedication intertwined in the army's next chapter of political interference. The officers had expected the new government to take harsh measures against all the supporters of Sidqi and Sulayman, be they in the army or in the country at large. But Midfa'i decided to heal societal wounds and let bygones be bygones. That did not sit well with the nationalist officers who were itching to show off their muscular resolve. Intent on finding a firmer man at the helm than Midfa'i, they saw in Nuri al-Sa'id the perfect candidate, a choice cemented by Nuri's strong Arab nationalist credentials.

What made the institutions of state even more captive to the "men on horseback" was the acceptance by civilian politicians of the military's involvement in politics. Thus, even someone of the prudence and farsightedness of Nuri al-Sa'id would in fact encourage military meddling in politics. Realizing that he could not get to power without the army, he actively plotted to remove the Midfa'i government from office.[17] The military conspirators made their move in December 1938, and demanded the resignation of the Midfa'i Cabinet, otherwise they threatened a major rebellion.[18] Nuri "advised" the beleaguered Prime Minister to accept the fait accompli on the grounds that the army had been successful twice already in forcing governmental resignations, and resisting would only lead to the spilling of blood.[19] Midfa'i thus tendered his Cabinet's resignation to King Ghazi. To emphasize their emerging military predominance, the occasion at the Royal Palace was attended by army officers. And when the King intimated that he would accept anyone but Nuri for the position of prime minister, he was told in no uncertain terms that Nuri was the army's candidate.[20] King Ghazi duly complied and invited Nuri al-Sa'id to form the next government.

Over the next year, Nuri, through forced retirements, gradually allowed his supporters among the army officers, particularly the four colonels, known as the "Golden Square," Salah al-Din al-Sabagh, Fahmi Sa'id, Mahmud Salman, and Kamil Shabib, to consolidate their control of the armed forces. In the spring of 1940, Nuri, after close consultations with the four colonels,[21] decided to resign and pass on the premiership to Rashid 'Ali al-Gaylani, with Nuri assuming the foreign affairs portfolio. With the eruption of war in Europe, the wily politician felt that he could more easily pursue his pro-British policy as foreign minister working under a popular politician with strong pan-Arabist credentials, such as Rashid 'Ali. A committed friend of Britain, Nuri saw Iraq's destiny as inexorably tied to that of Britain, and as such was instrumental in breaking relations with Germany. As an Arab nationalist, he also fervently believed that the interests of not only Iraq, but the Arab world as a whole would best be served by an allied victory. He thus advocated an unambiguous declaration of war against the Nazi power, even offering to send two divisions to the North African theater, and approaching al-Sabagh to lead the expeditionary force.

His military friends, however, were moving in an opposite direction, being increasingly influenced by the anti-British views of the charismatic Haj Amin al-Husayni, the Mufti of Jerusalem. Fleeing Palestine, after the British put down his Arab rebellion, he took refuge in Iraq in late 1939, and quickly became the ideational magnate for the nationalist movement within the armed forces and the non-military civilian sectors. Moving increasingly away from the views of the determinedly pro-British Nuri al-Sa'id, the four colonels and Rashid 'Ali would advocate a position of neutrality in the world conflict. In fact there was no dearth of fascination among this group, and increasingly the country a large, with the rise of Germany from the ashes of World War I to great power status. Many thought that the German experience should become a model for Iraq and other Arab countries.

The tide of political sentiment in the country as a whole was indeed shifting away from Nuri's position, a development that was reinforced by the fall of France in the summer of 1940. Rashid 'Ali's government was now publicly espousing "absolute neutrality" while pursuing secret contacts with the Germans at the same time that the Mufti and his entourage were negotiating with the Germans and Italians through their own independent channels. In January 1941, the Mufti, representing the opinion of the pan-Arabists in Iraq, sent a letter to Hitler stating "Rashid 'Ali's willingness to fight Britain if Germany would recognize the independence of Iraq and the other Arab countries."[22] It was obvious that the Mufti would not have made such a bold promise had he and Rashid 'Ali not had the four colonels and the army in their corner.

The army by now had become the most consequential institution in the country's political structure. Governments were deferring to the army not only on issues that fell within the military's competence, but also in economic and technical matters. For example, the army objected to the building of an oil refinery a hundred miles north of Baghdad, with the result that it was built on the outskirts of the capital, polluting the environment for the country's densest population center. The army also sabotaged for a long time connecting Iraq's rail lines with those of Turkey and Iran.[23] Such cases of interference were a testament to the army's mounting power, which also could be discerned from the disproportionately higher wages and many privileges accorded to the officer corps.

It was Regent 'Abd al-Ilah, the uncle of the infant Faysal II, in concert with Nuri al-Sa'id, who realized that he had lost his hitherto erstwhile military supporters to Rashid 'Ali, who decided that the time had come to clip the wings of the four colonels, and reduce, even reverse, the army's influence in the political affairs of the state. They began by engineering the forced resignation of Rashid 'Ali on January 31, 1941. They then induced the succeeding prime minister, General Taha al-Hashimi, to order the transfer of at least two of the colonels to more distant posts. But such was the colonels' power now that when they protested, the prime minister was compelled to ignore his own orders.

Nevertheless, suspecting that the Regent and Nuri were determined to neutralize them, and believing that Iraqi and Arab interests were being sacrificed at the alter of friendship with Britain at all costs, the colonels decided to act with haste. On April 1, they moved troops into Baghdad, surrounded the Palace and other public buildings, and demanded the resignation of Hashimi and the re-appointment of Rashid 'Ali. The Regent, however, managed to escape to British positions, and from there to Transjordan, and he was soon followed by a number of prominent Iraqi politicians, including Nuri al-Sa'id, who probably was the man most responsible for stimulating the colonels' appetite for political power.

It was, however, a matter of time before Britain would confront the new rulers and their publicly espoused anti-British sympathies, and, given the international situation, this was bound to happen sooner than later. On May 2, the British attacked Iraqi army and air force positions, and a week later the Mufti of Jerusalem declared *jihad* against the British. But by May 29, the Iraqi war effort had been spent, and its military and political leaders had made their own escape to neighboring countries. The Regent and his entourage of pro-British Iraqi politicians returned to Iraq, and exacted harsh revenge on the military plotters, who one by one had been captured over a period of four years. The four members of the famed "Golden Square" were all sentenced to death and summarily hanged. The most charismatic and acknowledged leader of the four, Colonel Salah al-Din al-Sabagh, was the last to be caught and hanged in 1945, and in an act of wonton vindictiveness, his lifeless body would be publicly suspended at the gate of the Ministry of Defense, to be taken down only after Regent 'Abd al-Ilah drove by the grisly scene on his way to the Royal Palace.

From then until the end of World War II, through emergency laws and authoritarian structures and regulations, successive governments worked to impose the will of the state on all sectors of Iraqi society in order to root out any remaining vestiges of anti-Palace and anti-British agitation. The military establishment was the first and foremost target. The army had grown from 20,300 in 1936 of which 800 were officers, to 28,000 in 1939 with the number of officers jumping to 1,426. But the dramatic increase occurred over the next two years. By 1941, the army had soared to 47,000 men, and the officer corps had stood at 1,745.[24] In the aftermath of the war with Britain, the Iraqi authorities, especially Prince 'Abd al-Ilah, embarked on a systematic policy of undermining the army's capabilities, and ensuring that leadership positions went to supporters of the monarchy. Within few months over 605 officers were either arrested or retired, including all division and brigade commanders. The army's strength was reduced from four to three divisions, and its numbers fell to around 25,000 men.[25] Not only did the army endure a huge decline in numbers; its state of well-being and readiness suffered considerably as well. A British eyewitness describes the woeful conditions of military personnel and institutions:

> [Army] boots were mostly unfit for wear in marching, its supply of cloths short, its leave long overdue, its pay meager, and its rations had been reduced to a figure a thousand calories below the minimum considered necessary by European medical men for Eastern Europe. Money for repair of barracks and camps had been stopped. The Police were forbidden to assist in tracing or arresting deserters and by the summer of 1943, out of an established strength of thirty thousand men, twenty thousand were deserters.[26]

It would take the army till the end of the monarchical period to reach the lofty numbers it had before the war with Britain.

The policy of weakening the army was backed, indeed encouraged by the British. One dispatch from the British Foreign Ministry to the embassy in Baghdad would emphasize the necessity of working with the Regent to ensure that the army did not move again against British interests, a goal that would best be achieved through a wholesale reduction, even elimination, of the army, and by appointing friends of the Palace and Britain into leadership positions. "Such an opportunity," the Ambassador was reminded, "will not arise again, and the Regent must not let it slip from his hands."[27] It is interesting that in the years, 1936–1941, the two security ministries, those of Defense and Interior, were filled by ex-Sharifian officers only 22 percent of the time, whereas in the following five years, with the increasing need for "reliable" men at the helm, the percentage more than doubled.[28] The modus vivendi of the era was to put a stop to the army's seemingly insatiable appetite for meddling in politics, a domain that should have been outside its competence and responsibilities. Of course, not everyone agreed. Taha al-Hashimi, a scion of the old guard, puts up a spirited defense of the military involvement in politics. In his memoirs, he says:

> Before people demand the distancing of the army from politics, they need to look at Iraq's recent past, where no real parties existed, where parliament had no control over public affair, where it would scramble to gain the blessings of government, rather than have government defer to it . . . , and where political personalities used politics simply to increase their wealth and serve the interests of their supporters. . . . In a country such as this where uprisings proliferate because of administrative incompetence and corruption, how can the army be deaf to the bitter complaints and blind to the sad realities. How can the army be asked not to care about the state of domestic politics."[29]

Be that as it may, successive governments worked hard in the wake of World War II to break the back of the army and degrade its capacity to effect political change. The ruling elite also made sure to suppress "seditious" (i.e., anti-British and anti-Palace) activity by ruling through a highly restrictive martial law throughout the duration of the war.

It is worth noting that in the post-1941 period, the relationship between Iraq's Executive Branch and British officialdom was much smoother than the one that existed during King Faysal's reign. The Regent and Nuri al-Sa'id were ever ready to seek the advice of the British Ambassador in both domestic and foreign affairs, and in turn the Ambassador was generally active in suggesting and endorsing Cabinet members, and other high officials.[30] Even when the British would grow frustrated with Nuri's seeming inflexibility, with his inability to broaden the ruling circle by easing into the political process a younger generation with a new vision to reform the country's political and economic structure, the embassy would still advise London that Nuri "has served Britain well, and therefore deserves continued British support."[31] Very much in the vein of earlier periods, the British seemed to be constantly in two minds about Iraq's political elites: their commitment to their friends on the one hand, and their distaste for the inflexibility and non-reformist proclivities of these very friends that were impeding the development of the country.

A major concern was the state of Iraq's economy. World War II had a devastating effect, creating dysfunctional inflationary pressures that between 1939 and 1945 reached almost 500 percent.[32] Between 1939 and 1942, the grain price index rose from 100 to 773, and the textile price index rose from 100 to a staggering 1,287.[33] The result was considerable erosion in the purchasing power of the vast majority of people. Two reasons contributed to this crisis. The first was the high expenditure of the British army in Iraq which, according to the British Ambassador, increased the volume of currency circulation in the domestic economy fivefold between 1941 and 1943.[34] This was compounded by landowners and merchants who hoarded produce to push up prices. Many of those profiteers were either members of the political elites themselves, or were connected in some way to government officials.[35] Another ploy was the control of the highly profitable import licenses. Among the registered license importers were ministers, senators, and deputies![36]

Inevitably, the section of society that was hit hardest was the lowest stratum, which saw its income remain static while prices of basic foods and material rose in some cases by more than tenfold.[37] Rising unemployment inevitably hit the lower sector of society hardest. By the end of this period, less than 30 percent of the population was in some form of employment. While rampant female unemployment might have distorted the percentage, the fact was that no more than half of the male population was economically active.[38] A number of demonstrations took place, some led by women carrying children they were unable to feed. The salaried middle class too suffered perceptible erosion in its standard of living. During this period of debilitating inflation, the wages of salaried employees rose a mere 25 percent.[39] Undoubtedly, the war years and their economic impact widened the gulf between the very narrow upper stratum of society, which constituted the bulk of the political elite, and which was mired in corruption and greed, and the rest of the population consisting of the poor and the salaried government employees.

British officials in Iraq were well aware of the dysfunctions of Iraqi society, and they worried that the snail pace of political and economic change would ultimately lead to an eruption that would greatly undermine British interests. Yet they also recognized that these interests were well served by a group of dominant politicians who, while loath to change, were committed to the old mandatory power. In the end Britain did not upset the status quo, not least because after the end of the mandate, British officials could advise, even cajole, but no longer had the power to determine policy.

By the end of 1945, popular hostility to the ruling elite was rampant. The country had moved from one economic crisis to another, and successive governments seemed indifferent to the economic miseries of the average citizen. Governments ruled through emergency laws, aided by a pliant Parliament, whose members were more interested in using their positions of access and influence to exploit the extraordinary conditions of the war to enrich themselves, their relations and friends, than to attend to the concerns of their long-suffering constituents. Wholesale corruption extended through all branches and layers of government, reaching a level that impelled a few parliamentary deputies to demand that the Cabinet put a stop to it. The response of the government came in the form of a bill that it sent to Parliament which included penalties that were hardly harsh enough to achieve the outcome of rooting out corruption. Even so, when the bill reached Parliament, most deputies spoke out, and eventually voted, against the bill that would have penalized their relatives and friends, even themselves.[40] If Parliament was in no mood to act against the interests of the majority of its members, the public was certainly willing to up the struggle, but manifestations of public dissent and dissatisfaction were suppressed by trigger-happy security forces. The deteriorating political and economic conditions that pervaded the country pointed to the real possibility of a societal eruption of dire consequences.

The government seemed neither willing nor able to address the country's many maladies through the enactment of political and economic reforms. The British, however, who by the end of 1945 were no longer constrained by the demands of the war, and were well aware of the general malaise overtaking the country, began to nudge Regent 'Abd al-Ilah to liberalize the political system.

The Regent finally succumbed to the pressure. In late December 1945, he gave an unscheduled address to members of the Senate and the Chamber of Deputies in which he outlined the country's policies for the postwar period. He blamed the lack of liberal institutions and policies on the "unnatural conditions" created by the military's persistent interventions in politics and the global instabilities engendered by World War II. "But now months after war had ended with a great victory for democracy," it was time to reassess the country's political direction. He then promised the return of multi-party life to Iraq. "The country can not continue without national political parties and organizations," the Regent said. "[These parties] will be presenting their programs, and whoever wins will assume (governmental) responsibilities."[41]

The speech, it seems, took many by surprise, including the sitting Prime Minister, Hamdi al-Pachachi,[42] for while not necessarily a despot, neither was the Regent a devotee of Jeffersonian democracy. But in addition to gentle British pressure, the Regent, anticipating a few controversial political initiatives that would re-define Iraqi-British relations, recognized the need for some broadening of the country's sphere of political participation.

A LESS STRIDENT STATE AUTHORITARIANISM, 1946–1954

The Regent's speech signaled the onset of a decade of relatively liberal politics. As we shall see in the following chapter, the standards fell far short of true institutional and political liberalism, but taken as a whole and by comparison to the preceding periods (and what would follow), this era was undoubtedly less authoritarian and more open to oppositional views. In the wake of the Regent's speech, several parties were formed and licensed. Some, such as Nuri al-Sa'id's *Hizb al-Ittihad al-Dusturi* (Constitutional Union Party) and Saleh Jabr's *Hizb al-Umma al-Ishtiraki* (Nation Socialist Party) were defenders of the status quo, particularly as it pertained to the thorny issue of relations with Britain. Others, however, proved at various times to be vigorous opposition parties, such as the centrist *Hizb al-Ahrar* (Liberal Party), the right leaning *Hizb al-Istiqlal* (Independence Party), and the left leaning *Hizb al-Watani al-Dimuqrati* (National Democratic Party), the last two boasting impressive mass following. Two more parties worth noting were *Hizb al-Sha'ab* (People's Party) and *Hizb al-Ittihad al-Watani* (National Union Party), both of which were led by political activists with strong Marxist leanings, and both soon dissolved in the face of governmental harassment and because their popular base remained small.[43] The probable reason for the weak popular base of these two Marxist-oriented, yet legalized, political parties was the competition for the same ideological space that they were bound to encounter from the clandestine Communist Party which had for many years built up a reputation for effective and popular opposition. *Al-Sha'ab* and *al-Ittihad al-Watani*, along with the *al-Watani al-Dimuqrati* emerged from *Jama'at al-Ahali*, which in the 1930s had attracted many of the reform-minded younger generation.[44]

With this revival of party politics, Iraq's political scene differed markedly from the earlier 1936–1945 period. The vigor with which oppositional political parties and their newspapers went after governmental policies in the 1946–1954 period breathed new life into a dormant democratic spirit and established new norms in which the concept of a legitimate opposition became institutionalized into the body politics of the country. This happened not because, but in fact in spite, of state policy-making institutions that were disinclined to moderate their habitual authoritarian ways and as such proved less than welcoming of the new political arrangements.

The Anti-Liberal State in the (Relatively) Liberal Era

It would of course take much more than a speech by the Regent to moderate the innate authoritarianism of the governing elite, represented not just by the "older politicians," but also by the Regent himself. Predictably, it would not take long before the Regent would begin to question the wisdom of his decision to liberalize the political process. He had asked a respected politician, Tawfiq al-Suwaydi, to form a government that would implement the Regent's promises. Taking the Prince at his words, Suwaydi filled his Cabinet with younger, seemingly reform-minded ministers.[45] The new Cabinet enjoyed the confidence of Parliament, particularly its "oppositional figures." This, however, soon became an object of concern for the Regent and the usual group of elder statesmen. Prince 'Abd al-Ilah saw in the liberal orientations of the Suwaydi government the possibility (real or imagined) of a resurgence of radical, anti-monarchical forces. In one dispatch, for instance, 'Abd al-Ilah would ask the British to help him "limit the increasing activities of the leftist elements in the country."[46] On their part, the elder statesmen, ever suspicious of liberalism, conspired to bring the government down from the first day of its inception. They finally were able to achieve this at the end of May; a mere three months after the Suwaydi government had taken office.

It was hardly a coincidence that the Regent would entrust the formation of the new Cabinet to Arshad al-'Umari, who was known for his authoritarian proclivities. He immediately set out to limit the freedom of the press, curb the activities of the just licensed political parties, and throttle any expression of public dissent with resolute force. In one instance in the city of Kirkuk, over twenty oil company workers who were demonstrating for better wages were killed by police fire, a tragedy that occasioned the resignation of 'Umari's Minister of Interior, who had insisted on disciplining the responsible officials, but had been overruled by the Prime Minister.[47] It seemed that nothing would dissuade the Prime Minister from his determined authoritarian course. He simply responded with more restrictions and greater oppression, so that four months into its tenure, the government had closed down more than three fourths of Baghdad's newspapers and put on trial a number of newspaper editors and party leaders.[48] The deteriorating situation did not escape the attention of the British who counseled the Regent against the retention of the Prime Minister,[49] whose actions they likened to those of a "raging bull."[50] Petitioned strongly by the opposition parties and sensing the increasing volatility of the political situation, the Regent hastened to "accept" 'Umari's resignation, but not before the state had shown its limited tolerance of democratic practices.

Not that the succeeding government of Saleh Jabr, which began its life in March 1947, would exhibit more tolerance for the opposition. It embarked on "managing" political dissent by closing down the two left-leaning parties, *al-Sha'ab* and *al-Ittihad al-Watani*. While a third off-spring of *Jama'at al-Ahali, al-Watani al-Dimuqrati*, was allowed to continue functioning, its leader Kamel al-Chaderji was brought to trial on charges of public sedition. Jabr also imposed strict censorship on the press, and closed down for a number of months *Sawt al-Ahali*, the widely read mouthpiece of *al-Watani al-Dimuqrati*, and the most virulent of the oppositional newspapers.

Jabr's crackdown on the press and the oppositional parties was in anticipation of a rough passage for the centerpiece of his government's program: the revision of the 1930 Anglo-Iraqi Treaty. The increasingly politically restive urban middle class was so hostile to the treaty that anything short of its annulment was bound to engender a public outcry, which, Jabr felt, would be exploited by the parties and their newspapers.

Not surprisingly, the initial negotiations were conducted in the utmost secrecy in late spring 1947. During the summer, the Regent went to England and talked privately to Ernest Bevin, the British Foreign Secretary, passing on to the government in Baghdad the gist of the talks. Secret negotiations resumed in Baghdad from October to early December, this time in the British embassy. Senior British officials would arrive secretly in Baghdad and meet with the Regent and senior Iraqi government officials in the Palace. This was interspersed with the Regent's own talks with Bevin in London. While rumors abounded, only the very few at the top of the policy-making stratum knew of the negotiations.[51] Only in late December, after more than seven months of secret contacts and negotiations did the Regent invite twenty-two "elder statesmen," but no one from the opposition, to a meeting in the Palace. Even then, the meeting merely broached the topic of Iraqi-British relations generally, with participants commenting on the fundamentals of the alliance with Britain. There was not the slightest effort to debate some of the issues that had been discussed during any of the many secret negotiations, nor was there the merest suggestion that the Regent or Jabr would be bound by the participants' views or recommendations.

When the news of the meeting and the intended new treaty broke out, massive demonstrations took place in the major cities, but especially in Baghdad among college students and trade unionists. These groups were egged on by the parties, as well as by clandestine organizations such as the

Communist Party. The government responded by issuing orders to the police to shoot at demonstrators, and when casualties occurred, the public, seething with rage, attacked public buildings and police stations. The police again were forced to fire into the crowd, and more deaths were reported, but the police were beginning to lose control. Faced with the real possibility of a collapsed security situation, Saleh Jabr and his Cabinet felt it had little option but to order the army to intervene. The Regent, however, with the events of 1941 still fresh in his memory, was reluctant to facilitate the re-entry of the army into politics. At the same time, the country was on the verge of a full-scale popular uprising. The Regent decided to force Jabr to resign, and later repudiated the new treaty.

Much of the blame for the chaos that had ensued has to be attributed to the government's penchant for formulating and implementing consequential policies in isolation from the broader political environment. The Regent's speech of December 1945 had raised hopes for a liberal era in which the opposition would participate fully in the political process. But in reality the custodians of political power, having become accustomed to authoritarian rule, perceived the democratic process as a willful intrusion into the process of policy-making, which they treated as their own exclusive domain. They might have tolerated verbal assaults and condemnations, but in no way would they acquiesce to, even contemplate, sharing power or diluting their political control. The unwillingness of Jabr and his government to partake in broad-based discussions and consultations over the revision of the treaty was a symptom of increasingly entrenched political attitudes that pitted state institutions and structures against legitimate demands by political parties and personalities for broadening the narrow political power base.

The man who followed Saleh Jabr was Senator Muhammad al-Sadr, who was known for his neutrality, and who commanded public support. Al-Sadr and the Regent knew that the primary task of the incoming government was to calm the still incendiary situation. Thus within less than a week, the Sadr government repudiated the new treaty with Britain. It then proceeded to dissolve Parliament, which had become the object of the public's ire when it voted for the treaty. At the same time, it reversed a number of its predecessor's harsher policy decisions that had led to press closures and the harassment of political parties, a main feature of which was to arrest and try party leaders on flimsy sedition charges.

The new government's more tolerant approach raised hopes that at long last a true liberal era was at hand, in which the state would not find it necessary to constantly manipulate and control the political environment in order to undermine and stunt the growth of democratic institutions. That this was to prove to be a forlorn hope became evident when the government, through the individual efforts of Cabinet members who were encouraged by the Regent, managed the elections for the new Parliament with such efficiency that opposition parties were able to win no more than six of the 138 seats. According to Majid Khadduri, however, this skewed result may not have been fully attributable to state malevolence. Khadduri credited the poor showing of the opposition parties also to their lack of organization as well as to their inability to match up to the more experienced older politicians.[52] Still, the Iraqi historian, 'Abd al-Razzaq al-Hasani, provides a plethora of evidence regarding the manipulation of the electoral process in the provinces including the many threats against individual candidates, and indeed the assassinations of local leaders of opposition parties. These infractions led to the resignation of two Cabinet ministers whose letters of resignation specifically cited widespread intimidation and numerous threats aimed at individuals for the purpose of dissuading them from declaring their candidacy.[53] Once the elections were over in June 1948, Muhammad al-Sadr, whose initial appointment as Prime Minister had engendered so much optimism, tendered his Cabinet's resignation.

Now that the incendiary conditions of the immediate post-Jabr period had subsided, the Regent returned to the small group of older politicians who had controlled Iraqi politics since the inception of the state. The gathering clouds of war over Palestine gave these politicians, who innately had a palpable distaste for sharing power, a convenient excuse to introduce martial law and press censorship. By the end of the year, two opposition parties, *al-Watani al-Dimuqrati* and *al-Ahrar* decided to temporarily cease operations. In the following three years, particularly during the relatively long tenure of Nuri al-Sa'id's eleventh Cabinet (September 1950–July 1952), state antipathy to democratic practices continued unabated with the constant harassment and arrests of leaders of the public opposition and clear human rights violations against the underground opposition, particularly members of the banned Communist Party.

There was hardly any let up when Nuri resigned and more or less passed on the premiership to yet another elder politician who as usual promised much but delivered little. This was particularly unwise, since a military takeover in Egypt in July 1952 pledged to undertake sweeping political and social reform of a system not unlike that of Iraq. In November, large-scale street demonstrations erupted in Baghdad. The opposition parties, as well as the underground Communist Party, might not have organized these demonstrations, but they certainly facilitated and encouraged them.[54] They soon turned violent when shots were exchanged leading to casualties among demonstrators and police. The size of demonstrations grew by the day and the violence correspondingly increased. Demonstrators burned down police stations, and they attacked British and American agencies and companies. As chaos ensued, the Regent felt that the civilian government had lost not just control but its nerve. This time he saw no alternative but to ask the army to intervene.

The Chief of Staff was asked to form a government, which he duly did and immediately instituted martial law, followed by sending troops into the streets to quell the disturbances. This was accompanied by disbanding all political parties and closing down their newspapers. A number of independently owned papers that did not consistently tow the government line were also suspended. Additionally, the military government carried out wholesale arrests of demonstrators who were then summarily tried on sedition charges, and to impress upon everyone the seriousness of its intent, over 220 political leaders, including ex-ministers, members of Parliament, party leaders, and journalists were taken into custody under the newly instituted emergency laws.[55] With such overwhelming state power, order was soon restored, but the spectacle of tanks and armored vehicles rolling down the streets of Baghdad could not but bring back the specter of 1941 to the very politicians who had fled for their lives when the army acquired a taste for political power.

It was thus hardly surprising that the Regent would engineer the dismissal of the military government a mere two months after it came to power.[56] Apart from restoring order, the military government was able to change the electoral law to allow for direct elections. For over a decade, the political parties had demanded that the two-step elections be abandoned on the grounds that the small number of secondary electors facilitated greater governmental interference. This became one of the primary rallying cries of the demonstrators in Baghdad and in other Iraqi cities. In order to calm the waters, the military government changed the electoral procedure to allow for direct elections, which indeed occurred in January 1953, a week before the resignation of the Cabinet. But to think that electoral reform would yield free and fair elections was to misjudge the willingness of the governing elite to loosen their tight grip on power. Governmental interference was as widespread in this election as in past elections. Almost 60 percent of the winners were unopposed, and the long hand of the state was evident in the affiliations of those who "won" the rest of the seats. This prompted one ex-Prime Minister to remark that some of the past indirect elections were more honest than the new direct one.[57]

One last effort at a true liberalization of the political system, entailing a decreasing involvement of the state in political life, occurred a year later in 1954. It was born out of the rivalry between the two "strong-men" of Iraq: the Regent and Nuri al-Sa'id. Parliament was dominated by Nuri's supporters, which meant that the wily politician could frustrate all kinds of schemes and policies desired by the Regent. Twice during 1954, the government headed by Fadhil al-Jamali, which was seen as doing the Regent's biding, fell for lack of parliamentary support. Taking advantage of Nuri's absence in Europe, the Regent engineered the dissolution of Parliament and called for new elections, which he promised would be free and fair. And to the surprise of many, the June 1954 elections went down into the annals of history as perhaps the freest of all Iraqi elections. The political parties, including all the forces of the opposition, participated in the elections,[58] and the electoral campaign was vibrant and relatively free of governmental interference.[59] And it produced the desired outcome: a shift in the balance of parliamentary representation toward the Regent. But the new Parliament also contained no less than fourteen out and out opposition figures, who, on some issues, might count on the support of another fifteen or even twenty members.

It did not take long for the Regent to realize that winning his personal battle against Nuri might have compromised the state's capacity to formulate and execute policies unencumbered by parliamentary opposition. With consequential policies looming on the horizon, such as the long delayed revision of the Anglo-Iraqi Treaty and the possible entry of Iraq into an Anglo-American anti-Communist security alliance, opposition within the ranks of Parliament could spell real trouble for the ruling elite. When consulted by the Regent, the old politicians, almost to a man, believed that only Nuri would be capable of effectively containing such a potentially volatile situation.[60] The British, too, would forcefully endorse the necessity of entrusting the ship of state to Nuri. Quickly retreating, the Regent asked the wily politician to return to Iraq and form a new government. Nuri's conditions were typical of the man's innate authoritarianism: the dissolution of the Parliament, the disbanding of the parties, the revocation of press licenses, and the suspension of organizations and associations that were deemed seditious by the government, with sedition covering even the most benign forms of opposition.[61] In the elections that were organized by Nuri's government in September 1954, 116 members entered Parliament unopposed, while the remaining nineteen seats were contested by a mere twenty-five candidates.[62] By the fall of 1954, Nuri had acted on all of the conditions that he had presented to the Regent prior to becoming Prime Minister. And with that, the relatively liberal, or at least the less stridently authoritarian, era came to a decisive end.

PURPOSEFUL STATE AUTHORITARIANISM RESURGENT, 1954–1958

Nuri's return to power after the blatantly fraudulent elections of September 1954 signaled a determined and unrelenting assault on any trace of liberalism that characterized the preceding decade. In early August, the Prime Minister, in a gesture that underscored the path that his government would follow, disbanded his own party, *al-Ittihad al-Destouri*, explaining that Iraq no longer had any need for political parties. Using a deviously self-interested line of reasoning, the Prime Minister argued that the elimination of party politics would allow all those who wished to represent their country in the new Parliament to do so on equal footing without the bias and divisions provided by party affiliations.[63] In an official communiqué read on Baghdad Radio on September 28, 1954, Nuri's Minister of

Interior, Sa'id Qazzaz, announced the disbanding of all existing political parties, societies, and clubs in the country, the number of which had stood at 458.[64] Soon after, the government revoked the licenses of 130 newspapers and magazines in Baghdad (in reality, of these only twenty-nine were actually printed and distributed),[65] twenty in Mosul, seven in Basra, and another thirteen in other Iraqi provinces.[66] With these draconian measures, the earlier era, in which opposition if not embraced, was at least not fiercely hounded, came to an abrupt and definitive end. From now until the end of the monarchical era, the state under the stern supervision of Nuri, the Regent, and the other members of the ruling elite would intrude in all societal matters with next to no regard for civil liberties and political representation. Any democratic pretense had by now completely disappeared. The stringent control of the electoral process remained utterly unchecked throughout the last four years of the monarchy's life. A clear exhibition of this was the last elections under the monarchy which took place on May 5, 1958, less than ten weeks before the military coup of July 14 that sealed the fate of the Hashemites. In the expanded Chamber's 143 seats, no more than twenty-seven seats were contested. The other 116 parliamentarians were elected by *al-tazkia* (the by now familiar official phrase, meaning unopposed). This election was such a non-event that newspapers "reported the voting and its results in inside pages as perfunctory matters."[67]

Whatever natural authoritarian proclivities that Nuri and Iraq's other "oligarchs" possessed, these were cemented and in a sense rationalized by dramatic changes in the country's external environment. There was of course a pressing need to renegotiate the Anglo-Iraqi Treaty which had remained dormant since the 1948 insurrection. But Iraq's bilateral relations with Britain were now a function of a much larger international configuration of forces that was shaped by the gathering global East-West confrontation. The 1950s saw the determined entry of the United States into Middle East politics. The United States' purpose was the creation of an alliance that would range the "free world" against the Soviet Union and its Communist surrogates and allies. Having created the North Atlantic Treaty Organization (NATO) in 1949 and the South East Asian Treaty organization (SEATO) in 1954, the United States wanted a Middle Eastern alliance that would link with NATO through Turkey and with SEATO through Pakistan to complete the encirclement of the international Communist powers.

To bring this vision to fruition, the U.S. Secretary of State, John Foster Dulles, approached Egypt to act as the linchpin of this new alliance. But Gamal 'Abd al-Nasir, the young military leader of Egypt, was lukewarm at best. Nasir seemed utterly unconcerned about threats from the Soviet Union, which, as Nasir would remind Dulles, was "five thousand miles away."[68] In the wake of his visit to Cairo, Dulles was persuaded that he needed another Arab country to enter a pact with Turkey and Pakistan and hopefully bring other Middle Eastern countries with it into the bargain.

Iraq was a natural choice. With the virulently pro-West and anti-Communist Nuri at the helm, particularly now that he had a pliant Parliament and a muzzled press, there would be precious few obstacles to the passage of such a pact. Nuri, in contrast to Egypt's Nasir, could not conceive of a political path not just for the Iraqis, but for the Arabs as a whole, that was divorced from the West. He was later to write that Nasir "failed to understand that the West would not tolerate Russian influence in the Middle East. He failed to understand that the West would not grant the Arabs the luxury of neutralism, that this area is too decisively vital for this sort of foolishness. He failed to understand that the Middle East is inextricably tied to the West economically—there is no bigger market for Arab oil, for example. Despite a soldier's background, [Nasir] overlooked the military reality of Russia's incapacity to defend the Arabs if they made an enemy of the West."[69] By thrusting Iraq as the central player in this new configuration of forces, Nuri felt that his bargaining posture would be strengthened in negotiations for a new Anglo-Iraqi treaty. Disregarding the protestations of the radical Arab forces which saw this kind of alliance as sacrificing Iraq's foreign policy independence at the altar of Western "imperialism," Nuri signed a security treaty with Turkey in February 1955, which became known as *Mithaq Baghdad*, the Baghdad Pact, conceived as the first step of a larger regional alliance involving Pakistan and Iran, to be cemented by Britain and the United States.

After a short debate that was distinguished by the paucity of oppositional comments, to say nothing of criticisms, the Chamber of Deputies approved the Pact by an overwhelming vote of 112 to 4. The Senate followed suit, ratifying the Pact by twenty-six votes to one. If the docility of

Parliament was to be expected from a membership that was literally selected by the Prime Minister, the near absence of popular outrage did constitute a major surprise. The Egyptian radio station, "The Voice of the Arabs," which was listened to avidly by Iraqis, lambasted Nuri and the Palace for their traitorous act and their general infidelity to the Arab cause,[70] exhorting "brother Iraqis" to rise against the "lackeys of British colonialism and American imperialism."[71] As we shall see such verbal onslaught would have a major impact on the Iraqi street later on, particularly during the Suez crisis, but the ratification of the Baghdad Pact was concluded without major incidents in Iraq. The previous fall's assault on the opposition—elimination of political parties, closing down of newspapers, jailing of prominent oppositional leaders, rounding up of known underground, particularly Communist agitators, and strengthening of internal security and the secret police, paid the desired dividends through the perceptible, and to many surprising, lack of public protest. There were of course isolated incidents of sedition. A few explosives had been planted under a major bridge that connects the two sides of Baghdad, but thanks to the revamped internal security system, these were discovered and disabled. A few donkeys were paraded in a marketplace in Baghdad with signs attacking the Turkish Prime Minister 'Adnan Menderes. But that seems to have been the extent of the protest. Indeed, when some of his ministers advised the imposition of martial law, Nuri adamantly refused, expressing confidence in the police and security forces to maintain law and order.[72] To further blunt possible popular anger, Nuri announced the termination of the Anglo-Iraqi Treaty and the return of air bases still under British control to the Iraqis. On schedule, British evacuation of its troops from Iraq began in May of that year.

The Baghdad Pact may not have induced political instability in Iraq, but it was without doubt a seminal event in the sense that from this juncture until the end of the monarchy, political discourse and activity inside Iraq would be dominated by issues and events arising from the clash of competing interests and policies in world and Middle Eastern affairs. While the anticipated popular eruptions did not materialize in February 1955, the attack by Britain, France, and Israel on Egypt in the fall of 1956, that was a response to Nasir's unilateral nationalization of the Suez Canal Company, did create the kind of instability that posed an immeasurable challenge to the legitimacy of the government and state institutions in Iraq.

While anger at the attacks swept through the streets of Baghdad and other major Iraqi cities, the official response was tepid, even gleeful. In fact, Tawfiq al-Suwaydi, a long- standing member of the ruling elite maintains that Nuri had known beforehand of British and French plans to attack Egypt, and in a meeting in London had actually advocated it.[73] This is confirmed by Naji Shawkat, another high-ranking member of the elite. Shawkat relates in his memoirs that he had asked Saleh Jabr on his return from London whether Nuri knew about the impending attack on Egypt. Jabr confirmed this and went further saying that in fact Nuri had "advised the British government to do whatever it could to eliminate 'Abd al-Nasir before he eliminated Britain's interests and influence among the Arab countries."[74] But if Nuri had thought that he would be able to put the lid on peoples' anger, as he had done earlier in the case of the Baghdad Pact, the following days would prove him profoundly wrong.

The seething populace took to the streets in huge numbers.[75] Riots erupted in Iraq's three main cities of Baghdad, Basra, and Mosul, and in the Shi'ite cities of Najaf, Kufa, and Hilla, where the clandestine Communist Party was particularly strong.[76] The situation deteriorated so badly in Najaf that a battalion of special forces from Mosul, all of whose members were Sunnis, was sent to bolster the overmatched police and restore order in the Shi'ite holy city.[77] In Baghdad, in just two days of rioting, 378 demonstrators were arrested.[78] This time, the government was compelled to impose martial law, with orders to the police to shoot at demonstrators if necessary. A mini-insurrection in the southern town of al-Hayy was put down with unrestrained brutality, including the public hanging of the ringleaders.

The state's resolute response was in fact a fig leaf covering the mounting isolation and uncertainty of the ruling elite. A revolutionary situation was at hand, and the security forces seemed overextended in its efforts to contain it. The British Ambassador reported to his government that he had never seen Nuri "more deeply discouraged and depressed,"[79] and in a Baghdad Pact meeting, the Prime Minister of Turkey thought that Iraq's leaders were in a state of "near collapse."[80] Indeed, this was one of the very few occasions when Nuri would be subjected to scorching criticisms from his own inner circle of older politicians. In his memoirs, 'Ali Jawdat, Nuri's friend and an ex-Prime Minister, relates that in a meeting of trusted politicians that the Regent called to go over the rapidly deteriorating situation, criticisms of Nuri were rampant. Jawdat himself lambasted Nuri for encouraging Britain's premier, Anthony Eden, to invade Egypt. He advocated stronger language to show London Iraq's displeasure, and even said that nationalizing the oil companies was a legitimate endeavor in the circumstances.[81] While the crisis eventually passed without the collapse of the political order, it did nevertheless demonstrate that the political system was becoming more vulnerable as it grew more authoritarian. Moreover, while Nuri and the ruling elite could foresee and try to manage internal problems, they were discovering that they had next to no control over external events and policies that spilled over into Iraq's domestic political environment.

THE LIMITS OF STATE CAPACITY

Looking back at the performance of the Iraqi state, it is clear that in the political domain, the results were mixed at best, with the ruling elite, getting older and more entrenched with the passage of time, unwilling to put in place much needed political reform, but sufficiently benign not to administer a draconian tyranny. Thus, the state meandered, uncertain of its direction, oscillating between an authoritarian impulse and a political need for liberalizing initiatives. The problem for the ruling elite was that the political stagnation which characterized the last four years of the monarchy's life tended to cloud some positive achievements of the state in other aspects of public life.

There were, for instance, perceptible improvements in educational attainment. The number of students attending secondary schools jumped from just over a thousand in 1927 to almost 100,000 in 1958. In 1927, there were only seventy-seven college students, yet by 1958, the number had risen to 8,568.[82] Educational improvement had a dramatic impact on the bureaucracy. At its inception, the state employed 3,000 men, the vast majority of whom were uneducated. By the end of the monarchical period, the state directly employed over 20,000 men and women, with just under half having attained at least secondary education.[83] The educated urban middle class also expanded considerably, numbering 740,000 (28 percent of the population) in 1958. However, only one fourth of it was privately employed.[84] The problem for the ruling elite was that while socioeconomic and educational advances would contribute to a more "national" rather than "communal" outlook, it would also open people's minds and horizons to incendiary ideologies, such as radical nationalism, that were sweeping the Third World in the 1950s, as well as to the political and social ills of society, thus on balance making the "student" and the "professional" an adversary, rather than a "friend" of the state.

The growth of the middle class was also reflected in the rapid economic changes that occurred during the last decade and a half of the monarchy's life. In 1958, the country's earnings from exports stood at $566 million, while it imported $307 million worth of goods. Both figures were about a third higher than corresponding totals five years earlier.[85] The income from petroleum royalties rose from just over $7 million in 1947 to $300 million in 1958. The government created a Development Board in 1950 to which it allocated no less than 70 percent of its earnings from petroleum.[86] Just under half of the Board's budget went to agricultural irrigation and flood control (which for generations had been a major menace in the country, particularly Baghdad). A number of dams were built, and by 1957, the threat of flooding had all but ceased, and the agricultural domain significantly expanded. A fourth of the budget was allocated to transportation, so that by 1958, over 1,243 miles of main roads and 932 miles of secondary roads, as well as twenty bridges, had been built, while the port in the southern city of Basra was modernized and expanded and a new airport was constructed in Baghdad.[87] The rest of the allocations went to construction and industry, which, in addition to a major refinery, financed a few light industries.

The problem was in the Board's emphasis on long-term projects whose gains were not discernible immediately, or at least in the short term. A British report criticized this orientation, faulting the Board for "thinking its task almost exclusively in material terms, in brick and mortar." It then went on to recommend that "capital investment may be suitably and more often beneficially made in improving the quality of human beings."[88] The report's conclusions were no doubt influenced by the conditions that the report's authors had observed while in Iraq, for allied with, and indeed contributing to, the growing political alienation were deep socioeconomic disparities that continued to plague the country. Thus, with all the educational advancements, two thirds of the country's younger generation, mainly in the rural areas, and in the poor neighborhoods of the urban centers, remained illiterate. For most of the population, living conditions were atrocious. Eighty percent of residences were without electrical power,[89] and as late as 1956, only 21 percent of the population lived in permanent dwellings that had piped running water.[90] This gave rise to a stark material divide between some 30 percent of the population comprising the rich upper class and the comfortable middle class, and the remaining 70 percent that was situated at the bottom rungs of the socioeconomic ladder, and that lived in abject poverty. The disparity was harshest in the rural domains where less than 1 percent of landholders owned 55 percent of the land, whereas three fourths of the peasant population owned less than 17 percent of the land.[91] Indeed the vast majority of the peasant households were "landless or almost landless."[92]

The dire living conditions of the peasant engendered wholesale migration into urban areas, which confronted newly arrived poor with the ways and styles of the urban rich, many of whom had used their political clout (they were ministers and members of Parliament, or people associated with them) to make their fortunes in real estate and import-export licensing businesses. All this served to highlight and emphasize even more the vast socioeconomic gulf that existed in the country and that showed no sign of narrowing. And as stated earlier, in the midst of all this, a middle class, educated, salaried and professional, was rapidly expanding and becoming increasingly susceptible to revolutionary ideas. It grew to resent the wealth of the upper class, its corruption and conspicuous consumption, its dogged hold on power, and its seeming symbiotic relationship with, indeed dependence on, the despised old colonial power—more than enough elements and conditions for a cataclysmic change in the political order.

CHAPTER SIX

Potholes in the Democratic Road, 1936–1958

During the period spanning the decade 1936–1945 democracy could hardly be expected to fare well. Any growth of democratic ideas and institutions that had been achieved earlier came to an abrupt halt in 1936, as military coups do not as a matter of principle and custom provide the ideal terrain in which representative institutions can grow and prosper. Army officers, custodians of political power between 1936 and 1941, cared little, if at all, about democratic institutions and practices. They were succeeded by civilian governments, openly abetted by the Palace, which systematically interfered in the workings of the country's supposed representative institutions. Political parties and groupings operating within the straitjacket of military government and martial law had all but disappeared from the political scene. And successive governments made certain to emasculate Parliament of even the flimsiest pretense of independence and impartiality.

It was not as though this was not recognized by Iraqis. An editorial in the leading oppositional paper, *al-Ahali*, which appeared as late as 1945, derided governmental pretense that Iraq was a constitutional monarchy possessed of a Parliament with legislative authority. The paper dismissed the claim of "parliamentary democracy" as a lacerating illusion. It reminded Iraqis that in a real democracy Parliament is the institution that represented the interests of the people, because it was elected by the people, and as such should have total authority over government. The result of this "true" parliamentary democracy was that the government could not but work to achieve the interests of the people. In Iraq, however, Parliament had no power over government, which allowed the Executive to rule unhindered, with the result that its policies were aimed to serve not the people as a whole, but the narrow interests of the ruling elites.[1] And indeed, during the Bakr Sidqi era, even parliamentary immunity went by the wayside, as members of both the House of Deputies and the Senate were expelled from Parliament and put in prison. A number of those were tribal leaders who vehemently opposed the populist ideals of the Ahali group, which they considered to be socialist, even communist.[2] Indeed, at one point a respected (and in the circumstances, courageous) senator stood up to declare that no less than a third of the membership of the Senate had been maltreated by the government.[3] The functions of Parliament as a legislative body and a watchdog over governmental actions and policies were cavalierly cast aside by the government of the first coup.

The Cabinet of Nuri al-Sa'id, which, as we have seen, was put in place by the military was perhaps less ruthless in its treatment of Parliament, but still exhibited complete lack of deference to the institution. In Nuri's initial days as Prime Minister in early 1939, a few parliamentarians cast dispersions about the circumstances under which the new government was formed. To their astonishment, at the outset of the following parliamentary session, a royal decree was read dissolving Parliament on the grounds that "constitutional procedure requires complete harmony between the executive and legislature. [Since the Cabinet felt] that no such harmony existed between itself and the Chamber, it had decided . . . to dissolve the Chamber of Deputies and hold new elections."[4] Not surprisingly, the new elections yielded not a single opposition member.

In the wake of the Regent's escape from the country after the 1941 military coup, Rashid 'Ali and his army backers resolved to depose the Regent and appoint a replacement. Such a consequential constitutional issue, however, was vested in Parliament, which could only be convened through a royal decree. The Regent of course was no longer available, and in any case would hardly be expected to set in motion a process aimed at his own removal from power. The expectation was that a constitutional crisis would ensue. But Rashid 'Ali and the army officers were not going to be sidetracked by some pesky constitutional nitpicking, and went ahead and convened Parliament. While most of the deputies were supporters of the Regent and Nuri, they could well see the writing on the wall and pliantly voted to depose 'Abd al-Ilah and appoint another member of the Hashemite family to take his place.

Much of the Parliament's weakness could be attributed to the continuing practice of rigging the elections, where the bulk of deputies would be chosen before elections took place. One such instance of governmental management of elections is detailed by an Iraqi historian who consulted dispatches from the British Ambassador in Baghdad to the Foreign Office in London.[5] Prior to the 1943 elections, Nuri al-Sa'id and his minion, Saleh al-Jabr, prepared a list of candidates acceptable to them and, they believed, to the Palace. They were then surprised by the Regent who presented his own list of 105 candidates (the total number of parliamentary seats), some of whom were not acceptable to either Nuri or Jabr. The two politicians threatened to resign, and a mini crisis followed until a compromise was reached. Nuri accepted ninety-nine candidates from the Regent's list, and the names were duly circulated to regional and districts officials. The ensuing "Regent friendly" Parliament immediately confirmed an amendment to the Constitution that essentially took away the right of Parliament to dismiss the Prime Minister and his Cabinet, and bestowed it on the King (or in this case, the Regent).

Here again, the British were at best silent on the question of electoral rigging and parliamentary weakness. While in their dispatches to the foreign office the ambassadors complained about the rigidity and corruption of the political elites, there is little evidence of a concerted effort to impress upon the Iraqi leaders the advisability of conducting free and fair elections that would yield a Parliament that was independent of the executive. Indeed, the British seemed content to stay with the status quo for fear that anti-British opposition groups would influence parliamentary debate to the detriment of British interests in Iraq. At a minimum, therefore, the British acquiesced to the flagrant intervention by the government in the electoral process.

The press, however, was not treated so cavalierly. Opposition papers were indeed harassed, and more often than not shut down. For example, *al-Ahali*, the mouthpiece of *Jama'at al-Ahali*, was not published from 1937 to 1942. But those that were published found ways to express oppositional views, and the political leaders responded with the kind of patience that they did not accord to Parliament or opposition political parties. Editorials, some of them carrying stinging criticisms of governmental policies or the British presence, continued to be published and read avidly throughout the 1930s, and gained in intensity as the clouds of war began to gather in Europe.

When the war started, the government enacted emergency laws that placed newspapers and magazines under direct governmental censorship in an effort to put a lid on anti-British sentiment. Yet throughout 1940 and 1941, various newspapers continued gleefully to publish accounts of German victories, which naturally angered the British Ambassador.[6] This prompted then-Prime Minister Taha al-Hashimi to invite editors and members of the media to a meeting to ask them to be more responsible in their news coverage, given the emergency situation during the war and the censorship laws that were in existence at that time. His address to the newsmen is interesting because it was a mix of veiled threats and friendly indulgence that was a microcosm of the hesitant relationship that the authorities had with the press. "Yes, the press is free," Hashimi confirmed, "but the difficult conditions that the world is going through necessitate vigilance on our part, and the emergency laws give us the power to constrain the press. There is no justification for the press to support the (country) which is the enemy of our ally, and there is no need for seditious news. . .that would negatively impact our political and economic well-being. Nor [should] the press attack or demean the dignity of the officials of the monarchy [since in the present circumstances] the country needs all of its sons to come together." Hashimi then ended the meeting by thanking the press for behaving responsibly and "for recognizing the perils of the present situation."[7] The tenor of the Prime Minister's comments was clearly intended to compel members of the press who attended the meeting not so much to desist from voicing opposition, but to merely tone down the stridency of their criticisms.

It is not clear why the authorities treated the press more benignly than Parliament or political parties. Perhaps the very low literacy rate (less that 10 percent at the time) played a role. And in the majority of cases, this narrow readership was already set in its political orientation, so the ability of a newspaper to change attitudes and opinions was limited. Moreover, allowing newspapers to criticize governmental policies and personnel, even in a limited form, would bestow a veneer of legitimacy on the ruling elite.

The Prime Minister, for example, would be able to point to his relatively relaxed attitude toward the press to counter accusations of authoritarianism. At any rate, anti-British news items continued to appear, and during the short-lived 1941 Rashid 'Ali's government, the press embarked on venomous tirades against the British and their Iraqi "agents" and "lackeys."[8] But these papers were soon to be closed after the Iraqi defeat at the hands of the British and the collapse of the Rashid 'Ali government. Most would remain inactive throughout the duration of World War II. Not until the end of 1945 would Prince 'Abd al-Ilah promise in a major address a significant relaxation of the policies and practices that had characterized the authoritarian decade of 1936–1945.

DEMOCRATIC ATTITUDES AND PRACTICES IN THE RELATIVE LIBERALISM OF 1946–1954

In light of the analysis in the previous chapter that detailed constant and blatant state restrictions on the institutions and procedures of democracy, one is apt to question the extent of political liberalism in the "liberal" era. Needless to say that what pertained during 1946–1954 was by no means a shining example of Jeffersonian democracy. The progress of democratic ideas and practices was indeed slow and uncertain, and was constantly impeded by state institutions with insatiable appetite for political control. On the other hand, however, democratic ideas that would not be considered benign by the governing elite were allowed to air, and even be taught in schools. For instance, as early as 1946, a social studies textbook for secondary (high) schools extolled the virtues of democracy as the most appropriate system of governance for Iraq. It claimed that democracy had made perceptible advances, but admitted the slowness of these advances, attributing it to a number of sociopolitical factors including "the weakness of political institutions." It then went on to cite a number of conditions that needed to be attained for democracy to grow. These included some recommendations which the book conceded were "politically risky," such as "the obliteration of the feudal order," and "imbuing the governing elites with the democratic spirit."[9] As we shall see in the following discussion, the political system, while dominated by state structures that were inhospitable to liberal attitudes, was still open enough to allow for oppositional ideas to circulate among the population, and for opposition figures to launch effective anti-governmental campaigns.

At various times during this period, the opposition parties mounted vitriolic and ceaseless onslaught on the British and their policies and on successive Iraqi governments for being umbilically tied to British interests in the country. Thus, the parties were at the forefront of those who opposed the new Anglo-Iraqi Treaty signed by Prime Minister Saleh al-Jabr in 1948. When news of the signing of the Treaty reached Iraq, the streets of Baghdad and other major cities soon filled with thousands of anti-Treaty demonstrators. The massive demonstrations were vigorously encouraged, even egged on, by the opposition parties.[10] Vigorous condemnations of the "Portsmouth Treaty" (labeled after the city where it was signed) were issued by the parties. *Al-Istiqlal* called it "a national disaster . . . which was facilitated by a parliament that does not represent the nation, and which was negotiated by a delegation that did not emerge from the will of the people, [and as such] the Party proclaims its fervent opposition to this treaty and urges the people to reject and resist it."[11] *Al-Watani al-Dimuqrati* issued a statement that attacked the treaty as the work of an unrepresentative government intent on "shackling Iraq with new chains, negating its sovereignty, and tying it firmly to the wheels of British imperialism." The treaty was thus nothing less than "a blatant assault on Iraq's very being, its sovereignty and its political future." The statement concluded by appealing to "the Iraqi people to defeat this new imperialist project and resist it with all its might."[12] Even the moderate *al-Ahrar* Party in a public declaration characterized the treaty as "a mortal danger to the independence and sovereignty of the [Iraqi] monarchy and an unyielding hurdle to the country's progress and to the realization of its national interest and aspirations." The Party then went on to urge the Iraqi people to "stop the ratification of the treaty by all legitimate means possible."[13] Moreover, the official newspapers of the parties launched streams of incendiary attacks on the treaty that fanned the flames of the insurrection.

As demonstrations grew in size and intensity, the Regent called the leaders of the opposition parties, as well as other prominent politicians to a meeting at the Palace.[14] The ensuing discussion was remarkable for its candor, and it contained open criticisms of the governing elite, which naturally included the palace, for the way they ran the country. "The people want the constitution to be implemented," complained Kamel al-Chaderji of *al-Watani al-Dimuqrati* to the Regent, adding that the people were demanding full freedoms—"of the press, association and opinion." He then addressed the Regent directly: "You in your capacity as defender of the constitution must penalize the government when it behaves [antidemocratically]."[15] Muhammad Mahdi Kubba of the virulently anti-British *al-Istiqlal* focused on the ills of the treaty and, eschewing accepted etiquette, told the Prince that his much revered uncle, King Faysal I, did not have the support of the Iraqi people when he signed the 1930 Anglo-Iraqi Treaty. Kubba then threatened openly that if nothing was done about the Portsmouth accord, he and members of his party would be "at the forefront of the demonstrations."[16] Given that one of the most prominent and favorite slogans of the marauding crowds was the overthrow of the monarchy and its replacement with a republican order,[17] Kubba's words were bold indeed, and speak to a relatively forbearing political milieu.

While it was the opposition that led the verbal assault against the Portsmouth Treaty, the Regent could not but recognize the near unanimity among all those present in rejecting it. It was thus resolved that a declaration in the name of the Regent would be broadcast on the radio assuring the people that their demands would be met. The declaration was read on the main news that evening. It explained that the Regent had met with a number of political personalities, including representatives of the opposition parties, and they had concluded that the Portsmouth Treaty "did not fulfill the country's aspirations, nor did it constitute the proper means to cement the friendly relations between the two countries. Accordingly, His Royal Highness, the Regent and Crown Prince, promises the Iraqi people that no treaty would be signed that does not guarantee the country's rights and its national aspirations."[18] Immediately upon hearing the Royal pronouncement, the frenzied situation in the streets abated. The general response of the citizens was overwhelmingly positive and a semblance of normalcy returned to the cities.

The euphoria did not last. Armed with British insistence to put the accord in front of Parliament, Prime Minister Saleh al-Jabr returned to

Iraq and affirmed his continued commitment to the treaty that he had just signed in Portsmouth. He coupled this with threats against "the anarchical elements whose heads he was prepared to crush."[19] Acting on his threat, he ordered the police to come out into the streets of Baghdad in full force. The following day, riots and massive demonstrations erupted in Baghdad in which several people were killed by the police. Leaders and members of the opposition, disillusioned by the abrupt turn of events, were active during that day: some participated in the increasingly violent demonstrations, others distributed leaflets, and still others liaised with student organizations and labor unions.

Even the usually pliant parliamentarians, most of whom owed their parliamentary seats to the government, were getting restless and less cooperative, particularly as armed clashes between the demonstrators and the police became more commonplace resulting in a mounting loss of life. The tone and substance of speeches made on the floor of the Chamber grew more and more critical, and a group of thirty members of the Chamber of Deputies tendered their resignation, accusing the government of "using terror tactics to coerce the people into accepting a treaty that everyone rejects."[20] This was followed immediately by the resignation of the President of the Chamber, which for all intents and purposes left a crippled Parliament that would lack the authority to bestow constitutional legitimacy on the treaty.

Toward the end of the day, as the Prime Minister was rapidly losing control, the leaders of the opposition met and decided to demand the immediate resignation of the prime minister. And they duly communicated the demand to the Regent.[21] By then, the situation had become so untenable that Jabr was forced to tender his resignation, and immediately fled Baghdad to his tribal domain in the south.

The Regent, having achieved the necessary lowering of the political temperature, began to contemplate the various possibilities for the premiership. With relative calm returning, the Regent's authoritarian instincts pushed for a "strong" prime minister who would not think twice about clamping down on anti-government elements. His preference was for the uncompromising Arshad al-'Umari, an ally of the Regent. But 'Umari's relations with the political parties and their leaderships were far from cordial. Consequently, the opposition coalesced in rejecting the nomination, using their newspapers to publicize their position, and supporting instead the moderate Muhammad al-Sadr.[22] By now the Regent had become greatly concerned about a prolonged political stalemate and a possible return of anarchy to the streets. Indeed he was beginning to lose his nerve. In a cable to the Foreign Office, the Deputy British Ambassador related a conversation with Nuri al-Sa'id, in which the latter claimed that the Regent had burst out crying when he met with Saleh al-Jabr, demanding his resignation, and that he was listening to no one's advice except those of his increasingly paranoid mother and sisters. Apparently, Nuri had been so embarrassed by the Regent's behavior that he had personally apologized to the British, but was realistic enough to tell the Deputy Ambassador that no Iraqi politician could any longer publicly support the Treaty.[23] By then it was a foregone conclusion that the Regent would acquiesce to the demands of the opposition and invite al-Sadr to assume the premiership.

The first order of business for the new government was the inescapable repudiation of the "Portsmouth Treaty"; a task that was accomplished quickly and seamlessly. This represented an undoubted triumph for the opposition parties. They, however, were not able to exploit the vulnerability of the ruling elite and build on their victory, not least because of differences that separated them.[24] Still, these parties, especially *al-Istiqlal* and *al-Watani al-Dimuqrati*, played an "important and effective role in the rejection of the treaty."[25] Indeed, in this instance, the opposition not only proved to be a capable medium for transmitting, as well as advocating, the demands of the people to the ruling elite, but also was willing to take the lead in securing important changes against the wishes of the ruling elites.

Three years later, yet another instance of consequential party activism occurred. Buoyed by the military coup in Egypt that toppled the monarchy in July 1952, and encouraged further by the forced resignation of the President of Lebanon at the insistence of the opposition in September of the same year, three political parties in Iraq took the opportunity of the formation of a new government tasked with preparing the country for new elections to send stinging memoranda to the Regent encapsulating their political demands for fundamental political reforms, including limiting the powers of the Head of State himself. What was even more remarkable was that these memoranda were published in the newspapers of the parties. *Al-Istiqlal* minced no words when it began its memorandum by declaring that in the present Iraqi conditions, every citizen found himself "regretting being born in this country, and living under its political tyranny." The party then demanded that the independence of the judiciary be affirmed, that the two-stage indirect elections be discarded and replaced with direct elections, and that widespread corruption be eliminated. But the most pugnacious of its demands was the insistence on an amendment to the Iraqi Constitution "so that the King (in this case the Regent) would desist from interfering in matters of government."[26] The second opposition party, *al-Jabha al-Sha'biya*, asserted that it had become common for successive cabinets to thrust aside their legitimate governmental responsibilities, complaining that "the Regent made a habit of interfering in all matters large and small."[27] The memorandum of *al-Watani al-Dimuqrati* was presented as a "summary of the complaints of the Iraqi people," which ranged from poor living conditions, economic stagnation, and corruption to denying people their democratic rights and subordinating the country's vital interests to British ambitions and designs. Again there were a number of strident criticisms of the Regent himself. The party rebuked the Regent for disregarding the Constitution, thus making it irrelevant, and pointedly accused him of being the one "responsible for this aberrant situation." It castigated him for interfering in governmental decisions, and for expropriating governmental powers, so that all Cabinet decisions were conditional on his approval, a situation that was "absolutely contrary to the democratic process." In light of these and other derelictions, the memorandum asked that "all such infringements be stopped."[28]

In assessing the extent of the system's authoritarianism, it is interesting to speculate what the response of some one like Saddam Husayn would have been had these memoranda been written fifty years later! Yet Prince 'Abd al-Ilah replied promptly admitting "that reforms were necessary and that [he] was ready to welcome any advice on this matter from any public man or organization."[29] Ironically, the parties hardly applauded the Regent's response; they thought that its promptness betrayed a dismissive attitude toward not only the parties, but also the people and their concerns. *Al-Ahali* newspaper, the mouthpiece of *al-Watani al-Dimuqrati*, wrote: "such an important issue in such conditions deserved the full and unswerving attention of those responsible for this country's political affairs. But the speed of the response proves the offhandedness and dismissiveness with which the affairs of the state have been treated in the past, and which was, and continues to be, an important reason for the deterioration of conditions. This also shows the persistence of a mentality that cares little about the people and their wishes."[30] Similarly, the newspaper of *al-Jabha al-Sha'biya* characterized the response of the Palace as "precipitant and offhanded," contrasting it with "the parties' memoranda which were minutely studied to the extent that every sentence was subjected to detailed criticism and analysis."[31] The expectation, therefore, was that nothing would come out of this. However, three days later, the Prince invited the leaders of the three parties and other political notables to the Palace to discuss the conditions of the country and the grievances articulated in the memoranda. While the meeting eventually resolved very little if anything, it nevertheless did speak to an environment of relative liberalism that allowed political parties to level biting public criticisms at the highest echelons of government with little fear of real retribution.

Much of the parties' public assault on various governments was voiced through their newspapers and other independently owned opposition papers. When, after the Regent's 1945 speech, the governmental ban on newspapers was lifted, the oppositional papers went on the offensive immediately. In early 1946, for example, *al-Bilad*, the independent opposition paper, counseled the Regent to stay out of party politics in accordance with constitutional conventions.[32] Later on, in the summer of 1946, *Liwa al-Istiqlal* and *Sawt al-Ahali*, the mouthpieces of the opposition parties *al-Istiqlal* and *al-Watani al-Dimuqrati*, respectively, mounted virulent campaigns against the allegedly ruthless and dictatorial Prime Minister Arshad al-'Umari, who, according to *Liwa al-Istiqlal*, "had declared an unrelenting war of mythical proportions against public freedoms in general."[33] These attacks on the whole were directed at the policies of the government, but they also did not spare the Prime Minister. In one editorial, *Sawt al-Ahali*, dismissed al-'Umari as somewhat "unbalanced," and alleged that "many Iraqis . . . could not imagine that such a man would attain the important political position that he was now occupying," and as such "they treated his appointment with apathy, indeed with not a little ridicule."[34] When 'Umari decided that he had had enough, he took Kamel al-Chaderji, the paper's owner and the leader of *Hizb al-Watani al-Dimuqrati*, to court. With seventeen lawyers volunteering their services, the six months imprisonment for sedition was quickly appealed and squashed, and the paper reappeared after a hiatus of six weeks or so.

The same tone of press attacks continued to be launched against successive governments, until a few years later Nuri al-Sa'id, with very little tolerance for verbal attacks by members of the opposition, repeated 'Umari's tactic by taking Chaderji again to court and closing his paper. Even though Nuri was probably the most authoritarian of all of the "old politicians", his courts were hardly the kangaroo courts that Iraqis became accustomed to in the era of Saddam Husayn. Chaderji arrived in court this time attended by no fewer than twenty-one defense lawyers. He used the occasion to lecture the public prosecutor and the judge on democratic principles and practices, and the proceedings were quickly disseminated to the public, adding to the defendant's public aura. The court ended up sentencing Chaderji to six months hard labor, but the defense team successfully had the appellant court rescind the decision. These were the most high-profile, but not the only, cases where editors of oppositional newspapers were taken to court. However, the editorial staff of *al-Ahali* in its various incarnations seemed to receive the lion's share of charges.

Between 1946 and 1954, charges against the opposition produced little actual sanctions, with the accused usually released for lack of evidence or after immediate appeal.[35] What is interesting here is that while the state, through its governing elite, was clearly inhospitable to democratic opposition, and did what it could to harass the opposition and undermine their effectiveness, it was reluctant to consistently use its coercive power to allow it to completely neutralize the opposition. Nor was it inclined to publicly impose its will on the legal institutions.

The opposition press continued to assail governments and their prime ministers throughout the 1940s and early part of the 1950s. During the 1948 "Portsmouth Treaty" talks, the press attacked Prime Minister Saleh al-Jabr mercilessly, going beyond determined criticism of his policy to unashamed incitement of the public to revolt. *Al-Wathba*, the resultant uprising, was aided by incendiary newspaper reports and opinions that not only hailed the actions of the demonstrators, but actually egged on the population to join in the mini-insurrection. The rousing reports and exhortations were in fact distributed to the protesters by the journalists of the opposition themselves, many of whom marched at the head of demonstrations that specifically called for a free press and the doing away with governmental bans on newspapers.[36]

Closing down newspapers or at a minimum increasing the censorship on what they were able to write were the weapons employed by various Iraqi governments to limit press criticisms, and these methods of curbing the freedom of the press were used frequently during the monarchical period. But here again, the political environment in the 1946–1954 period was hardly so procrustean as to prevent newspapers from circumventing governmental interference. This was particularly true of the practice of closing down newspapers.[37] Whenever the Ministry of Interior issued an order to close down a paper, the ownership would immediately file a request to the Interior Ministry to bring out a new paper under a modified name. And more often than not the ministry would comply, usually within a short period of time. Hence *al-Ahali* went through several reincarnations as *Sawt al-Ahali*, *Sada al-Ahali*, and *Nida' al-Ahali*. Similarly the mouthpiece of *al-Isiqlal* Party appeared as *Liwa' al-Istiqlal* and then as *Sada al-Istiqlal.* The official newspaper of the Marxist-oriented *Hizb al-Ittihad al-Watani* came out as *al-Siyasa*, and after it was closed down, it reappeared as *Sawt al-Siyaasa*.[38] Each would pick up the readership of its immediate predecessor, and would follow the same vigorously oppositional editorial policy.

So complex was the general relationship of the opposition to the Iraqi governments during this period that at times the opposition was able to influence, even change, policies; yet at other times it was not. But that is hardly different from practices that we find even in the mature democratic systems of the contemporary era. The point to be remembered is that at various times the opposition provided an effective channel of articulating and transmitting peoples' demands and interests, and because they had sufficient confidence in the relative liberalism of the system, they were able to do so purposefully and publicly. It is not that the state did not harass them or did not try to silence their criticisms; it is simply that the system was never so tightly closed that the opposition could not challenge the policies of the state or outmaneuver its institutions.

After a hiatus of rigid authoritarianism during the years 1936–1945, where opposition practically disappeared from the public sphere, the political parties and their newspapers that re-entered the political arena in 1946, participated vigorously and effectively in the country's political life until 1954. As such they were responsible for resurrecting and re-implanting the concept of *al-mu'aradha* (opposition) as an accepted and legitimate political endeavor into the public consciousness. *Ahzab al-Mu'aradha* (parties of the opposition) and *Jara'id al-Mu'aradha* (newspapers of the opposition) once again became a staple of the country's daily political lexicon.

An argument can certainly be made that the relatively liberal political attitudes and practices during this period were little more than empty political theater lacking in any real substance. What is missed by those who have such a view is the existence of a spirit of dialogue, a willingness to listen to an opposing viewpoint, and an ability to compromise if the situation deemed it. As was illustrated earlier, the meeting that Prince 'Abd al-Ilah called at the height of the chaos that followed the signing of the "Portsmouth Treaty" was replete with critical opinions not just of the Prime Minister but of the Regent himself. Participants did not shirk from using strong, sometimes pointedly biting, language, but discussions were conducted in an atmosphere of civility that is the hallmark of liberal politics and institutions. And when this civility was contravened, apologies generally followed.

One of the most pertinent examples of the civility that tended to imbue the relations among members of the political elite, whether these were affiliated to the government or the opposition, occurred in 1952, when responding to oppositional calls for immediate reforms, the Regent invited political leaders that included members of the opposition to a meeting at the Palace. Taha al-Hashimi, the leader of one of the opposition parties, *al-Jabha al-Sha'biya*, who himself was a Sharifian (member of the original group that accompanied King Faysal I into Iraq), and who was an ex-Prime Minister and had been a universally respected Chief of the armed forces, warned the Regent that the situation in Iraq was beginning to resemble the conditions that pertained in Egypt just prior to the military coup that toppled the Egyptian monarchy. He then asked the Prince to desist from interfering in politics. 'Abd al-Ilah apparently took great exception to this, and launched a personal attack on those present accusing them of lying about his role in the politics of the country, and blaming them for the deteriorating situation in Iraq. When Hashimi objected to the tone and substance of the Regent's remarks, the Prince ordered him to be quiet. Incensed by the Regent's insult, Hashimi walked out of the meeting, followed by Chaderji of *al-Watani al-Dimuqrati*.[39] The next day, having heard that the attendees, even those who were loyal supporters of the Crown, were singularly unhappy with his outburst, Prince 'Abd al-Ilah made a point of visiting the homes of most of the participants.[40] The gesture was meant to convey the Regent's regret over his intemperate words.

Another incident demonstrates this prevailing milieu of relative civility and tolerance. In one meeting of the Iraqi Senate, Muhammad Rida al-Shibibi, who was a bitter critic of Nuri al-Sa'id, as well as being a prominent poet, asked to speak at the same time that Nuri's hand went up. Nuri yielded the floor, remarking flippantly with a dismissive gesture of the hand: "Let the sheikh recite his poem."[41] Feeling insulted by Nuri's comment, Shibibi departed the Chamber angrily. That evening, Nuri drove to the Senator's house and personally apologized. He did, however, remark rather prophetically that the day might come when the opposition would mourn the demise of the monarchical system.[42] This gesture coming from the "most feared" man in Iraq betrayed a respect not just for a prominent oppositional figure, but also for the institution that he represented.

The picture that emerges is of a governing elite imbued with an authoritarian impulse, determined to keep its hold on the levers of power, yet at the same time willing to accept that dissent did not necessarily translate into sedition or treason. Efforts at stifling the opposition were undertaken throughout the decade spanning 1945–1954, yet the same decade abounds with instances of tolerance and willingness to compromise and of civility in political argument. One is hard put to find, for instance, the kind of feral viciousness that was the hallmark of the Saddamist order.

The era of relative liberalism came to an end in September 1954. The return of Nuri to power and his determination to pursue unpopular policies such as subscribing into the Western alliance system and confronting the government of Egypt and its popular leader Jamal 'Abd al-Nasir, closed the book on any hope for the continuation, let alone progress, of liberal practices. The state's rigid control of the public sphere and its zealous intolerance of the slightest hint of opposition gathered momentum during the last four years of Iraq's monarchy. Political parties and civil society associations were disbanded, press licenses were cavalierly withdrawn, leaving a token skeleton of few cheerleading newspapers,[43] elections were severely rigged, and rights were generally assaulted. By July 1958, as the enemies of the monarchy decided to make their predatory move the ruling elite could hardly count on a popular support base that would come to its rescue in its hour of greatest need.

CHAPTER SEVEN

Nationalism and the Ethnosectarian Divide, 1936–1958

In addition to momentous changes in governance and political institutions, the Bakr Sidqi coup brought to the surface a simmering ideational clash amongst the political and intellectual classes, which, not surprisingly, found its way into the military ranks, centering on the parameters of Iraq's national identity. The conflicts that beset the Bakr Sidqi era which led ultimately to the demise of the Sulayman government speak not only to the power constellations and rivalries among the various members of the political and ruling elites, but also to two differing conceptions of what constituted Iraq's national identity: an Iraqi identity that recognized and catered for the country's various ethnosectarian groups, and an Arab identity that saw Iraq not just as an indivisible part, but a leader, of the Arab world. The latter vision had an ever-increasing appeal among the ranks of the armed forces, particularly among Sunni officers, whereas the former, that of a localized "Iraqi first" identity, was propagated mainly by groups that lay outside the traditional Sunni center of political power. The government that was established as a result of the Bakr Sidqi coup not only wrested political power from the Sunni center, but with its commitment to the "Iraq first" vision, endeavored to dilute the Arab nationalist ideology of its predecessor. Thus, the aftermath of the coup can be seen as an effort by the out-group to move into the center not just politically, but ideationally as well.

The ideational orientation of the new political order was immediately evident in the composition and policies of its political elite. The three pillars of the policy-making group were Sidqi (a Kurd), Sulayman (a Turkomen), and Abu al-Timman (a Shi'ite). The government's first statement to the Iraqi public focused almost exclusively on the country's problems, promising to foster national unity and overcome communal divisions. "Arab unity," the aspiration of every bona fide Arab nationalist, was mentioned only once in passing.[1] Throughout its tenure, the Sulayman Cabinet continued emphasizing its "Iraq first" policies, and this was seen by the nationalist forces and, crucially for the government, by the Sunni nationalist officers as a veiled attempt to decrease Iraq's involvement in Arab affairs. And indeed, the major foreign policy initiative during this government's short life was the Sa'dabad Treaty, signed with Turkey, Iran, and Afghanistan.

The government's policies aroused the ire of "Arab" nationalists who objected to the seemingly purposeful distancing of Iraq from what they considered to be its natural habitat. "No success will ever be achieved," opined the virulently nationalist *al-Istiqlal* newspaper, "if the government were to abandon the nationalist creed."[2] What was more disquieting for the new government was a realization that such Arab nationalist sentiment was pervasive among the officer corps, whose appetite for political power already had been awakened by Sidqi's military intervention, and whose interest in Arabist issues had been stirred by the 1936 Arab revolt against the British and the Jews in Palestine. Thus, needing to explain to the British Ambassador his government's strident rejection of the British partition plan in Palestine, Prime Minister Sulayman conceded the existence among Iraqis of a powerful feeling of fraternity with fellow Arabs in Palestine, telling the unhappy British envoy that "no Iraqi government would be able to remain in power without giving some degree of satisfaction to the public hatred of the proposals for the partition of Palestine."[3]

The gathering alienation of Arab nationalist officers was heightened by a belief that under Sidqi recruitment into the military college favored Kurdish candidates. Rumors began to fly, all pointing to a deliberate policy of shifting the ethnic balance in the army away from the Arabs. In a conversation between Sa'ib Shawkat, a prominent Iraqi politician with strong Arab nationalist proclivities, and Fritz Grobba, Germany's Chargé d'affaires in Iraq, that took place after the assassination of Bakr Sidqi, Shawkat complained that "Sidqi pretended to care about the interests of the Arabs, but really cared only for the Kurds." This, according to Shawkat, was ascertained from Sidqi's policy that aimed at "substituting Kurdish for Arab students in the military college, with the result that Kurds ended up constituting 70 percent of the cadets in the military college."[4]

Since the vast majority of the officer corps was Sunni, most espousing strong Arab nationalist views, the move against Sidqi would come sooner than later. In August 1937, a carefully planned plot to assassinate Sidqi came to fruition in the northern Iraqi city of Mosul, known for its Arab nationalist proclivities. And when Prime Minister Sulayman ordered the arrest of the plotters, garrisons commanded by Sunni Arab nationalist officers proceeded to mutiny. In the circumstances, the Prime Minister and his Cabinet were left with no choice but to resign. The demise of the Bakr Sidqi era signaled the ascendancy of Arab nationalism over Iraqi particularism.

Arab nationalist concerns also played a role the next time the military intervened in the political process, when they succeeded in forcing the government of Jamil al-Midfa'i to resign and compelled the King to ask Nuri al-Sa'id to become the new Prime Minister in December 1938. Beyond personal interests, the nationalist officers also felt that in the person of Nuri al-Sa'id, with his impeccable "Arabist" credentials, they had someone who shared their commitment to the Arab nationalist creed, its ideational vision, and its political goals. Salah al-Din al-Sabagh, one of the leading army conspirators, wrote glowingly of Nuri as a man "committed to the Arab world and dedicated to its unity."[5]

It is of course difficult to assess the relative importance of considerations of national identity on the determination of political strategies. It could very well be argued that their impact was highest when they happened to coincide with the personal interests of the protagonists themselves. While, as we have seen, this was true of most instances, there were also cases where personal considerations seemed to have played a subsidiary role to ideology. For example, the alienation of the nationalist officers from Nuri al-Sa'id, who was for a long time their chosen politician, and who himself had facilitated the officers' entry into politics, occurred primarily as a result of an increasing ideological dispute over what was best for Iraq and Arab nationalism: Nuri's pro-British policies or the officers' increasing pro-German sentiments. At a minimum, therefore, questions of national identity should not be dismissed as simply tangential to the political process during this tumultuous period in Iraq's modern history.

Indeed, the policies of the Iraqi government in the wake of the Rashid 'Ali episode and the ill-fated Iraqi-British War of May 1941 is a testament to the perceived significance of nationalist considerations. Immediately on their return to Baghdad after their forced departure, the Regent and the other members of the ruling elite embarked on a wholesale reform of educational institutions, which basically amounted to the "cleansing" of schools and colleges of anti-British, Arab nationalist teachers. Sati' al-Husri himself had his Iraqi citizenship withdrawn, and over 300 teachers who had been imported by Husri to implant the nationalist ideal in the hearts of Iraqi youth were pushed out of the country.[6] That ideal would now be appropriated by the pro-British political elite, who would cleanse it of its revolutionary impulse, and turn it into various state-sponsored plans and schemes for uniting the Arab lands.

In 1943, Nuri presented to the British his plans for a "Fertile Crescent Union". Nuri purposely omitted any reference to "Arab" unity to placate the "Iraq First" constituency and avoid the kind of ideational and political polarization that characterized the late 1930s.[7] Nuri's memorandum emphasized the symbiotic national bonds that tied Iraq to Syria, Lebanon, Transjordan, and Palestine, the other Fertile Crescent regions (none, apart from Iraq, was an internationally sanctioned state), but it also recognized the differences that existed among them. So, rather than advocate immediate organic unity, Nuri proposed a two-stage process, where in the first stage Syria, Lebanon, Transjordan, and Palestine would unite into one state. Once this state of "Greater Syria" had been formed, it would join Iraq in an "Arab League" to which other Arab states could later adhere if they so wished. The League would have responsibility for defense, foreign affairs, currency, communications, customs and the protection of minorities (a particularly sensitive issue for the Christians of Lebanon and no doubt the Jews of Palestine).[8] The plan was presented as the first of a number of steps that would lead eventually to a union of the Arabic-speaking world,[9] the governmental form of which would depend on the preferences and ultimate decisions of the Arab populations.

There can be little doubt that the plan had as much to do with Hashemite ambition as with any consuming attachment to the cause of Arab nationalism. But the two motivations need not be mutually exclusive. After all, Nuri and the other Sunni elder statesmen constituted the backbone of the Arab revolt against the Ottomans. That commitment to the Arab cause was attested to by no lesser figures than the Arab nationalist officers who considered Nuri to be one of their own. Thus, Nuri had a plan that he believed would serve the Arab nationalist, as well as the Hashemite, cause.

On the popular level, however, it is not clear what support the plan had. It would have received its greatest backing from the Sunni educated class, the most committed of Iraq's communities to Arab nationalism. But even among Sunnis, there would be many who would suspect that a Machiavellian Hashemite impulse was behind it all. On the other hand, the Kurds would see any scheme leading to an Arab unity, which would reduce them to the status of a small island in an ocean of Arabic-speaking people, as nothing short of a nightmare. Nor were the Shi'ites that enamored with the plan, which they saw mainly as a plot by the minority Sunni group to cement Sunni hegemony and further marginalize the Shi'ites.[10] To the Shi'ites, Arabs themselves, their wariness of the union scheme did not predicate on national (or ethnic) considerations, but on a strategic political calculation relating to the distribution of political power.

It is, however, important to note that debates on identity issues, ranging from the "Arab" to the "Iraqi" resided mainly at the political elite level. At the level of the poor and illiterate masses, who constituted the vast majority of the population, matters of identity were an esoteric subject of which they had no real cognizance, and to which they accorded little importance, let alone much loyalty. In his memoirs, 'Abd al-Karim al-Uzri, a Shi'ite member of the monarchical political elite, relates that during Iraq's 1941 war with Britain, he observed Iraqi soldiers whom he had expected to be at the front get back to their tribal domain around Baghdad, adorn the tribal garb, and behave as though the struggle with the British "occupier" was in no way their concern. Indeed, if anything, he implies that the tribesmen were working in tandem with the British against the Rashid 'Ali government and the Arab nationalist forces.[11] Even with the committed efforts to create a national identity, and through it loyalty to state institutions, it was perhaps too much to ask the state, a mere two decades or so into its life span, to imprint its national ideas beyond the thin layer of the educated and middle-class sector of the country's urban population.

It was mainly from the ranks of the middle class (students, bureaucrats, army officers) that the anti-monarchy revolutionary impulse emerged and prospered. Members of this class were the most susceptible to nationalist ideas and ideals, and there can be little doubt that education and urbanization played essential roles in this process. In urban centers especially, some important gains were made in bridging the ethnosectarian divide. The result was that in the 1950s, particularly among the educated classes in urban areas, national loyalties were beginning to supplant the more particularistic affiliation to smaller sub-state groups, such as sects and tribes. This was especially true in the case of the Shi'ite community.

There was significant economic progress among the Shi'ites. Suffice it to say that the Shi'ites were the largest land-owning group in the country, and by 1958 fourteen of the eighteen members of Baghdad's Chamber of Commerce were Shi'ite.[12] Parallel to increased prosperity, the Shi'ite educational status perceptibly improved.[13] Secular schools, teaching mathematics, the sciences and foreign languages, and using modern instructional methods, replaced the old religious *maddrassas*. At the beginning of the 20th century, over 8,000 students attended Shi'ite *maddrassas* in the holy city of Najaf. By 1957, the number had dwindled to 1,954.[14] The secular, state-sponsored schools emphasized the "oneness of Iraq" and the "Arab" character of the country. By the 1940s and 1950s droves of young, well-educated Shi'ites had entered the ranks of the middle class, working in governmental institutions, the private sector, and the professions. Their social mobility undoubtedly created some erosion in the social and cultural barriers that had separated the two sects. For example, "Sunnis began giving their daughters in marriage to [the Shi'ites] when only a few decades before the impediments to such intermarriage seemed insurmountable."[15] Moreover, the exodus of the Jews from Iraq in 1951 allowed the Shi'ites to expand their presence in the country's commercial life.

Along with this came improvement in the Shi'ites' political status. Between 1947 and 1954, four prime ministerial positions went to Shi'ites, whereas not one Shi'ite had attained the position before 1947. In the first decade of the monarchy, Shi'ites occupied just under 18 percent of the ministerial positions, yet in the monarchy's last decade, their share of ministerial positions had gone up to almost 35 percent.[16]

This meant that by the end of the 1950s, the Shi'ites were gradually getting integrated into Iraq's body politic. To be sure, friction between the two sects, especially pertaining to Shi'ite grievances about the unremitting Sunni domination of Iraqi politics, continued to hover under the surface. And even though some of the richest Iraqis were Shi'ites, the community as a whole was economically, as well as socially, still considerably inferior to the Sunnis. Nevertheless, while these disparities would cause a few eruptions, these were limited in scope and purpose. The bottom line was that as a group not alienated ethnically from the rest of society, the Shi'ites in the 1950s were beginning to see themselves increasingly as functioning citizens of Iraq. Sure enough, they would agitate to improve their sociopolitical status in the country vis-à-vis the Sunnis, but they had little or no reason to extricate themselves from the country. By the 1950s, many Sunnis too shared the same perception, at a minimum questioning the hitherto widely held belief within their community that Shi'ite affinity with their co-religionists in Iran, was stronger than their loyalty to the Arab state of Iraq.

It is not that Iraq was becoming an egalitarian society. Sunnis were by far the more prosperous and better educated of the two communities, and they continued to the very end of the monarchy to dominate the two pivotal areas of politics and security. In the political domain, while Shi'ites certainly had made political strides which came to fruition in the last decade of the monarchy, their political participation, to say nothing of their share of political power, was in no way commensurate with their demographic weight. Thus, around 60 percent of the membership of the Chamber of Deputies belonged to the Sunnis, even though they constituted no more than 20 percent of the population. More often than not, Shi'ite cities tended to be represented by more Sunni than Shi'ite deputies. In more than one case, a Shi'ite city did not have a single Shi'ite parliamentarian representing it. In other cases, more seats would go to Christians and Jews than to Shi'ites in a city such as Basra where the population was 90 percent Shi'ite.[17]

As for security, the officer corps in the armed forces was dominated by Sunni officers. 'Abd al-Karim al-Uzri, a Shi'ite pillar of the monarchical regime comments caustically in his memoirs on the paucity of Shi'ite officers more than thirty years after the inception of the Iraqi state. Al-Uzri says that he brought this problem to the attention of the King and the

Regent, telling them that Shi'ite youth had become so disheartened with the prejudicial policies of the Military College that they no longer bothered to apply. He also maintains that entry into the ranks of the police was even more difficult for the Shi'ites. This problem came up in parliamentary debates, but apparently to no avail.[18] Thus, while state institutions dominated by the Sunni establishment did endeavor to integrate Shi'ites into the body politic of Iraq, the effort lacked a wholehearted commitment to fully rectify the political and socioeconomic imbalance that existed between the two communities.

Halfhearted as they might have been, the efforts by the Sunni-dominated state institutions to break down sectarian barriers with the Shi'ites were not replicated in the case of the Arab-Kurdish ethnic divide, which seemed to be perceived by all parties as intractable. Consequently, governmental overtures always smacked of indifference at best, and outright loathing at worst,[19] and deep down, the Kurds never gave up on their own fervently held national aspiration for an independent Kurdish state. The lack of an impulse for assimilation into the Iraqi state meant that unlike the Shi'ites, the Kurds were touched less by the processes of urbanization and education. Phebe Marr attributes this to the many Kurdish rebellions which, because they were based on tribal structures, lasted well into the 1940s, and that meant that government-induced modernization projects, including education, did not enter Kurdish areas, the bulk of which was rural, until the 1950s. By 1958, for example, the Kurds had less than half the percentage of Sunnis and Shi'ites in secondary schools.[20] This in turn cemented the cultural and political distance, borne out of a durable ethnic divide, that existed between the Kurds on the one hand and the Arab Sunnis and Shi'ites on the other.

In fact what was sustaining and indeed cementing the cultural and political gulf between Arab and Kurd was the same ideological force that was bringing Sunnis and Shi'ites together in the 1950s. Arab nationalism which had competed with other ideologies had by the mid-1950s emerged triumphant, eclipsing other national and sub-national identities, and in doing so was having a major impact on the development of Shi'ite political identity. Thus, in the 1920s and even in the 1930s, much of the Shi'ite community clung to their sectarian identity. While the state's propagation of secular Arab nationalism fired the imagination of the Sunni population, the Shi'ites, preferring their *madrassas*, generally kept the new secular creed at arms length. When secular education and urbanization turned the Shi'ites to political activism, demanding of the state a change of the political balance in their favor, many of the new activists turned to the clandestine Communist Party. One of the reasons for this was Shi'ite concern that Arab nationalism was essentially a Sunni project aimed at uniting the Arab states, whose populations were predominantly Sunni, thus rendering the Iraqi Shi'ites (a majority in Iraq) an insignificant minority.

If there was one period where the ideational divide between Sunni and Shi'ite was at its lowest, it was during the 1950s, and particularly in the second half of the decade. It was not as though all Shi'ites became ardent nationalists, but more and more of them were being seduced into the Arab nationalist ranks, be it as Nasirists or Ba'thists. The Ba'th Party was a particular beneficiary of the intensely ideological milieu of the 1950s. The Ba'th Party had begun its clandestine activities in Iraq in 1951, but recruitment proceeded slowly due to intense governmental repression and the competition provided by a long-established Communist Party. The Ba'th Party's growth accelerated in the middle of the decade, coinciding with Nasir's onslaught against the Western alliance system which had become centered in Baghdad. The Party received its greatest boost in the wake of the Suez crisis, so that by the Iraqi revolution in July 1958, the Ba'thists had become a recognized element of the "progressive" forces that were instrumental in the demise of the Iraqi monarchy.[21] And the Shi'ites were playing an active role in the party. Indeed, of the seventeen members of Iraq's Ba'th Party leadership in the 1950s, eight were Shi'ites, including the secretary-general, Fuad al-Rikabi.[22] More significantly, in the second half of the decade, the nationalist creed increasingly defined the identity of educated and politically cognizant Shi'ites, where sectarian affiliations, we are told, were beginning to be dismissed as not worth even inquiring about. Taleb Shabib, the first foreign minister in the Ba'thist government that took over power in 1963, and who was a Shi'ite member of the Party in the 1950s, says that members of the Party Command were unaware of each other's sectarian denominations.[23] It was as though the young nationalist generation was proclaiming the death of Shi'ite identity and the dawning of a new, all-encompassing nationalist era. This, of course, was as premature as it was simplistic. Sectarian impulses were too resilient to die at the hand of the ideational juggernaut of Arab nationalism. It was simply that for the time being Shi'ite identity was superseded by a seemingly triumphant Arab nationalist creed.

The bad news for Nuri and Iraq's old political establishment was that the acknowledged leader of Arab nationalism, the man who gave it a distinct and potent revolutionary direction, was Egypt's President Jamal 'Abd al-Nasir, Nuri's foremost Arab nemesis. This revolutionary impulse was cemented by the events surrounding the Suez crisis and the tripartite invasion of Egypt, from which Nasir emerged unscathed, indeed triumphant. So potent was this impulse that it became a threat to the Iraqi state. Nuri and the other members of the ruling elite, those who for so long had been the custodians of the Iraqi state, well recognized the immense dangers of trying to stem the seemingly unstoppable nationalist tide. Nuri tried to ride the bandwagon, by invoking his Arab credentials as a leader of the 1916 Great Arab Revolt who continued to struggle for the unity, independence, and glory of the Arab nation. He tried to paint Nasir as an upstart lacking Nuri's long-standing commitment to the Arab nationalist cause. In a radio address to the Iraqi people at the height of the extensive and violent disturbances that pervaded almost all Iraqi cities during the Suez crisis, Nuri expounded on his own long-standing Arab nationalist credentials:

> Compatriots; you have known me as a struggling young man who advocated and worked for the independence of the Arabs and their unity and for raising the prestige of the Arab at a time when the word "Arab" would have cost the speaker his neck. This was at a time when those who are today advocating nationalism were prostrating themselves at the feet of the oppressors and the imperialists and accusing us of treason and atheism. I have been exposed to danger more than once, and proceeded on my way seeking nothing but the independence of the Arabs, the glory of the Arabs, and the dignity of the Arabs. . . . The call to Arab nationalism is not accidental to me, but is my very being. I am proud of it and I strive to promote it and to safeguard it whether I am inside or outside the government.[24]

Nuri's plea, regardless of how heartfelt it might have been, would find few takers. By now, radical Arab nationalism, perpetrated by charismatic young men, had come to dominate the political discourse in the Arab world and the political consciousness of the Arab people. Increasingly, the legitimacy of any political order was becoming a function of that order's pronounced fidelity to the radical Arab nationalist creed. The problem for Nuri and the Iraqi leaders was twofold. First, Nasir had already cornered the ideational debate, and other Arab leaders had to hang on to his coattails or play catch to no avail, thus running the real risk of abject defeat and possible eradication. Secondly, the nemesis of Arab nationalism, its "other" that gave it its vibrancy was the West, its influence, and meddling in the Arab world. And Iraq, through the policies of Nuri, Crown Prince 'Abd al-Ilah, and other members of the ruling elite, had become almost symbiotically tied to the despised West. Nuri's feverish effort to assure the skeptical Iraqi public of his nationalist credentials was guaranteed to fall on deaf ears.

In the ideational struggle for the hearts and minds of the Arab public, Egypt's Nasir had comprehensively prevailed. And in that part of the Arab world, where Nuri and the Crown Prince had political control but rapidly receding legitimacy, the political order had become so fragile that it could not withstand any further psychological defeat.

The sudden news of the unity of Syria and Egypt and the creation under Nasir's leadership of the United Arab Republic (UAR) in February 1958 was the bombshell that would soon lead to the unraveling of the monarchical order. Met with "an overwhelming sense of exuberance and ardor" by Iraqis,[25] the UAR engendered such contempt for the Baghdad government that many Iraqis were prepared to take great risks simply to register their approval of the Egyptian-Syrian merger.[26] This intense public endorsement of the UAR left Iraq's ruling elite in a state of near despair. Prince 'Abd al-Ilah confided to a friend that the UAR "was a mortal threat to Iraq's existence."[27] He prophetically told the British Ambassador that the political situation in Iraq had deteriorated so much that "the whole thing could crumble in a matter of months."[28] And crumble it did.

On July 14, 1958 a military coup toppled the monarchical political order, killing in the process Nuri al-Sa'id, Crown Prince 'Abd al-Ilah, the young King Faysal II, and all other members of the royal family. All of the pillars of the monarchical order who were in Iraq were arrested and later put on trial. To the universal jubilation of the populace, the officers proclaimed the birth of the Iraqi Republic. Unable to sustain a moderately liberal political stance after 1954, unwilling to infuse new younger blood into the policy-making elite, seemingly unperturbed by the widening socioeconomic disparities in the country, and determined to pursue a foreign policy that ran against the ideational spirit of the times, the monarchical political system, rejected and abandoned, was to meet its end with very little, if any, resistance.

CHAPTER EIGHT

The Monarchy's Political System, 1921–1958

A number of reasons coalesced to bring about the demise of the monarchy in July 1958. Some of these were structural, embedded in the constitutional arrangements and political relationships inside the country. Others were precipitated by political and ideological developments that gathered momentum in the regional and international arenas, and thus, to a certain extent, were outside the control of Iraq's governing elite. But on both levels, Iraq's politicians were slow, at times completely unwilling, to adapt.

Looking back at the monarchical era, it is hard not to place the major responsibility for the collapse of the political system squarely on the shoulders of the palace and the old politicians: their penchant for authoritarianism, their distaste for acceding authority to a younger generation, their petty squabbles among themselves, and their inability to reach out to new constituencies in a rapidly changing political milieu. These changes were happening not just domestically, but in the broader Arab environment, where the force of nationalism was sweeping the region, and was being appropriated by a new generation of leaders. In the 1950s, Iraq's politicians, old and rigid in thinking, were being left behind, increasingly vulnerable and exposed, by the new custodians of this powerful ideological force.

And it was not as though the Iraqi rulers had built a broad support base to be able to keep at bay this new dangerous world. Their response to domestic demands for democratization was uncertain and haphazard. Thus, on the one hand, they were obsessive in their efforts to control elections and thereby degrade the ability of Parliament to legislate and oversee governmental activities. On the other hand, they were not so single-minded in their attitude to the political parties and the oppositional press. Here they tended to dither and vacillate. At times, Iraq looked like a functioning democracy, with a vibrant multi-party system and freewheeling press. But then the government would get cold feet, clamp down, and the parties would be harassed and ultimately closed down. Simultaneously, the heavy hand of the government censor would descend on the newspapers, not only doctoring news and opinions, but ultimately herding editors and reporters to court, and sometimes to prison.

As the winds of change gathered momentum in the 1950s, the question remains whether the monarchy would have survived had it taken determined steps to adjust to a changing ideological and political milieu. The answer must by definition remain in the realm of conjecture. It should be noted, however, that by the 1950s, Iraq's ruling elites, set in their ways, were in their fourth decade of governing the country. They had built political structures and nurtured political and economic interests that would have been (and indeed ended up being) almost impossible to change or even modify. Thus, the seeds of the ultimate collapse of the political system under the monarchy lay in the very structures and relationships that had imbued the political order since the birth of the state in 1921.

RIGIDITY OF STATE INSTITUTIONS

In examining the almost four decades of monarchical rule one is struck that the notion of the "circulation of elites," so vital for vibrant political structures, hardly existed in Iraq. While the average life span of Iraqi Cabinets was a mere five and a half months, the names and faces of the occupants of Cabinet ministries changed little. This was particularly true of the pivotal portfolios—the premiership, defense, interior, foreign affairs, and finance, where over 50 percent of these portfolios in the entire monarchical period were held by no more than fourteen men.[1] This concentration of political power was most apparent in the office of Prime Minister. Thus, for example, of the forty-eight cabinets between 1930 and 1958, twenty-one were headed by two men: Nuri al-Sa'id fourteen times and Jamil al-Midfa'i the remaining seven.[2] Men who were members of the political and military entourage of King Faysal I during World War I were still holding sway over the political fortunes of Iraq in 1958.

Whatever elite circulation there was occurred within the very top of the societal strata and rarely extended downward. More damaging was the excruciatingly slow pace with which the younger generation from within the ranks of the top stratum itself would be granted entry into the seemingly exclusive domain of the top policy-making elite. A few members of the governing elite did create political parties that could have become channels for generational change, but these organizations were tied tightly to the personality and policies of the leader. Membership bestowed access and the opportunity to maintain the privileged status quo, but not the capacity to influence, let alone change, policies or modify political practices. Joining Nuri's party, for example, was for the majority of members simply a quick route to personal gain, to an undeserved promotion or to a much sought after relationship with a foreign company. Tribal leaders flocked to these parties to ensure the maintenance of their economic and political privileges. Cementing the status quo was the operational code of these parties; it was not just that debate, efforts at reform, voicing the slightest skepticism were not tolerated; these were not even contemplated. Opposition was left to the opposition parties and these participated in the decision-making process on very rare occasions, and usually for periods so short that any impact on policy was negligible.

Nuri al-Sa'id, who literally defined the politics of the era, was probably the biggest culprit. To begin with, he had been the dominant political personality for so long that, according to a protégé of his, he treated Iraq as "a father would treat a child: take personal charge of his upbringing, look after his welfare, and discipline him when necessary."[3] This paternal attitude, necessarily dismissive of youth, was fortified by Nuri's mistrust of change, which contributed to his unwillingness to effect a generational transformation. This frustrated even the British, his most ardent admirers. As early as 1943, the British Ambassador, despairing of the rigidity of Nuri and the "old gang," tried to alert Prince 'Abd al-Ilah to the stagnation of the ruling elite and "the need for introducing new blood, otherwise peoples' discontent might take violent forms."[4] A decade and a half later, the Ambassador's fears would be realized, not least because the recommended transfusion of new blood was at best perfunctory. While Nuri consulted with the British Embassy regularly and was known to take the counsel of the Ambassador and his government seriously, he did not budge on his proclivity for dependence on old and trusted faces.

The old and trusted faces were not limited to the closely knit ruling circle; it extended to the leaders of tribes and other feudal lords who, because of their economic interests, were symbiotically tied to the old politicians who along with the British were responsible for cementing and enhancing the sheikhs' economic power. It was first the British who transformed the Ottoman system of leasing land to the sheikhs to outright possession, even conferring extra tracts of lands on the sheikhs.[5] After 1921, successive indigenous Iraqi governments legalized the arrangement. "Not only was the [sheikh's] title to the land confirmed by law," the American Ambassador at the time tells us, "but he was simultaneously given representation in Parliament."[6] The increasing political strength of the tribal leaders allowed for greater impunity in usurping for themselves communal tribal lands, even land areas owned by the state. While the sheikhs amassed fabulous wealth, the annual income of the dispossessed peasant amounted to five dinars (about $15) in the 1930s and 30 dinars (about $90) in the cripplingly inflationary post-World War II period.[7] The result was some of the most appalling living conditions imaginable, in which infant mortality was pegged at a staggering 35 percent.[8] Inevitably, the migration of peasants to urban areas, particularly to Baghdad and Basra, gathered momentum to an extent that agricultural income was affected.[9] This problem had become evident to the land-owning sheikhs as early as 1933, and correspondingly they induced the ruling elite to promulgate the notorious Rights and Duties of Cultivators' Law, in which peasants were literally reduced to the status of serfs.

Other legislation favoring the sheikh over the peasant in following years testified to the political power of the land-owning class accrued through its alliance with the Palace and the old politicians. The sheikhs used their parliamentary representation, which in the 1950s never fell under 35 percent,[10] to their advantage in the legislation of laws. This led to the widespread belief that governments simply did the sheikhs' bidding.[11] And indeed that perception was hardly far from the truth. Thus, all efforts to create a regularized agricultural property tax were sabotaged by the sheikhs through their presence in Parliament and alliance with the ruling elites. When a number of parliamentarians urged the Regent to intervene on the issues of property taxes and land reform, he responded with not a little irony that parliamentarians kept telling him of his growing unpopularity in the cities, so if that were true, then why would he turn the countryside against him too?[12]

The Regent was particularly sensitive, even beholden, to the sheikhs and their demands and interests. Following the riots of 1952, Prince 'Abd al-Ilah appointed a military government under the premiership of General Nur al-Din Mahmoud to restore order. In the process, however, he insisted that the agriculture portfolio should be given to Haj Raih al-'Attiya, a sheikh of a large southern tribe, whom the Prince counted as a loyal supporter, but who happened to be barely literate![13] In the perception of 'Abd al-Ilah and the old politicians, such committed defenders of the monarchical order were increasingly hard to come by in urban areas during the turbulent 1950s. In 1954 the Minister of Finance, 'Abd al-Karim al-Uzri, introduced a new taxation bill for agricultural lands and a fairer distribution of land among the sheikhs and peasants. 'Abd al-Ilah invited the tribal sheikhs to a meeting with al-Uzri at the Palace, whereupon they threatened to use arms to stop the implementation of the bill. While their belligerent response irritated the Prince, he nevertheless took their side; privately explaining to al-Uzri that public interest would not be served by angering and alienating the sheikhs since they represented an important, even crucial, pillar of the political order. "We depend on them," the Prince concluded, "to stop the revolutionary tides that threaten the security and stability of the country."[14] And when the Prime Minister, Fadhil al-Jamali, took up the cause of his Finance Minister with the Prince, he too was summarily rebuffed.

The British Embassy, in fact, had for some time advocated a radical reform of the laws relating to socioeconomic conditions among the tribal holdings, including new taxes on feudal landowners and a more equitable redistribution of land. But 'Abd la-Ilah backed by Nuri al-Sa'id, stood steadfast against British pressure arguing that they could not afford to lose the support of the sheikhs, increasingly the only significant segment of society that was unbendingly committed to the monarchical order.[15] In the post-World War II period, as turbulent times were sweeping not just Iraq but the region, the old politicians and the Palace found solace in an ever-narrowing societal support base of familiar segments of the social strata at the expense of a broader social milieu that included a rapidly expanding and influential, yet increasingly alienated, urban middle class. Sharing in the same patriarchical authoritarian beliefs brought the rulers and tribal sheikhs into a symbiotic partnership. The sheikhs' application of their rigid authoritarian structures in their tribal domains, cemented by laws that transformed the peasants into serfs in almost everything but name,[16] was in many ways a microcosm of what 'Abd al-Ilah, Nuri, and the old politicians wished they could (and indeed tried to) impose on the country as a whole.

At times, the political environment would necessitate some tempering of the elites' political control. Liberal policies would be promised and a pledge to loosen political structures would be dangled seductively in front of the populace. But the course of the seduction was never allowed to go the distance, because lurking under the surface would be the despotic culture of the ruling elite, which would eventually, often pretty quickly, impel a restoration of the authoritarian status quo.

The immediate post-World War II period is a case in point. In December 1945, after a decade of military coups, a war with Britain, crippling economic inflation, and suffocating dictatorship, the Regent, motivated principally by political expedience, announced with much fanfare measures to liberalize the political order: political parties would be formed and allowed to contest elections, which would be fair and free of governmental interference. The task was entrusted to Tawfiq al-Suwaydi, who brought into his Cabinet younger personnel whose political outlook was less inflexible than that of the old politicians.

The new government quickly acted on the Regent's directives, legalizing a number of opposition parties and promising free elections. As the parties, enjoying unprecedented freedom began to exercise their right to oppose and criticize, the old politicians decided that the liberalization "gig" had gone too far, and that it had become "a real challenge to their authority."[17] The Regent, who himself had set the liberalization process in motion, was getting cold feet too. Thus, a constitutional plot was hatched to unseat the al-Suwaydi government. Using the Senate, whose members were appointed by the Palace, they engineered a procedural maneuver that forced al-Suwaydi to submit his government's resignation.[18] That the innate authoritarianism of the ruling elite was too entrenched to allow for any real liberalization of the political order was attested to by a senior member of the opposition, who along with other cohorts from the opposition were not so sanguine about the Regent's announced liberalizing initiative, or his general commitment to democratic transformation. Muhammad Mahdi Kubba, the leader of the *Istiqlal* Party, one of the newly formed oppositional parties, would write in his memoirs:

> Neither the Regent, nor the ruling class nor their British allies were serious about implementing the new (liberal) policy advocated by the Regent. Nor were we and the other national elements that formed the new political parties and organizations confident about the good intentions of the rulers in following the Regent's declared policies. But we and the comrades from the other parties felt that it was our duty to use this opening to gather and organize the national elements in the country, and spread political awareness among the people.[19]

The policy of undermining the liberal and nationalist political parties and pushing them to the margins of political life ultimately would prove the undoing of the political order itself. The inability of the ruling elite to allow opposing points of view to influence public policy meant that eventually those opposition parties, that had been willing to operate openly and within the system under what they had hoped to be the democratic umbrella, would eventually shift their operations underground to work in tandem with the far more radical clandestine Communists and Ba'thists. The resulting clandestine National Union Front, formed in February 1957,[20] did much to foment public opinion and promote anti-government activities which, in many ways, if it did not create the environment, at least it prepared the way, for the 1958 revolution.

Undermining political opposition, manipulating political institutions, and exploiting constitutional opportunities were all manifestations of the entrenched authoritarian proclivities of the ruling elite. Such was this innate authoritarianism that, if all else failed, governments would think nothing of suspending the Constitution, or circumventing it with new laws. The enactment of emergency laws became a main tool of successive Iraqi governments to neutralize political opposition activity. And it is hardly coincidental that the practice was started by Nuri-al-Sa'id during his first Cabinet in 1931. After that it became almost the stock of trade of Iraqi Cabinets, so that between 1931 and 1958, no less than twenty-seven emergency laws were instituted, an average of one per year.[21] During the same period, martial law was declared sixteen times, and between the 1941 Iraqi-British War and the demise of the monarchical order in 1958, the country lived under martial law for almost nine of the seventeen years.[22] It is obvious that the predominant feature of the Iraqi state under the direction of the Palace and the old politicians was the ingrained mistrust of opposition and the innate determination not to cede an ounce of power.

The British, who continued to sustain a powerful presence throughout the life of the Iraqi monarchy, could have reversed, or at least considerably tempered the proclivity to authoritarianism. But the strategic and economic interests of the imperial power trumped any commitment it might have had for genuine and fully fledged democratic development.[23] The British approved of only those democratic practices that did not clash with their interests.

This blinkered view of democracy manifested itself particularly in the troubled relationship the British had with the Iraqi Parliament. They made their intent early on in the life of the Iraqi state. In 1922 the High Commissioner closed two political parties and expelled their leaders because they opposed the terms of the proposed Anglo-Iraqi Treaty. And while they encouraged the creation of Parliament in 1924, British officials cast weary eyes at the institution, being constantly concerned about its potential rebelliousness,[24] and in order to stem this, the British did not shy away from strong arm methods, ranging from threats to the use of physical force. For instance, when the 1924 debate over the ratification of the Anglo-Iraqi Treaty in the Constituent Assembly took longer than anticipated, the British let the parliamentarians know that this might have an impact on the fate of the northern Wilayat of Mosul, which at that time was a point of dispute between Iraq and Turkey.[25] And, as we have seen, when vehement opposition continued and it seemed that the Treaty would be either rejected or amended radically, the British High Commissioner stormed into the Royal Palace with an ultimatum that the Treaty be passed forthwith or the Assembly would be dissolved.[26] That same evening deputies were rounded up and hustled into vehicles, many without knowing their destination, until a quorum was reached and the Treaty was passed.[27] This pattern of regular interference in the workings of Iraq's Parliament continued throughout the Mandate period.[28] As the presiding power in the country, Britain was not going to allow a few opposition figures, of whose stature she thought little, to question its imperial dominance.

British encouragement of Executive authoritarianism continued after the end of the Mandate period in 1932. Obviously, however, it could no longer be as blatant as it was when Britain was the legal guardian. While British officials prodded the Palace and the old politicians to initiate a few reforms, such as bringing into the decision-making circle a younger generation, their abiding concern was naturally with the maintenance of their privileged political position in the country, which in turn meant that they would prod, but not push, let alone shove, their natural allies—the Palace and the old politicians. In short, throughout the monarchical period they were in effect active participants in the authoritarian political structure.

Indeed, even the Americans would put the stability of an ally ahead of that ally's more than spotty record on democratic rights and freedoms. When in 1954, ten members of opposition parties were elected to Parliament, creating a theoretical opposition bloc of thirty-two members, which was less than a fourth of parliamentary membership,[29] the American Embassy considered that to be "a very dangerous occurrence that would lead to a dark future."[30] No wonder that neither the British, nor the Americans would offer even a whimper of protest when Nuri al-Sa'id was brought back by the Regent and immediately proceeded to dismantle democratic life in Iraq. Heirs to the two greatest democratic traditions, the British and the Americans, when dealing with Iraq seemed to have decided to leave their democratic ideals at their own front door. Could Iraq's ruling elite be faulted for following this precedent in their own indifferent response to democratic ideas and institutions?

Governance in Iraq emerged not out of the interactions of multiple institutions, but of the political dominance of a narrow elite that was bound by a rigid and exclusivist definition of its interest and well-being. Within the parameters of such a definition, however, petty squabbles would exist, indeed abound. It was perhaps to the misfortune of the monarchy that in the most volatile decade of its life, the 1950s, the most significant rivalry among the top policy-makers was the one that existed between Nuri al-Sa'id and 'Abd al-Ilah.

At the core of the complex, often troubled, relationship was Nuri's determination to be the sole gatekeeper of everything political in Iraq. His long years of service, his frequent occupation of the office of Prime Minister, and his broad network of strategic allies and cronies, bestowed upon him, he fervently believed, a position of centrality and political dominance above that of the other politicians. 'Abd al-Ilah, on the other hand, younger and less shrewd, but fortified by the powers of the Royal prerogative, would try on a number of occasions to clip Nuri's wings. Thus, at times he would pointedly bypass Nuri's advice and seek the counsel of other politicians, most of whom, after all, were as seasoned as Nuri. But even such a small matter would be considered by Nuri as a scornful insult and a measured slap in the face.[31] On a more serious political level, 'Abd al-Ilah would confide to friends and to the British his concern over Nuri's monopoly over the policy-making structure and process.[32] He would thus try from time to time to loosen Nuri's grip by entrusting the government to some of those he considered his allies. Nuri would respond by engineering a governmental crisis by instructing his supporters in Parliament to sabotage the workings of the existing government.

A revealing instance of this tug of war occurred in 1954. 'Abd al-Ilah asked his ally Arshad al-'Umari to form a government, and recognizing the predominance in Parliament of *Hizb al-Ittihad al-Distouri*, Nuri's party, he dissolved Parliament and called for a new election. While the new elections did not break Nuri's hold over the institution, 'Abd al-Ilah was able to bring many of his supporters into the new Parliament. Nuri still had a majority, but a considerably reduced one. By the time the elections had taken place, Nuri had already left the country in a huff, traveling to Britain for ostensibly medical reasons. In London, however, Nuri convinced the Foreign Office that British vital interests would be jeopardized by his exclusion from power, an argument he did not have to make too strongly to his British friends and admirers. These were turbulent times; there were escalating fears of a Soviet penetration in the area and of a disquieting upsurge in anti-British nationalist fervor. Britain needed its trusted "strong man" at the helm and would convey this sentiment in no uncertain terms to the Prince.[33] In Baghdad, Khalil Kanna, Nuri's trusted protégé, under instructions from his mentor, would use Nuri's parliamentary majority to frustrate governmental policies, prompting 'Abd al-Ilah to summon Kanna to the Palace and tell him to his face that "much as he has tried to like him, he simply could not."[34] Having been completely outmaneuvered, the Prince had to swallow his pride and fly to Paris to meet with Nuri al-Sa'id and accept all the conditions that were laid out by the wily old politician.[35] In an increasingly volatile region, radicalized by the nationalist onslaught and Cold War machinations, the constant tension between the two most powerful political personalities did little to cement the political order in the face of gathering political storms.

The troubled relationship between Nuri and 'Abd al-Ilah was anything but unique; it was in fact a microcosm of the kind of relationships that existed among the old politicians generally. Fueled mostly by personal rivalry and political greed rather than honest ideational or public policy disagreements, these squabbles, petty they might have been, would lead to political stagnation within the Cabinet, and on a number of occasions precipitate the fall of governments.[36] A British Ambassador would write in despairing tones to the Foreign Office that repeated governmental crises were the result of "the inability of ministers to put the national interest ahead of their personal rivalries. . . ."[37] While this ambassadorial lamentation was written in the 1940s, it in fact reflected an institutional frailty that characterized the entirety of the monarchical period right through to its end in July 1958.

One of its most dysfunctional consequences was the military's intrusion into the political process, which ultimately was to seal the fate of the monarchy. The practice of using the army to unseat rival politicians started in earnest in the mid-1930s when, as we have seen, members of the *Ikha'* Party conspired with military officers to overthrow the government of Yasin al-Hashimi. While the populist *Ikha'* had genuine differences with the dictatorial Hashimi, the entire ploy was driven by Hikmat Sulayman, whose objection to Hashimi had more to do with settling personal scores than with ideational differences.[38] It was the same Sulayman who, a year earlier, had conspired with tribal sheikhs to overthrow the government of 'Ali Jawdat al-Ayubi.[39] Even Ja'far Abu al-Timman, known for his decency and lofty ideals, would be driven to collaborate with the army to unseat the recalcitrant Hashimi.[40] And in one of those gruesome historical ironies, Nuri al-Sa'id, whose body was mutilated by an angry mob in the wake of the 1958 military coup, was one of the first politicians to use the army to achieve his own political ends in the second half of the 1930s.[41] Indeed, he was the darling of the "Golden Square,"[42] the four army officers who literally controlled the direction of Iraqi politics in the late 1930s and ended up plunging the country into a preposterous war with Britain in 1941.

That war sidelined the army for the next few years, and its capacity to act was severely curtailed by the political leadership, especially the Regent. But its position and status began to improve in the late 1940s when the politicians found a new role for it. As nationalism swept through the region, gripping the hearts and emotions of a new generation increasingly alienated from the old politicians and their British backers, 'Abd al-Ilah and other members of the ruling elite looked to the army to maintain public order. In the popular insurrections of 1952 and 1956, public order was restored only through the imposition of martial law and the introduction of army units into the streets. While the army would "save" the monarchical order in these instances, in the long term, every such event would heighten the army's appetite for political power and control, and thus constituted simply another nail in the monarchy's ultimate coffin.

What is strange was that while one or two of the politicians would caution against too much reliance on the military, the ruling group as a whole seemed pretty sanguine about the army's loyalty. Nuri was absolutely certain of the loyalty of the military to the throne and the existing political order, and would angrily dismiss any suggestions to the contrary.[43] Nor was the Palace otherwise persuaded. In one meeting in 1954, 'Abd al-Ilah told an Egyptian minister, who had been a senior member of the army putsch which toppled King Farouk in Egypt two years earlier, that contrary to the troubled relationship that existed between Farouk and his army, Iraqi officers were loyal to the Hashemite monarchy. He listed the many benefits that the officers enjoyed: they were given villas, their pensions were generous, and they received a full year's salary as a bonus on retirement. 'Abd al-Ilah's conclusion was that the military putsch in Egypt would not be emulated in Iraq.[44] Indeed, a few days before Iraq's own military coup of July 14, 1958, King Husayn of Jordan learned through his intelligence services of the conspiracy and the impending insurrection.

Not only did he have the details, but also the names of the main conspirators. The Palace in Baghdad dispatched the Commander-in-Chief of the armed forces to Amman. But the latter remained unmoved, looking "politely bored" at the recital of evidence. Before taking his leave, he assured the Jordanian King that "the Iraqi army was built on tradition [and was] generally considered the best in the Middle East." If anyone should be concerned about the loyalty of his army, the Iraqi general concluded, it should be King Husayn himself.[45] That the ruling elite would be so cavalier while rumors of plots and conspiracies abounded was a testament to the political and cognitive isolation of the Palace, Nuri, and the other politicians from the country, which by the summer of 1958 had reached chronic proportions.

DEMOCRATIC VACILLATIONS

The ultimate inability of the monarchical regime to withstand the mounting pressures on it from domestic and regional forces was a function of the increasing isolation of the ruling elite from society as a whole. The monarchy could have fared better had the legitimacy of the political order been fortified by a genuine and effective democratic system. As we have seen there were democratic institutions, such as the press, that at various periods proved relatively successful in propagating the notion of institutional opposition. However, other institutions and mechanisms, such as Parliament, the electoral process, and political parties fared less well. In all this, the most central and consequential institution has to be the Parliament. In mature democracies Parliament acts as the legislative arm of the political system, the representative of peoples' demands and interests, and as the watchdog over governmental policies with enough powers to curb executive excesses. In Iraq, it fell far short of discharging these essential functions and responsibilities.

A number of factors contributed to the institutional weakness of Parliament, but the delineation of its constitutional powers vis-à-vis the executive had to be the most damaging. While the 1924 Constitution made the Cabinet responsible to the Parliament, in fact during the reign of King Faysal I "not one of the fifteen Ministries . . . owed its downfall to a direct vote of no confidence by the Chamber. In almost every instance, the resignation of the Cabinet was due to either the direct wish of the King or to the belief that it no longer possessed His Majesty's confidence."[46] And indeed, of the 58 Cabinets and 778 ministers that populated the entire political history of the monarchical state, not one resigned or was dismissed as a result of a parliamentary vote of no confidence.[47] The predominance of the Executive over Parliament was in fact cemented in 1943 when a constitutional amendment increased the prerogatives of the King by granting him the power to dismiss the Prime Minister and Cabinet.[48] Ministerial changes occurred as a result of the displeasure of the King or the Regent and sometimes because of personal conflicts.

The Constitution also stated that sovereignty lay with the people, and thus by definition with the peoples' representatives. But it then made the King its actual trustee. Tawfiq al-Suwaydi, a Prime Minister and active participant in the country's political life, suggests that this provision weakened the Parliament and gave the King (or the Regent) an excuse for authoritarian rule.[49] Moreover, the Monarch was constitutionally safeguarded and was not responsible. He had the right to prorogue and dissolve Parliament, and when Parliament was not in session, the King could issue ordinances that had the authority of law. One parliamentarian, lamenting the near impotence of his institution, simply would declare that the King was "the sovereign, the master and the sole custodian of power and authority."[50] If Parliament was supposed to balance the powers of the King, this balance in fact was tilted in favor of Royal prerogatives throughout the monarchical era.

Parliament might have had a chance to withstand the assault of the Executive, even the constitutional disadvantages, if it had been filled with members who were fortified by the knowledge of their own legitimacy; a legitimacy that is endowed by a fair and credible electoral process. But such legitimacy was hard to come by given that almost every election was rigged by the ruling elite. The process, in fact, started with the much revered King Faysal who "made his personal approval obligatory before candidates received government support."[51] And it would only get worse in the years after Faysal's death. In the 1940s and 1950s the Regent and the ministers, abetted by the British, would agree on a list of candidates that would be distributed to the mayors and leaders of the various councils,[52] sometimes without even informing the lucky candidates themselves, who would hear of their election to Parliament on the radio.

Such brazen disregard for the institution's integrity occurred consistently enough to make it into a pattern of the ruling elite's single-minded determination to ensure the compliance of the Parliament. In his memoirs, 'Abd al-Karim al-Uzri recalls one morning when a relative telephoned him offering his congratulations on his electoral success. The problem was that al-Uzri had no inkling that he was even a candidate.[53] In another episode during one election a candidate for the southern province of Diwaniya did not spend any time electioneering in that city, and in fact was in Baghdad on the eve of the election. The candidate explained that he needed to remain in the capital to ensure that his "appointment" would not be reversed.[54] This meant that most members saw themselves as representing the Palace and government, rather than their constituents. When an American journalist on a visit to Iraq at election time asked a candidate what his political platform was, the candidate immediately answered: "Whatever the Prince (Regent 'Abd al-Ilah) orders."[55] Even after 1952 when Iraq finally moved away from the easily manipulated two-tier elections to the direct format, governmental interference continued unabated.[56] And it is not as though the Palace or the old politicians were shy about admitting their control of the Parliament. In one famous speech to the Chamber of Deputies, Nuri al-Sa'id, seemingly exasperated with criticisms from the nationalist opposition, angrily retorted:

> Tell me, is it possible that anyone would be elected to the Chamber of Deputies, regardless of his position in the country and regardless of his service to the state, unless he were to be nominated by the government? I challenge anyone here who boasts about his popularity and his nationalism to tender his resignation, and we will call another election and exclude him from the government list, and let us see whether this highly popular deputy with his droves of supporters is able to get elected.[57]

The prestige of Parliament was further devalued by the poor quality of many of its members. Perhaps because of constant governmental intrusion, members saw their institution merely as an agency for securing official favors and public gain. A substantial percentage of the membership did not avail themselves to be elected out of a concern for civic duty, but to serve their own narrow interests and those of their clans and tribes. The majority of deputies were uninterested in, and more often than not, intellectually incapable of comprehending and following the intricacies of parliamentary debates and procedures.

In the midst of this sea of seeming parliamentary futility, there were indeed islands of purposeful activism. Admittedly not many, they nevertheless constituted a core of articulate and educated parliamentarians that took the fight to the ruling elite. Despite governmental manipulation of the electoral process, and the Herculean efforts of successive governments to exclude anyone but the pliant supporter, opposition figures continued to be elected. They may have been few in number but they were determined in spirit and vociferous in their criticisms, and saw to it that governmental control would not be cost-free. Thus, while governments tended to consistently win the day, the existence of an opposition, small as it undoubtedly was, ensured a sustained watchdog role for Parliament. Governments were indeed able to pass bills, but these did not go through without vigorous debate, which as a rule would be fully reported in the press.

In fact, while governments did not fall as a result of "no confidence" votes, a number of them ended up resigning because of parliamentary hostility spearheaded by a raucous and aggressive opposition, or because of the incendiary impact on the population of strident oppositional speeches.[58] The "young Turks" in Parliament also on a number of occasions forced their ideas and demands on government, thus modifying governmental policies, sometimes even reversing them.[59] This defiance was particularly evident on the issue of British influence. The proceedings of parliamentary debates in the monarchical period are replete with instances of deputies, and sometimes even senators, assailing the British directly, or indirectly through their association with, and influence among, Iraq's ruling elite.

It is thus not entirely accurate to dismiss Parliament during the monarchy as a thoroughly lifeless and inconsequential institution. While the majority of members acted as cheerleaders, others attacked prime ministers mercilessly, belittling their policies in the harshest of terms. "Government to [you] is nothing but a whim," was the accusation leveled by one deputy at Prime Minister Fadhil al-Jamali in 1954. A litany of sins from subservience to the British, to authoritarian proclivities, to lack of domestic achievements were trotted out, followed by the contemptuous conclusion that a governmental resignation would leave the country far better off.[60] Even the supposedly much-feared "strong man" of Iraq, Nuri al-Sa'id, would be characterized in one memorable parliamentary instance as a "perpetrator of terrorism," and his era as one of "calamities distinguished by a culture of revenge."[61] Interestingly, bitter criticisms of the 1955 Nuri-engineered Baghdad Pact were voiced in what is considered to be the most pliant of all Iraqi parliaments.[62] On this point, the Iraqi historian, 'Abd al-Razzaq al-Hasani, writes that of all the Cabinets of monarchical Iraq, the two consecutive Cabinets led by Nuri between August 1954 and June 1957, the era in which all opposition was reportedly silenced, were the target of the "bitterest criticisms and most strident condemnations."[63] Admittedly, Nuri had such a stranglehold over the institution that he could magnanimously allow the shrill few to vent their frustrations. However, on the whole, parliamentary proceedings of the 1940s and 1950s clearly show that prime ministers and senior ministers consistently participated in the Chamber's debates, and would seriously and thoughtfully respond to questions and criticisms from deputies. Finally, as a testament to the relative liberalism of the era, parliamentarians who assailed governmental figures, sometimes in the most lacerating of terms, did so generally without fear of retribution.

Bitter denunciations of governmental policies and personnel were also voiced constantly in the press, much of it the mouthpieces of opposition political parties. There can be little doubt, for instance, that the 1948 insurrection against the Saleh Jabr government which had signed the treaty with Britain was fueled by the streams of ferocious attacks mounted by the opposition political parties through their newspapers. The campaign was so fierce that Jabr's government fell and the treaty was overturned. One other of many such instances occurred during the early part of World War II, as Britain was suffering major setbacks. Iraqi newspapers gleefully published accounts of German victories and berated Iraq's leaders for blindly and obediently hanging onto British coattails. The British Ambassador was so incensed that he complained to the Prime Minister, who then pleaded with journalists to tone down their support of the "enemy of our ally," and "not to demean the dignity of the (officials) of the monarchy."[64]

Yet, the attacks continued to appear in the opinion columns of the newspapers, to be stopped only after the institution of emergency laws that followed the collapse of the anti-British coup in 1941.

As we already have seen, in spite of governmental interference and constant efforts by state institutions to gag the voice of the opposition and subdue its spirit, the opposition, throughout the monarchical period, continued to be a political force that the ruling elite would be wise not to dismiss or even ignore.[65] Even leaders of the opposition who in their memoirs are given to detailing what they call the "sham democracy" of monarchical Iraq, thus leaving the impression of a beleaguered opposition suffocated by governmental malevolence, do in general concede the relative liberalism of the system (particularly in comparison with what followed it),[66] and the contribution of the opposition and its press to "cementing democratic values."[67] The point here is that while the state did harass the opposition parties and undoubtedly did endeavor to stifle their criticisms, state control was neither so universal nor so draconian as to completely neutralize oppositional ideas and activities.

Nationalist Woes

Not that this relative liberalism would win the ruling elite much kudos among the population. Generally, the old politicians, their grip on power uncontested, were seen increasingly as inflexible and out of touch. As they gradually lost credibility among important segments of the Iraqi populace, they might have lifted their sagging fortunes with alluring appeals to national ties that bind all members of society regardless of status or class. Citizens, even alienated ones, are prepared to sacrifice much and forgive a lot when the national spirit is aroused. Nationalist leaders targeting the combustible emotions of willing followers can paper over human misery and turn defeat into a famous victory. And in the intensely nationalist decade prior to the monarchy's demise, that vehicle for salvaging their diminished standing would be needed more than ever before by the leaders of Iraq.

By the 1950s, however, Iraq found itself on the margins of the nationalist upsurge, where the center had been expropriated by Egypt and its charismatic leader, Jamal 'Abd al-Nasir. Yet less than two decades earlier, it was intellectuals and political activists residing in Iraq who were the leading lights in the nationalist march. Sati' al-Husri and his disciples set out to make Iraq the beacon from which nationalist ideas, exhorting the oneness of the Arab nation, would spread to other Arab lands. To those intellectuals, who were gradually cornering the political debate, Iraq would play the role that Prussia played in uniting German-speaking domains in the previous century.[68] By the 1930s, these ideas had penetrated deep into the consciousness of important sectors of Iraqi society, particularly the student population and the officer corps of the army. In the second half of the decade, nationalist officers were in command of the army, and as we have seen became pivotal players in the political arena. The culmination of the process was the 1941 coup that installed a vigorously anti-British, Arab nationalist government; all this while Egypt was continuing to struggle unsuccessfully to stride out beyond the intellectual confines of its own Egyptianness.

So why was Iraq displaced from the nationalist center a mere decade and a half later? A number of explanations can be offered. To begin with, nationalism's greatest victory in Iraq in 1941 turned out to be its most enduring misfortune. After British troops defeated the Iraqi army in the same year, the ruling elite embarked on a comprehensive cleansing of the nationalist officer corps as well as the clubs and organizations that were populated by nationalist professionals and intellectuals. By the 1950s, Iraq did not possess the ready cadre of young charismatic leaders that Egypt would produce in its 1952 revolution. This was coupled with the chronic unwillingness of the ruling elite to promote a younger generation of leaders who would propagate an Iraqi definition of nationalism that would compete with that of Egypt's Nasir. Nuri would remind his Iraqi compatriots of his impeccable nationalist credentials,[69] but these had been earned in the Ottoman era before World War I, and for the 1950s generation they were no more than specks in some distant historical memory.

The "other" in nationalist discourse was not the long departed Ottomans, but the British who to Iraqis exerted an inordinate amount of political control over their leaders, as well as possessing two military bases in their supposed sovereign country. To people like the Regent and Nuri, the relationship with Britain was symbiotic, based on a confluence of mutual and overlapping interests. They would thus argue that the economic and strategic ties between the Middle East and the West were so inextricable that any talk of neutrality in the Cold War was sheer foolishness.[70] Beyond the confines of rational calculation, there were also deep-seated emotional ties that bound Iraq's two dominant political figures to Britain. Barely a month before the 1958 revolution, Nuri, sensing the mounting popular displeasure in his ties with Britain, told the British Ambassador:

> Throughout all my life I have followed one policy from which I have not deviated, namely a policy of unbending friendship with [Great Britain]. . . . I can become a great national hero if I were to embark on an [anti-British path]. But I am too old to change my [ways]; I would rather give up politics and retire to a small village . . . than to have you accuse me of [turning against you].[71]

Nuri's emotional connection to Britain was more than replicated by 'Abd al-Ilah. The Prince could never forget the help extended to his family after it was forced to flee Hejaz in the wake of his father's defeat at the hands of 'Abd al-'Aziz bin Sa'ud. When one of his ministers, with whom the Prince was close, once urged him to get tough with the British in order to bolster his sagging popularity among the Iraqi population, he replied: "How can I stand against the British? I still remember when we were thrown out of Hejaz, they maintained us at a time when I owned little more than my underwear."[72]

This unbending resolve not to extricate themselves and their country from Britain's sphere of influence made it easy for Egypt's Nasir to put Iraq's rulers constantly on the defensive, depicting them time and time again as the agents of British imperialism and by definition the enemies of Arab nationalism.[73] As Nuri and other Iraqi leaders recognized that they were losing the ideational battle to Nasir and his brand of anti-West, radical nationalism, they sought protection in the West, entering into military alliances with Britain and its allies in the region. Strategically, this made sense, but politically it further weakened the Iraqi leadership by feeding into the alienation of the increasingly powerful sectors of Iraqi society, most notably, and as it turned out consequentially, the officer corps in the army.

And, it was not as though Iraq's rulers could resist Egypt's propagation of Arab nationalism by balancing it with a competitive identity based on an attachment to the Iraqi homeland. While an Iraqi identity certainly had been developing since the birth of the state, it had not developed sufficiently to overcome the innate fissures of Iraqi society. As we have seen, from the very beginning of the state, King Faysal and his nationalist entourage well understood that creating a coherent Iraqi nation was as vital to the future of the country as building the institutions of governance. They accordingly developed a state directed national and secular educational curriculum meant to replace the parochial teachings of religious institutions, and made state schools the gateway to higher education and government employment. By the 1940s and 1950s more and more Shi'ites (less so Kurds) were flocking into the various agencies of the bureaucracy, and in major cities, especially Baghdad, the cultural divide among the country's sects and ethnicities was becoming less visible among the urban middle class. Even the ranks of the military, a near Sunni monopoly in the first decade of the state, were opened to Shi'ites, Kurds, and Christians. At no time did the Iraqi ruling elites talk about, refer to, or advertise their political order as anything but national.

The problem was that even though pockets of multi-ethnic harmony did exist by the 1950s, the state had not been able to neutralize broadly across the country the deep ethnosectarian loyalties. These remained potent enough to impede the nurturing of an all-encompassing Iraqi identity. The primary culprit was of course the continuing Sunni domination of state institutions. While the Sunnis did endeavor to absorb other ethnicities and sects into state structures and agencies, such efforts did not proceed with sufficient speed or commitment to erase the sociopolitical imbalance that favored the Sunnis. The latter dominated governmental bureaucracies and constituted the bulk of the officer corps in the army. A Shi'ite senior minister, in his memoirs of monarchical Iraq, would lament the dearth of Shi'ites among army officers and employees of the Foreign Ministry,[74] insisting that the country was full of well-trained Shi'ites able to competently fill these positions. As for the armed forces, while some senior positions such as divisional commanders did go to Shi'ites, the Chief-of-Staff was always a Sunni.[75] The imbalance was even starker in the political domain. Hence, in examining the sixty Iraqi Cabinets that covered the thirty-eight years of monarchical rule, one finds that only four of those were led by Shi'ites, spanning a period of two years and five months, and three by Kurds over a time span of two years and eleven months,[76] even though the Shi'ites constituted more than half of the population and the Kurds around 18 percent. The process of integrating Shi'ites and Kurds into the higher echelons of government did accelerate in the last decade of the monarchy, but it was hardly a radical departure from past practices. In the ten years between 1948 and 1958, Kurds and Shi'ites held the premiership for eight and seven months, respectively.[77]

In spite of their efforts to propagate the national ideal, the Sunni ruling elites lacked a real commitment to radically rectify the ethnosectarian imbalance. After all, they well knew that such realignment would inevitably undermine their political dominance. Yet at the same time, lingering resentments and suspicions among Shi'ites and Kurds would impact negatively on the efforts to create a universally effective national identity that could be used to counter the larger Arab identity propagated with increasing vehemence by Nasir's Egypt.

CONCLUSION

The problem for the monarchy was that the state, embodied in its policymakers, was never able to resolve two contending dilemmas: how to acquire legitimacy without losing political control and how to respond to revolutionary ideas without undermining traditional strategic relationships. The resultant policies were stop-and-go, half-hearted efforts that did little to enhance the resilience of the state; indeed they might very well have weakened it. Thus, the periodic efforts to achieve limited liberalism proved less than sufficient to create the necessary legitimacy to protect the political order against its internal and external enemies. Yet, to the misfortune of the monarchical order, it was enough to highlight, even exaggerate, governmental frailties which in fact became a catalyst for further weakening the state and its institutions. And, in many ways, this was a function of the schizophrenic attitudes of the ruling elite to democratic ideas and practices that characterized the entire monarchical period. On the one hand, the Regent and the senior politicians desired the legitimacy that came with liberalizing the political system, yet on the other hand they feared the torrent of political frustration that might be unleashed by political liberalization. Opening up the system, while maintaining the country's stability, was a delicate balancing act, and on a number of occasions the ruling elite showed that they were not up to the task. The tendency to push through policies without proper consultations, harass and revoke the licenses of the political parties, censor and close down newspapers, manipulate the electoral process, and on occasions prorogue Parliament, all worked to the long-term detriment of the ruling elite themselves, who furthermore seemed not particularly concerned about calling in the army and dispatching it into the streets of Baghdad in order to confront public anger and frustration.

This weakened state with diminishing political legitimacy and not much to show on the social and economic front would be forced to confront in the 1950s a menacing nemesis in the form of an Arab nationalist tide that with every passing year was becoming an unstoppable juggernaut driven by the charismatic and aggressive young leader of Egypt, the most powerful Arab state. Efforts by the Sunni ruling elites to absorb the other communal groups into the political order, thus creating a countervailing Iraqi identity, proved less than sufficient. Instead Prince 'Abd al-Ilah, Nuri al-Sa'id, and the old politicians would increasingly place their trust in traditional tribal-based internal allies, as well as in their perceived protector, the ex-colonial power. The problem with such a strategy was that the allies of the political order and its protector were the very target of the nationalist onslaught that was riding the wave of socialism and anti-imperialism. The more the Iraqi rulers sought these traditional forces for support and protection, the more they made themselves easy picking for the nationalists and their leader, Egypt's Nasir. And in all this, the army, which had been called on so many times before to re-stabilize the ship of state that it was bound to develop a voracious appetite for power, and whose admiration was directed increasingly at the Egyptian leader, would finally make the momentous move that would signal the passing of the monarchical era.

CHAPTER NINE

The Authoritarian Republic, 1958–1968

In the early hours of July 14, 1958, the clatter of moving armor through the streets of Baghdad awakened some of the residents of the country's capital. If they were somewhat bemused by the rare occurrence, the ruling elites were not: orders had been issued to two brigades to move into the other Hashemite Kingdom in Jordan to fortify it against the mounting revolutionary menace of Nasir's United Arab Republic (UAR), and to caution Nasir against any military move from Syria into Lebanon, yet another beleaguered pro-Western country. The military units, however, never made it to Jordan; instead they occupied Baghdad, announced the end of the monarchical order, declared the birth of the Iraqi Republic, and proceeded to kill or imprison the bulk of the prominent figures of the *ancien régime.*

There can be little doubt that the demise of the monarchy was met with almost universal approval by the Iraqi people. Indeed the unbridled rage of the seething multitude in the first days of the revolution, which saw its ugliest expression in the sadistic mutilations of the lifeless bodies of ʿAbd al-Ilah and Nuri al-Saʿid, testified to the abyss that had grown between the people of Iraq and the men of the monarchy.[1] The support base for the Kingdom had been narrowing throughout the 1950s, so that by the summer of 1958 it had shrunk to a paper-thin layer of privilege of feudal sheikhs, urban rich, and a coterie of opportunistic followers-on. The bulk of the population, the impoverished peasants and the urban ghetto-dwellers, could hardly be expected to embrace a political order that had been active in its exploitation and suppression. The urban middle class— students, traders, professionals, and even government employees— was by 1958 totally alienated from a ruling elite that was inflexible in its political vision, mired in corruption, and out of touch with peoples' political preferences and economic expectations.

During the first week after the military coup, huge demonstrations filled the streets of the country's major cities, all proclaiming their devotion and commitment for the infant republic, their support for the new military leaders, even when they still had no clue who these were and what they stood for, and their pledge, repeated time and time again in colorful rhythmic chants, to offer their lives for the defense of the Republic against all "imperialist" conspiracies. If such designs by the great powers were indeed contemplated, they would be discarded in no time in the face of the obvious mass support for the revolution.

The only discernible element of the new and seminal change was the preponderant role of the army. The military officers who, in earlier episodes of the country's history, had intervened, albeit briefly, in the country's political life were now ready for a lengthier and more sustained tenure at the apex of Iraq's political power structure. While the military's initial political moves suggested a promising proclivity for sharing power with like-minded civilians, it would not be long before those who had a monopoly over coercive force would hold sway over all institutions of the state. For the following decade, the military would radically and consequentially impact the ideas and institutions of governance, democracy, and identity.

GOVERNANCE IN THE QASIM ERA

The announcement on July 14 of the new "republican" Cabinet and armed forces positions gave more than ample hints as to where the center of power would reside. Among the new senior policy ranks, two officers stood at the helm of the political edifice: Brigadier 'Abd al-Karim Qasim and Colonel 'Abd al-Salam 'Aref. Prior to the coup, the committee of "free officers," which for over two years had been planning the military operation, had agreed to emulate Egypt's policy-making structure, where ultimate authority rested in an officer-dominated Revolutionary Command Council (RCC). Once in power however Qasim and 'Aref deflected all queries from their "brethren" officers on the subject.[2] After all, 'Aref explained that it was he and Qasim who had risked their necks while the other officers slept peacefully next to their wives.[3] The two were now the custodians of power: they claimed the premiership and deputy premiership as well as the two security ministries of defense and interior. Additionally, they assumed control of the entire armed forces, with Qasim becoming the Commander-in-Chief and 'Aref assuming the position of his deputy.

The political affiliations of the ministers who filled the remaining eleven Cabinet portfolios reflected the two leaders' early efforts at inclusiveness: there were four Arab nationalists (one being the secretary-general of the Ba'th Party), two constitutionalists, two independents, one Kurd, one communist, and one army officer. While the ideational spread among the new ministers promised a unity government of sorts that catered to all anti-monarchical political forces, it also laid the seeds for ideological confrontations and political conflict; an eventuality that could have been averted had the two "leaders of the revolution" continued on the path of cooperation and unity of purpose which had characterized their relationship when they were conspiring to overthrow the monarchy.

That a united front did not come to pass was a function of the divergent personal ambitions of the two leaders that became enmeshed in the conflicting ideational pulls of the time. From the very beginning, 'Aref, the younger and less measured of the two, would travel the nationalist path going as far as advocating, without reference to Qasim or the Cabinet, immediate unity with Nasir's UAR. It is not clear when this individualist, even maverick, proclivity developed; perhaps as soon as July 19, five days after the revolution, when 'Aref traveled to Damascus to meet his hero, the UAR's President.

Buoyed by the occasion which had afforded him, an unknown officer a few days earlier, the opportunity to sit and talk on equal basis with Nasir, who by then had become the towering political figure in the Arab world, 'Aref unilaterally promised Iraq's deliverance into the UAR. When asked whether Qasim would agree, 'Aref cavalierly dismissed his more senior partner as inconsequential, labeling him "Iraq's Neguib"[4] (the early figurehead of Egypt's 1952 revolution who was later ousted by the younger Nasir). If Qasim were to resist, 'Aref asserted confidently, a bullet would decide the argument. Taken aback, Nasir responded with a friendly rebuke, recommending instead dialogue and persuasion.[5] If the events of the next few weeks were anything to go by, then Nasir's wise counsel must have fallen on deaf ears.

Back in Iraq, 'Aref blazed his way through the length and breadth of the land, making numerous speeches to mass rallies in which he extolled the virtue of Arab unity and the leadership of Nasir. He consistently referred to the UAR president as "our champion" and "our beloved leader."[6] While, as we shall see, 'Aref in later years would be more than circumspect about playing second fiddle to the Egyptian leader, there can be little doubt that in the early days of the Republic, he exhibited an almost adolescent infatuation with Nasir, to the extent that one foe was moved to remark that 'Aref was elevating Nasir above Qasim, as though it was Nasir not Qasim who had led *al-Thawra al-Mubaraka*[7] (the "Blessed Revolution" which was what the military coup had become in the everyday lexicon of the Iraqi media and official pronouncements). Signs of discord began to surface as each would devalue the other's contribution to the coup in their interviews with the foreign press.[8] However, as 'Aref gallivanted around the country, the more calculating Qasim worked quietly to clip his wings by undercutting his power base in the army. By September, Qasim felt strong enough to dispatch 'Aref as Ambassador to Germany, and when the latter resisted, he was arrested "on the charge of plotting against the security of the homeland."[9] Qasim could now justifiably claim to be *al-Za'im al-Awhad* (sole leader), a title that his supporters had begun to work into their public expression of support, and which he did little to discourage.

The Qasim-'Aref rift was a microcosm of a broader political polarization in the country between the "unity now" forces and the "Iraq first" elements. Foremost among the latter were the communists, who in the last decade or so had been active in the underground opposition to Nuri's rule. Their position was strengthened after July 14, as a number of their membership and supporters attained key positions in the army and bureaucracy. Ideologically opposed to the nationalist creed generally and to unity with the UAR particularly, their interests overlapped with those of Qasim. It was a marriage of convenience, for Qasim was no communist, but at least for the time being the communists became the anchor of Qasim's popular base.

One of the first institutional initiatives of the communists was the creation of the Popular Resistance, a militia which ostensibly was tasked with defending the infant republic against foreign interference and conspiracies. Significantly, in the communist discourse and their public pronouncements, "foreign" was no longer restricted, as it had been before, to the "imperialist" forces, but was now extended to the UAR, and even to its nationalist supporters inside Iraq. Exploiting their proximity to the center of power the communists also raided the many professional organizations, with the result that most of these associations returned leaderships that shared their ideology. But the emphasis was on the street, on the power of the mob. So, in addition to the Popular Resistance, the communists formed the "Peace Partisans," an amorphous smorgasbord of people, ranging from the peasant to the lawyer and the professor, who in their hundreds of thousands would fill the streets in a spectacular show of power specifically meant to intimidate. While other groups such as Kamel al-Chaderji's party, *al-Watani al-Dimuqrati*, shared the communists' allergy to the nationalists' demand for organic Arab unity, it was the communists who, by the end of the year, had become the single most influential political force in the country.

It was inevitable that any semblance of national unity that was encapsulated by the ideological diversity of the republican Cabinet formed in the first hours of the revolution would disappear in the face of the communist advance. In February 1959, registering their disquiet with the growing power of the communists, the "nationalist" members of the Cabinet resigned. Qasim could hardly be displeased with the removal of the last vestiges of pro-unity elements in the cabinet, and he duly replaced the departed ministers with independents whose primary ideological label, it seemed, was their unequivocal allegiance to the "sole leader." The communist newspapers cheered the removal of the anti-communist ministers,[10] but they must have reflected with some trepidation on the dearth of communist sympathizers in the newly reshuffled Cabinet. Still, with a number of key security and military positions in the hands of their sympathizers, and with growing dominion over the streets in the country, the communists could be excused not to feel too despondent over their lack of Cabinet portfolios.

If anything, their power was to considerably increase in the wake of a failed anti-Qasim coup in March 1959. The leader of the conspirators was 'Abd al-Wahab al-Shawaf, a nationalist officer who commanded the military garrison in the northern city of Mosul, a conservative Sunni city with strong nationalist leanings. It was the determined insistence of the communists to hold a rally of the "peace partisans" in Mosul that triggered the coup. The communists undoubtedly played an active role in suppressing the coup which had received strong verbal and material support from the UAR.[11] In the few days that followed the failed revolt, communists backed by Kurdish tribesmen unleashed bloody and indiscriminate reprisals against the inhabitants of the city, many of whom were in no way associated with the Shawaf revolt, but whose sin was the bearing of nationalist credentials. The victory of the communists in Mosul was endorsed a month later when, on April 12, over a million "partisans" filled the street of Baghdad in a show of force not seen before in the capital.

The ascendancy of the communists was reinforced by the seeming realization of their primary foreign policy goal. The backbone of the "Iraq first" coalition, the communists did everything they could to sabotage the nationalists' call for good relations with the UAR, and this was dramatically realized in the wake of the executions of the coup leaders in Iraq. Nasir and the UAR unleashed a bitter campaign against Qasim, famously labeling him "Qasim al-'Iraq" (the divider of Iraq),[12] belittling his role in the coup against the monarchy, insinuating instead that it was 'Aref who had been the real leader of the revolution.[13] Qasim did not need to personally retaliate; his many minions were up to the task, calling Nasir a "little pharaoh," "a fascist," and "a servant of the imperialists."[14] Qasim later would join the fray, declaring that the time had come to liberate Syria from the clutches of the UAR.[15] As these mutual insults and recriminations flew across the airwaves, no longer would anyone inside or outside Iraq doubt the seeming hegemony of the communists in the country's politics.

At no time since the birth of the Iraqi state did a political group exert so much influence on the political process. This the communists did not so much through participation in decision-making, but because of their dominion over the streets of the major cities, and their domination of professional organizations.[16] They trumped other groups through superior organization learned from years of underground activity. Their tactic was to quickly put people in the streets thereby preempting competitive groups from mounting a challenge to them. The dictum devised by the communist leaders was: "Let's consume them for lunch before they devour us for dinner."[17] Consciously or otherwise, this "street power" could not but constitute a perceptual limitation on the process of policy-making. There may not have been a Parliament, nor were the communists a legalized party, nor did they constitute a majority of the officer corps,[18] but during the first year of the Republic, they constituted a parallel political structure to governmental institutions.

To the party leaders, as well as to the rank and file, the time had come to demand a greater role in the higher echelons of policy-making that would reflect their undoubted power at the mass level. On May 1, 1959, celebrating the International Workers' Day, a huge demonstration filed its way through the main streets of Baghdad chanting: "*Hatha za'imi 'abd al-karimi, wa hizb al-shiyou'i bil hukum matlab 'adhimi*" (my leader is 'Abd al-Karim, and the Communist Party in government is a lofty demand). On the same day, the executive committee of the Communist Party publicly demanded Cabinet portfolios. While not specifying which ministry, they put the word out that foreign affairs, interior, and agrarian reform would suffice.[19] To show their seriousness and resolve they organized a massive demonstration of the peace partisans who swarmed the streets in their hundreds of thousands, chanting for the inclusion of the Communist Party in government.[20] After all, other parties and groups had been represented in the Cabinet; why not the communists, who, as they were to remind Qasim, had been the sole leader's most loyal and effective supporters.

Ironically, the by now unrivaled ascendancy of the communists was to become their great misfortune. They now encountered powerful foes represented in the conservative religious hierarchy, which in 1959 and 1960 saw a remarkable coming together of Sunni and Shi'ite clerics in their opposition to the ascendancy of the "atheist" communists.[21] But the communists' most telling adversary was to be found in Qasim himself. The communists had been allowed to accumulate power because Qasim needed them in his struggle with 'Aref and the other UAR-oriented nationalists. Now that the latter's significance had been greatly reduced (at least for the time being), the "sole leader" was not about to cede some of his powers to yet another group, regardless of that group's services to him. It was indeed such labels as the "sole leader," "noble and magnanimous commander," "beloved savior," and others,[22] which were energetically used by the communists in their efforts to neutralize the nationalist 'Aref, that soon would come to haunt them. Beholden to no one, as the title would suggest, it was quite natural that the sole leader would show little tolerance for any group attempting to rise above its station.

Qasim began the process of reducing the communists to size by relaxing the severe sanctions that had been imposed on the nationalists in the wake of the Shawaf revolt. Within a month anti-communist newspapers began appearing again, taking the communists to task, blaming them for implanting the seeds of anarchy in the country. Prominent nationalist figures that had fled from Iraq after Shawaf's failed coup were pardoned and allowed to return to Iraq. A number of communist and leftist officers were transferred to less sensitive commands, and for the first time, the communists' uncontested control over unions and professional organizations was being challenged through direct appeal to Qasim. These were successive blows meant to soften up the communists for a decisive hit. All that remained was an opportune moment.

This was to occur on July 14, 1959, the first anniversary of the revolution. For some time, the city of Kirkuk had been contested by Kurds and Turkomen, each group basing its claims on historical rights and demographic preponderance. Adding to the tension was a palpable socioeconomic schism, where the Kurds were mostly oil workers and menial laborers, whose meager wages contrasted sharply with the comfortable lifestyles of the Turkomen merchants, traders, and artisans.[23] It was natural that a confluence of interest would emerge between the dispossessed Kurds and the communists. Thus, a procession organized by communist-led organizations to celebrate the first anniversary of the Republic quickly turned into a Kurdish vendetta against the Turkomen, the result of which was the wanton murder of scores of Turkomen, some dragged in the streets and mutilated, others buried alive. Most of the perpetrators were Kurds affiliated with communist organizations, seemingly who had been given free rein by the security forces in the area, dominated as they then were by communists and communist sympathizers. The carnage did not abate until three days later when, on July 17, army units arrived from Baghdad and disarmed Kurdish soldiers and militiamen.

Furious and visibly shaken, Qasim in an address delivered appropriately at the inauguration of a Christian church railed against those given to perpetrating *fawdha* (anarchy), promising to crush anyone who dared challenge the authority of the state.[24] If the communists felt secure in the amorphous nature of the term *fawdha*, Qasim would be more explicit a week or so later. He held a meeting with editors and journalists, in which he vented his fury at newspapers that spread false rumors about imaginary plots against the Republic. No other newspaper was as guilty of such an infraction as the communist *Ittihad al-Sha'ab*. He then pointedly and vigorously attacked the practice of parties and groups that had filled the streets with demonstrators armed with slogans that encouraged the Kirkuk violence.[25] Once more, he repeated his threat to "crush" any such anarchy if it were to happen again. The apologetic and "self-critical" response of the communists, printed on the front pages of *Ittihad al-Sha'ab*,[26] signaled the beginning of their retreat, and the ending of any hope they might have harbored about communist inclusion into the much coveted ranks of the policy-making elite.

Barely a year after the military coup, the contour of the emerging political power structure in the new republican era was taking shape. Power was being concentrated at the center in a way not known before. In the monarchical era, politics was indeed dominated by Prince 'Abd al-Ilah and Nuri al-Sa'id, but there existed sufficient diffusion of power among the "old politicians," in addition to modest limitations imposed on the policy-making process by the opposition, that a semblance of power pluralism operated in that system. Now, however, Qasim was gradually becoming the "sole leader" in every sense of the phrase. Having neutralized 'Aref and the nationalists and reduced the communists to size, Qasim's goal went beyond the simple concentration of power; from now on the public sphere would evolve around him, and him alone.

This galloping egocentric proclivity would receive added ammunition on October 7, 1959. Qasim was on his way to a diplomatic reception when his car was blanketed by submachine gun fire and hand grenades. The perpetrators were members of the underground Ba'th Party, who had begun plotting the attack after the failure of the Shawaf revolt. One of the attackers was a young man by the name of Saddam Husayn. Qasim was injured and rushed to hospital, but that he had not perished given the horrific condition of his bullet-riddled car was seen by him and many Iraqis as a sign of his *Baraka*, his God-sanctioned good fortune. Convinced of the righteousness of his mission, even of his own infallibility, Qasim would brook no other political orientation except that measured by loyalty and affection for the "sole leader." He sometimes would take this to ludicrous proportions. On one occasion in late 1960, the commanding officer of Shu'aiba air base near Basra was summoned to the Ministry of Defense in Baghdad to meet with Qasim. At some point during the meeting, the officer felt the need to reiterate his loyalty and devotion to the sole leader, at which point Qasim asked pointedly: "Why then did I not receive a telegram from you on the anniversary of my miraculous escape from the bullets of the traitors?"[27] That Qasim would monitor the thousands of telegrams that were sent to him and pinpoint the delinquents speaks volumes about the personalization of political power in Iraq after 1959.

In such a milieu, it was no surprise that earlier efforts at political pluralism and diffusion of power would go by the wayside. As we have seen, the original Cabinet of the Republic, appointed on the day of the revolution, consisted of a wide array of ideological and political orientations. It took less than three months for the nationalist contingent to be eased out of the Cabinet. Ministerial changes would continue so that by early 1960 only a few ministers were left whose political sympathies extended beyond the strict parameters of devotion to the sole leader. The narrowing of the ideational spectrum continued during the course of the year when three "leftist" ministers and one with an affinity to Islamist concerns were relieved of their posts, so that by year's end the Cabinet could not be characterized as anything except "Qasimite." This state of affairs would persist until the ouster of Qasim in February 1963.

One of the surprising, even anomalous, manifestations of the Qasim era was that the conflict then stagnation that beset the political/ruling elite had little impact on policy making, which on the whole was activist and goal-oriented. A number of policies were enacted in the Qasim era that constituted radical departures from monarchical policies. Two weeks after the demise of the monarchy, the "revolutionary" government announced the abrogation of the separate legal status of the tribal domain, and the imposition of progressive taxes on tribal sheikhs and landowners, who had used their clout under the monarchy to escape paying any taxes on their land.[28] Then, on September 30, 1958, Qasim announced a sweeping reform of agrarian laws and practices. The new law restricted the maximum holdings of any one person to about 1,800 acres. While the enactment of the law encountered substantial procedural and legal difficulties that had not been anticipated initially and which resulted in slowing the process considerably, the government was still able to seize almost 3 million acres of land, of which by the end of 1963 over a million had been distributed to hitherto landless peasants, and the rest leased by the government to peasant families.[29] By 1966, as the process became routinized, over 300,000 families had received land.[30] For all intents and purposes, the agrarian Reform Law put an end to the immense economic and political power of the tribal sheikhs that had gone virtually unchallenged under the monarchy.

It was clearly the intention of the new rulers to alleviate what had been the monarchy's Achilles heel: the pitifully wide gap between the obscenely rich and abject poor. Baghdad was to be the model of the reformist policies of the new Republic. The biggest eyesore had been the huge slums on the eastern and northeastern outskirts of the capital, where people, most of them peasants who had escaped the harsh exploitation of tribal sheikhs in the south of Iraq, lived in mud shacks that lacked all amenities of the most basic existence. The conditions were so appalling that the stench carried for some distance beyond the slums. Identifying this as a major priority, the government allocated a large chunk of the budget for housing and construction, and within two years of the revolution, the mud slums had been replaced by a whole new city of brick houses, with running water, schools, and medical facilities. *Madinat al-Thawra*, the Revolution City, was to become the model for similar, albeit less spectacular, projects in other parts of Iraq. In his speech on July 14, 1960, celebrating the second anniversary of the revolution, Qasim proudly declared that no less than 25,000 new homes had been built and distributed to the poor, and a project of 5,000 more homes would begin immediately.[31] Additionally, more than 300 hospitals and medical facilities were built in the first three years of the revolution,[32] many of them in poor and outlying areas.[33] Even a critic of Qasim, the leftist poet Muhammad Mahdi al-Jawahiri, would concede that Qasim transformed the life of the poor classes, restoring to these downtrodden people a sense of worth and dignity.[34] The construction boom also helped reduce unemployment.[35] Moreover, for the first time, a new generation of peasants, illiterate for centuries, was receiving proper schooling. Indeed, education was another governmental priority. With the doubling of the education budget, the number of students attending primary and secondary schools in 1963 was three times the number in 1958 at the end of the monarchy.[36] Obviously, a consequential social transformation, born out of a potent reformist impulse, was taking place in Iraq.

A reformist spirit alone would not realize the socioeconomic goals of the new Republic. Increased resources were desperately needed, and to get these, Iraq's leaders would turn predictably to petroleum, a resource that in 1961 provided 27 percent of total national income.[37] From the very beginning of the revolution, Qasim and the other leaders had voiced their displeasure with what they perceived to be the lopsided relationship that had existed between the British-owned Iraqi Petroleum Company (IPC) and the monarchical order. The new Iraqi leadership felt that the royalties received by Iraq from the IPC were exploitatively low, a sentiment universally shared by Iraqis of all persuasions. The IPC did accede to some Iraqi demands and Iraq's revenue from oil increased by almost 60 percent during the life of the Qasim regime.[38] But that was merely an opening gambit. The Iraqis wanted larger royalty share and significant expansion of oil production. When negotiations between the government and IPC dragged, Qasim invited four oil-producing countries (Iran, Kuwait, Saudi Arabia, and Venezuela) to Baghdad in the summer of 1960 to discuss solutions to stagnant oil prices. The result was the creation of the international cartel, the Organization of Petroleum Exporting Countries (OPEC). The point was not lost on IPC; it made some significant concessions that the Iraqis might have accepted earlier in the negotiating process. But the emboldened Iraqis continued to up the ante over the course of the following year, and when negotiations stalled yet again at the end of 1961, Qasim unilaterally promulgated a law that expropriated all of the concession areas from the IPC, leaving the British company in control only of the oil fields it had already prospected. Simultaneously, Qasim created the state-owned Iraqi National Oil Company (INOC).[39] These moves earned Iraq considerable control over its prized resource, as well as earning Qasim much kudos inside the country for a policy that constituted a significant departure from those followed by the monarchical order.

Another policy that radically departed from earlier practices, and that exhibited the reformist spirit of the new political elite was the Personal Status Law of 1959, which aimed "to ensure to women their legal rights and family independence."[40] This law was truly revolutionary for its time not just for Iraq, but indeed for the Muslim world as a whole. It fundamentally transformed the status of women in the country. It prohibited underage marriage as well as polygamy, and enhanced the wife's rights and protection in the case of divorce. Straying from the rules set forth by *al-Shari'a* (Islamic law), the new law accorded equal rights for men and women in matters of inheritance. Another departure from religious strictures was making a woman's testimony in court equal to that of a man. Pointedly, the law would apply to Sunnis and Shi'ites. Unsurprisingly, the law's provisions created much consternation among Muslim clerics, the most vociferous critique coming from the Shi'ite clergy.[41] Half Shi'ite himself, Qasim publicly contested the clerics' interpretation of Qur'anic strictures on the subject.[42] That this would earn him and his government the enmity of the religious establishment speaks not only to the spirit of reformism in the new Republic, but also to the spirited activism that characterized the policies of the new Republic even when governmental institutions were beset first by instability, and later by stagnation due to the suffocating impact of excessive personalization and centralization of political power.

GOVERNANCE IN THE NATIONALIST ERA

The Qasim era was to come to a violent end in February 1963 in a military coup orchestrated mainly by members of the Ba'th Party. While the leadership of the 1958 coup that toppled the monarchy consisted exclusively of military personnel, the leaders of the Ba'thist coup were a mix of civilians and military officers. On the day that pictures of the executed Qasim were shown on television, a new Cabinet was announced that had a preponderance of civilians who controlled some of the most sensitive portfolios, such as interior, foreign affairs, finance, and oil. In his memoirs, Taleb Shabib, the new Foreign Minister and a pivotal participant in the conspiracy, contends that the civilians made sure not to allow officers to monopolize the planning of the coup, and once zero hour was agreed on, the civilian wing participated fully in the actual execution of the coup.[43] Indeed, Shabib insists that no more than twenty-six officers were privy to zero hour.[44] While the presidency was given to the non-Ba'thist officer 'Abd al-Salam

'Aref in recognition of his status and seniority, and while the Prime Minister and Defense Minister were also officers, it was the civilians 'Ali Saleh al-Sa'di, Taleb Shabib, and Hazem Jawad, through their seniority in the Ba'th Party, who influenced the content and direction of domestic and foreign policy, a state of affairs that did not escape the attention of the British Ambassador in Iraq, and on which he commented favorably.[45] Indeed right through to October 1963, the civilians did hold sway, with military officers seemingly unwilling to publicly challenge their authority.

In their effort to balance the coercive power of the army, the civilians, under the direction of al-Sa'di, created a paramilitary institution, the National Guard, which was made up primarily of Ba'thists (or at least those who claimed fidelity to the party), and which by August 1963 was 34,000 strong.[46] Al-Sa'di, who was fast emerging as "first among equals" was the most vociferous of the civilians in his opposition to military influence. Not known for his tact or equanimity, he once, in a meeting of the ruling elite, called the Minister of Defense a coward, and in another instance described President 'Aref as a worthless military figure "who would not be allowed to steal power from the [civilians]."[47] Backing words with deeds, al-Sa'di bestowed on the National Guard powers that infringed on the military itself, so that members of the Guard "often stopped, searched and even abused army officers."[48] That kind of behavior, the Ba'th Party would later learn, would not bode well for its rule.

Just as deleterious to Ba'thist health was the internal struggle brewing within the Party among the civilian leaders themselves between the left and right. It is not clear what this meant in purely ideational terms, but what is indisputable was al-Sa'di's increasing penchant for appropriating neo-Marxist credentials for himself and a few of his comrades, while referring to other senior civilians, especially Shabib and Jawad, as rightist and chauvinist. In September, in elections to the leadership of the Iraqi Ba'th Party, al-Sa'di and a number of his leftist allies were easily returned, while Shabib was defeated and Jawad barely survived. Al-Sa'di now had the bulk of the Party's rank and file as well as the National Guard behind him. But he lacked the pivotal support of the Ba'thist officers, enraged as they had become by the behavior of the Guardsmen toward them, which they blamed on al-Sa'di. In a Party congress in November army officers stormed the meeting, intimidating the assembled Ba'thists into voting al-Sa'di and his supporters out of office. These individuals were then bundled into a plane and unceremoniously dispatched out of the country. Two days later, Shabib and Jawad left the country to avert a confrontation between the National Guard and the army, thus leaving a political vacuum that 'Aref soon exploited in a military coup on November 11. 'Aref gave himself extraordinary powers, formed a new Cabinet replete with his own supporters, embarked on a ruthless campaign to decimate the National Guard, and began a process of army de-Ba'thification. By early 1964, there was hardly a trace of the Ba'th Party in governmental policy-making structures.

The Ba'thist era had lasted a mere nine months that were pervaded by political turbulence, ideological discord, and personal rivalries. No wonder that apart from the decision to repeal the Personal Status Law which had been enacted by the Qasim regime in 1959, on the grounds that it was inconsistent with *Shari'a* (Islamic) law,[49] the Ba'thist era lacked any substantive domestic policy achievements. That is unless the witch hunt against the communists and their sympathizers is to be placed within the realm of public policy.

If the Ba'thist regime of 1963 is to be remembered for anything it is for the single-minded determination to thoroughly de-racinate communist influence from Iraqi politics and society. And if this were to be achieved through wholesale killings and torture, the Ba'thists would suffer hardly a twinge of conscience. Thus, one Party member would derisively dismiss a charge of murdering twelve communists with the comment that "he would only go to execute five hundred and would not stir for twelve."[50] In one instance, the Minister of Defense, Saleh Mahdi 'Ammash, would personally pick twenty communists from Iraq's overflowing prisons and order their summary execution.[51] This wanton, yet systematic, brutality succeeded in quickly reducing the Communist Party to an immaterial skeleton of its former self, able to operate only at the inconsequential margins of the political domain.

The eradication of any semblance of communist power would of course be welcomed by President 'Aref. One less issue to deal with, he could focus his early energy on consolidating power, primarily by excluding Ba'thists. With that any notion of civilian partnership with, let alone civilian dominance over, the military was laid to rest. 'Aref's power base centered on the army, in which trusted, on the whole non-Party based, officers, that included his brother, occupied the most sensitive security-related positions. Iraq was reverting again to the tradition of a narrow ruling elite revolving around a dominant central figure, this time President 'Abd al-Salam 'Aref.

As we have seen, 'Aref already had exhibited his distaste for sharing power in the early days after the 1958 Iraqi revolution by adamantly resisting the formation of a policy-making Revolutionary Command Council (RCC) that would consist of the senior officers who had plotted the coup. Those who had access to the leadership of the 1958 coup suggest that while Qasim was vacillating, and might have been persuaded, 'Aref was clearly not enamored with the idea,[52] insisting that "he did not make the revolution in order to hand it on a plate to others."[53] That he was self-obsessed came through five years later in February 1963, when the leaders of the coup against Qasim formed themselves into a kangaroo court, assembling in the television studio where Qasim would be executed minutes later. While others mercilessly questioned and denounced Qasim's policies, 'Aref's only concern seemed to force his old colleague and senior partner to admit to 'Aref's leading role in the 1958 military putsch.[54] As small and inconsequential this incident might have been, it nevertheless did hint to the new president's resolve not to allow others to dilute, or in any way undermine, his predominance over the governmental structure and policy-making process.

The tactic this time, however, was different. Reversing his 1958 stance, 'Aref did not object to the formation of an RCC, but made sure to fill it with officers who were loyal to him, so that any opposition to his policies would be minimal. Moreover, he unilaterally endowed on the office of the presidency extraordinary powers that allowed him to act outside the jurisdiction of the RCC and Cabinet for a full year that could be extended by the President as he saw fit.[55] Pointing to the chair in the presidential office, 'Aref would tell one of his colleagues: "it eluded me once. Now I'll even use my teeth to keep it in my possession."[56] And his teeth would bite deep into the power structure. Potential competitors, mostly senior army officers, were eased out of Cabinet and army positions and replaced by devotees of his. And when the Prime Minister, who also happened to be the commander of the air force, engineered a botched up military coup, 'Aref used the opportunity to cut his military contestants down to size by not only civilianizing the Cabinet, but pointedly asking the respected politician and eminent lawyer, 'Abd al-Rahman al-Bazzaz, not known for fraternal feelings to the military, to form the Cabinet in September 1965.

Al-Bazzaz was the first civilian to become Prime Minister since the demise of the monarchy in July 1958. The program of his Cabinet promised a return to constitutional life and contained biting denunciations of the military's meddling in politics.[57] He received the support of a broad sector of Iraqi society that had become disillusioned with army officers and their seemingly endless interference in the political and economic direction of the country. But al-Bazzaz well knew that regardless of the breadth of his popular base, his ability to formulate and implement policies ultimately depended on the continued patronage of the President. This was to be put to the test when President 'Aref was killed in a plane crash in April 1966, but the prompt passing on of the presidential baton to his brother, General 'Abd al-Rahman 'Aref, and the latter's immediate appointment of al-Bazzaz as his Prime Minister averted possible disruptions and instability. Al-Bazzaz would continue in his post until August 1966.

The main domestic initiative during the first 'Aref presidency was a body of socialist economic polices that were instituted in July 1964 under the banner of "Arab socialism," which was first propagated by the UAR's President Nasir. Decrees for the nationalization of all banks, insurance companies, and thirty "primary" industries, as well as a number of import companies, were announced, bringing these into the public sector, and providing for workers to sit on their boards of directors. The nationalization measures were supposed to bring Iraq's economy in line with Nasir's UAR in preparation for some future unity between the two Arab states.[58] Thus, the primary motive behind the initiative was less economic, more political, and as such found favor with the new ruling elite, the bulk of whom were officers of nationalist, pro-Nasir proclivities.

The suddenness of the wide-ranging socialist decrees and the seeming unpreparedness of governmental agencies to effect a smooth transition would have an adverse impact on the performance of the country's economy. The measures led to a considerable flight of capital, and the dearth of technical and administrative expertise needed to run the nationalized enterprises resulted in rapid decline in production and mounting unemployment,[59] all of which led to a sizeable increase in imports. During the Qasim era, from 1958 to 1963, the value of Iraqi imports had risen from $307 million to $319 million, a less than 4 percent increase over the entire five-year period. In 1964, the year of the socialist decrees, the value of imports climbed to $413 million, an increase of almost 30 percent in one year. By 1966, the figure stood at just under $500 million.[60] This of course would place immense strains on the country's budget, to say nothing of the mounting anger and hostility not only of the business community, but also of a large segment of the middle class, increasingly frustrated with the lack of basic commodities and with price inflation.

The socioeconomic conditions had deteriorated to such an extent that it could hardly escape 'Aref's attention. As early as 1965, the President would be heard personally disassociating himself from the nationalization initiative, blaming it instead on the flawed advice of subordinates.[61] Not surprisingly, when al-Bazzaz became Prime Minister in the fall of 1965, 'Aref did not object to al-Bazzaz's policy of tempering down the socialist measures. While the nationalization decrees could not be reversed, al-Bazzaz enacted a number of policies aimed at stimulating the free market economy. He also encouraged financial partnerships between the private and public sectors. In his speeches he would discard the term "Arab social-ism," labeling his measures instead "prudent socialism." Under al-Bazzaz, Iraq espoused a mixed economy, in which the public and private sectors would co-exist, even cooperate, to achieve higher production while not losing sight of fair distribution of resources among the population at large.

Al-Bazzaz would continue his economic policies under the new presi-dent, 'Abd al-Rahman 'Aref, in the face of mounting opposition by nation-alist forces that saw in his policies a conscious effort to distance Iraq from Nasir's Arab socialism. The most vehement of these were elements within the armed forces. In truth, however, it was not al-Bazzaz's management of the economy that earned the ire of the officers, rather his disregard for their status, and his scorn for the military's role in politics, upon which he blamed much of the ills of the country.[62] It would not be long before the President would accede to mounting military demands to appoint an army officer as prime minister.

To his credit, al-Bazzaz fought as long as he could to keep a semblance of civilian control over the governmental structure and to keep at bay the military's unbridled longing for political power. As we shall see later, he endeavored to make civilian rule routine by promising elections and pluralist politics, but neither of the two 'Arefs, military men themselves and sensitive to military interests, would find the idea palatable. Given the prevailing power culture since 1958, the surprise was not al-Bazzaz's ultimate failure to institutionalize civilian rule; rather it was his ability to last in office for so long—almost one whole year.

Over the next two years, governance in Iraq was at the mercy of a factionalized military divided not by different conceptions of ideological or policy directions, but by personal jockeying for power and the personal gain that comes with it. 'Abd al-Rahman 'Aref, weaker and less ruthless than his brother, acted simply as a referee over the various contestations, with the consequent deleterious effect on the process of policy-making. It is thus hardly surprising that little of substance emerged during this period, except for one important policy that placed the rich Rumayla petroleum field in the south of the country in the hands of the Iraqi National Oil Company. Otherwise, a weak and factionalized government with few concrete achievements operating in a milieu of mass ennui was in fact living on borrowed time until a more determined and ruthless group would usurp power in July 1968, and in the process chart a singular and ultimately tragic destiny for the country.

Democracy on Life Support

As we have seen, authoritarian practices had already been instituted in the last four years of the monarchy after a decade of relative liberalism which had produced discernible democratic advances. From September 1954, the monarchy witnessed a considerable contraction of democratic institutions. Political parties were shut down, the licenses of most opposition newspapers were withdrawn, and elections were so rigidly controlled that they produced pliant parliaments, the bulk of whose membership acted simply as cheerleaders with no more than a handful of vociferous opposition members. When the 1958 revolution took place, many hoped that democratic institutions and practices, in abeyance for those last four years, would be quickly restored.

The initial hopes for democratic restoration, interestingly enough, lay in Qasim's own personality. Almost all of his acquaintances, even his enemies, testify to his abhorrence of violence and his penchant for forgiveness.[63] Even those Ba'thists who participated in the attempt on his life in late 1959, and who had been sentenced to death, had been released from prison by the end of 1961. He also was ever ready, certainly in the first year of the revolution, to listen to others and change his mind if need be. He began his reign a humble man who was concerned, in light of peoples' public adoration, about keeping his vanity in check.[64] And the formation of his first Cabinet in July 1958, which contained civilians of various political orientations, was a hopeful sign of his proclivity to inclusiveness.

The progress of political transitions, especially in the volatile years of the 1950s, was subject not only to the good intentions or otherwise of leaders, but also to unintended and unanticipated developments. Thus, days before the execution of the coup, Qasim sent an emissary to Kamel al-Chaderji, the leader of *al-Watani al-Dimuqrati*, to ask him to become Prime Minister of an exclusively civilian Cabinet.[65] Chaderji declined, advising the formation of a military government which, once stability was attained, would hand over power to civilians.[66] Had Chaderji, an unwavering believer in democracy, accepted, then perhaps the revolution and the Republic would have trodden a different, less authoritarian, political path.

Later, as Qasim's conflict with 'Aref erupted not only in the corridors of power but also on the streets of Iraq's cities, the anti-nationalist forces, in their efforts to neutralize the greatest asset of the "unity now" crowd, the charismatic Nasir of Egypt, endowed on Qasim the title of "sole leader," a phrase increasingly chanted by tens, even hundreds, of thousands, sometimes on a daily basis. 'Aref's defeat ignited the mass resignation of nationalist members of the Cabinet and their replacement with Qasim loyalists, who themselves began to echo the streets' adoration for Qasim. This process reached its peak in the wake of the failed assassination attempt on Qasim's life, which was seen, as well as portrayed, as nothing short of divine intervention. Thus by early 1960, events and purposeful advocacy by his supporters had transformed Qasim. This transformation is best described by Hashim Jawad, Iraq's foreign minister under Qasim:

> At the beginning, Qasim was accessible, open minded and very anxious to learn. . . . But events brought more and more power into his hands [and] ministers would not take any initiative or decide on anything without referring to him. . . . So the un-opinionated, unassuming Qasim whom I knew in 1958 gradually got the taste of being the only man in the country. In other words, we built a dictator. . . . Our people are in truth builders of dictators.[67]

Even with the label "sole leader" occupying an ever greater space in his own consciousness, Qasim continued to be relatively tolerant of criticism and accepting of some form of political pluralism. In the first year of the Republic, he made a number of references to the desirability of a multi-party system,[68] and indeed in January 1960, the Cabinet passed an association law that allowed for the licensing of political parties. In the following six months the Ministry of Interior received applications from eight parties: three with connections to the communists, two that were broadly constitutionalist, one Kurdish, and two Islamist. Of the eight, four were licensed: one communist, deemed by the Minister of Interior to be the least radical of the three that had applied, one of the two religious parties, called the Iraqi Islamic Party (IIP), and both constitutionalist parties. In an affirmation of the relatively tolerant mood of the era, the application of the religious IIP had been initially rejected by the Minister of Interior, but appealing their case to the Court of Cassation, the Party leaders were able to reverse the Ministry's decision.

Regardless of the system's relative tolerance, the licensed parties would operate in an environment already defined by the dominance of the sole leader. The parties would soon discern the contradictions in their situations. The raison d'être of any political party is its role as a mediating agent, transmitting the demands of the populace to the government, providing access, and contesting elections.[69] The new parties, however, came against a leadership style that, two years after the revolution, would negate any mediating functions for the parties. Qasim's populist style of rule dictated a direct and unchallenged relationship between him and the masses,[70] so that by definition political parties would have no option but to reside outside the envisaged direct link. Driven by little more than their hopes for the oft-promised elections, the parties meandered aimlessly, holding meetings and conferences, but serving no purpose other than allowing Qasim and the government to show off Iraq's alleged pluralism. No wonder that by the summer of 1962 when hopes for multi-party elections had all but disappeared, the political parties either had physically ceased to exist, or if not, would have vanished from peoples' cognition anyway.

If political parties had failed as the main venue for political articulation and aggregation, that space was to be occupied by professional associations and trade unions. The more activist of these organizations were instrumental in influencing, even at times initiating, governmental policies, an instance of which was the prodding by the Women's League to enact the Personal Status Law. Professional associations had indeed existed under the monarchy, but in the Qasim era they acquired distinct and vehement political dispositions. In one way or another, they became the domains for the wider political and ideological contestation that was being fought out nationally. During the first two years of the Republic, the communists dominated most of the associations. They were particularly strong in the workers and peasant unions, but also won control of the pivotal students, journalists, and teachers associations. It is a testament to communist organization that even when the political tide, vigorously led from above, was turning away from the communists by the middle and end of 1960, students, journalists, and teachers continued to re-elect communist representatives.

But the outlook for the communists was anything but rosy. Regardless of how often the communists reiterated their fidelity to Qasim, the sole leader, as we have seen, resented their seeming power at the mass level. The process of undermining the communists' associational power began in wresting their control of the workers and peasant unions. Flagrant governmental interference and harassment returned non-communist leaderships to the two union federations.[71] Three other communist-controlled organizations, the Peace Partisans, the Women's League, and the Federation of Democratic Youth, were either shut down or saw their power greatly depleted. By the end of 1961, the teachers and journalists, who had continued to elect communist leaderships in the face of governmental displeasure, finally shifted allegiance and elected non-communist leaders.

Only the student association would maintain its fidelity to the communist cause right until the very end of the Qasim era.

Not that all the ideological shifts and changes meant much any longer. By the middle of 1961, three years after the birth of the Republic, neither political parties nor professional associations were able to mediate societal demands or influence the direction of policy. The political fortunes of the country lay hostage to the will and whim of one man. Even the Cabinet had been purged of anyone with even a whiff of political or ideological independence. When in late 1962 Kamel al-Chaderji was asked about the prospect of a return to constitutional life, the inveterate politician replied: "only in a form determined by him (Qasim)."[72]

The resultant political stagnation, encapsulated in the atrophy of representative institutions, fed into a governance structure that in spite of its activism evolved around the preferences and judgments of one "sole leader." This excessive personalization of politics, especially in the second half of the Qasim era, minimized the ability and willingness of other members of the political elite to have a meaningful input into the policy-making process. It was thus Qasim who decided, against the advice of others,[73] not to eschew a military confrontation with the Kurdish leader, Mulla Mustafa al-Barazani, causing a perilous fracture in the delicate identity balance that he and Iraq could ill afford. All this coalesced into a general malaise that undermined the Qasim regime sufficiently for nationalist officers, predominantly of Ba'thist persuasion, to successfully execute the February 1963 coup.

DEMOCRACY EXPIRES

It was hardly a propitious sign for democracy when it became clear soon after the success of the coup that the new leaders belonged to the Ba'th Party. The early formulators and custodians of Ba'thist ideology would say much about the usurpation of power and the forced unity of the Arab people, but precious little about democratic institutions. While the constitution of the Party paid lip service to the concepts of people's sovereignty and constitutional elective systems, it in fact gave the Party and the envisaged Ba'thist state the central role in determining the scope and extent of political freedoms. Ba'thist ideas were endowed with a "strong statist strain" in which individual rights were subsumed into the "general will of the community."[74] This illiberal streak would be reaffirmed in the Party's Sixth National Congress, held in 1963 after the Ba'thist coups in Iraq and Syria. The meeting would reject unequivocally the notion of liberal parliamentarianism, espousing instead the Soviet concept of "democratic centralism" linked to the Party's role as the vanguard political institution in the state. To put it simply, why would the Ba'thists risk losing, or even sharing, power through sanctioning a democratic multi-party political system when they could simply hijack the term "democratic" and attach it to what essentially was a one-party dictatorship.

At least, the Party faithful would tell you, there were open debates among members of the Party over ideological directions and policy choices, and indeed, as we have seen, ideational rifts between left- and right-leaning Ba'thists did occur and more often than not were publicly aired. Such a semblance of pluralism, even in this flawed form, would disappear after the Ba'thists were cast aside by 'Abd al-Salam 'Aref. Imbued with a military hierarchical culture, looking to the army, rather than society as a whole, to build his support base, and having tasted power, only to lose it then regain it, 'Aref, as he would say again and again, would allow no one to deprive him even partially of total political control.

While a number of "democratic" initiatives were advertised with unfettered ritual, none would come to fruition. The most elaborate was the provisional constitution, promulgated in May 1964, which contained the usual "buzz" words, such as democracy, the inviolability of peoples' fundamental rights, equality before the law, prohibition of ethnic or religious discrimination, et cetera.[75] Yet what stood out were the sweeping constitutional powers accorded to the President: he appoints the Premier and Cabinet; he sanctions laws and Cabinet decisions, he appoints judges, governors, civil servants, diplomats and officers, and in the latter's case, he pensions them off; and he declares martial law and a state of emergency.[76] In terms of policy, the constitution affirmed that "decisions, proclamations, orders and decrees by the president of the republic . . . shall have the power of law and shall annul all [existing] provisions to their contrary. . . ."[77] Of the 105 articles, no less than 21 addressed the powers of the

Chief of State, whereas only three dealt with the role and responsibilities of the envisaged legislative institution.

The marginality of democracy to the central intent of the Constitution was evident also in the manner of its presentation to the public. For such an important document that was advertised as a seminal event for the country's political development, it was subjected to hardly any discussion outside the Cabinet in the period prior to its announcement, not even among some pivotal members of the ruling elite,[78] let alone the population at-large. And when the veteran politician Kamel al-Chaderji wrote a letter criticizing the absence of any mention of a multi-party system, and bemoaning the lack of debate over the document, the emissary who volunteered to take his communication to the Presidential Palace was immediately arrested.[79] In the process of personalizing power, criticism of 'Aref's method of conducting the affairs of state would not be tolerated, especially as the main thrust of the provisional Constitution was the cementing of the President's own powers.

The document, through numerous references to the UAR, aimed at replicating the principles and rules embodied in the latter's own Constitution. Chief among those of course were the many powers accorded to the Chief Executive, so that the President of the UAR was not "constitutionally responsible to any institutional checks upon his authority."[80] To 'Aref, the Constitution's utility lay in its institutionalization of presidential (that is, his) powers and privileges.[81] Indeed, during a three-year transitional period before the promulgation of a supposedly permanent constitution, all legislative prerogatives were accorded to the President and Cabinet. In short, executive and legislative institutions, necessarily separated in a democracy, would be fused into each other, and all responsibilities, functions, and privileges of governance would legally be the domain of the executive branch of government.

The other manifestation of democratic vibrancy, the existence of competitive political parties, had remained lifeless since the announcement of the Association Law during Qasim's time (which itself had produced very little). Under 'Aref, the idea was decisively expunged from the country's political consciousness and lexicon through creating in July 1964 a one-party organization, called the Arab Socialist Union (ASU). 'Aref basically was emulating the UAR's institutional structure, which in the case of the latter's President was aimed at cementing his authoritarian rule. While Nasir trumpeted the one- party organization as possessing real powers over the formulation and implementation of policy,[82] in reality its main raison d'être was to mobilize the population behind the regime.[83] That, of course, fit in perfectly into 'Aref's own view of the functions and responsibilities of political parties. And indeed, once created, the Iraqi ASU was expected not just to serve, but also not to exceed, its purpose of mobilization.[84] The ASU published its own newspaper, which in effect became yet another news outlet for the regime. The absence of a parliamentary institution, a multi-party system and a diverse range of printed political opinion spoke volumes about the dearth of even the most rudimentary democratic proclivities and practices.

The premiership of the civilian 'Abd al-Rahman al-Bazzaz did engender renewed hopes for a restoration of some democratic ideals and institutions. In his public statements and interviews after assuming the office of prime minister, he exuded a commitment to inclusiveness and tolerance of opposition.[85] He also assaulted the military's practice of usurping power by force, and invited them to stay in their barracks and leave politics to civilians. And while he did not publicly advocate a multi-party system, he did voice reservations about the ability of the ASU to represent the interests of all the people.[86] In his second period of tenure, he announced that his government was committed to the holding of general and local elections.[87] But by then, as military opposition to civilian rule grew in intensity, his days as Prime Minister were numbered. He thus was hardly able to put through a measure so out of step with military traditions and preferences, nor was he helped by mounting popular apathy.

The military government that succeeded al-Bazzaz did promise elections and indeed produced an electoral law in January 1967. But its heart was not in the project, and few people considered the proposal seriously, especially as it negated any role for political parties, recognizing only the cheerleading ASU. Again, after much trumpeting, the electoral law was allowed to recede from public memory and discourse, and was never enacted—yet another affirmation of the authoritarian culture of the period that would create ideal conditions for the procrustean totalitarianism of the Saddamist era.

Nationalisms and Ethnosectarian Preferences in the Qasim Era

It would be patently naïve to suggest that the early bitter struggle between Qasim and 'Aref was a function of divergent ideological positions. There can be little doubt that aspirations of political power and personal aggrandizement were the key driving forces that separated the "two leaders of the revolution." But the personal rift fed into, and soon reflected, a wider ideational schism that existed in the country as a whole.

The Arab nationalist camp was one pole that was populated in the main by Ba'thists and Nasirists, but a few belonged to other Arab nationalist organizations. This camp believed that the peoples who inhabited the various states of the Arabic-speaking world constituted a cultural unity, and the fact that state borders separated them was a residue of perfidious colonial policies. To the Arab nationalists, Arabs would be unable to achieve their full potential until all those "artificial" states are fused together into the natural condition of one Arab nation-state.[88] To Sati' al-Husri, the Arabic-speaking people "constituted one indivisible nation that had to be housed in a unified state."[89] It was no surprise therefore that the Arab nationalist camp would immediately go on the offensive, supporting organic unity with Nasir's UAR, itself a fusion of Egypt and Syria that was barely five months old.

On the opposite pole a loosely-knit coalition of various groups were camped that opposed organic unity with the UAR, advocating instead a localized Iraqi identity. Some of these were political organizations, such as the Communist Party, whose internationalist ideology was diametrically opposed to nationalism, and Chaderji's *al-Watani al-Dimuqati*, whose commitment to democratic ideals and practices was at odds with the UAR's authoritarian one-party political system. Then of course there were the Kurds, who were ethnically non-Arab and considered Arab unity a mortal danger not only to their own national identity, but even to their very existence as a community. While some Shi'ites, themselves Arabic-speaking, embraced Arab nationalism, the majority was wary about a unity plan that would reduce the Shi'ites, a majority in Iraq, to a permanent (and irrelevant) minority status in the Sunni-dominated Arab world. Perceiving organic Arab unity as essentially a Sunni project, the Shi'ites on the whole were more partial to those espousing an "Iraq first" proclivity. This loose coalition demanded that the new republic ought to focus its energies on the Herculean task of improving the socioeconomic conditions of Iraq, before entertaining such grandiose undertakings as organic political unity with other Arabic-speaking countries. This group was not necessarily averse to some form of Arab union, but theirs was a much vaguer conception than that held by the nationalists, at most a loose federal arrangement in which Iraq would retain considerable independence. In short, the "Iraq first" group was adamantly opposed to subsuming its Iraqi identity within the larger Arab identity.

As we have seen, the two groups who had found their champions in Qasim and 'Aref entered the political fray with untold vigor. For two months the clash of the two nationalisms (Iraqi vs. Arab) was fought with mounting violence on the streets as the political struggle gathered momentum within the ranks of the governing elite. The ferocity of the clashes between the two polar groups testified to their realization that this was a zero-sum game—a winner take all situation, dominion for one group, extinction for the other.

It was the collapse of the Shawaf revolt in March 1959 that signaled the defeat of the unity now forces. The UAR was blatantly involved in the ill-fated rebellion, and its inability to change the course of the conflict in favor of the Arab nationalists signaled the retreat of the unity now forces. From now until the demise of the Qasim regime, the groups espousing an Iraqi identity, emphasizing the national unity of the various ethnosectarian elements of Iraqi society, would be in the ascendancy. In a major speech, Qasim, at once a motivator and a reflector of the Iraq first orientation would spell out his and the Iraqi position: "The Iraqi people consist of brotherly nationalities which have amalgamated in order to defend the existence of the eternal Iraqi Republic. [This is] why we always declare 'long live true Iraqi unity', for in it lies our strength."[90] Going beyond mere words, Qasim would enshrine the ascendancy of the Iraqi identity in new designs of the country's national symbols. Emphasizing Iraq's historical status as the cradle of luminous civilizations that predated the Arabization of the country, Qasim pointedly added the Akkadian eight-point star of Ishtar to the national flag, as well as incorporating the insignia of the sun god Shamash to Iraq's national emblem.[91] This constituted a purposeful reminder that Arabism is but one component of Iraq's rich history and its multi-faceted identity.

Of all the groups in Iraq, the Kurds were undoubtedly the happiest with the turn of events. But if they had thought that their time-honored troubles with the Arab-dominated Baghdad governments now would be resolved, events would soon prove their optimism misplaced. Until mid-September 1961, more than three years after the revolution, the Kurds had cordial and constructive relations with the Qasim regime. Qasim, whose mother was a Shi'ite Kurd, genuinely desired an end to the perennial conflict with the Kurds. In a truly significant development, and for the first time in the history of the Iraqi state, the new republican Constitution recognized the national rights of the Kurds. To emphasize the change of attitude, a department for Kurdish education was created to oversee the teaching of the Kurdish language and culture, a move supplemented by the printing of educational books written in Kurdish, as well as opening a department of Kurdish Studies at the University of Baghdad.[92] Kurdish newspapers thrived during this period of spirited cultural opening. The Qasim regime made every effort not just to acknowledge the separate national identity of the Kurds, but also to show that it could co-exist with other Iraqi identities in one unified political structure. All this was happening at a time when Ba'thists and Arab nationalists persisted in denying the existence of Kurdistan as a homeland for the Kurds inside the Iraqi Arab domain.[93]

All this portended the increasingly cordial political relations between the Baghdad government and the Kurdish leadership, which was crowned less than two months after the revolution when the Kurdish Leader Mulla Mustafa al-Barazani, his family, and other members of his clan returned to Baghdad from exile. Not only were they received with much pomp and ceremony, but they were given generous governmental salaries and subsidies. Mulla Mustafa lived in the confiscated home of Nuri al-Sa'id, and the car that had belonged to Prince 'Abd al-Ilah was put at his disposal.

It is interesting that this time of tranquility and mutual esteem continued to live in Kurdish consciousness into the 21st century. In September 2006, the Kurds unilaterally stopped flying the Iraqi flag which had been unchanged since the days of Saddam Husayn. They demanded instead the resurrection of the Iraqi flag that was designed during the Qasim era because "of the many positive achievements for the Kurdish people that occurred under Qasim's rule, especially his sincere efforts to solve the Kurdish question in a peaceful and democratic way."[94] But, perhaps reflecting a natural human instinct to remember the good and block out the bad, Kurdish memory seems to put less emphasis on the last eighteen months of Qasim's rule when the situation for the Kurds became discernibly less rosy.

The corrosion in relations occurred as a result of the age-old Arab suspicion harbored by successive Baghdad governments of Kurdish national aspirations, coupled with the traditional rivalries indigenous to the Kurdish domain. It might be that some of Qasim's inner circle had always been wary about Kurdish national rights as enshrined in the republican Constitution, and the insistent and shrill advocacy by the Kurdish Democratic Party (KDP) of these rights was seen, and presented to Qasim, as proof of Kurdish separatist sentiments.[95] Be that as it may, there can be little doubt that by 1961 earlier promises and initiatives had been put on the shelf or gone by the wayside. "Kurdish nationhood" was gradually deemphasized in governmental pronouncements, Kurdish newspapers publicizing this governmental infraction were closed down and their editors put on trial, and promised funds from the central government were drying out, so that whatever economic development projects had been embarked upon had come to a screeching halt by the summer of 1961. A further contributing factor to Baghdad's displeasure was the flight of many Kurdish tribal leaders to Iran, as well as, according to Qasim, their conspiratorial dealings with British-owned petroleum companies.[96] By this time Kurdish leaders had become convinced that Baghdad was deliberately reneging on its earlier promises. The early cordial relations gave way to an environment of mistrust and suspicion, and in such an atmosphere, movements among units of the Iraqi army in the early summer of 1961 served only to heighten the increasing tension.

Army movements had occurred in response to the eruption of hostilities among Kurdish tribal *aghas* (leaders). The proximity of Barazani to Qasim alarmed other tribal leaders, and fighting ensued between the Barazanis and their rivals, the Zibaris and Bardosts, who received material support from the Shah of Iran. Barazani saw this as a golden opportunity to neutralize his competitors, a goal he had almost realized in the summer of

1961. Trying to cement his new dominion in Kurdistan, Barazani publicly demanded a considerable degree of autonomy for the Kurdish region.[97] Qasim, wary not just of Barazani's intentions, but also of his new power responded by emphasizing the oneness of Iraq. He "spoke of treating the Kurds as an indistinguishable as well as indivisible part of the Iraqi people."[98] Soon after Qasim would allow his army units to support anti-Barazani Kurdish forces. From this point onward the Kurdish conflict continued to escalate so that by the end of the Qasim era more than three fourths of the Iraqi army was mired in the conflict.

The Kurds had been a crucial component of the "Iraq First" coalition, which propagated an "Iraqi" as opposed to an "Arab" identity. And while the Kurds would continue to reject the ethnically exclusive Arab identity, their commitments to the notion of various ethnic, sectarian and ideological groups all united in one overarching Iraqi identity was being severely tested. On the opposite side, Iraqi Arabs, who had been allies within the Iraq first coalition, would wonder whether the Kurds truly would ever be loyal to anything but their own Kurdish national identity.

A separate national identity was never a concern or a demand of the Shi'ites, the other component of the "Iraq First" coalition. From the very beginning of the Iraqi state, the Shi'ites had consistently demanded of successive governments a redistribution of resources to improve the community's poor socioeconomic conditions, and to absorb more Shi'ites in the governmental and bureaucratic structures that would reflect their demographic weight. To many Shi'ites the Qasim regime seemed genuine in its determination to respond to Shi'ite grievances, and indeed the energetic steps undertaken to alleviate the plight of the dwellers of Baghdad's slums, the vast majority of whom were Shi'ites, went a long way to endear Qasim to the mass of Shi'ite poor. No wonder that the main resistance to the Ba'thist military coup that was to topple the Qasim regime in February 1963 came from predominantly Shi'ite areas of Baghdad.[99] It is undoubtedly true that the almost unstoppable Arab nationalist bandwagon that swept through the Middle East in the 1950s impelled many Shi'ites to join the ranks of the Ba'th Party and other nationalist organizations, espousing the more universal Arab nationalist identity. Still, the majority of Shi'ites remained true throughout the Qasim era to the "Iraq First" coalition, with its expressed advocacy of an Iraqi identity that subsumed the country's various ethnic and sectarian groups.

While Sati' al-Husri and the early framers of nationalist ideology in Iraq endeavored to show that the two identities need not be mutually exclusive, that indeed they were mutually reinforcing, the relations between the adherents to the two identities in the Qasim period were so laden with suspicion and mistrust that compromise and accommodation was literally untenable. Those who espoused an "Arab" identity were mainly Sunnis with a few Shi'ites who were drawn from the urban educated classes, while advocates of an "Iraqi" identity tended to come from the Shi'ite community with some Sunnis who belonged to political parties, such as *al-Watani al-Dimuqrati*, that emphasized "Iraqi" political and economic development. Of the two orientations, the Kurds strongly espoused the Iraqi identity—that is, as long as it did not conflict with their Kurdishness, their primary sense of belonging. While this combustible mix of identities was not unique to the Qasim period, but could be found in the monarchical era, the 1958 revolution brought it essentially to the mass, more specifically street, level, whipping up incendiary tensions and hostilities that would span the entire Qasim period, and beyond.

CONTESTED IDENTITIES IN THE NATIONALIST ERA

The first communiqué announcing the demise of the Qasim regime spoke of enhancing national unity, restoring freedoms and establishing the rule of law, but said little about Arab unity apart from a cursory mention toward the end of the communiqué. Indeed, the commitment to United Nations principles, to the anti-imperialist struggle, and to the policy of non-alignment all preceded the reference to the unity of the Arab people.[100] Listeners to the first communiqué would have been doubtful about the ideological credentials of their new rulers.

That would be surprising since the new ruling elite had not in the past hesitated about proclaiming their Ba'thist beliefs publicly and emphatically even in the face of imprisonment and exile. These beliefs had been first annunciated by Michel 'Aflaq, a Christian Syrian intellectual. As a student in Paris in the 1930s, 'Aflaq was exposed to the intellectual ferment of that European era, and would later formulate the concept of an "indivisible Arab nation" that had been forcibly divided by colonialism and imperialism into a number of "illegitimate" Arab states. To 'Aflaq, this willful fragmentation of the Arab nation had led to the degeneration of the Arab spirit itself. Ba'thists therefore would strive to reverse this trend, reunite the various Arab entities, and do it quickly and by force if necessary.[101] From this emerged the need not to shy away from alliances with the military.[102] It was such an alliance, as we have seen, that facilitated the Ba'thist coup in Iraq, which allowed it to put its ideals into practice.

The explanation for the new rulers' reticence on Arab unity probably lies in the uncertainty of the coup makers over the ideational direction of the Iraqi population, which after five years of Qasim's rule would have found comfort in the notion of an Iraqi national unity based on its various ethnic and sectarian demographic elements. While in the early uncertain days of the coup it was prudence that prevented the new Ba'thist rulers from aggressively advertising their Arab nationalist creed, once in power they would soon grasp the wide gulf that existed between stirring slogans demanding organic Arab unity and concrete policy that could not but take into account Iraq's demographic realities. The new Iraqi leaders thus would advocate a more realistic, less emotional, conception of Arab unity,[103] and this orientation would come through in the "unity talks" that took place in Cairo with Egypt and Syria in March 1963.

The talks were precipitated by the two Ba'thist coups in Iraq and Syria in February and March 1963, respectively. The new leaders in Baghdad and Damascus traveled to Cairo in March 1963 to urge a tripartite unity on Egypt's President. The talks, however, would soon flounder not only because of deep mistrust brought on by the earlier break up of the UAR, but also because of the varying political, demographic, and socioeconomic conditions of the three countries. On their part, the Iraqis stressed their country's local conditions, and advocated a confederate arrangement in which Iraqis would have considerable autonomy over policy, an ideational stance that constituted a considerable departure from the Party's determined insistence on organic and comprehensive unity. Additionally, they counseled for a slow transitional period before any unity arrangement was put in place.[104] And indeed, the final communiqué of the talks, labeled the Cairo Charter, announced a transitional period of two years of cooperation, at the end of which a federal constitution would be promulgated. While this skeletal and vacuous arrangement would fall far short of true Arab nationalist aspirations, for the Iraqis at least it showed a pragmatic recognition by the Ba'thist leaders of the country's fractured national identity.

The lowering of Ba'thist ideational expectations would be replicated by the successor regime of 'Abd al-Salam 'Aref. But whereas in the Ba'thists' case this occurred as a result of pragmatic considerations of domestic imperatives, Aref was simply seduced by power, so that the notion of sharing it became too costly a personal sacrifice. This was the same man who five years earlier had literally offered Iraq to 'Abd al-Nasir. But then he was an obscure officer who was a true devotee of the Egyptian leader. Five years of a political career that spanned the extremes of a death sentence and the presidency of the Republic had brought about an attitudinal metamorphosis. In 1958, his devotion to Nasir and commitment to Arab unity brought about his downfall; now he would not try to hide his displeasure when he was met in public meetings with cries eulogizing Nasir or extolling unity with Egypt.[105] Ideological fidelity had become decidedly subservient to personal advantage, which obviously would not be served by playing second fiddle to Nasir.

The problem was that 'Aref's nationalist credentials and history, as well as his need not to alienate his natural support base in the army, which was concentrated among Arab nationalist, pro-Nasir officers, imposed real limitations on his freedom of maneuverability. He could not be seen to purposely shirk away from the pursuit of unity, or at a minimum political union, with Egypt. Aref thus proved adept at enthusiastically entering into agreements and signing accords, yet doing precious little to realize them. His government's program, announced in December 1963, promised to pursue the cause of Arab unity, by advancing the Cairo Charter that was signed by the Ba'th in April, into a full-fledged unity. Then to a chorus of blazing publicity, 'Aref went to Cairo in May 1964 and signed with Nasir a preparatory agreement of union between the two countries. However, the accord simply enumerated the many steps that needed to be taken for a union to take shape. Some time later a unified political command was formed, but not before 'Aref explained in detail to Nasir his country's difficulties in carrying out the tenets of an agreement on unity.[106] And when Arab nationalist officers sent a telegram urging 'Aref to grab the moment and enter into full-fledged unity, he derisively commented: "It is I, not they, who will lose."[107] Indeed, back in Iraq he took to lambasting Egypt as a country of "corrupt values and lax morals full of female singers and dancers and prostitutes,"[108] presumably not the kind of country with which Iraq would want to be united.

Such puritanism was the product of a conservative Sunni upbringing that would have made him a strange bedfellow to the secular Nasir. Indeed the speeches he made in Egypt would always begin with a Qur'anic text and would constantly infuse Islam in references to nationalism and socialism. Contrary to the secular spirit of the times, 'Aref's pronouncements would raise many an eyebrow. But in Iraq it would have more deleterious effects.

In many ways, 'Aref was a Sunni bigot who would not think twice about using the derogatory term, *'Ijmi* (which in Iraq means Persian) in reference to Shi'ite members of his own political leadership.[109] In the first communiqué of his coup against the Ba'thists he labeled the Ba'thist leaders, a number of whom were Shi'ite, *shu'ubi*, another term that questions the Arabness of Iraqi Shi'ites.[110] Even the Sunni members of the leadership attest to his sectarianism. 'Abd al-Karim Farhan, a member of the RCC, relates that in one meeting 'Aref announced that forty-two Iraqi cadets would be sent to a technical college in Alexandria, Egypt, but that Nasir would prefer them to be Sunni. Farhan exonerates Nasir from such blatant sectarianism, blaming it rather on 'Aref's own bigotry and his innate abhorrence of Shi'ites,[111] a loathing that the Iraqi President harbored for Christians as well. Once he would tell a Syrian Minister who belonged to a party led by a Christian that it was unnatural for "the youth of Muhammad" to follow the dictates of a Christian."[112]

'Aref's personal fanaticism would have an impact on the policy-making domain. The President would assign some of the most sensitive security and political positions to Sunnis from the Anbar province, from which he himself emanated.[113] This was particularly the case with pivotal military positions, such as the Chief of Staff, Military Governor, Commander of the Baghdad Garrison, Commander of the Republican Guard, Deputy Head of Military Intelligence, and Minister of Interior (in charge of police and internal security). Moreover, when further recruitment for the Baghdad Garrison and the Republican Guard was opened it was restricted to residents of the Anbar province. The Shi'ites on the other hand would be purposely marginalized. Thus in 'Aref's first Cabinet, minor portfolios were given to two Shi'ites, both known to be vehemently secular and very much divorced from Shi'ite impulses and concerns. Shi'ite writers contend that additionally, the Shi'ite community suffered a disproportionate share of imprisonment, torture, and job loss in the 'Aref era.[114]

No societal eruptions would occur in response to these particularistic and bigoted tendencies primarily because the public face of the government was defined by its nationalist policies, particularly its many overtures to Nasir and his UAR. In his public pronouncements and frequent television addresses, 'Aref insistently projected an all-inclusive demeanor, ever ready to embrace all Iraqis of good will who, like their President, naturally would be fervent believers in Arab nationalism. Missing from this public stance were the *shu'ubis*, the undefined admirers of Iran, and of course the Kurds.

The Kurds were not to be spared 'Aref's palpable hostility. A Minister in the first 1958 Cabinet relates that in one meeting of the military conspirators prior to the 1958 coup, 'Aref had intimated that in addition to dealing with the Shi'ites and Christians, a goal of the revolution would be "to expunge the Kurds and their problems."[115] More than his predecessors, 'Aref would be dismissive of Kurdish national uniqueness. Thus, Kurdish sensitivities were the last thing on 'Aref's mind when he signed an agreement that committed Iraq to work with Egypt to achieve "the union of the Arab nation . . . emanating from the unity of language and history, unity of the Arab struggle and destiny."[116] To 'Aref, therefore, Kurdish existence was a gross inconvenience; a predicament that the country could well do without, but in reality could not. Consequently, the Baghdad government would not stray too far from earlier efforts in which promises to satisfy Kurdish national demands would be made but not acted upon. While 'Abd al-Rahman 'Aref was less of a bigot than his brother, he nevertheless continued the tradition of successive Iraqi governments in neglecting Kurdish demands and concerns. In a January 1967 letter from Barzani to 'Abd al-Rahman 'Aref, broadcast from a clandestine radio station, the Kurdish leader would list no less than twelve crucial governmental promises relating to Kurdish institutional and cultural developments that had not even been attempted, let alone fulfilled.[117] By the time the era of the two 'Arefs came to an end in July 1968, ethnic polarity between Arab and Kurd was reflected on the ground in the military stalemate in the north of the country, where control over the villages and countryside belonged to the Kurdish insurgents while the cities and main roads were in the tenuous hands of over-stretched army units that were poorly prepared for warfare in mountainous terrain.

CONCLUSION

Was the republican era simply an extension of the authoritarianism of monarchical Iraq, particularly the last four years that preceded the 1958 military coup? The foregoing analysis of the 1958–1968 decade clearly would give the lie to any such fanciful assertions. As we have seen, during the worst years of Nuri's authoritarianism, opposition to, and disapproval of, the political order were voiced, even in the much maligned "pliant" Parliament of 1954–1958, and there was sufficient pluralism among the ruling elite that no one person, not even Nuri, could make policies without at least an effort to consult, with the expectation of some criticism, even censure. Apart from the few months of chaotic Ba'thist rule, the republican era produced a system of power centralization and personalization that went far beyond monarchical political practices. Under the Republic, politics and policies became hostage to the will and whim of leaders perched at the very top of a strictly hierarchical power pyramid. "Skilled at manipulating systems of patronage and coercion,"[118] leaders like Qasim and 'Abd al-Salam 'Aref, imbued with a militarist culture and thus dismissive of democratic ideas and practices, regarded political power as though it was a personal possession.

Populism was the order of the day. Political institutions, such as political parties and parliaments, were viewed as a hindrance to the direct link between the leader and the people, and worse still, these institutions could compete with the leader for the loyalty and affections of the masses. Whether it was Qasim or the first 'Aref, the name of the game was the implantation of the prominence of the President in the consciousness of the people. The result would be either the negation of mediating institutions or at best a grudging tolerance of a single political organization which, in any case, did no more than mobilize support for the leader. Along with that would come the natural and inevitable suffocation of the press, which would now come under strict control by the ministry of guidance, dedicated to "guiding" political opinion in accordance with the leader's revolutionary vision and wise counsel.

Nor would the winds of political change in the Middle East as a whole come to the rescue of democracy. The Arab nationalist creed, sweeping the region under its charismatic custodian, Nasir of the UAR, was at best indifferent, and at worst hostile, to democratic ideas and institutions. Nationalism generally would produce more malevolent effects in Iraq. Violence would grow exponentially among competing Iraqi factions, some espousing Arab nationalist loyalties, others following a more local variety. This growing ideational schism, most pronounced in the Qasim era created a culture of violence, of settling scores, of eliminating foes, and of sending tanks rumbling through the streets of cities. This became embedded in people's expectations as the probability of waking up in the morning and hearing communiqué number one announcing the news of yet another successful or failed military coup.

It is not as though the culture of violence was absent in the monarchical period, but it certainly was not endemic; there was enough civility and sufficient diffusion of power that limited the frequency, scope, and intensity of violent outbursts. These attributes would recede in value and significance during the republican era, as power was centralized, and representative institutions were discarded. In this milieu, a high premium would be placed on the ability to utilize not just the coercive agencies of the state, but also the less than amiable instincts of human beings—perfect grounds for the 1968 military coup, which opened the door for the most violent era in modern Iraqi history.

CHAPTER TEN

The State Rules without Rules, 1968–2003

On the morning of July 17, 1968, Iraqis woke up to martial music and the by now familiar Communiqué Number One announcing the removal of the government of 'Abd al-Rahman 'Aref. If the population showed little more than cursory interest, it was because this was the seventh announcement over the last decade heralding a military coup. Three of its predecessors had succeeded, the other three had failed. People had learned to wait a few days before even bothering to find out the new list of who is who in the power hierarchy. What they had not anticipated was a second "corrective" coup two weeks later that would usher in the Ba'thist/Saddamist era.

The July 17 putsch against 'Aref had been planned by a few veteran officer conspirators who had been involved in some capacity in military coups and plots since the 1950s. The most senior officer was Ahmad Hassan al-Bakr who had been a key figure in the 1963 Ba'thist coup, and who had been eased out of power by the first 'Aref. In retirement he had become the Secretary-General of the Regional Command of the clandestine Ba'th Party, and had begun plotting to grab political power during the two years of weak central control and officer infighting that characterized the rule of the second 'Aref. At Bakr's side was the ferociously ambitious and ruthless Saddam Husayn, who at 31 was second only to Bakr in the Party's power hierarchy.

In planning the coup against President 'Aref, Bakr and Husayn realized that 'Aref loyalists controlled pivotal military units and organizations, particularly in Baghdad, that would make a successful execution of a coup difficult. But given the military's sharpened appetite for political power and all its attendant privileges, it proved easy for the Ba'thists to seduce away from 'Aref his two most trusted loyalists, 'Abd al-Razzaq Nayef, Head of Military Intelligence and Ibrahim 'Abd al-Rahman al-Daud, Commander of the Republican Guard. With the defection of these two, 'Aref's fate was sealed, and he was duly upended and dispatched abroad. A new Cabinet was announced with Bakr as President, Nayef as Premier, and Daud as Defense Minister. Saddam Husayn's name was conspicuously absent, but continuing to be the Deputy Secretary-General of the Party, the young conspirator kept his real power base. And this would become evident within two weeks of the July 17 coup.

The Ba'thists, having learned from their 1963 experience with 'Abd al-Salam 'Aref, were in no mood to share power with officers claiming fidelity to the nationalist cause but eschewing membership in the Ba'th Party. Particularly adamant on the necessity for the Party to monopolize power was Saddam Husayn. On the eve of the July 17 coup, he told the assembled Ba'thist plotters that the elimination of Nayef and Daud after the coup was as necessary as the alliance with them before the coup. He also insisted that he be given the responsibility for carrying out the putsch against the non-Ba'thists at a time and place of his own choosing.[1] On July 30, while Prime Minister Nayef was having lunch at the Presidential Palace with President Bakr, Saddam and a group of loyal Ba'thists burst into the room, weapons in hand, and bundled the distraught premier into a plane out of Iraq. Daud had already been maneuvered out of Iraq on some pretext of a military cooperation mission in Jordan, and was now told not to return to Iraq, but to immediately take an ambassadorial appointment. On that same day, a new Cabinet was formed and announced to the Iraqi public. As the names of the Cabinet Ministers were read, no one would have any doubt that this time the Ba'th Party alone would shape the structure, and command the direction, of the Iraqi state.

THE BA'THIST/SADDAMIST STATE

While Saddam Husayn did not assume the presidency of Iraq until July 1979, and while in the years after the 1968 coup he would publicly defer to President Bakr, and would appear prepared to consult with, even debate, other senior members of the Party, in reality, from the very beginning of the Ba'thist era, he behaved and was perceived as the surest bet for appropriating political power. An adroit political manipulator and determined street fighter, Saddam was never concerned about getting his hands dirty with the blood of those he considered a danger to the Party generally, but mainly to himself.

The membership of the Revolutionary Command Council (RCC), the highest executive and legislative body, and of the Cabinet which was announced after the removal of Nayef and Daud suggested a collective leadership of senior and powerful Party members. Saddam, however, had worked hard to win the confidence and affections of Bakr, whom Saddam would publicly refer to as *al-Abb al-Qa'id* (the father leader). That they both originated from the town of Tikrit in the midst of Iraq's Sunni heartland only cemented the bond of trust and mutual reliance that existed between the elderly military man and his young civilian deputy. Bakr thus would rarely contradict and clash with Husayn. Since between the two of them, they occupied the two most powerful positions in the RCC, the Cabinet and the Regional (Iraqi) Command of the Ba'th Party, Husayn was able to consistently push his preferences through.

Less than two years after the coup, as Iraq entered the 1970s, Husayn was well on the way to becoming the primary formulator and implementer of Iraqi policy. As an admirer of Joseph Stalin,[2] Husayn well realized the value of the infamous 1930s purges to the longevity of the Soviet dictator's absolutist rule. Matching Stalin's ruthlessness and manipulative acumen, he spent the first two years consolidating his hold on power by promoting to positions of influence in the party and the security organizations men who were loyal to him personally, and eliminating potential rivals by uncovering real and imagined plots against the government.

Husayn's first concern was with taming the military. A two-pronged policy was followed. He would ensure that officers were well provided for materially. Salaries of all levels of the armed forces were raised, and officers would consistently receive preferential treatment, such as priority listing for house and car purchases. During the Iraq-Iran War, Western reporters were always surprised by the frontline quarters for officers, which were lavishly equipped with beds, television sets, video machines, carpets, and had direct telephone lines to Iraqi cities.[3] Such inducements were meant to make the officers' well-being dependent on Husayn's munificence.

Alongside the generosity, Husayn was ruthless in his crusade to ensure the subservience of the defense establishment to the civilians in the political leadership. In one of his early pronouncements, he declared that "the ideal revolutionary command should effectively direct all planning and implementation. It must not allow the growth of any other rival center of power. There must be one command pooling and directing the subsequent governmental departments, including the armed forces."[4] Husayn, having used the military to get to power, was not about to fall victim himself to the same gambit. "With party methods," he stated in an interview, "there is no chance for anyone who disagrees with us to jump on a couple of tanks and overthrow the government."[5] And he would act on these words decisively and without pity. By 1971, his main rivals, Generals Hardan al-Tikriti and Saleh Mahdi 'Ammash, had been removed from power, along with their supporters in the armed forces. The Intelligence Services, by now controlled almost exclusively by Husayn loyalists, had made a point of infiltrating the ranks of the military. And by amalgamating the membership of the Party's Regional Command into the RCC, the latter institution, the highest policy-making body in the land, was now dominated by civilians.

Not that civilians were spared. As conspiracy after conspiracy, some real, others manufactured, were unearthed, imprisonment and executions claimed their share of civilians as well as military officers.[6] In the new regime's first decade, Husayn, while legally the number two man in the Party and governmental structures, was in fact consolidating power around himself, methodically cleansing Party, administrative, and security institutions of competitors and their supporters. By the second half of the 1970s, Saddam was secure in the knowledge that civilian leaders who were popular and influential among the Party's rank and file had been eliminated. The army had been tamed, particularly now as the Minister of Defense, Adnan Khayrallah, was his first cousin and childhood playmate. Thus, while it is true that only in July 1979, after easing out Bakr, would Husayn rise to the summit of the political edifice, in the actual constellation of power, Husayn had been the top dog some years before that.

And it is not as though he had not been publicly visible. The bulk of the seminal policies undertaken during 1968–1978 had the stamp of Husayn printed all over them.[7] It was Husayn who conducted the exhaustive negotiations with the Kurds that produced the much heralded 1970 agreement that granted considerable administrative and cultural autonomy to the Kurds. And when the agreement collapsed and the ensuing war with the Kurds, who were actively aided by the Shah of Iran, would sap Iraqi resources and energy, it was Husayn who met the Shah under the auspices of the Algerian president and signed the 1975 treaty with Iran which effectively ended the Kurdish rebellion. Again it was Husayn who planned, pushed through, and personally supervised the nationalization of the Iraqi Petroleum Company in 1972.[8] In the same vein, it was Husayn who, on two highly publicized trips to the Soviet Union, laid the foundation for the 1972 Soviet-Iraqi Treaty of friendship and cooperation. And it was Husayn who in 1975–1976 negotiated with the French the purchase of a nuclear research reactor.

Husayn's ascendancy to the presidency in July 1979 was in effect the formal institutionalization and legitimation (perhaps an inappropriate usage of the term in the context of Saddam's Iraq) of his already established predominance over the governmental structure and decision-making process. He once said that initially he had thought of giving up power after a few years, but then apparently the relationship between him and the people in the 1970s had developed to such an extent that he felt "relinquishing his responsibilities would be tantamount to abandoning the people and the party and stabbing them in the back."[9] Saddam's assumption of the presidency, one presumes, exhumed any fear of abandonment his people might have had. But in a preview of the kind of rule he would impose on Iraq, the changeover would be accompanied by the obligatory violence, when in one murderous stroke he would set the tenor of his rule, daring anyone to challenge, even question his supreme authority.

The blood-soaked drama began to unfold innocuously enough on July 16, 1979, when President Bakr appeared on television, looking weary, almost sickly, to announce his resignation, and to entrust the ship of state to Saddam Husayn, "the brave and faithful struggler who enjoyed the respect and trust of the party's strugglers . . . , the brilliant leader who was able to confront all the difficulties and shoulder all the responsibilities."[10] Whether Bakr resigned willingly or was pushed out by his deputy must remain a topic of historical conjecture. There was, however, one crucial policy that had been initiated by Bakr, and which must have given Husayn sleepless nights. Iraq and its hitherto rival Ba'thist Syria had decided a year earlier to forego their differences and work toward unity. The date for this momentous decision was fast approaching, and in the case of its actualization, Husayn was bound to continue his "deputy" status, this time to the Syrian president, Hafiz al-Asad, who was older and more experienced, and whose stature in the Arab world could not be matched by Husayn. It is thus hardly coincidental that one week after Bakr's retirement, the new President would "discover" a plot against him that would implicate the Syrians, thus allowing him to terminate the process prior to its feared consummation. Bakr, it seems had anticipated Husayn's move, and shortly before his resignation had pleaded with Asad to speed up the process for the union, as he warned of a political current in the Iraqi leadership which was "anxious to kill the union in the bud before it [bore] fruit."[11] In fact, the "discovered" conspiracy allowed Husayn not just to neutralize the Asad threat, but in a macabre rendering of "killing two birds with one stone" he would also eliminate remaining potential rivals at the dawn of his absolutist and totalitarian rule.

It may very well have been that some members of the RCC preferred Bakr to stay in office, fearing the autocratic proclivities of Saddam Husayn, but the evidence of a wide-ranging plot to forcibly topple Husayn was paper thin, dependent on the testimony of one RCC member who had been relieved of his post and showed clear signs of torture. In all, sixty-six senior Party members, including five members of the RCC, were summarily tried. Fifty-five were found guilty and twenty-two sentenced to death. Not only were the executions immediate, subject to no legal appeal, but they were carried out by the colleagues of the accused, themselves senior members of the political leadership. Saddam Husayn insisted on filming the whole grisly affair, with instructions to distribute copies among the membership of the Party. This served two purposes: spreading culpability and demonstrating the consequence of dissent. In the following weeks and months, Husayn would carry out wider purges within the party as a whole, and among the military, bureaucracy, and professional associations.

By the end of 1979, a new system of government had been imposed on Iraq, one in which supreme unquestioned power was vested in Saddam Husayn. At the very basis of the system was the institution of a reign of terror that would hold an entire population hostage to the will and whim of the President. Husayn would simply build, excessively and indiscriminately as it turned out, on Ba'thist penchant for wholesale coercion. In a speech to Party cadres, emphasizing the inter-connectedness of Ba'thist principles and insurrections, Michel 'Aflaq, the founder and philosopher of the Ba'th Party, had candidly identified "cruelty" as the most reliable instrument to effect a conforming ideational change. "When we are cruel to others," 'Aflaq wrote, "we know that our cruelty is meant to bring them back to their true selves, of which they are ignorant."[12] In the Saddamist scheme of things, the use of cruelty translated into a breathtaking expansion of the institutions of coercion. Intelligence services proliferated, the numbers of secret police and spies multiplied, and party militia roamed the streets. Kanan Makiya makes an interesting claim that by 1980 "one fifth of the economically active Iraqi labor force was institutionally charged . . . with one form or another of violence."[13] The slightest divergence (not even dissent) from state policy would result in years of dreadful incarceration and unspeakable atrocities.[14] People would be picked up from their homes, imprisoned and tortured for no reason other than appearing amused by an innocuous joke about the regime. School teachers were in a state of constant panic lest they said something in class that might contradict a passing utterance by Saddam. Even inside the supposed sanctity of the home, parents would be weary about saying something that might be related outside the home by their children. Families conversed in accordance with an Iraqi dictum, *ilhitan 'idha adhan* (the walls have ears). And when the reckless few attempted a move against the President, the sadistic wrath of the state would descend not just on the perpetrators, but on their families, clans, and villages as well. A horrific example of this were the assaults of genocidal proportions that the state waged against the Kurds in the late 1980s, and again in 1991, this time along with the Shi'ites.

The primary purpose of the machinery of government was to facilitate the President's absolute political control and psychological hold over peoples' lives. In addition to the considerable increase in the use of terror, what separates the post-1979 period from the earlier decade of Ba'thist rule, politically as well as culturally and intellectually, was the extraordinary personalization of political power; the effort to appropriate every cultural symbol onto the person of Saddam Husayn; the determined elevation of his persona to the forefront of the consciousness of every Iraqi. It was essential that the President be perceived as the sole arbiter of power, the lone dispenser of justice, the unitary figurehead to whom the loyalty of all true citizens would be directed. After July 1979, a more fitting and correct designation of the Ba'thist state would be the Saddamist state.

Saddam enacted institutional reforms to cement not just the centrality of the presidency, but the personalization of the office. He made sure that members of the RCC owed their elevated status to him personally and not to such outdated notions of "Party seniority" and "Ba'thist fidelity." Indeed, in years to come, real political power in Iraq would devolve gradually to men who were tied to Saddam by tribal and familial bonds. This was a natural development that signified the waning of ideological ties as the Ba'th Party continued to lose its earlier institutional luster, turning into yet another agency for mobilizing the masses for the leader, getting thousands of school and college students into the streets shouting their devotion to Saddam and hurling abuse at the President's enemy du jour, erecting huge billboards of the President on almost every street corner, spying on unsuspecting citizens, and insuring conformity and punishing the slightest whiff of dissent. This could be discerned from the not so subtle changes in the daily discourse within the Party regarding Saddam. In the 1970s, he was introduced in Party meetings and conferences as *al-rafiq* (comrade), but after 1979 that designation quickly disappeared, and was replaced by *al-ra'is* (President), soon to be embellished by a variety of adjectives, such as *al-munadhil* (struggler), *al-batal* (hero), *al-mufakir* (thinker), et cetera. The extent of Party subordination to the President is captured in the deliberations of the ninth Congress of the Ba'th Party in the summer of 1982. This was a time when Iraq's military effort against Iran, which was closely identified with the person and policies of Saddam Husayn, was going very badly. Yet, not only was the Congress ecstatic about Iraq's achievements under Saddam, but it attributed to the President every success and exonerated him from any failure. In its final report, the Congress

> praised the ethical leading role of comrade Saddam Husayn in rebuild-
> ing the Party . . . praised his historic success in leading the party . . .
> praised his decisive and historic role in planning and implementing

the revolution . . . praised his rare ability and immense courage in confronting the conspiracies against the revolution . . . praised his unique capacity to plan, devise and implement all the party's prominent successes . . . praised his creative leadership in designing and implementing the economic development plan . . . praised his commanding role in the war—in all its military, strategic, mobilizational, political, economic and psychological aspects—in a creative, courageous and democratic manner.[15]

Simultaneously, state agencies in charge of cultural production focused their attention exclusively on the glorification and aggrandizement of Saddam Husayn. A deluge of books and articles by journalists and academics, underwritten by the ministry of Culture and Information, raved about Saddam's unparalleled genius, best captured by the ramblings of a professor of literature at Baghdad University. According to this starry-eyed groupie, Saddam's genius "covers all aspects of the lives of individuals, their societies, countries, nations, and humanity as a whole, through the submissions, treatments, values, practices, explanations, writings, speeches, declarations and responses which are the hallmark of the personality, genius, wisdom and humanity of Commander Saddam Husayn."[16] Beyond the written word, the Ministry of Culture and Information began also to dig deep into Iraq's illustrious history and draw a continuous cultural and political route starting from the luminous civilizations of ancient Mesopotamia,[17] running through the famed Baghdad-based Islamic empires, and ending with modern Iraq under Saddam Husayn. Whether the idea came from Saddam or from one of his cultural cronies, immense resources were allocated to the endeavor that included the reconstruction of temples and arches of ancient Babylon, in which the bricks used had the name of Saddam Husayn inscribed on them. In Baghdad, a billboard, portraying Saddam and the 6th century BC King of Babylon Nebuchadnezzar shaking hands, had Saddam looking down on the legendary Babylonian King.[18] By the early 1980s, it had become commonplace to see Saddam being mentioned not just as one of the luminaries of Mesopotamian and Islamic history, but decidedly as the overachiever among them.

This pervasive cultural invasion would be represented in the most garish and sinister of ways in the huge four- to five-story portraits of the

President that adorned the streets of Iraq's major cities. Here was the ubiquitous President looking down on a population afraid even to gaze upwards. Such a psychological milieu of purposeful subjugation would impact not just ordinary citizens, but inevitably the political elites as well, even the most senior members of the political leadership. Increasingly, these would not dare debate or argue a point that had been decreed by Saddam. Indeed, none of these supposedly "key" decision-makers considered himself any longer a "colleague" of Saddam, simply a subordinate who owed his privileged position to the President. No wonder then that in 1995 'Adnan 'Abd al-Majid Jasim, the Minister of Industry, traditionally one of the more important Cabinet ministers, since war production was part of his jurisdiction, would publicly promise Saddam that the Iraqi people would "sacrifice themselves and what they have for your sake so that you will continue to be a bright sun."[19] In a similar vein, Tariq 'Aziz, who, as a long-standing member of the RCC was no political slouch himself, would write an article about Husayn that read like a teenager's gushing love letter, eulogizing his beloved "hero-president" as "the struggler, the organizer, the thinker and the leader."[20] Not to be outdone, the Deputy Chairman of the RCC, 'Izzat Ibrahim al-Douri, supposedly second only to Saddam himself in the political hierarchy, would publicly, and seemingly without a hint of embarrassment, remind his audience of their good fortune for having a president who had been "enlightened by God" so that "he can meet his destiny . . . to be the leader of this nation and its march and history and achieve glory for it."[21] Such panegyrics were in no way exceptional or out of place; they were typical of the times as people responded to, and were swept into, the all-encompassing aura of the personality cult.

So extreme was the cult of personality that even those who belonged to the venerated first Ba'thist generation, such as Michel 'Aflaq, the founding father of the Ba'th Party, and others of similar stature, pivotal players who for years had stood at or near the center stage of ideological and political influence at a time when Saddam was in charge of nothing more than running messages from hideout to hideout, were purposely reduced to the role of toadying cheerleaders, and were brought out periodically to render their obligatory praises of the new icon for the ages. It is within this context that someone of the political and ideational stature of Ilyas Farah, the long-standing Syrian Ba'thist leader, who because of doctrinal differences was forced to leave Syria and live in Iraq, would agree to writing a laudatory forward to a book on Saddam that was published in 1994, three years after the disasters brought upon Iraq by Saddam's decision to fight the world over Kuwait. Farah would write: "the Arab nation has selected from its sons and heroes a historical leader, embodying all the characteristics of cultural heroism, in order to implant the foundation for a new civilizational order."[22] It must be noted that Farah was simply echoing the tone and rhythm of the book, written by a well-known Iraqi writer and journalist, Hani 'Ashour, who dedicates his book to Saddam in these words: "To you who taught a nation to be; and taught history to write itself; to you the towering spear in an era of bowed heads, to you O great commander, Saddam Husayn; I dedicate this book."[23] Such was the intellectual capitulation of the era.

The policy consequences of such stranglehold over state and society interestingly enough need not be always negative. Sometimes a wise and activist authoritarian leader can push through much needed reforms, and enact visionary policies that might be deemed "dangerously revolutionary" by others, with a speed and decisiveness that simply can not be matched by democratic leaders, encumbered as they are by the diffusion of power and responsibilities among various, constitutionally separated and balancing, institutions. There can be little doubt that substantial socioeconomic reforms and improvements took place in Iraq under Saddam Husayn. Much of this occurred in the days of plenty that were sandwiched between 1974 after the dramatic hike in oil prices and the early 1980s before Iraq's economy would come to a grinding halt as a result of the war with Iran.

Personally involved in directing socioeconomic changes, almost micromanaging reforms, Saddam was determined to put the dramatic increase in oil income, which jumped tenfold between 1972 and 1974, to constructive use. Eschewing the practice of the Gulf kings and princes of building palaces and purchasing large private jets (excesses to which the Iraqi leader himself would fall prey later on), Saddam in the 1970s embarked on an ambitious development plan that brought unparalleled prosperity to Iraq by the end of the decade. The GDP per capita literally took off from $382 in 1972 to $2,726 in 1979.[24] While Saddam continued to mouth Ba'thist socialist slogans, he encouraged private enterprise by incentivizing market forces and expanding the share of the free market in the state's economy. By the end of the decade Iraq's middle class had grown considerably and become manifestly more affluent. A revealing statistic is the number of privately owned cars in the country which rose from 67,400 in 1970 to 170,100 in 1978.[25] This could not but bolster the regime's stability, since a content middle class would be less likely to undermine a political order from which it benefited.

At the same time, Saddam's development plans were instituted with an eye toward reducing the gap between rich and poor.[26] He thus introduced a variety of governmental initiatives aimed at the poor classes, including a substantial building program of modern dwellings for the poor, free education right through university level, and an expansion of free hospitals, clinics, and other medical facilities. Saddam also enacted legislation on social security, minimum wages, and pension rights, as well as building electrical grids and generators so that electricity could be extended to remote villages, to people who had hardly seen a light bulb, let alone a refrigerator or television set. Beyond the "social justice" aspect that Saddam and the Ba'th preached, there was a palpable political benefit in these extensive reforms in that they significantly expanded Saddam's support base, as the largest beneficiaries were the Shi'ites of the south, traditionally the poorest and most socially disadvantaged of Iraq's communal groups.

Education was a major priority for Saddam in this period. Motivated by a modernist outlook and a desire to elevate himself above other leaders of Arab countries, Saddam poured significant resources into education and culture. Between 1973 and 1980, student enrollment in secondary schools rose from 600,000 to almost a million, and at universities it almost doubled from 49,000 to 96,000. In the same seven-year period, the number of university teachers increased from 1,721 to 6,515.[27] Thousands of Iraqi university graduates, armed with generous government scholarships, were arriving in West and East European capitals and cities in search of higher degrees. In all this, women were primary beneficiaries. They made impressive strides, particularly in educational attainment and participation in the work force. By 1980, women constituted 70 percent of all pharmacists, almost half of all teachers and dentists, and just under a third of all physicians.[28] In 1978, Saddam launched a governmental campaign to eradicate illiteracy within three years,[29] and while this ambitious goal was never achieved, by the end of 1980, about 2 million Iraqis between the ages of 15 and 45 had been taught rudimentary reading and writing. Since much of the impetus behind the program was to add to Saddam's stature, the state propaganda agencies made sure that international organizations were well aware of Iraq's Herculean efforts. UNESCO duly obliged by awarding Iraq a prestigious international prize.

There can be little doubt that all these momentous policies and reforms were Saddam's own initiatives and were applied and realized under his personal direction and supervision. No other institution challenged or debated these policies or the strategies behind them, and those tasked with implementing them, went about their work diligently and incorruptibly (somewhat of a rarity in the Arab world) for fear of the wrath of the all-powerful man at the helm. That Iraq was able to achieve so much in such a short time was in no small measure attributed to the absolute control and unforgiving power of the centralized policy-making institution.

It could very well be argued that all of these successes and achievements might not have materialized, with such speed and efficiency, had Iraq possessed a democratic structure in which every policy is scrutinized and debated minutely, sometimes ad infinitum. In those days of abundance Iraqis might look at their situation, consider the good times, and legitimately wonder what value could be ascribed to political debates, to an opposing point of view, to all the niggling little hindrances of discussion, disagreement, and dissent that were the necessary baggage of democracy.

If Iraqis had begun to feel comfortable with the many offerings of authoritarianism, they soon would be jolted out of their comfort zone. The lack of discussion and debate, and the absence of an opposing point of view would plunge them and their country, hitherto looked at with wonder and envy by others in the Middle Eastern neighborhood, into an abrupt change of direction, a downward cycle, toward a destination that the contented and unsuspecting citizens of Iraq, had they been asked or consulted, would not have chosen.

The decade of success would come to a halt in September 1980, when Saddam, having had enough of the aggressive rhetoric of the new Islamic republic in neighboring Iran, decided to use his much vaunted military power to silence the shrill and unfriendly ayatollahs next door. The crisis with Iran had begun in 1979 when a revolution led by a frail old cleric succeeded in toppling Iran's powerful Pahlavi dynasty and creating a Shi'ite Islamic republic. To Saddam, the Iranian revolution represented a clear danger in its potential to stir incendiary sentiment among the majority Shi'ite population of Iraq, a concern hardly abated by the aggressive posture of the new republic and its leading cleric, Ayatollah Khomayni, who purposely and purposefully projected the demise of the secular, and hence infidel, Pahlavi order in Iran as the model for all true believers in other Muslim countries ruled by equally misguided rulers.

The Ayatollah's message did find an echo in Iraq. A Shi'ite underground movement, by the name of *al-Da'wa*, which had been operating clandestinely for some time in Iraq and had organized a number of demonstrations, took heart from the momentous happenings in Iran, asked for and received arms, training, and equipment, and proceeded to up the ante. By the summer of 1980 *al-Da'wa* had conducted a number of sabotage operations against political and security targets, that included assassination attempts against Tariq 'Aziz, a member of Iraq's RCC and Latif al-Jasim, Minister of Information and Culture. Clearly shaken by the growth of *al-Da'wa* and the boldness, even effrontery, of its operations against his political order, Saddam arrested and later put to death Muhammad Baqir al-Sadr, the most influential Iraqi Shi'ite cleric of the time whose charisma and learning were to inspire many of Iraq's post-2003 Shi'ite leaders. And lest anyone would doubt Saddam's pitiless resolve, he executed Sadr's sister for good measure and expelled tens of thousands of Iraqi Shi'ites, many of whom were herded into trucks and dumped on Iraq's border with Iran.

The problem lay in the very nature of Saddam's vision of his political order. While in 1980, he was at the height of his popularity, he still could not be convinced of the solidity of his peoples' support for him and his regime. Lacking the assured security that fortifies legitimate democratic institutions, Saddam at best could only guess at the strength or fickleness of his support. He had of course expended enormous resources on the Shi'ites, and all outward manifestations pointed to solid support among the community. But a conspirator himself, he would not bet on Iraqis, particularly Shi'ites, not falling prey to the appeals of the ayatollahs. He thus would treat *al-Da'wa* as an advance bridgehead for the ayatollahs' ambitions in Iraq, and would, in perhaps an exaggerated fashion, see it as a mortal danger to his political order. Consequently, Saddam would act quickly and decisively, as only authoritarian leaders are apt to do.

On September 22, 1980 Saddam sent thousands of Iraqi forces into Iran supported by blistering aerial attacks on Iranian positions. The strategy was to occupy the oil-producing southern part of Iran, which Saddam believed would not be difficult as it was inhabited mainly by an Arabic-speaking population. Not much military resistance was anticipated as Khomayni had cashiered much of the Iranian officer corps. Controlling the oil, and thus starving Tehran of its only financial resource, would, Saddam believed, precipitate an early and unceremonious demise of the ayatollahs. The strategy was solely Saddam's, and for the first few weeks of the war, he would micro-manage the operational theater, expecting his generals simply to implement his directives.[30] He expected swift victory, and with it he would not only rid himself of this impending threat, but his certain triumph would catapult him into the very center of Arab leadership, bestowing on him a status not earned by an Arab leader since the death of the charismatic Jamal 'Abd al-Nasir of Egypt a decade earlier.

None of these grandiose aspirations would come to pass. After a two-week period in which the Iraqis scored a few successes, the most notable of which was the capture of the Iranian city Khorramshahr, the initial momentum petered out, which allowed the Iranians to catch their breath after the initial shock of the surprise attack, and to gradually slow down the Iraqi advance. By December 1980, it had become apparent that the expected famous victory would evade the imperious Saddam. The Iraqi President, his army, and his country would soldier on fighting a stalemate of a war that, by the time of its messy conclusion in 1988, had had a catastrophic effect on both countries.

Iraq suffered over half a million casualties and its once dynamic economy was in tatters. The country's main oil terminals, refineries, and petrochemical plants in the south had been completely destroyed early in the war, and with that Iraq's daily oil production had fallen ominously from 3.4 million barrels in August 1980 to 800 thousand barrels exactly a year later.[31] It did recover to just over a million barrels a day in subsequent years, still only about a third of the country's pre-war production level. When the war began, Iraq had over $35 billion in foreign reserves; by 1988, it had accumulated foreign debts of over a $100 billion.

Saddam's inability to realize his pre-war objectives speaks to the flagrant limitations of authoritarian decision-making. Going to war might have been a simple error of judgment, but it was an error that could have been averted with broader scrutiny and wider discussion. And the tragic irony was that the same personal authoritarianism that had made the country so vibrant and prosperous would now set it firmly on the road to its ultimate undoing.

The second stop on the country's path to eventual ruin occurred in August 1990. Barely two years after emerging debilitated and virtually bankrupt from the Iraq-Iran War, Saddam plunged Iraq into another personally directed misadventure that would turn out to be even more disastrous than the war with Iran. Overwhelmed by Iraq's financial abyss, which by 1990 had shown few signs of improvement, Saddam demanded that Kuwait cut back on its oil production, stop an alleged encroachment on Iraqi oil fields, forgive Iraq's debts, and make further cash gifts to alleviate Iraq's economic crisis. After all, Saddam argued, all Iraq's hardships were incurred while the country was defending not just itself, but also Kuwait, the Gulf, indeed all Arabs from the irredentist designs of Iran's ayatollahs. While he talked of resolving the emerging crisis through diplomacy, he kept the veiled threats coming. When the unexpected happened, and Kuwait did not cower, Saddam took it as a calculated insult to him personally, a public slap in the face that had to be punished.

Invading the oil-rich, yet small and powerless, southern neighbor seemed a particularly attractive idea that could be accomplished swiftly and with little cost. The only problem was international reaction. Here, Saddam felt that the global community might rise in shrill condemnation of the Iraqi operation, but its actions would fall far short of its words: America still suffered from the Vietnam syndrome, Europe was preoccupied with the extraordinary happenings in the Communist abode, and Arab and Muslim leaders would be contemptuously dismissed with a flick of Saddam's hand. By late July, Saddam had resolved to invade Kuwait and rub the noses of its sheikhs in the blistering sands of mid-summer.

Until a meeting on the eve of the invasion, there is no evidence that the RCC, the Cabinet or the regional command of the Party, supposedly the pivotal decision-making institutions in the land, were involved in any meaningful discussion, any analysis of the pros and cons, of the looming international crisis. If anyone was consulted or told of the impending decision, it would have been the few members of Saddam's immediate family and clan.[32] On August 2, 1990, Iraqi forces poured into Kuwait, and within a few hours were in control of the country. The Kuwaiti ruling family escaped to Saudi Arabia, and soon watched Saddam officially annex their country making it the nineteenth province of Iraq.

The first inklings of Saddam's miscalculation came immediately when a joint U.S.-U.S.S.R. statement condemned the Iraqi action, and the United Nations Security Council called for an immediate withdrawal. This was compounded when five days later, American troops began to deploy in Saudi Arabia. The Americans and British then made unequivocal statements declaring that the crisis would end only with the unconditional withdrawal of Iraq and the return of full sovereignty to Kuwait. Within a month, an impressive international coalition, which included a plethora of Muslim and Arab partners, had been amassed, with many contributing troops. Legitimation of the coalition's goals followed when, at the end of November, the United Nations sanctioned the use of force if Iraq had not withdrawn from Kuwait by January 15.

If ever there was a time for compromise, it was in this crucial six-week period before the onset of the deadline. But Saddam did not budge, rebuffing a number of mediation offers from the United Nations, the European Community, France, the Soviet Union, and others. At some point around mid-December, Saddam had decided that Iraq could, indeed would, win a war against America and the world. Given the daunting arsenal that was being assembled on the borders of Kuwait by the Americans and their allies, Saddam could not have misjudged the inevitable devastation that would be wreaked on his country and people. But in a catastrophic turn of fanciful and callous self-delusion, he believed that his army, seasoned in ground warfare against the Iranians, would eventually bog down the invaders, inflict huge casualties on them, and force them to turn back and sue for peace.[33] His "mother of all battles" would be the ultimate proof of his genius, perhaps his infallibility.

But that was sheer fantasy. After almost six weeks of unrelenting bombardment from the air, the ground campaign began on February 24, 1991 and, in just over two days, Kuwait had been liberated. Two days after that, when coalition forces stopped their lightning and almost unchallenged advance, which had brought them deep into Iraqi territory, over two thirds of Saddam's much vaunted and lionized army had been decimated, and some 90,000 Iraqi troops had been captured. Saddam had handed his country and people one of the most comprehensive and devastating defeats in contemporary warfare.

Immediately, major insurrections erupted in the southern Shi'ite part of the country and in the Kurdish north. The regime was at such a state of political disarray that it probably would have taken the United States no more than a gentle prod to dismantle the entire political edifice. But the Americans stayed put, giving Saddam the breather he needed, and had not expected, to launch a counter assault on the Shi'ite and Kurdish rebels that, in true Saddam fashion, exacted savage retribution on everyone regardless of culpability. In the south, Saddam dispatched Republican Guard divisions, consisting mainly of Sunni troops, backed by some of the most unrestrained elements of state and Party security. Purposeful bombardment was aimed at houses with little regard for its occupants, and people were indiscriminately shot in the streets. Rotting bodies were left in full public view, and those attempting to retrieve them for burial were themselves shot at and killed. Within less than three weeks, over 30,000, including women and children, had been killed, and some 70,000 had fled the country, mainly to neighboring Iran.[34] Turning to the north, Saddam's troops followed similar tactics which were to lead to the flight of more than 2 million Kurds, who, terrified of the regime's renowned cruelty, made their way to the mountainous borders with Iran and Turkey. With barely any food or belongings, braving the most appalling conditions, thousands were to die, many of them children and infants. The human tragedy unfolded on television screens and led to an international outcry. In response, the United States, supported by the United Kingdom and France, imposed a no-fly zone above the 36th parallel, which effectively sealed the Kurdish areas from the Iraqi army and allowed the Kurdish population to return to their homes.

Saddam would never regain control over the northern part of his country. From 1991 until the forcible ouster of the regime in 2003, the Kurds would lead an autonomous existence from the central government in Baghdad. Meanwhile, crippled by international economic sanctions, the now tarnished President, a symbol of unbridled excess, would reside over a decaying state and a teetering economy, infested by graft, corruption, and nepotism. In the decade that followed the first Gulf War, the GDP remained literally stagnant, growing from $29 billion in 1992 to $31 billion in 1999, a measly seven percent over the entire seven years.[35] It was hardly surprising that during the 1990s, much of the spectacular advances that had been achieved in the 1970s had all but disappeared.[36]

The contention here is not to negate any possibility of reasoned argument and rational assessment in Saddam's decisions over Iran and Kuwait. A balanced and objective calculus of the costs and benefits, and of the probabilities of success, could certainly be constructed to show that Saddam's actions were not mere fanciful misadventures. Saddam could extrapolate a number of indicators pertaining to the seeming fragility of Iran's political order in 1980 and to the ideological and geo-strategic competitions within the international system of 1990 to show that his decisions were measured and deliberate. That things ultimately did not work out should not signify an absence of decision-making rationality.

The problem is that any such rationality would at best be limited by two variables, one intrinsic to Saddam himself, the other extrinsic. Saddam might have thought things through, but this thought process was inexorably linked to the President's uncommonly elevated opinion of his capabilities and perception of his stature. Impacted by such emotional and non-rational impulses, not only would the process of decision-making be impaired but the likelihood of reassessing the decision, or turning back from it altogether, is that much less likely. Rationality is further degraded by the chronic shortage of other assessments and opinions against which the President's decision would be evaluated. Saddam's incomparable supremacy over all aspects of life in Iraq was such that no one dared question his wisdom. The possibility, therefore, that an opposing, even probing, viewpoint would be put on the table was sheer fantasy. And that pattern of governance, of the all-knowing, all-controlling, imperious President surrounded by a compliant loyal flock, exacting savage punishment on perceived rivals and foes would continue until he was finally ousted by foreign troops in 2003.

THE DEGRADATION OF DEMOCRACY

It hardly comes as a surprise that neither the institutional structure nor the ideational milieu of the Ba'thist/Saddamist political order was in any way conducive to democracy. The founding fathers of the Ba'th Party had stressed Arab unity and socialism, but when they spoke of freedom, they generally referred not to individual liberty but to a peoples' independence from outside control and interference.[37] They denigrated Western democracy as exploitative and capitalistic,[38] opting instead for democratic centralism, a system in which one ideological party or organization reigns supreme.

Hopes for some kind of pluralism were raised at the end of 1971 when President Bakr announced a "National Action Charter" which declared the regime's intention to establish a "National Front" of all progressive forces. This initiative was primarily an effort by the regime to allow the communists, by then fully domesticated, a measure of participation in government, and by doing so pacify the Soviet Union, the country's main supplier of arms and major global ally at a time when the Iraqis had few friends internationally or in their immediate region. In March of the following year, two communists joined a reshuffled Cabinet, and in 1973, the communists finally joined the Progressive National Front, which had eight Ba'thists, three communists, three Kurds, and two independents. Notwithstanding the fanfare that accompanied these moves, and Ba'thist claims that the Front represented the wish of the political leadership "to cement democracy and to include the masses and all national forces in the new political undertaking,"[39] in fact no real diminution of Ba'thist political control would occur, indeed at no time was it even contemplated. Peripheral and lowly portfolios (primarily of the Minister of State variety) were given to non-Ba'thists, and the ruling party had made sure to have an absolute voting majority in the Front itself. And in any case, real executive and legislative power remained concentrated in the RCC which, apart from one token and helpless figure, the Kurd Muhyi al-Din Ma'rouf, was exclusively Ba'thist. Moreover, the non-Ba'thists would be ominously warned by the President that "no party other than the Ba'th Party [would] be allowed to carry out any form of political or organizational activity within the armed forces."[40] The rulers, conspirators themselves, well appreciated the necessity of keeping the non-Ba'thists, particularly the communists, at arm's length from the security institutions.

In any case, as we have seen, the rapid emergence in the 1970s of Saddam Husayn as the central decision-maker and formulator of policy would substantially diminish the powers, privileges, and responsibilities of the Ba'th Party. Whatever "democratic centralism" there was, manifested in debates and argument among various currents within the Party, quickly disappeared as the institution became an appendage of presidential authority. Rather than argue and oppose, Party members would sit in meetings, organized by the Office of the President, and take notes as he held forth on Ba'thist ideology, sometimes revising fundamental party beliefs.[41] Looking back at the Ba'thist period, apart from possibly the first two years after the 1968 seizure of power, any talk of Party autonomy was pure whimsy.

After July 1979 when Saddam finally institutionalized his de-facto political control, he began to hint at broadening and liberalizing the political order. As early as 1977, in an exhibition of candor wholly uncharacteristic of Arab leaders, he would warn in one of his public lectures that "because Arab leaders have not come to power through liberal democratic means, then they should expect to leave power also in non-democratic ways."[42] Saddam was thus evaluating democracy not necessarily for its own intrinsic value to the public good, but as an agent for the consolidation and resilience of the political system.

This concern must have continued to percolate in his mind, as he would come back to it again after assuming full control in 1979. In a revealing speech in April 1980, Husayn intimated that instability resulted from "the isolation of the ruler from the people. When any ruler reaches this situation he is finished. The problem is not one of time, or one of occupation by an external power, the real crisis, fundamental and historical, is the isolation of the ruler from the people."[43] Only the hopelessly naïve would think that Saddam was now ready to submit himself and his political order to the will of the people. What he wanted was to give the Iraqis a sense of involvement in the political process, which, regardless of how circumspect, would still release pent up frustrations, and create in them a sense of accessibility to their President and the ruling elite. Simultaneously, his stock would rise regionally and globally. It did not take long for him to announce that national elections for a Parliament would be held soon.

The first Iraqi elections in more than twenty years took place on June 20, 1980. Six million Iraqis went to the polls to elect a National Assembly (*al-Majlis al-Watani*) in a process that was visibly free of harassment and intimidation. The results were not unexpected. Three fourths of the elected members belonged to the Ba'th Party, including RCC members and ministers who had decided to stand. Still, forty percent of the total assembly were Shi'ite and twelve percent Kurdish.[44] The exercise would be repeated periodically every four or five years until the demise of the Saddamist political order.

The preponderance of the Ba'thists was the result of a thorough screening process of all candidates. Although they did not need to be card-carrying members of the Party, candidates had to declare themselves to be adherents to the principles of the 1968 "revolution." A commission of five high-ranking members of the leadership, under the chairmanship of an RCC member, was responsible for a painstakingly thorough evaluation of the candidates.

Even with such loyal cadres, Saddam would take few chances with the Assembly's assigned powers. In theory, the Assembly was supposed to propose and draft laws, confirm budgets and development plans, ratify international treaties, debate all aspects of domestic and foreign policy, argue departmental performance, and even propose the resignation of ministers. In reality, however, although some debates, whose parameters were strictly set, did take place, the Assembly's jurisdiction was restricted to endorsing policies and enacting laws submitted to it by the RCC. Very quickly it became a favored venue for the President to announce grandiose initiatives and make speeches assailing adversaries, and then sit back and bask in the adulation of the deputies who must have set many records in the length and intensity of their frenzied expressions of support. Born in a circumstance of high hopes and expectations, in the end, the assembly was anything but the democratic breakthrough; more like a theatrical stage for the principal actor to show off his many gifts and matchless talent.

If there was one era in Iraq's history of statehood, where the democratic ideal was consistently denigrated and degraded, this was it. This was because, unlike other periods, Saddam and his cronies talked of democracy, sometimes incessantly, but took to defining it in ways that were meant to enhance and justify their stranglehold over the political process, and in so doing inflicted untold harm to the very essence of the concept. Saddam could make sterling speeches about the perils of a ruler's isolation from his people, thus raising hopes for the liberalization of the political order, but the institutions he created were in fact calculated to restrict and stifle the political openness he preached. Whether this had always been his design or whether he got cold feet once the time came for the idea to be implemented is not clear, but either way, it spoke to the arrogance of absolute power.

Much in the same vein, when Saddam and his cronies described their political system, they would revel in attaching all kinds of adjectives, such as "popular," "revolutionary," "socialist," et cetera to their brand of democracy, anything but the "Western" kind, which they constantly degraded as a wicked imperialist creation, but that just happened to include notions of human rights, tolerance of opposition, civil liberties, and the rule of law. Bored after awhile with what to him had obviously become an asinine debate, Saddam would tell a Western journalist, who was questioning the features of Iraqi "democracy," that regardless of what democracy was or what it represented, in the final analysis, the Iraqi people were "convinced that the leadership in charge was democratic."[45] Like other narratives, the definition and interpretation of democracy was subject wholly to the President's assessment of his own interest and advantage.

FORCED IDENTITY FLUCTUATION

The denigration of democracy as an idea, as well as a system of institutions, was simply a function of a procrustean authoritarian order that subjected all thoughts and formulations to its interests, preferences and ways of thinking. Even fundamental Ba'thist beliefs were unilaterally expropriated by the President, modified and changed, to become the new official orthodoxy. In one of his frequent revisions of Ba'thist beliefs, Saddam would tackle the sacred cow of the Arab nation.

It must be understood that at the very heart of Ba'thist philosophy lies the revered and oft-quoted concept of "one indivisible Arab nation." In this intellectual schema, "state" is seen as too grandiose a label to assign to entities that are much more modest, no more than regions of the Arab nation. To Michel 'Aflaq Arab states were in essence illegitimate, mere "artificial and counterfeit statelets" created by colonialists and imperialists who were determined to keep the Arab nation from attaining its full creative potential.[46] It follows that, in Ba'thist doctrine, the overriding loyalty of all Arabic-speaking people, regardless from which geographic area they emanated, had to be directed to the Arab nation. This identity prioritization can be seen in the administrative structure of the Party leadership. Each state ("region" in Ba'thist lexicon) would have its own regional command, but on the central issues of ideological and political direction the regional commands would be subservient to one paramount national command, representing the Arab nation as a whole.

Saddam, however, was hardly one for sacred cows. As early as 1975, he would feel unrestrained in tackling the issue of Arab and Iraqi identity. He had been told that in meetings and rallies, Party members, in their efforts to educate people in core Ba'thist principles and beliefs, had been raising a flag they depicted as an "Arab flag," and substituting it for the Iraqi flag. Saddam in a major address would reformulate the notion of "region" and the relationship between the Arab nation and the Iraqi region, decidedly to the latter's advantage because, he would argue, of its actual and non-abstract nature; an entity that is "felt" by the Iraqi citizen:

> When we put our faith in the Arab flag, which the party has raised on some occasions, we should be aware not to commit the error of making the citizen believe that the Iraqi flag is less than sacred. And when we talk about the Arab nation, we must remember to educate the "Iraqi" to cherish this parcel of land, "the Iraqi region," on which he lives, and which constitutionally is his country, and for which he must be ready intellectually and emotionally to martyr himself. [The Iraqi region] is his existential country, with which he interacts in a practical way on a daily basis, whereas he interacts with the Arab nation in a general ideational way.[47]

Without intimating a necessary abandonment of the Arab identity, Saddam was signaling a new direction in promoting and nurturing an Iraqi identity. To this end, words would be backed by deeds. The regime embarked on a political and cultural program designed to create a continuous link between modern Iraq and the ancient civilizations that had resided in the same land.[48] Plays depicting the achievements of Sumeria, Akkadia, Babylonia, and Assyria were performed throughout Iraq, as well as internationally. Massive archeological work was done to resurrect and/or to reconstruct such ancient cities as Hatra, Assur, Nineveh, and Babylon. New museums of Iraqi history were built and old ones were lavishly refurbished. The political leadership made sure they became "a focal point of pilgrimage for the adult populations as well as for school children."[49] And artists and intellectuals were encouraged to incorporate Iraq's pre-Arab heritage in their work.

The effort at identity reformulation was not just some infatuation with the country's unrivaled ancient civilizations. It served a clear political purpose. In the jockeying for predominance in Arab and Middle Eastern politics and international affairs, it would remind Iraqis and other Arabs, particularly the Arab kings and presidents, that in addition to geo-strategic and economic advantages, Iraq possessed an unrivaled civilizational history that ought to place the country (and by definition its leadership) at the epicenter of the Arab world. Such predominance in the region, in itself a sought after goal, would also cement the status and prestige of Saddam and the Ba'th inside Iraq.

This early penchant for unilaterally formulating identity would repeat itself more assertively and frequently in later years. From the beginning of the Iraq-Iran War in 1980, through the Kuwaiti crisis and sanctions regime of the 1990s, until the end of the Saddamist era, the issue of identity in Iraq would simply become a ploy to serve the President's political needs, particularly as he would marshal all the state's totalitarian agencies of cultural production and information dissemination in an effort to penetrate the consciousness of Iraqis and shape their conception of who they are.

Core and fundamental concepts, such as notions of identity, which analysts usually treat as independent variables were thus transformed by Saddam into dependent variables, used to serve the paramount interests of the state, which in actuality meant his own interests, since to Saddam the two sets of interests were coterminous. Thus in 1979, as talk of unity with Syria became rampant, Saddam would tell a high-level meeting in Iraq: "If we are in control, then we welcome unity with open arms. The larger and richer country (which Iraq was) should be in control. And Baghdad has to be the unity's capital."[50] After all, he had not invested all the political and intellectual capital in cementing an independent Iraqi identity through "educational" addresses and speeches and resurrecting Iraq's pre-Arab Mesopotamian history to see all of it at the service of Syria's president, Hafiz al-Asad!

The outbreak of war with the Islamic Republic of Iran in September 1980 faced Saddam with a dilemma that soon forced on him a re-evaluation of identity preferences and options. A major factor in Saddam's decision to invade Iran in September 1980 was his fear of the possible appeal of Iran's Shi'ite ayatollahs to the majority Shi'ite population in Iraq, and there can be little doubt that the ayatollahs themselves were aware of this particular vulnerability. From the very beginning of the war, their appeals to the Iraqis were couched in unabashed religious terms, consistently invoking the Shi'ite venerated holy sites in the Iraqi cities of Najaf and Karbala.[51] In formulating a response, Saddam calculated that the ayatollahs' Persian ethnicity constituted their major point of weakness. It was around this time that Saddam's uncle and father-in-law, Khayr Allah Tilfah published a best seller in which he asserted that "God erred in creating three things: Persians, Jews and flies."[52] Saddam would thus use the ethnic banner of Arabism as the most effective identity that would separate the "Arab" Shi'ites from the "Persian" ayatollahs of Iran, regardless of the sectarian proximity that existed between the two communities. Accordingly, Saddam undertook an "identity shift," this time vigorously promoting historically based Arabist symbolism. Thus, the war was quickly likened to the famed battle of al-Qadissiya, when the Arabs of the Peninsula defeated Sassanid Persia in AD 637 and expelled the Persians from Iraq. Indeed the war, popularly and in vigorous governmental propaganda, came to be known as *Qadissiyat Saddam*, the Qadissiya of Saddam.

Another example of the use of historical imagery in emphasizing the ethnic divide between Arab and Persian Shi'ites was to extol the Arab ethnicity of the founders of their sect. Saddam and his agents of cultural production would place a huge banner at the entrance of the Imam 'Ali mosque in Najaf, the holiest religious site in Shi'ite Islam, which declared: "[W]e take pride at the presence here of our great father 'Ali, because he is a leader of Islam, because he is the son in law of the prophet, and because he is an Arab."[53]

This emphasis on Iraq's Arab identity did not mean that other identities were not invoked. Many references were made to the unity of the "Iraqi nation," reminding the Iranian "Persians" that Sunnis, Shi'ites, and other sects formed a unified Iraqi nation that is "fighting to safeguard its values and new spirit."[54] Yet more often than not such invocations of Iraqi nationalism would be linked to the larger ethnic Arab bond,[55] particularly since by the 1980s, Saddam and his propagandists had fused the Mesopotamian and Arab identities into each other.[56] On other occasions, faced as he was with Iran's religious onslaught, Saddam found it prudent to reiterate the country's commitment to Islamic principles. Thus, for instance, responding to the ayatollahs' accusation that Iraq's practices and policies were un-Islamic, the government's mouthpiece, *al-Thawra*, retorted: "The people and the leaders of Iraq believe in Islam as a religion and as a heritage."[57] Again, citing the "heritage" of Islam is hardly coincidental as, both Iraqis and Iranians know, Muslim heritage is fundamentally Arab.

Not only were allusions to other identities infused almost always with an Arab dimension, the frequency of references to the Arab character of Iraq dwarfed all other identity representations. The fact that throughout the duration of the Iraq-Iran War no real dissension occurred among the rank and file of the Iraqi army, the majority of which was Shi'ite, suggests more than just a passing coincidence between regime and populace over the centrality of the Arab identity.

By the end of the 1980s, however, a new orientation had begun to slowly erode the full-fledged commitment to Arab identity. Perhaps because the Iranian threat had receded after the death of Iran's uncompromisingly belligerent leader, Ayatollah Khomayni in 1989, or because of the poor performance of the cadres of the virulently Arabist Ba'th party in the Iraq-Iran War, or because of the reluctance of the urban middle class to sacrifice its sons in the war, or a combination thereof, a more primordialist identity, that of tribal solidarity, began to creep into public discourse and policy. In the second half of the 1980s, Saddam made a number of complimentary allusions to tribal values such as courage and sacrifice, and indeed in 1990, the tribal tradition of *ghasl al-'ar bil dam* (erasing dishonor with blood), which allowed relatives of an adulterous woman to kill her, was incorporated into the legal system.[58] However, the real turning point in the latest redefinition of identity occurred in the wake of Saddam's monumental defeat at the hands of the international coalition in February 1991.

Iraq's military collapse precipitated major revolts in the Shi'ite south and Kurdish north, which Saddam was barely able to survive. What followed was the most intense crisis of his rule. His prestige severely tarnished and his hold on power uncertain, Saddam also had to contend with debilitating international sanctions. As his support base narrowed among the urban middle classes, who were severely hit by the sanctions-induced economic deprivations, Saddam turned to tribal solidarity and loyalty.

On the surface, this was a curious choice for a leader who had always publicly extolled the virtues of modernity, and had consistently reiterated his commitment to the vigorously anti-tribal Ba'th Party. Yet, as a personal value not publicly trumpeted, tribalism was embedded in Saddam's psyche. From the very beginning of his rule, Tikrit, the town of Saddam's birth, had provided a disproportionate number of the country's ruling elite, as well as the support base for the regime. A tribesman at heart, the Iraqi leader well appreciated the advantages of *al-'Asabiyya al-Qabaliyya* (tribal solidarity) in defending the regime. Members of tribes and clans from Tikrit and the Sunni heartland filled pivotal political and security positions, as well as the ranks of the elite Republican Guard divisions. But painstakingly projecting the image of the modern, forward-looking, and impassioned believer in Ba'thist principles that denigrated tribalism as the "epitome of backwardness and social reaction,"[59] Saddam was careful not to advertise his regime's dependence on tribe, region, and clan or to define tribalism as a central element of Iraq's national identity.

The events that immediately followed the Iraqi defeat, particularly the March 1991 Shi'ite revolt in the south, persuaded Saddam of the benefits of tribes and tribal values to his regime. The troops that quickly and savagely put an end to the rebellion were drawn mainly from tribes that inhabited the Sunni provinces of Anbar and Salah al-Din. Additionally, a number of southern Shi'ite tribes which Saddam had visited, and to which he had extended financial support, either sided with the regime or remained neutral.[60] The lesson was not lost on Saddam.

Over the following years, as the country sank into an abyss of endless economic woes and social disintegration, brought about by international sanctions, the beleaguered President, by word and deed, began elevating tribal identity to the forefront of Iraqi consciousness. He was now no longer coy about extolling the centrality of the tribe in Iraq's social structure or the virtues of tribal values and custom. He would declare in major gatherings and under the full glare of television lights that tribes represented "all of the Iraqi people [and] all of the nation's principles."[61] Indeed the Iraqi state was an extension of the tribes in the way both cherished certain values and traditions and rejected others.[62] The people of Iraq, Saddam would affirm, had become "a single tribe."[63] Even the virulently anti-tribal Ba'th Party would be characterized by the ever more eager president as "the tribe encompassing all tribes."[64] Saddam's reluctance in the 1970s to project a tribal identity had all by disappeared in the 1990s.

And it is not as though this was a strictly one-way process. The tribes responded with public demonstrations of support for their hero president, *Shaykh al-Shiyukh* and *Shaykh al-Mashayikh* (Chief of All Chieftains), which appeared with ever greater frequency on the television screen. More crucially, supportive tribes would become increasingly a security arm of the regime. A number of anti-government disturbances in the 1990s in the south were put down with tribal help. This would be followed by public declarations of tribal fidelity to Saddam.[65] A grateful Saddam would label the loyal tribes "the swords of the state" and in a significant expansion of tribal jurisdiction, would decree that all those who were pursued by the law and who sought refuge within the tribal domain would not be prosecuted.[66] This decree covered even what to Saddam constituted the most heinous of crimes, army desertion.

Saddam's *al-hamla al-imaniya* (the faith campaign), begun in the early 1990s, while religious in nature, was nevertheless fundamentally in tune with the traditional beliefs and values of tribesmen, and consequently cemented the increasing projection of tribal identity. New laws were enacted that were aimed at curbing practices which, to tribesmen and villagers, epitomized the corrupt ways of city life. In May 1992, the regime cracked down on nightclubs and alcohol consumption. Opening hours were reduced and the issuance of new licenses was stopped. The number of nightclubs in Baghdad was reduced from forty to eighteen.[67] Two years later, in a decree signed by Saddam, alcohol was banned in all places except the home and private parties.[68] Furthermore, a series of governmental decrees concerning theft and desertion reflected tribal conservative proclivities. The RCC introduced hand amputation for theft and robbery, and foot amputation for a second offense,[69] while deserters would be liable to have their ears amputated.[70] The same fate was visited on educated and well-trained Iraqis who were caught on the border trying to illicitly leave the country.[71] Women, too, would have their freedoms curtailed as they now, in this last decade of the 20th century, would be prohibited from travel abroad unless accompanied by a male relative from the paternal side of their immediate family.[72] All this was done to a chorus of mounting emphasis on religious symbolism, which in itself constituted a repudiation of the modernism and secularism of city attitudes, so alien to tribal sensitivities.

The prevalence of tribal values was highlighted in 1996 in a savage act of retribution that was as bizarre as it was deadly. This time it would involve members of Saddam's own family. In August 1995, an inner family conflict that was precipitated by Saddam's son, 'Uday, was to lead to the defection of two of Saddam's cousins who were also his sons-in-law. They then proceeded to spill the beans on Saddam's weapons of mass destruction. After a five-month stay in Amman, Jordan, the two took leave of their senses and decided to return to Iraq, having been promised forgiveness and safe passage by Saddam and his equally homicidal son. Once in Iraq, they were separated from their wives (Saddam's daughters) and quickly killed. As a clear testimony of this tribally laced era, their defection was treated not only as a treasonous act against the state, but also as an unforgivable infidelity against tribal honor. Indeed, their ritualized execution was carried out not by state institutions, but, as the official *al-Thawra* would proudly declare on its front page, by "heroic youths from the (clans of) Al 'Abd al-Ghaffour and Al Abu Sultan,"[73] members of Saddam's own Majid clan of the Bayjat tribe.

There is ample evidence that the emphasis by the state and its institutions of cultural production and information dissemination on glorifying tribal values and in the process building a tribal identity seeped through to the public at large. In the first decade of Ba'thist control, when there was concerted denigration of tribal proclivities as retrogressive and out of step with modernity, people did not advertise, indeed were consciously embarrassed about, tribal affiliation. In the 1990s, however, there was almost a tribal revival, a bandwagon effect, as people took their cue from their President. Why would anyone be coy about their tribal lineage, when that heritage was glorified constantly on television screens and in newspapers. This phenomenon became publicly discernible as an ever-increasing number of people attached their tribal or regional affiliation to their names. The list of names of those elected to the National Assembly in March 1995, printed in newspapers and broadcast repeatedly on radio and television, would read like a *Who's Who* in contemporary Iraqi tribes.[74] And then there was the scene, shown repeatedly on television, of the hospital bed occupied by 'Uday after the unsuccessful attempt on his life in December 1996 as it was visited day after day by people dressed, almost uniformly, in tribal garb. Indeed, the *'Abaya*, the cloak worn by tribesmen, became a fashion statement for urban males in the streets of Baghdad and other major cities. As an indicator of the increasing prevalence of tribal values in urban society in the 1990s, studies showed a discernible decline in the status of women and in the opportunities accorded to them.[75] And in the days just prior to the collapse of Saddam's regime in 2003, it was almost surreal to see a parade of Iraqi officials, specialists, and experts on *al-Jazeera* and *al-'Arabiya* television, all of them urbane and impeccably groomed, with doctorates from Western universities, some married to Western women and speaking English at home, make references to tribal honor and solidarity as they spoke about American perfidy, its hegemonic ambitions, and the lies it spread about weapons of mass destruction in Iraq.

As a sub-state identity, tribal solidarity would inevitably compete with and ultimately undermine attachment to the all-encompassing Iraqi identity. As state and society turned to particularistic loyalties, other particularisms gained momentum as well. With the gradual contraction of the regime's support base in the 1990s, Saddam's tribalism inevitably would become progressively partial to his Sunni domain,[76] where the bulk of the state's privileges and resources would be directed. There was of course little reason for the Sunni population to advertise a Sunni identity, since by the mid-1990s state politics were in essence Sunni politics, and state institutions had become enwrapped by a Sunni ideational cloak. Conversely, in the south the intensification of tribal identity was accompanied by a parallel cementation of Shi'ite identity. The difference between the two identities was that while the former could be publicized, the latter had to be concealed for fear of the sinister and unforgiving power of the Sunni state. No such hedging existed in the north, where the Kurds, under the protection of the American-imposed no-fly zone, embraced a fully fledged Kurdish identity that was nourished by purposeful policies of cultural exclusiveness. The consequent fragmentation of Iraqi identity was to come to the fore fully after the institution of American dominion over Iraq in 2003.

Conclusion

The political and social landscape of the Iraqi state under Ba'thist rule, particularly Saddamist rule, constituted a marked and fundamental departure from the earlier periods of Iraqi history. One can argue that certain features of the monarchy's tribal proclivities or Qasim's personalization of politics or 'Aref's Sunni tribalism were the building blocks, effectively the "usable past,"[77] that allowed for the monstrous political and social order that Iraq became under Saddam. There can be little doubt that traces of earlier tendencies, practices, and policies can be discerned in the Saddamist era. But to argue that these somehow informed (or worse, were responsible for) the development of Saddam's political order is at best a gross oversimplification.

Saddam's Iraq was the exclusive creation of the man who effectively ruled the country for almost thirty-five years. He constructed and, over time, refined a relentless police state that was defined almost solely by its pervasive and barbaric agencies of coercion. Such coercion was not only physical but intellectual as his institutions of cultural production facilitated an adulatory milieu that was dedicated to no other purpose but the indulgent aggrandizement of the President. The authoritarianism of Nuri, Qasim, and the 'Aref brothers is so dwarfed by Saddam's procrustean totalitarianism that comparisons are not only untenable, but invidious as well. No policy of any other leader or government of Iraq even approximates to Saddam's genocidal assaults on his own people, his malevolent intrusion into the lives of its citizens, and his cavalier exploitation and manipulation of national symbols and institutions, such as identity and democracy. At no time since the birth of the monarchical state of Iraq in 1921 were fundamental values, rights, and beliefs so utterly subjugated to the dictates, quirks, and ramblings of the country's hero-president. Unlike earlier authoritarian periods in Iraq, and much like the Soviet Union under Stalin, Saddam's Iraq was a country that was held hostage to the will and whim of one omnipresent tyrant.

CHAPTER ELEVEN

Politics in the New Era, 2003–

On March 20, 2003, The United States and Britain, aided by smaller forces from a few other countries, crossed into Iraq from Kuwait and in a swift and overwhelming military campaign defeated the Iraqi army in less than three weeks, formally occupying Baghdad on April 9. On that day, television cameras captured the unforgettable and, a few years earlier, un-imaginable scene of a U.S. tank, cheered on by Iraqis, topple a huge statue of Saddam Husayn in central Baghdad. That simple, yet momentous, act of bravado signaled the end of the thirty-five-year Ba'thist/Saddamist era. Saddam, his two sons, key members of his clan, and all of the other high-ranking figures of his regime went into hiding, many in the Sunni sections of Baghdad or in the Sunni tribal heartland north and west of the capital city. By the end of the year, however, the vast majority of those had sur-rendered or been captured or killed. Saddam's two sons, 'Uday and Qusay were killed in July. And any hopes harbored by those who desired a return to pre-invasion days were fully dashed, when on December 13, 2003, Saddam himself was captured.

The publicly stated reason for the invasion was Saddam's possession of weapons of mass destruction (WMDs) and his links with international Islamist terrorists. On February 5, 2003, U.S. Secretary of State Colin Powell told the United Nations Security Council that Saddam was manu-facturing WMDs, which, given his terrorist associations and his hatred of the United States, constituted a grave danger to the American people.[1] The subsequent failure to find these WMDs and to establish credible Iraqi links with the Islamist terrorist organization, al-Qa'ida, seriously under-mined the legitimacy of American claims. It is probably more likely that from the very beginning the Bush Administration, or more precisely in-fluential elements within it, made the removal of Saddam Husayn a central plank of the administration's policy. According to Paul O'Neill, Bush's first secretary of the treasury, it was almost immediately after the inauguration, that toppling Saddam became "topic 'A'" in meetings of the National Security Council. "There was a conviction," relates O'Neill, "that Saddam was a bad person and that he needed to go."[2] It might have been the realization that the severe economic sanctions imposed by the United Nations were no longer tenable. Manipulated by a pitiless regime, the dire impact of the sanctions was felt by the Iraqi people, not their targeted President. International public opinion, along with more and more Third World and European governments, were turning against the sanctions. The chorus of "end the human tragedy in Iraq" was getting louder by the day and drawing thousands of demonstrators. The possibility, even probability, of an end to the sanctions regime would have added urgency to Washington's concern over a tyrant who was suspected of possessing WMDs, who at various times during his rule had harbored, supported, and used the services of a plethora of terrorist groups, and whose past was replete with irredentist and aggressive threats and behavior.

DIRECT RULE, APRIL 2003–JUNE 2004

Whatever the reasons for the invasion, the United States found itself on April 9, 2003 the hegemonic power in Iraq, faced with the responsibilities of governance. And indeed until June 28, 2004, when sovereignty was transferred to the Iraqis, the United States (with some input by the British) ruled Iraq directly through a mostly American administration in Baghdad called the Coalition Provisional Authority (CPA). A month into the occupation of Iraq, L. Paul Bremer, a hardened diplomat became the head of CPA with the title U.S. Presidential Envoy and Administrator.

The CPA was confronted over the following months with an array of difficulties, some of which at times, to the surprise of many, seemed insurmountable. In an interview in September 2003, Powell would confide that an "unanticipated aspect of the post war occupation was the extent to which the entire structure of military and civil society collapsed so completely as the war ended, leaving a vast problem for the American troops to handle."[3] Much of the trouble came from the Sunni areas, recipients of Saddam's generous largess. But beyond the monetary and economic shortfall, the minority Sunnis, who, as we have seen, had ruled Iraq since the formation of the state in 1921, seemed unable to accept the inevitable loss of their status and the eclipse of their political fortunes. The area north and west of Baghdad, which had staffed much of Saddam's military apparatus and secret police, quickly became the center of resistance to the American occupation. Compounding the problem was a seemingly endless stream of infiltrators from neighboring countries, most of whom were Islamist *jihadists* ready to martyr themselves for the cause of inflicting abundant harm on the infidel Americans. To the local Sunni insurgents the addition of these suicidal and murderous fanatics was a sure sign of God's blessings.

The escalating resistance to the occupation was hardly helped (some would say was caused) by major policy blunders committed by Bremer and the CPA. Less than two weeks after assuming his responsibilities, Bremer issued two orders; one dissolving all regular Iraqi military forces and another banning all Ba'th Party members from taking part in public life. These would prove to be costly mistakes. The point is not that these two institutions should have been allowed to carry on "business as usual." By any measure, Saddam's bloated army was the mainstay of his coercive rule, and the Ba'th Party functioned as an instrument of intimidation to dragoon Iraqi society into line behind the hero-president. The CPA was not amiss in thinking that Iraqis would be better off without such predatory entities in their midst.

The consequential error lay in the timing. Looking over the horizon instead of just down the road, Bremer and the CPA forgot to ask themselves what it might mean to turn thousands of military officers loose on the streets without at first even the promise of monetary compensation. Similarly, to proscribe all Ba'thists without exception from taking part in reconstruction was to exclude most of the very Iraqi professionals whose services will have proved crucial in rebuilding the country. Given the ideological decay that permeated the ranks of the Party in the 1990s, the bulk of the Party's rank and file were nominal members at best, whose Party card simply meant better job prospects. It would have been wiser for the CPA to have begun with wide-ranging investigations aimed at identifying human rights violators and active Saddamists among Party members and military officers before dismissing them without imbursement.

It is almost a certainty that in the first year of the occupation the initial sparks of the insurgency were masterminded by Ba'thists and ex-soldiers. As the year went on, the insurgency spread, grew more violent, and became more sophisticated, showing clear signs of professional military expertise. As the range and intensity of attacks increased, American soldiers responded with mounting belligerence and waning regard for Iraqi cultural norms and sensitivities.[4] American and coalition forces soon found themselves in the unenviable position of responding ever more harshly to attacks while supposedly trying to win civilian hearts and minds.

Beyond its costs in life and material, the deteriorating security situation had a deleterious impact on the socioeconomic development of the country that, more than any other factor, contributed to the mounting malaise. In the words of Larry Diamond, an eminent academic who had joined the CPA as an advisor to Paul Bremer, the gathering insurgency undermined

> postwar construction at every turn. Electricity grids could not be revived, oil facilities could not be repaired, reconstruction jobs could not be commissioned, supplies could not be delivered, civil society could not organize, and a transition to democracy could not move forward because of the pervasive terrorist, criminal and insurgent violence.[5]

The violence also had significant political ramifications. Initially, the Bush Administration entertained the idea of a longer-term occupation, similar to the situation in post-World War II Japan.[6] The violence soon dissuaded Washington from such folly. Instead, a decision was made to transfer sovereignty to the Iraqis by the end of June 2004. In the meantime, an Iraqi Governing Council (IGC) was appointed in mid-July 2003 to provide an Iraqi face to decision-making. Bremer decided that membership of the IGC should reflect the ethnosectarian composition of the country. While this move was initially applauded for giving fair representation to groups such as the Shi'ites and Kurds who had been excluded by Saddam Husayn from participation in the political process, it was in hindsight the one decision that would open the way for the institutionalization of ethnosectarianism in the country's body politic.

While the IGC, hindered by the spread of violence, niggling dissensions within its ranks, and Bremer's veto powers, effected precious little economic or social progress, the committee tasked by Bremner and the IGC with writing a temporary constitution was able to come up with the Transitional Administrative Law (TAL) which was signed by the IGC on March 8, 2004. This cleared the way for the transfer of sovereignty to the Iraqis. In early June, the IGC dissolved itself and created a government under the premiership of Ayad 'Allawi, an ex-Ba'thist who in the early 1990s had created an anti-Saddam organization based in London. On June 28, 2004, Paul Bremer left Iraq and the CPA era came to an end.

High Hopes for Democracy, July 2004–May 2006

'Allawi's government, which followed the same ethnosectarian formula in the apportionment of Cabinet portfolios, would be a caretaker administration empowered by TAL to prepare for Iraq's first elections. The TAL had set a strict timetable for the country's transition to democracy: elections by the end of January 2005 which would produce a transitional parliament and government that would draft a permanent constitution and put it to the country for approval in a referendum no later than the middle of October, followed by general elections to take place by mid-December. The 'Allawi government would work closely with an independent electoral commission that Bremer made sure to establish before leaving Iraq.

But if the long-suffering population had thought that stability would come with the transfer of sovereignty to the Iraqis they would immediately have their hopes cruelly dashed. The fledgling political order would come under a concerted two-pronged assault that in the summer and fall of 2004 would create the worst conditions of instability since the fall of Saddam. West of Baghdad in the Anbar Province, the city of Fallujah had become the center of the Sunni Arab insurrection and the headquarters of the foreign *jihadists*. To the capital's south, a young Shi'ite cleric with a revered family name made a power grab by hurling armed followers against coalition forces. It was clear to 'Allawi's new interim government and its U.S. military advisors that these forces—each essentially opposed to democracy—would have to be defeated in order for elections to go forward on time.

The easier of the two tasks was tackled first. After clashing with Muqtada al-Sadr's Mahdi army in Baghdad in April 2004, coalition forces along with some Iraqi troops mounted a more a effective campaign against the Shi'ite militia in August for over two weeks in a number of southern towns, especially the Shi'ite shrine city of Najaf. Defeated and with nowhere to go, remnants of the Mahdi militia holed up inside the revered Imam 'Ali Mosque. But the narrowness of their support base in Najaf became clear around the month's end as thousands of Shi'ites, acting at the urging of Iraq's most senior cleric Ayatollah 'Ali al-Sistani, marched to the mosque and compelled the remaining few hundred fighters to leave without encountering any serious resistance.

Fallujah presented a more menacing challenge. Long home to many members of Saddam's military and police forces, Fallujah and the other towns of the Sunni domain had no stake in a new order that was obviously and inevitably going to diminish their political and economic status. Fallujah in particular had been a haven for militant Sunni fundamentalist preachers even under Saddam. These clerics had made the place a hotbed of radicalized Islam that became a magnet for foreign Muslim extremists after Saddam fell. These bloodthirsty Islamists formed an alliance of convenience with Saddam's old cadres, and the two groups orchestrated daily attacks on government and coalition forces in Baghdad, and established increasingly unchallenged dominion over many parts of the Sunni districts. A half-hearted effort in April failed to dislodge the Sunni militants. But in early November U.S. Army and Marine Corps units supported by Iraqi commandoes began an assault on the city that would involve fierce house-to-house fighting and would last for over six weeks. By mid-December the city was secured with insurrection elements either killed or expelled from the city.

The capture of Fallujah was seen at the time as a defining victory not just for the United States and the nascent Iraqi security forces, but also for the government of Ayad 'Allawi. The Prime Minister had shown toughness and a determination not to cower to particularistic interests, which many thought would auger well for his electoral chances in January. With military victory, however, came political fallout. While the fighting was still going on, Sunni leaders started a determined campaign to delay the elections, citing bitterness over Fallujah as well as the continuing grave lack of security in the Sunni areas. The stress on 'Allawi's ethnosectarian Cabinet was mounting, calling into question its ability to meet the deadline for elections. And, when moderate Sunni leaders such as Interim President Ghazi al-Yawer joined the chorus for postponing the elections, it appeared as though the Sunnis would get their way. But senior Shi'ite clerics, most notably Ayatollah Sistani, would not allow it. From the very beginning, these men had understood that a democratic transition would work in favor of Iraq's Shi'ite majority. Sistani and his associates had accordingly become Iraq's most consistent and effective advocates of elections and parliamentary representation, demanding that the Sunni Council of Muslim Scholars support the January vote and rallying Shi'ite opinion with religious edicts on the sacred duty of going to the polls. The Kurds, for their part, needed little encouragement to vote in large numbers; they had a major stake in designing a constitution that would safeguard their cultural and political autonomy.

With the postponement strategy failing, Sunni leaders began trying to spoil the election in advance. Calling publicly and vociferously for a general boycott, and greeting the murderous acts of Sunni terrorists with a blind eye if not a subtle nod, these leaders were hoping to see turnout depressed far enough to undermine the vote's legitimacy. Here again, however, the new political reality made itself felt. In the elections that took place on January 30, 2005, a turnout of over 70 percent among the Shi'ites and over 80 percent in Kurdish areas resulted in an overall national turnout rate of better than 58 percent, making the elections a huge and indisputable success.

From a packed field of more than 7,500 candidates belonging to a bewildering range of parties, three groups emerged as the powerhouses of the new 275-seat National Assembly. The biggest player, with 140 seats (or just over 51 percent, a slight "seat bonus" given its 48 percent vote share), was the United Iraqi Alliance (UIA), a collection of mostly Shi'ite groups that enjoyed Sistani's unofficial but widely known blessing. The Kurdistan Alliance, a fusion of the forces of the two major Kurdish political figures, Mas'oud al-Barazani and Jalal al-Talabani, followed with 75 seats while the Iraqi List of Premier 'Allawi mustered 40 seats. Nine minor parties accounted for the remaining 20 seats.

Given the breakdown of the vote, it was abundantly clear that Iraqis overwhelmingly voted in accordance with their ethnic and sectarian identities. Almost all Kurds (probably over 95 percent) voted for the Kurdistan Alliance, some 75 percent of Shi'ites voted for the UIA, and at least 75 percent of Sunnis opted for their sectarian choice—boycott. Consequently, only 17 of the assembly's 275 members were Sunnis, and most belonged to secular and nationalist lists. In this predominantly sectarian environment, it was inevitable that 'Allawi's secular Iraq List would garner only 40 seats, less than 15 percent of the Assembly's membership.

The ethnosectarian character of the voting left some puzzled, particularly as 'Allawi and his party waged the most sophisticated and expensive electoral campaign. Using secular and Iraqi identity symbolisms, and publicizing its professional membership, the Iraqi list projected itself as the only party with the expertise, toughness, and national commitment to lift the country from its downward security and socioeconomic spiral. But to no avail. Whether ethnosectarian identities had become entrenched in the Saddamist era and then institutionalized in the makeup of the IGC and the 'Allawi Cabinet, or whether the insurgency so undermined party organization and activities that the electorate would revert to traditional allegiances, was not clear at the time. Yet in retrospect, it was the first concrete indication of the primacy of sub-state ethnosectarian loyalties, a fact to be endorsed in the next general elections eleven months later.

In the wake of the January 2005 elections negotiations of great length and complexity ensued. While the strict demands of the TAL were a factor in driving these, perhaps a more important cause was the conscious decision of the parties themselves, especially the UIA, to go for inclusiveness rather than speed. Soon after the polls closed, UIA leaders said publicly that they would seek to build consensus rather than press their majority status. Fearing the potential for more violence, secession, or civil war, they rejected the idea of trying to form an all-Shi'ite coalition to steamroll parliamentary opposition. Instead, UIA leaders promised a national-unity government that would include Kurds and Sunnis as full partners. To achieve this, not only a general climate of consensus but also a specific apportionment of powers (that is, Cabinet seats) was needed. It was hardly surprising that a Cabinet was not formed until April 27; the fruit of three full months of intense negotiations and bargaining.

The Kurds had made it clear from the start that they would bargain hard. They saw that the Sunni boycott had handed their alliance their biggest-ever seat share and with it a unique chance to press tall demands. These included the preservation of the Kurds' *peshmerga* militias as a separate armed force, a declaration that multi-ethnic Kirkuk is a "Kurdish" city, some choice Cabinet ministries, a sizeable share of national oil revenues, and even expansion of the territory of Kurdistan into parts of the predominantly Arab provinces of Diyala and Ta'mim. It took about two months for the UIA to convince the Kurds that, while early deals could address some of their concerns, such thorny issues as the status of Kirkuk would have to follow TAL strictures and await the deliberations and decisions of the full National Assembly.

The Sunnis posed a tougher challenge. The Kurds may have bargained hard, but their commitment to the democratic process was not in doubt. While the Sunnis' low turnout left them with just seventeen seats, both the UIA and the Kurdish Alliance saw the need to give the Sunnis Cabinet and other administrative posts, and so buckled down to protracted and at times stormy dealings with the small yet fractious Sunni caucus in the Assembly. Nevertheless, having emerged as the real losers, and not wanting the political process to pass them by, the Sunnis, at times shrill in their rejectionist public stance, in effect began to show traces of flexibility that had not been part of their earlier political repertoire.

The new government under the premiership of Ibrahim al-Ja'fari, leader of *al-Da'wa* Party, a constituent member of the Shi'ite UIA alliance was finally formed on April 27, 2005. Ja'fari apportioned Cabinet portfolios not just among Shi'ites, Sunnis, and Kurds, but also among Party members from within the UIA. While the concept of a national unity government was supposed to eliminate, or at least minimize, conflict, and thus move the country finally toward reconciliation, in reality it contributed to political and administrative stagnation. By the fall of 2005, it had become clear to all that Ja'fari's authority over his ministers was marginal at best. Indeed, each ministry became almost a separate canton, where the loyalty of the minister would be directed to the leader of his party or ethnosectarian group rather than to the hapless Premier. It was in such a milieu that militias and insurgency groups grew and became even more violent as they now could count on governmental and bureaucratic support.

The government's failure to subdue the escalating chaos manifested in its inability to rein in the Sunni insurgents or the array of anarchic Shi'ite militias was matched by its impotence to effect any improvement in the social and economic conditions of the country. If people would look for a silver lining it would be that the life span of the government was limited and its main task was to draft a permanent constitution, have it approved, and hold general elections by year's end.

On these two central issues Ja'fari's government fared better. The intense horse trading among the various groups, but particularly with the Sunnis, had delayed the formation of the constitutional committee, and hence deliberation could not begin until early July. Faced with an August 15 deadline, and a host of very contentious, yet far-reaching and consequential, issues, the disparate and cumbersome committee produced a compromise document, which contained no less than fifty-three articles that were left to be resolved at some point in the future. Even so, the Sunni members refused to validate the document. What concerned them most was the possibility that Iraq would collapse into a loose federal structure (almost a confederal system) of Kurdish and Shi'ite regions to the north and south, respectively, leaving the Sunnis with a central region bereft of resources and thus political influence.

As the October 15 date for the referendum approached, intense bargaining among the various groups continued, this time with heavy American involvement. The goal was to try and reach some political compromise that would address Sunni concerns, particularly those relating to the kind of federal structure envisaged for the country. Three days prior to the referendum, the Shi'ite and Kurdish leaders acceded to the demand of the largest Sunni party, the Iraqi Islamic Party (IIP), for an additional article that called for a new constitutional committee to be formed after the general elections, with the task of implementing within four months of its creation "necessary amendments to the constitution."[7] It was immediately announced that the IIP would urge its followers not only to participate in the referendum, but also to vote for the constitutional document.

If by bringing the IIP on board, the Shi'ite-Kurdish majority thought it had overcome Sunni opposition to the constitution and the referendum, they were soon to realize their error. While Shi'ite and Kurdish areas voted overwhelmingly for the adoption of the constitution, two Sunni provinces voted heavily against it, and a third registered a fifty-five percent negative vote. In fact, the Sunnis narrowly missed defeating the constitution altogether, since Iraq's Administrative Law had stipulated that a two thirds majority against the constitutional document in any three of Iraq's eighteen provinces would result in its rejection. While the Sunni negative vote exhibited the community's continued displeasure with its diminishing political fortunes, and while, like in January, the Sunnis failed again to achieve their goal, the feeling among their political leaders was that they made a far more potent statement through participation in the referendum vote than they had done in January when they boycotted the elections. This time around, therefore, there were hardly any calls for boycotting the December 2005 general elections, which were designed to elect a four-year National Assembly that would put in place a president, a presidency council, a prime minister, and a cabinet.

The Iraqi Independent Electoral Commission (IIEC) set a deadline of October 28 for party registration. The following day, the IIEC announced that 228 political parties, coalitions, and other entities had registered to contest the elections. It was obvious from the start, however, that in spite of the abundant assortment of parties and party lists, five coalitions would claim the lion's share of Assembly seats. These were the UIA, having now acquired stronger Islamist credentials with the withdrawal of some Shi'ite secularists such as Ahmad Chalabi's Congress Party and the incorporation of a group loyal to the firebrand cleric Muqtada al-Sadr, the Kurdistan Alliance, two Sunni lists, the Iraqi Concord (*al-Tawafuq*) Front and the Iraqi Front for National Dialogue, and Ayad 'Allawi's secular Iraqi National List.[8] Once the parties and coalitions were announced, the electoral campaign was to begin in earnest.

The most noticeable aspect of the campaign was its intensely localized character. The confluence of geographic and ethnosectarian lines in most areas of Iraq precluded public debates among the various parties and coalitions. Thus for example the UIA or the Concord Front hardly bothered to electioneer in the Kurdish areas of Duhok, Irbil, or Sulaymaniya. By the same token there was hardly any Kurdish presence in the southern Shi'ite provinces or in the Sunni provinces of Anbar and Salah al-Din. Even in the large supposedly multi-ethnic cities, such as Baghdad, Mosul, or Kirkuk, there was on the whole little crossing of ethnosectarian lines within these cities. Rather, the parties focused their energies on cementing support among their own ethnosectarian groups, and were doggedly intent on subverting intrusive efforts by others into their areas.

In such arrangements, the groups that stood to lose most were the secular non-ethnic parties and coalitions, whose performance in the elections depended on conducting an effective national campaign. For example, 'Allawi's Iraqi List, the most sophisticated and best financed of the secular parties, encountered staunch UIA resistance to the group's intrusion into areas considered by the UIA to be its own exclusive domain. 'Allawi's party headquarters were attacked by gunmen in the southern cities of Basra and Nasiriya, and fire bombed in the two holy Shi'ite cities of Najaf and Karbala.[9] Nor were UIA activists sanguine about the placement of Iraqi List banners and posters in Shi'ite areas of Baghdad.[10] No sooner would the 'Allawi posters go up, would groups of UIA supporters, some of them armed, arrive to tear them down. Indeed, in the later stages of the campaign, the UIA upped the ante by producing their own posters in which half of the picture was that of 'Allawi, the other half being occupied by Saddam Husayn, with the caption of "Ba'thists" placed under the pictures. Another UIA poster was emblazoned by the word "criminals," and was a montage forcing together three pictures representing 'Allawi, Saddam, and ex-Israeli Prime Minister Ariel Sharon, who are depicted to be casting appreciative smiles toward one another.[11] These activities ascribed to the UIA targeted not only 'Allawi's Iraqi List. The Sunni coalitions also accused the UIA of attacking its workers in Baghdad to prevent them from putting up posters of Sunni candidates.[12] For its part, the Kurdistan Alliance would complain bitterly that its own banners were removed presumably by Sunni Arabs from non-Kurdish areas in the northern city of Mosul. The Alliance, however, remained mum when the posters of its Kurdish competitor, the Kurdistan Islamic Union, were themselves torn down from walls in Kurdish cities.[13] It seems that what one group considered legitimate electioneering, the other saw as electoral trespassing that needed to be responded to in the most strident of ways.

More unsettling was a wave of assassinations and armed attacks that occurred in Baghdad and other Iraqi cities. A number of these were aimed at Sunni politicians who advocated participation in the elections and rejection of violence. Two days after announcing in a press conference that "non-participation in the coming elections is tantamount to treason,"[14] a prominent leader of the Sunni Iraqi Concord Front was gunned down in broad daylight just north of Baghdad. Indeed, the Front claimed that in one month after it had begun its campaign for the elections, no less than ten of its members were killed, including the head of its organization in the Sunni city of Ramadi. The man was dragged out of a mosque in full view of other worshippers and later executed.[15] Workers for other parties and groups were also killed either in individual attacks or in more coordinated assaults on party headquarters.[16] The then American Ambassador, Zalmay Khalilizad, was moved to publicly censure the spate of killings and other violence.[17] Similarly, the British Ambassador condemned this violence, saying that "any form of attack on or threat against political parties or individuals cannot be acceptable in the new Iraq."[18] Rumors naturally swirled and fingers pointed at a variety of suspects ranging from the al- Qaʻida types to Shiʻite irregulars, but no hard evidence was ever presented. While electoral violence was certainly a disturbing phenomenon, the reality was that neither in its intensity nor in its extensiveness did it go beyond violence levels experienced by other Third World countries during electoral campaigns.

Nevertheless, these problems did compound the difficulties already presented by the general lack of security in the country, which together imposed great limitation on the freedom of movement of party leaders. They consequently seemed to settle on campaigning through the electronic and print media. Satellite and television stations, such as *al-ʻIraqiya, al-Sumeriya,* and *ʻal-ʻArabiya,* broadcast incessant advertisements for the various parties. In this particular endeavor, it was more than evident that ʻAllawi's Iraqi List was by far the slickest and had the deepest pockets. But this was balanced by a plethora of features, interviews, and debates, involving prominent members of most parties, seen on television screens, heard on radio stations, or read in newspapers.

A number of themes emerged from this exposure of party leaders and spokesmen to the public. There was of course the perennial concern over the lack of security, basic services, and economic opportunity. The most blistering verbal attacks came from 'Allawi and other members of the Iraqi National List, who accused the UIA-dominated government of Ibrahim al-Ja'fari of indecisiveness, incompetence, and corruption. Believing it to be a vote-changing issue, 'Allawi zeroed in on the alleged ineptitude of the Ja'fari government, persistently pointing to the ills of the country—the broken down sewage system, the lack of sufficient electrical power, the dearth of job opportunities, inadequate health care, and above all the chaos of everyday life driven by an insurgency against which the government seemed at best unprepared and worst unresponsive. In a widely reported speech delivered at a major conference a few days before the elections, 'Allawi declared that Iraqis no longer "trust a government that has sunk into financial and administrative corruption, that is clueless about tackling a terrorism campaign that is aimed against citizens as well as assembly candidates, and that has left Iraq a weak and divided country on the verge of civil war."[19] Without saying it in so many words, 'Allawi later on in the speech strongly implied that a UIA government will be, as it supposedly was then, committed to doing Iran's bidding in Iraq, and therefore enshrining sectarianism that would inevitably result in the permanent dislocation of the country.

The two Sunni coalitions focused their campaign on what could be construed as a reversal of the security issue. They attacked the government and the Ministry of the Interior (which is in charge of police and security forces) for allegedly unleashing, or at a minimum giving the nod to, irregular Shi'ite militiamen to assassinate innocent Sunnis in retaliation for atrocities committed by the insurgency. They further accused the Minister of Interior of filling the ranks of the police with members of the Shi'ite militia, the Badr Brigade, to which he belonged, thus bestowing the cloak of legitimacy on police violence against the Sunni community. "The government talks of terrorism," a senior member of *al-Tawafuq* said in a TV interview, "but what about government terrorism?"[20] Echoing 'Allawi's accusation, leaders of the Sunni coalitions and parties invoked the ghost of bloody civil war, which they would place squarely on the shoulders of the Ja'fari government and its allegedly sectarian and partisan attitudes and policies.

The second major theme that dominated the campaign debates was the issue of federalism. This issue had been almost symbiotically tied to Kurdish aspirations since the defeat and consequent collapse of Saddam's regime in April 2003. From the very beginning of the new political order, the Kurds had made it clear that the price for their willingness to be part of Iraq was an acceptance by the Shi'ites and Sunnis of a loose federal structure in which Kurdistan, a region comprising at a minimum the three provinces of Irbil, Sulaymaniya, and Duhouk, would be accorded substantial autonomy within Iraq. While initially debate ranged over the issue, it was clear by late summer of 2005 when the constitutional committee was meeting that Kurdistan's autonomy had become a fait accompli. Even the Sunnis grudgingly accepted it.

What brought federalism back into the campaign with increased vigor and virulence was a series of statements made by 'Abd al-'Aziz Hakim, the acknowledged leader of the UIA, proposing a Shi'ite super region of the nine southern provinces, an idea that earned the ire of the Sunnis. Bitter denunciations of a move seen as a precursor for the dismantling of Iraq became a main staple of the Sunni political agenda in the campaign. The Sunni argument, forcefully repeated in the media, was summed up by Adnan al-Dulaimi, the leader of the Sunni *al-Tawafuq*, when he said: "We will not accept the creation of regions in the south and center of Iraq. We only accept the region of Kurdistan because of its historical, geographic and cultural specificities. . . . Such specificities do not apply in the rest of the country."[21] Sunni displeasure, however, did not dissuade Hakim from reiterating his proposal a number of times during the period immediately prior to the elections.

Another issue on which the parties clashed was the role of religion in politics generally, and in the campaign particularly. It was the secular Iraqi List that led the charge, railing against any move to insert religion into politics. Mostly by implication, occasionally in direct reference, the UIA, which as we have seen is composed mainly of Shi'ite Islamist parties, was the target of the verbal assault.[22] Interestingly the Sunni groups, one of its main components being the Iraqi Islamic Party, an offshoot of the Islamist Muslim Brotherhood organization, advocated the separation of religion from politics as well. Obviously, an Islamic state of the Shi'ite variety was hardly palatable to the Sunni fundamentalists. To all this, the UIA was visibly constrained in its defense of the inseparability of religion from politics. The gist of the UIA position was that political decisions are based on considerations of the national interest, but Iraqis after all are devout Muslims who will not be comfortable with Western-type secularism. It seems that the UIA sought to remain true to its religious essence, but it also needed to assure voters that religious beliefs would constitute only one of the many elements that determine public policy.

In this debate over the role of religion in politics, the shadow of Grand Ayatollah 'Ali al-Sistani, the most senior and revered Shi'ite cleric, hovered over all discussions and debates. The reclusive cleric himself did not make public comments or statements during the campaign. His office issued the occasional counsel, and assistants and disciples spoke on his behalf, essentially emphasizing his neutrality.[23] This did not stop the UIA and other Shi'ite groups from appropriating Sistani to their cause by invoking his name, declaring their fidelity to him, and putting his image on their posters,[24] a practice bitterly denounced by other groups, particularly the secular members of the Iraqi List.

Finally, many references were made to the issue of the "occupation" of Iraq by American and coalition forces. But this topic never lived up to the expectation that it was the one "burning" issue that would permeate and loom large over all discussions and debates. No party supported an open-ended occupation, and they all agreed to negotiate with the Americans and their allies some kind of a timetable for withdrawal, taking into consideration existing constraints. Sunni parties and groups, as well as Muqtada al-Sadr, wanted withdrawal to occur at a quicker pace than others. But in effect the more realistic option of a gradual, timetable-driven withdrawal had already been defined in an agreement that was reached a month earlier in a conference of conciliation that was held under the auspices of the Arab League in Cairo and was attended by almost all Iraqi groups and parties.

In light of the sustained and at times intense public debate, it could hardly be said that, by the day of the election on December 15, the public was not aware of where the main coalitions stood on the issues that dominated public discourse. These debates were generally absorbing and at times quite sophisticated, creating the impression that they might (indeed would) have an impact on voter behavior. It seems, however, that when voters finally went to the polling stations, shutting themselves off from the distractions of the campaign, they ended up turning to their primordial

TABLE 11–1
Breakdown of Provincial Voting in December 15 General Elections

Province	Turnout %	Province	Turnout %
Salah al-Din (Sunni)	98	Misan (Shi'ite)	73
Irbil (Kurdish)	95	Najaf (Shi'ite)	73
Duhok (Kurdish)	92	Dhi Qar (Shi'ite)	72
Anbar (Sunni)	86	Baghdad (mixed)	70
Kirkuk (mixed)	86	Nineveh (mixed)	70
Sulaymaniya (Kurdish)	84	Karbala (Shi'ite)	70
Babel (Shi'ite)	79	Wasit (Shi'ite)	68
Diyala (mixed)	75	Mutahna (Shi'ite)	66
Basra (Shi'ite)	74	Qaddisiya (Shi'ite)	65

Source: The Independent Electoral Commission of Iraq, January 20, 2006.

loyalties, very much as they did eleven months earlier in the January 30 elections.

Over 12 million turned up to vote on December 15, representing over 77 percent of the registered voters. Table 11–1 is a breakdown of provincial voting from the highest to the lowest turnout. It was not unexpected that the three Kurdish provinces along with Kirkuk, which has a Kurdish majority, would have some of the highest turnout percentages. The real surprise was the huge turnouts in the Sunni provinces of Salah al-Din and Anbar. The average turnout in the nine Shi'ite provinces was below the national figure at 71 percent, and Baghdad, plagued by daily violence, had one of the lowest turnouts, but still managed a respectable 70 percent. The elections represented the high tide of the country's democratic endeavor. The euphoria however would last but a brief moment as the results would bear witness not to the spread of the all-inclusive democratic spirit, but to the mounting entrenchment of ethnosectarian fissures.

THE PLUNGE INTO ETHNOSECTARIANISM, MAY 2006–FALL 2007

When partial results were announced a few days after the elections, showing a repeat victory for the UIA, a deluge of complaints alleging widespread fraud erupted in Baghdad and Sunni areas. Thousands of demonstrators took to the streets denouncing the Iraqi Independent Electoral

TABLE 11-2

Number of Assembly Seats Won by Parties and Coalitions
in the December 15 Elections

Party/Coalition	Assembly Seats
UIA (Shi'ite)	128
Kurdistan Alliance	53
Concord Front (Sunni)	44
Iraqi List (secular)	25
National Dialogue (Sunni)	11
Kurdish Islamic Union	5
Liberation & Conciliation (Sunni)	3
Risaliyoon (Shi'ite Sadrists)	2
Turkomen Front	1
Iraqi Nation (secular)	1
Yezidi Front	1
Rafidayn List (Christian)	1
Total	275

Source: The Independent Electoral Commission of Iraq, January
20, 2006, reproduced in Adeed Dawisha and Larry Diamond,
"Iraq's Year of Voting Dangerously," *Journal of Democracy*, vol. 17,
no. 2, April 2006, p. 99.

Commission (IIEC) and accusing it of doing the UIA's bidding. The pressure became so intense that the IIEC refrained from publishing the full and final results until an international commission, which arrived in Baghdad in late December, looked into the almost 2,000 complaints that were received by the Commission. By January 17, it had been decided that infractions had indeed occurred, but they were mostly minor in nature, and could not have impacted the final distribution of Assembly seats. Hence, the final and complete results, as shown in Table 11–2, were announced on January 17, 2006.

The results could not have been a clearer statement of the preponderance of ethnosectarian loyalties. Any hopes that the electorate would yield to secular demands to separate religion from politics or to transcend ethnic divisions were completely frustrated by the results of the election. The wish, certainly harbored by the Bush Administration, for a muscular showing by the Iraqi List which would cement 'Allawi's bargaining position, even allow him to emerge as the central character in a secular coalition, was shattered when he ended up losing about 40 percent of the seats his group had received in the January 2005 election. The extent of the ethnosectarian character of the vote is better illustrated when voting is broken down at the provincial level.

The results illustrated in Table 11–3 show that Kurdish parties received 100 percent of the vote in Kurdish areas, Sunni parties received 88 percent of the vote in Sunni areas, and Shi'ite parties received 86 percent of the vote in Shi'ite areas. The same pattern of ethnosectarian preference was repeated in the voting results in the four mixed provinces. Most surprising is that these particularistic proclivities emerged in the voting that occurred outside the country as well among Iraqi expatriates, many of whom had lived for many years and decades in secular democratic countries. Less than 20 percent of the expatriate vote went to 'Allawi's Iraqi List and other secular parties.

The critical difference from the earlier election was that the UIA fell short of an overall majority. And since many of the consequential decisions needed a two thirds majority, looking for coalition partners this time round was for the UIA a political necessity, not a gesture of magnanimity. But in constructing a viable coalition, factors other than just numbers had to be considered. The specter of the insurgency, for instance, made Sunni demands far weightier than their combined fifty-eight seats warranted. Thus while it was obvious to all parties that Sunnis had to be included in the government, the dilemma was how to balance the distribution of Cabinet portfolios among the prospective coalition partners. The debate in the aftermath of the election showed clear disparities in the aspirations and positions of the various parties.[25] While Sunnis talked of a national unity government, implying a kind of equality among the coalition parties, the UIA emphasized a governmental balance based on the results of the elections.

The political structure that emerged in the spring and early summer of 2006 bore an uncanny resemblance to the confessional system in Lebanon. Top-level decision-making positions were distributed along strictly ethnosectarian lines. The Kurd Jalal Talabani assumed the presidency, with a Sunni and a Shi'ite as deputies. The position of Speaker of the Assembly was reserved for a Sunni, and a Shi'ite and a Kurd were voted to be his deputies. The Prime Minister, being necessarily Shi'ite, would have Kurd-

TABLE 11-3
Ethnosectarian Distribution of Assembly Seats

Governorate	Allocated Seats	Shi'ite Lists	Iraqi List	Sunni Lists	Kurdish Lists	Others
Shi'ite						
Basra	16	13	2	1		
Dhi Qar	12	11	1			
Babel	11	9	1	1		
Najaf	8	7	1			
Qaddisya	8	7	1			
Wasit	8	7	1			
Misan	7	6	1			
Karbala	6	5	1			
Muthana	5	5				
Sunni						
Anbar	9			9		
Salah al-Din	8	1	1	6		
Kurdish						
Sulaymaniya	15				15	
Irbil	13				13	
Duhok	7				7	
Mixed						
Baghdad[1]	59	35	8	14	1	1
Nineveh[2]	19	2	2	10	4	1
Diyala[2]	10	2	1	5	2	
Kirkuk[3]	9			3	5	1

Source: The Independent Electoral Commission of Iraq, January 20, 2006, reproduced in Adeed Dawisha and Larry Diamond, "Iraq's Year of Voting Dangerously," *Journal of Democracy,* vol. 17, no. 2, April 2006, p. 100.

[1] Shi'ite majority
[2] Sunni majority
[3] Kurdish majority

ish and Sunni deputies. Indeed, the Herculean balancing act was reserved for the Prime Minister-Elect Nouri al-Maliki, who would try to fill thirty-seven Cabinet portfolios with an eye not necessarily for competence but for an ethnosectarian distribution that would satisfy the various parties nationally. No wonder the country, going through a critical phase, beset by violence, did not have a functioning government until May 20, more than five months after the elections. Maliki had finally been successful in including the bulk of the country's ethnosectarian groups in the Cabinet.

The ethnosectarian composition of the various structures of government was as much a function of, as it was a contributor to, a gathering descent of the country as a whole into ethnosectarian allegiances and loyalties, which soon began to have clear dislocative demographic effects. By late summer 2006, Shi'ites and Sunnis were killing each other in ever-increasing numbers. While certain calculated acts of sedition, such as the bombing of the *al-'Askari* Mosque, one of the most revered shrines in Shi'ite Islam, dramatically heightened tensions and increased Sunni-Shi'ite violence, the elevation of sectarian identity to the forefront of people's consciousness had occurred gradually and purposefully over time. As we have seen, ingrained ethnosectarian identifications and loyalties had existed since the Saddamist era, and the new, post-invasion state institutions would do little to weaken them. On the contrary from the creation of the Iraqi Governing Council a few months after the ouster of Saddam right through to the Maliki government, state institutions themselves seemed to endorse and legitimize particularistic loyalties through purposeful policies and decisions. Once ethnosectarian identity became the defining element in peoples' choices and preferences, and the central knot that tied people into a communal solidarity, violence against the threatening "other," represented in other identities, would be undertaken more readily and with less inhibition.

By the fall of 2006, violence between Sunnis and Shi'ites had measurably increased. Between 110 and 130 people were being killed every day in Iraq, and the vast majority were dying (to say nothing of the many more who were maimed and seriously injured) because of targeted sectarian attacks. Because of the indiscriminate nature of such conflict, people would be victimized simply by where they lived, and consequently, divisions along identity lines would consolidate along geographic boundaries. It was thus predictable that cross-migration would increase either as a result of intimidation or because of people's propensity to be with their own folk in situations of pervasive violence and fear. Thus Basra, the largest and most "mixed" southern Shi'ite city, saw an accelerating migration of Sunnis after a number of Sunni mosques in the city were attacked and Sunni clerics assassinated.[26] Sunnis also flocked out of other southern

Shi'ite cities such as Diwaniya and Nassiriya as Shi'ite militia, notably the al-Mahdi army, acted with increasing disdain for the state's security agencies.

As this was happening, a reverse process was occurring in the Sunni areas to the north and northwest of Baghdad. Shi'ites living in the few mixed areas, particularly the city of Samara and in the province of Diyala, were made to leave in large numbers, as Sunnis embarked on their own campaigns of "sectarian cleansing." Many of the departed Shi'ites headed south, in a way replacing the displaced Sunnis in southern provinces and in Baghdad.

In fact, most disturbing was the violence-perpetrated cross-migration that would occur within Baghdad itself. Because of its urbane and tolerant multi-ethnicism, the Iraqi capital which is home to around twenty-five to thirty percent of Iraq's population had always been perceived and advocated as the bedrock against the country's dislocation. The truth is, however, that probably as much as three-fourths of the city's population lived in largely non-mixed neighborhoods. And in the mixed areas, forced cross-migration gained momentum in 2006. One dramatic illustration of this was a series of incidents that occurred in late summer in *al-Jihad* District, which had a Sunni majority, but happened to be situated south of the airport road in what was conceived of as the northern tip of the Shi'ite domain. After a bomb exploded near a Shi'ite mosque, Shi'ite militia went on a rampage, shooting Sunnis on sight and burning houses, which resulted in an exodus of Sunni families out of the neighborhood. Similar tactics, leading to threat-induced expulsions, also occurred in no less than two dozen mixed districts of Baghdad in 2006.[27] Regardless of governmental efforts, aided by vigorous American military involvement, to respond to this rigidifying of sectarian boundaries ethnosectarian cross-migration would continue unabated.

According to figures from the United Nations Assistance Mission for Iraq, over 700,000 persons were forced to flee their homes due to sectarian violence in the twelve months spanning March 2006 to March 2007, and a large segment of these were displaced in Baghdad, where more than 120,000 moved, or were forced to move, to the relative safety of areas that were predominantly of their own sect.[28] By July 2007, according to the Iraqi Red Crescent Organization, 1,128,000 Iraqis had been internally displaced.[29] Baghdad had the largest concentration of displaced persons, some 200,000 who moved, or were forced to move. These migratory waves, as well as sectarian killings, did not seem to undergo a consequential deceleration even in response to highly publicized governmental security initiatives. Moreover, the figures did not take into account the thousands of Arabs and some Turkomen who were systematically forced out of Kirkuk by the Kurds.

This inevitably would feed separatist tendencies in Iraq, which in the Kurdish areas, as we have seen, had always been potent. Of all the Iraqi provinces, the Kurdish region, comprising the three provinces of Duhok, Irbil, and Sulaymaniya, acquired such broad autonomous powers that it might as well be independent. The Kurds of Kurdistan elected their own president and parliament, had their own cabinet, and boasted a 100,000 strong security force. Most pertinently, the Kurds designed and passed a Kurdish constitution that would override the Iraqi constitution on issues of constitutional disagreement. All this fell within the parameters of a purposeful national project in which young Kurds no longer cared to speak, or make an effort to learn, Arabic. Indeed, young Kurds who were inclined to take Arabic as a second language were looked at with bemusement at best and suspicion at worst.[30]

Shi'ites did not travel along the road of psychological separation as far as the Kurds had. But the difference in their attitude to a unified Iraq since the ouster of Saddam in 2003 was not inconsequential. The Shi'ite community, as a whole, may not have been particularly shrill in their demands for autonomy and/or independence, but they certainly did become more amenable and susceptible to calls from some Shi'ite leaders who agitated for a broadly autonomous region. 'Abd al-'Aziz Hakim, leader of the Supreme Council for Islamic Revolution in Iraq (SCIRI), continued to demand a Shi'ite nine-province region, akin to the Kurdish autonomous region, and parliamentarians from the Shi'ite United Iraqi Alliance (UIA) repeatedly asked for debates on federalism in which the southern provinces would be modeled on Kurdistan.[31] Of course, not all Shi'ites demanded autonomy, certainly not the young and influential Muqtada al-Sadr who liked to portray himself as an Iraqi nationalist, and who thus would reject a separate Shi'ite region. But the mere fact that demands for Shi'ite autonomy were made and discussed publicly pointed to the gradual acceptance of ethnosectarian identities.

One factor that continued to feed separatist sentiment was the state's inability to project power and provide security. According to the renowned 19th century German sociologist Max Weber, state institutions must have a monopoly over the use of physical force.[32] Iraq's security forces in the post-elections period were unable to establish their dominion over the array of military groups that operated in Iraq with carefree abandon. Nor were the state's security institutions considered to be legitimate. The biggest culprits were the police and other Ministry of Interior forces, of whom the Iraqi people perceived with utmost distrust and contempt. Even the Minister of Interior would concede that his ministry was wracked with "corrupt elements that have undertaken terrorist and criminal operations against the Iraqi people."[33] And in a statement that created much controversy, the Sunni Speaker of Parliament, Mahmoud al-Mashhadani, derisively asserted that those who speak of disbanding the militias should know that this would mean the dissolution of the ministries in charge of security.[34]

If the state is perceived as impotent in providing security and basic services, then what incentive do people have to stick with this failed agency? A discernible manifestation of the peoples' mounting indifference to state institutions was a greater tolerance by the population of the various militia groups. These militias may not have been hugely popular; indeed, many of their actions attracted bitter criticisms. Even so, the militias were either (in the best scenario for them) respected for providing a semblance of security and protection, and in some cases, services, or at worst simply feared. In the many clashes between state security forces and various militias, the performance of the government forces, particularly if they did not have the Americans by their side, hardly inspired confidence in their martial capabilities. There can be little doubt that the militias were increasingly perceived as a parallel and/or alternative security agent to the state.

Even when the militias indulged in blatantly errant and lawless activity, their influence vis-à-vis the state did not seem to suffer. On more than one occasion in 2006, blood was spilled over contested turf and over financial gain in the southern city of Basra. Various Shi'ite militias, al-Badr, Fadhila and al-Mahdi army, fought intense battles for control of the oil smuggling routes in the south of Iraq. The fighting necessitated the personal intervention of Prime Minister Maliki, who created an emergency council to run the city and curb militia activity, yet security continued to be contested and oil continued to be smuggled. The problem here was that while the Basra chaos might have heightened people's displeasure with the greedy militia groups, more significantly it dramatized the sheer impotence of the state and its institutions—a far more consequential cognitive and perceptual derivation that could not but auger badly for the future of Iraq as a viable and unified country.

The conflict among the Shi'ite militias in 2006–2007 reflected the personal rivalries that existed among their political leaderships. There was little doubt that the Islamist Shi'ite identity defined the raison d'être of the UIA's four main constituent groups: The SCIRI, al-Da'wa, al-Fadhila, and the Sadrists. But personal tensions and rivalries, as well as policy differences permeated intra-UIA relations. Even before the elections, when unity was at a premium, these differences came to the fore when al-Fadhila announced its withdrawal from the UIA citing unhappiness with SCIRI's leader 'Abd al-'Aziz Hakim, with some of his policies, and his handling of assembly seat distribution. Al-Fadhila ended up remaining part of the UIA only because the electoral commission would not accede to their request.[35] Differences surfaced again after the election when al-Fadhila, breaking with seeming UIA consensus, talked about the possibility of negotiating with the 'Allawi group, a statement that drew a particularly sharp rebuke from the Sadrists.[36] Underlying this was the uneasy relationship between the spiritual guide of al-Fadhila, Ayatollah Muhammad al-Ya'qoubi and the Sadrists' leader, Muqtada al-Sadr. Nor, for that matter, were relations between SCIRI and the Sadr group particularly fraternal. The Sadrists censured Hakim for negotiating with the Kurds after the election, calling it "a personal endeavor that did not enjoy the UIA's blessings."[37] Muqtada, who obviously resented Hakim's public demeanor as the acknowledged head of the UIA, and who, as we have seen, projected an image of himself as an Iraqi nationalist repeatedly rejected Hakim's pet proposal of a Shi'ite region in the south based on the nine predominantly Shi'ite governorates. Moreover, relations between the militias of the two organizations, SCIRI's Badr Brigade and the Sadrists' al-Mahdi army, erupted more than once in bloody clashes.

No wonder that the free and fair December 2005 general elections, so full of promise, gave the country a government but denied it governance. The Prime Minister's efforts to balance and satisfy the competing interests within the UIA and outside it among Kurdish, Sunni, and secular groups and parties created a milieu in which ministers were beholden first and foremost to their parties than to the Prime Minister. The notion of collective Cabinet responsibility was secondary to the loyalty of the ministers to their varying ethnosectarian groups. In such a structure the Premier's authority was bound to be diminished, and indeed soon it was apparent that the government had begun to resemble a collection of autonomous fiefdoms over which the Premier had nominal authority. It became common to refer to a government ministry not by what it was supposed to do, but by who "owned" it, which party or group had first claim on its loyalty, as well as its largess.[38] Particularly notorious, as we have seen, was the Ministry of Interior which became a haven for Shi'ite militia and death squads. The Shi'ites on their part would complain that the Ministry of Defense, headed by a Sunni, was endeavoring to make the army a Sunni domain. And it seemed that until the six Sadrist ministers jointly resigned in the spring of 2007, their ministries, including those of health and transport, were more concerned with enforcing Shi'ite Islamist strictures than with discharging their specialist responsibilities.

In such circumstances, when governmental ministries and agencies were incapable of executing their duties and responsibilities, democratic and civil society institutions were bound to suffer. Much hope was invested during the early years of the occupation in the mushrooming of civil society institutions. By the end of 2004, just under $1 billion had been allocated by the United States and other international donors for projects aimed at fostering civil society: civic education that promoted democratic values, especially the rule of law and civil liberties; support for an independent media, women's advocacy groups, and other non-governmental organizations and civic associations; and the establishment and empowerment of citizen participation at the local level. On all of these fronts significant strides were made early on. Professional syndicates, truly independent of government institutions, grew dramatically and organized politically, women's associations were influential enough to have an impact on policy, a discernible surge of activity at the level of local self-government occurred where many town councils were elected through peaceful and relatively consensual means, and more than 150 daily and weekly newspapers were sold on the streets of Baghdad.[39] As governance, security, and the provision of services stuttered and stumbled during 2003 and 2004, the growth of civil society institutions and practices provided countervailing hopes for the eventual success of the new order.

But it proved to be a forlorn hope. These promising institutions could not withstand societal and political developments that ultimately would restrict the growth of not just civic institutions but civic culture as well. As state capacity continued to retract, as the insurgency and militia activity escalated exponentially, as government withdrew to the safety of the Green Zone, creating a psychological barricade that separated it increasingly from its citizens, people would inevitably find solace in smaller groups defined by particularistic and primordial loyalties, and in the process eschew overlapping and bridge-building institutions and practices. By fall 2007, civil society institutions seem to have atrophied, their goals were restricted and their earlier vigor muted, as more and more of their members and advocates would succumb to the on-setting ethnosectarian milieu, or flee the country under threat of captivity or assassination.

A similar process occurred in the pivotal institution of representative democracy. Elected to their positions with so much hope and fanfare in 2005, the members of the National Assembly, reflecting voter preferences, would succumb to highly partisan and politically compartmentalized behavior that focused on promoting narrow interests at the expense of the general good. The Assembly seemed particularly allergic to any bill or initiative of consequence for the country. Efforts at revising the Constitution moved at a snail's pace, with Assembly members seemingly unconcerned by the constitutional committee's inability to meet a May 2007 deadline. A hydrocarbon law, regulating relations between the regions and centered on issues of petroleum control and resources, which was passed by the Cabinet in December 2006, had not gone through any serious discussion in the Assembly eight months later. And, the elected parliamentarians were mute on the subject of the much delayed provincial elections. Indeed, as governmental ineptitude and corruption and societal division grew with time, the Assembly members would accordingly distance themselves more and more from the country's pressing problems. Even one of the most promising aspects of the electoral law, the insistence on women being represented by no less than 25 percent of the membership, turned out to be a huge disappointment, as parties nominated pliant women, who would obligingly follow the lead of their male colleagues. Eventually even attendance would suffer as concern over the lack of security and perhaps a realization of futility made the trek to Parliament hardly a telling endeavor.

With governmental immobility, institutional indifference, and a security situation that was chaotic at best, the socioeconomic situation was bound to deteriorate, and living conditions would steadily worsen.[40] The inflation rate in Iraq jumped by some 70 percent by the summer of 2006, and the unemployment rate correspondingly rose to around 60 percent. Economic stagnation, coupled with the government's inability to provide services, had a devastating impact on society. In 2007, over half of the Iraqi population lived on less than $1 a day. Acute malnutrition had more than doubled since 2003, and by the summer of 2007 had affected no less than 43 percent of all children between the ages of six months and five years. This was compounded by the seeming collapse of the sewage system, where only a third of Iraqis had access to drinking water, while 43 percent of households were deprived of healthy sanitation facilities. The consequent acute need for medical attention was made more desperate by a lack of critical medical drugs and equipment, and by a steep reduction in the number of doctors and specialists, some 15,000 of whom by 2007 had been killed, kidnapped, or made to flee the country. And in the unforgiving summer heat, where temperatures in Baghdad regularly reached 45 degrees Celsius (116 degrees Fahrenheit), residents would be lucky to expect more than five hours of electricity a day.

To what extent did the first freely elected Prime Minister in Iraq's history bear the major responsibility for the incompetence of his government during this crucial period? On the index of performance alone, Nuri al-Maliki was weak and ineffective, seemingly unable to force ministers to eschew ethnosectarian considerations and embrace instead a political vision for an integrated and unified Iraq. Indeed, it was not clear that even he himself had actually developed such a vision. On a number of occasions the Prime Minister seemed as susceptible to particularistic and sectarian sympathies as his ministers were. He thus would accede, indeed encourage, American military attacks against Sunni insurgents in Anbar and Diyala provinces, but would hinder the same action against the Shi'ite al-Mahdi army in Baghdad's Sadr city.[41] His office was linked to efforts to detain or force out Iraqi officers who cracked down on Shi'ite militia, or conversely to reinstate Shi'ite officers American commanders had removed for turning a blind eye to violence committed by Shi'ite militiamen.[42] Even so, it is not clear whether Maliki took the lead in pursuing such policies, or simply acceded to powerful interests over which he had little control.

In a political structure and process that was fractured by competing identities and alliances it might have been too much to ask Mailki, or any prime minister for that matter, to show enough fortitude and toughness to bring everyone in line behind his vision for the future of Iraq. As we have seen, the democratic process itself ensured that any government would become hostage to ethnosectarian machinations. As a compromise candidate, he inevitably would be beholden to more powerful Shi'ite leaders, on whose support his position depended. This was particularly true of Muqtada al-Sadr and his Mahdi army. Beyond the Shi'ite circle, the Premier had to satisfy Sunni and Kurdish interests if the fragile unity government were to survive. And many of these interests were at odds with Shi'ite dispositions. The reinstatement of Sunnis into the army, which brought back the specter of Saddam's armed forces, was bitterly denounced by Shi'ites, and in fact led to publicly proclaimed fears by the Prime Minister himself of a possible military coup against him.[43] Kurdish demands to hold a referendum in the city of Kirkuk which would undoubtedly legalize the incorporation of the oil rich city into Kurdistan was strenuously rejected by the Sunnis and Muqtada al-Sadr. In such a tug of war among forces on whose goodwill the survival of his government depended, Maliki was bound to consistently choose the option determined by the least common denominator, aimed at not alienating anyone, but in terms of purposeful policy action achieving little.

All these concessions and compromises were of course taken in the shadow of the largest constraint on the Premier's freedom of maneuverability. Every decision Maliki would make, he was bound to have in the back of his mind the interests of the United States. True, Washington handed sovereignty to the Iraqis as early as the summer of 2004. And true, the Maliki government came into office as a result of free elections. But the hundreds of thousands of American troops, without which the odds on the survival of the Iraqi government would be very long indeed, meant that he would need to calculate the American response to any decision he made. Mimicking Faysal's dilemma with the British and the Iraqi nationalists in the 1920s and 1930s, Maliki would publicly take issue with some American policy or action in order to emphasize his independence, and then would bend to reality and relent. His dealings with the Americans in regard to military action in Sadr City were typical instances of the Prime Minister's political oscillations imposed upon him by the lack of independent power and capacity.

The hopes, so buoyant at one point, that the very successful December 2005 general elections would give birth to a democratic, united, and peaceful Iraq would diminish as particularistic loyalties rose to the forefront of peoples' considerations and political calculations. Governing Iraq became akin to a house of mirrors. Whenever one felt the road ahead led to escape and survival, one was confronted by yet another mirror that forced reassessment.

THE STATE RESPONDS

There can be little doubt that by early 2007 the authority of the government had sunk to a level that verged on irrelevance. Notwithstanding the pervasive corruption at all levels of government, the endless political deadlock on issues crucial to the health of the state, and the sheer inability to deliver on the most basic requirements of governance, the most damaging shortcoming was the perceived impotence of the security institutions to impose their will on seditious sub-state groups. As we have seen, groups such as al-Qaʻida and its allies and the Mahdi army had established a predatory and seemingly secure dominion in their respective areas, not only in the Sunni heartland and the Shiʻite south, but also in different areas and neighborhoods of Baghdad.

Recognizing that his troops were bogged down in what increasingly looked like a wasted effort, the newly appointed American commander in Iraq, General David Petraeus, devised a military plan to defeat al-Qaʻida that called for a substantial "surge" in troop numbers, and indeed the number of American forces in Iraq went up from 132,000 in January 2007 to 160,000 six months later. By the fall of 2007, the new muscular presence of American troops had already started to pay dividends. The media, to the surprise of many who had been accustomed to a constant barrage of dispiriting news from Iraq, was reporting cases of dramatic successes in towns, such as Fallujah and Ramadi, and in Baghdad neighborhoods such as Ghazaliya, all of which had been under the uncontested control of al-Qa'ida.[44]

The Americans however did not do it alone. A pivotal element in the seeming success of the surge was a dramatic shift of allegiance by the Sunni tribes in Anbar and Diyala provinces, hitherto the heart of the Sunni insurrection. Over four years of al-Qa'ida stifling orthodoxy and brutal practices had gone a long way toward alienating the tribal inhabitants of the Sunni provinces and their cities. The tribes had suffered considerable financial hardship as well, as economic activity was restricted by the armed confrontations between al-Qa'ida and the American forces. Consequently, from the spring of 2007 onward, first the Anbar then Diyala tribes broke with al-Qa'ida. Financed, armed and trained by the Americans, the tribes formed *al-Sahwa* (Awakening) councils that played a crucial role in expelling al-Qa'ida fighters from the provinces and their towns. This pattern was emulated in the Sunni neighborhoods of Baghdad with palpable success.[45] The most visible consequence was the reduction in violence. In June 2007, there were 1,646 civilian deaths and 101 American combat casualties in Iraq. Six months later in December, the numbers had gone down to 481 and 23, respectively.[46] By the summer of 2008, Sunni tribal sheikhs and American military commanders appeared to have established a working tactical alliance that, if resilient, should auger well for the return of normalcy to the Sunni areas.

The problem for the government in Baghdad was that the state seemed to have been excluded from this security relationship. As far as the tribes were concerned the bargain was struck with the Americans not with the Shi'ite-dominated government, which in fact was unhappy about the arming of the Sunni tribes.[47] If anything the Sunnis were bound to perceive any success in stemming violence as having happened not because of the state, but in spite of it.

Some of this doubt was to be tempered in the spring of 2008 when Prime Minister Maliki decided to move against his hitherto main backer,

Muqtada al-Sadr and his Mahdi army, which controlled Sadr City in Baghdad and much of the southern port of Basra. In Basra, the Mahdi army moved about the city with impunity, intimidating not only the population, but the security forces as well. It imposed Taliban-like orthodoxy, murdering as many as 133 women in 2007 for violating Islamic teachings, which in most cases meant wearing makeup or going outside the home without a headscarf.[48] Once a city known for its easy ways, Basra had become a grim reminder of the tyranny of religious zealotry. Repeated appeals from Maliki to Sadr to rein in his Mahdi army fell on deaf ears, and later on when Maliki threatened to use force, he was contemptuously dismissed as an American stooge.

In March 2008, Iraqi security forces launched a massive assault on the Mahdi army, and while initially the military effort spluttered, and a number of Iraqi soldiers laid down their arms or handed their weapons to the enemy,[49] by early May government forces supported by American and British air power had taken control of the city and established a measure of normalcy; a pattern that was repeated in other southern Shi'ite cities and towns. Later on that month, after repeated clashes with the Mahdi army, over 10,000 Iraqi troops entered Sadr City and quickly deployed throughout its neighborhoods, ushering a period of calm in the troubled area not experienced since 2003.

Concomitant with these military successes, there were a few significant political reconciliations. Sunni lawmakers and politicians, who had been estranged from the Prime Minister, perceiving him as totally beholden to his sect, were buoyed by Maliki's move against the Shi'ite militia, and publicly voiced their support for his policies.[50] Also during this period, there was at least one significant political breakthrough. The National Assembly was finally able to break the months-old deadlock and pass a Provincial Elections Law.

But doubts would persist. For all their public pronouncements affirming their commitment to reconciliation for the sake of the country, Iraqi politicians would continue to squabble, showing little appetite for compromise, over such critical issues as Cabinet representation, rules governing the provincial elections, and the right to sign petroleum contracts with outside companies. In each of these disputes, ethnosectarian concerns were at the fore. There was also the worry that increasing American reliance on the tribes and their sheikhs simply would cement the position of the tribe in the social structure of the country, bring tribal attributes to the forefront of Iraqi consciousness, and, as a consequence, solidify tribal identity at the expense of Iraqi national identity. And in all this, the actual physical and intellectual separation of Iraq's main groups would continue unabated,[51] hardening with every passing day.

A fractured Iraqi identity, fueled by ethnosectarianism and tribalism, would impact not just peoples' attitudes and relationships, but also, as we have seen, governmental performance. The political environment would become enmeshed in sub-state, particularistic proclivities and solidarities so powerful that it would beg the question: can Iraq survive as a united political entity?

CHAPTER TWELVE

W(h)ither Iraq?

The answer to the question whether Iraq would unravel need not be limited to the expectation of Iraq's total demise as a sovereign member of the global community. It does not necessarily anticipate its dismemberment into a number of independent parts. But we could ask the question whether there will be an Iraq that would resemble the country from its inception as a monarchy in 1921 until the demise of the Saddamist regime in 2003—a political entity brought and kept together by a central government that had the capacity to impose law and order, subdue sub-state fissiparous tendencies, and manage economic activity in the land?

The concern over Iraqi unity relates to the seemingly gradual eclipse of a national Iraqi identity by sub-state, ethnosectarian identities. But, as we have seen, that is hardly a unique or even contemporary phenomenon. Multiple identities and loyalties are as old as Iraqi history. Iraq after all was patched up together into a monarchy by the British in 1921 from three disparate provinces of the defunct Ottoman Empire. Divisions were so deep that when it came to choosing a ruler for the new state, the British realized that no local candidate would command the support of the whole population.[1] While the British decision to choose Prince Faysal of Hejaz to be Iraq's first monarch was of course multi-faceted, there can be little doubt that the ethnosectarian divisions in the infant state constituted one important factor. Twelve years into his reign, King Faysal I would still lament the yawning dislocations in his realm:

> Iraq is one of those countries that lack religious, communal and cultural unity, and as such it is divided upon itself; its power dispersed. . . . The Arab Sunni government rules over a Kurdish population, the bulk of which is ignorant, that is led by people with personal ambitions who use the [Kurds'] ethnic difference to advocate secession. [The govern-

ment also rules over] an uneducated Shi'ite majority that shares the same ethnicity with the government, but which was persecuted by Turkish (Sunni) rule . . . that [divided] the Arab population between the two sects. [This led] to the perception, which I have heard thousands of times, that taxes and death are the Shi'ites' lot in life, while public positions are reserved for the Sunnis. . . . In addition, there is the tribal mindset, plus the influence exercised by the sheikhs over the tribesmen, and the fear that [this influence] would wane in the face of enhanced governmental authority. . . .[2]

STATE POLICIES

The difference between 1933 and 2003 and after was not so much in the ethnosectarian-tribal structure of society, but in the policies adopted by the governing elites, as well as the perceptions of these policies by the population. Regardless of the country's fissures, which in fact were deeper in the first decade of statehood than what pertained in the post-2003 era, Faysal's government was committed to the ideal of a national state, and worked to subsume communal identities within an overarching Iraqi identity.[3] The man who spearheaded the undertaking was Faysal's protégé, Sati' al-Husri, Iraq's Director General of Education. From that position Husri and a group of committed disciples exerted profound influence on the educational and cultural orientations of the country, particularly in its crucial formative years. They disseminated their views on nation-building through purposeful educational policy, such as secularizing school and college curricula, and imbuing it with nationalist ideas.

While essentially Arab, not necessarily Iraqi, nationalists like Husri and his disciples did not consider the two positions to be mutually exclusive: all the nationalist notions of love of country, a feeling of community, a sense of togetherness, could be nurtured within the political boundaries of Iraq. Their formulations therefore presupposed a united Iraq, brimming with the nationalist spirit. The goal, according to one Iraqi analyst, was to "first melt the various Iraqi groups into the crucible of one country before moving on to achieve Arab nationalist aspirations."[4] In a history textbook for high school students published in 1946, King Faysal was portrayed as a believer in the Arab ideal, but whose sights were centered first and foremost on building the Iraqi nation-state.[5] Throughout Faysal's reign, his government's policies as well as its discourse, as portrayed by its agencies of cultural production, focused on fostering national unity, denigrating particularistic, sub-national identities. This was to be continued during the rest of the monarchical period and throughout the republican era.

This is not to say that successive monarchical and republican ruling elites were free of ethnosectarian bias. From the inception of the monarchy in 1921, governance was the domain of the minority Sunni population, and while the political fortunes of the Shi'ites and, to a lesser extent, the Kurds varied from one period to the other, Sunni dominance over the political power structure was not challenged. The important point here, however, was that ethnosectarianism was not allowed to become the key criterion in the public apportionment of governmental positions and responsibilities, nor in any way was it advertised as an element of public policy. Thus, Husri personally might have harbored anti-Shi'ite prejudices,[6] but his relentless pursuit of a secular, homogenized educational curriculum, which did disadvantage graduates of Shi'ite *maddrassas*, was done in the name of promoting all-encompassing nationalist values.[7] Later on, in the republican era, Iraq's president from 1963 to 1965, 'Abd al-Salam 'Aref, was known to hold bigoted views of non-Sunnis,[8] but neither he nor his agencies turned his personal ethnosectarianism into official policies and practices.

Similarly, for long periods during the 1970s, the upper echelons of the Ba'thist governing elite were dominated by Sunnis. The percentage of Sunni members of the Revolutionary Command Council and the Regional Command of the Ba'th Party was always considerably higher than their demographic weight would warrant. This would also have a socioeconomic dimension: of the thirty-one largest businesses in the country, which between them literally controlled the state's economic projects, twenty-three belonged to Sunnis.[9] Yet, the reality of Sunni dominance would be balanced by a spirited governmental campaign to extend extensive public largess to poor Shi'ite areas, to show that the state had no communal biases. This would be accompanied by a vigorously trumpeted public relations onslaught depicting Iraq as a secular meritocracy and extolling the country's long unified history and its vanguard role in the Middle Eastern region. Thus even in cases of actual ethnosectarian bias, an effort would be made not to reflect the communal imbalance in public policy or in publicly advocated elite preferences.

This anti-communal particularisms, or at a minimum the coyness to publicly admit to such particularisms, which on the whole permeated Iraq's public space from the country's inception until the 1990s was to disappear in 2003 and its aftermath. In the new era, countrywide ethnosectarianism was no longer something to overcome or balance with a national project or even national pretense. The state did not even feign neutrality on the subject. On the contrary, from the early days of the Coalition Provisional Authority right through the various governments in the period of Iraqi sovereignty, ethnosectarianism by word and deed was purposely and purposefully institutionalized in the body politic of the country, as well as being implanted into the mindset of the people.

Initially it was argued that inclusiveness was essential to democratic transition. Every group needed to feel that it had a stake in the new order, and apportionment of ministerial posts would allow for peaceful political bargaining and development. The danger in such institutional engineering was the potential routinization of this strategy whereby apportionment is extended beyond the top level positions, allowing it to become a settled and pervasive way of staffing the new state. This, as was the case in Lebanon's confessional system, would be a recipe for civil breakdown.

And it was to happen in Iraq. When state positions are apportioned according to some ethnosectarian formula that is advertised openly as the modus operandi of the new political order, then it is a matter of time before sub-national identities get embedded in the social fabric of society. Nor is it surprising that ministries become autonomous fiefdoms doing the bidding of ethnosectarian bosses and warlords, which they would do brazenly without trying to cover their tracks. In such a milieu, particularistic concerns, rather than the national interest, become the driving force behind governmental policies and parliamentary behavior. It is this break with attitudes and practices from earlier eras, this utter contrast in institutional engineering, that explains the seeming ascendancy of ethnosectarian identities more than five years after the toppling of Saddam's dictatorship.

State Capacity

State capacity played not an insignificant role in this shift in basic attitudes. For the national idea to compete with sub-national particularistic loyalties, the state has to literally woo the citizens away from their ethno-sectarian comfort zone. The state needs to show that the interests of the citizen will be served best (and sometimes exclusively) by the state, not the tribe, clan, sect, or region. A strong state, or more precisely a state that is perceived by its citizens to be strong, has to have the capacity to serve and care for its people, by responding to peoples' most essential needs such as jobs, health, education, and most of all a secure environment. Indeed, according to Max Weber security is paramount, for he defines the state as possessing "a monopoly over the legitimate use of physical force."[10] Thus, a necessary condition for the legitimacy of the state is the absence of forces within it that would challenge, or compete with it. In other words, the state should be able to project power throughout its geographic domain, and if a threat to its dominance should arise the state should have the capacity to subdue it.

The early history of the Iraqi state is a case in point. From the very beginning of Faysal's reign an essential element of the national project was the effort to penetrate the state into the lives of its disparate citizens. The countryside was not the priority; it was too large and too imbued with traditional primordial values to easily infiltrate and constructively change. Instead, the strategy turned to incorporating the traditional leadership into the body politic through the extension of generous material incentives to tribal leaders as well as allowing them formal and informal entry into the policy-making process.[11] The realization by the sheikhs in the south and *aghas* (Kurdish tribal lords) in the north that their economic and political interests were served better through an acceptance of the primacy of state institutions would go a long way toward curbing their feral and more anarchic impulses. And when on occasions that did not happen, as was the case of the tribal uprisings in 1935–1936,[12] the state would unleash its pitiless coercive capacity and successfully eliminate any challenge to its authority.

In the meantime the state would expand its presence and influence in the urban areas at the expense of traditional leaderships. Whether in the construction of roads, railways and dams, creating jobs through the expansion of the bureaucracy, providing essential public services, facilitating commercial opportunities, and extending secular and scientific education, which would serve as the gateway for material improvement and status enhancement, the state would progressively seduce citizens away from the ways of the past, characterized by sub-state loyalties and identities.[13] Urban population generally, and especially in the cities of the Shi'ite south, would associate their well-being more and more with the state and its national government and less with local traditional leaders, be they religious- or clan-based.

The same ability to project state capacity, whether in the provision of essential services or the imposition of coercive sanctions, was the mantra of successive governments in the republican era. Iraq continued to be modernized, and with that it became increasingly urbanized, dealing ever larger blows to traditional leaderships. Thus, the construction of cities with modern amenities during the Qasim era (1958–1963) attracted large numbers of men from the countryside and in so doing made them beholden to the central government.[14] Additionally, the reach of the state continued to expand into hitherto sparsely touched areas, so that, for example, under the Ba'thist regime in the 1970s, electricity was introduced to the remotest villages in the southern marshes, and state-subsidized health facilities were placed in nearby towns.[15] On the other side of the coin, when security infractions would occur, the state would put these down with its customary ruthless efficiency.

With varying degrees of competence and harshness, the state and its institutions of governance in the pre-2003 era were able to deliver services and impose sanctions that at once seduced and forced citizens away from tribal and ethnosectarian leadership, tying their interests and well-being to the state and its central governing authorities. And herein lay the stark contrast with the post-2003 era.

The removal of the procrustean regime of Saddam Husayn was bound to be a traumatic experience, leaving people naturally hesitant about committing their immediate and wholehearted support to the new political masters. In such uncertain circumstances, the exhibition of uncontested state capacity was thus unquestionably crucial. That, however, did not come to pass. Indeed, it would not be an exaggeration to say that the most defining characteristic of the state that emerged after 2003 was a chronic weakness that was palpable to all. Neither in the American, nor in the Iraqi, period, could governance be said to have been effective and resolute. The provision of essential services left much to be desired, indeed at times it was virtually non-existent. This was particularly true in the case of Baghdad, the capital city, inhabited by some 27 percent of the country's population. This not only would diminish the state and its institutions in the eyes of its citizens, but also would turn people to services provided by sub-national entities. In Sadr City, a district of Baghdad that is inhabited by over 2 million economically disadvantaged Shi'ites, people received most of their medical needs from health facilities run by a foundation that was controlled by the fiery cleric and warlord, Muqtada al-Sadr.[16] In a similar vein, whatever provision of services there was in the northern Kurdish cities or many of the southern Shi'ite cities, to say nothing of the Sunni heartland, it was associated not so much with the governing institutions in Baghdad, but with local leaderships that symbolized regionalism rather than the national ethos.

Five years after the demise of the Saddamist regime, the state was still not able to project coercive power over its geographic domain. To say that the Iraqi state did not meet Weber's criterion of possessing a legitimate monopoly over the use of physical force is an understatement at best. The security burden was placed squarely on the shoulders of the coalition, increasingly American, troops, which by 2008 had reached over 165,000. Iraqi forces did see action against Sunni insurgents and Shi'ite militias, but invariably in a supporting role. And when they were left to police towns on their own, they were more often than not no match for their belligerent adversaries.

This would occur more than once in a number of Sunni cities in Anbar and Diyala provinces, each time necessitating the reintroduction of American troops to rescue the overmatched Iraqi forces. The same dire situation pertained in the Shi'ite south, where Iraqi security forces would intermittently engage various Shi'ite militia, but were not able to secure uncontested and permanent political control over the cities.[17] The problem in all this is that while the chaos would hardly endear the avaricious militia groups to the people, more consequentially it would strikingly dramatize the relative impotence of the state and its institutions, which was bound to dampen hopes for a viable Iraq. The impaired ability of the state to project power is a stark contrast to the practices of the past, where the central government might have been lacking in many things, but not in imposing its will on potential competitive forces.

Returning to the proposition that citizens need to believe that their interests are served by the state, not by other sub-state groups and agencies, and that a strong state, therefore, had to have the capacity to respond effectively to its peoples' needs and demands through the extension of essential services and providing a secure environment, it is clear that on almost none of these requirements, did the post-2003 Iraqi state deliver the goods. The weakness, almost irrelevance, of state institutions was bound to be a critical factor in the deepening of ethnosectarian fault lines.

As we have seen, discernible progress in the performance of the state and its security institutions did occur in 2007–2008. The successes of *al-Sahwa* councils in combating al-Qa'ida fighters and the improvement in the performance of the security forces against the militias in the south of the country did raise hopes that the state was taking its first decisive steps toward a political and social consolidation of the country. But the authorities in Baghdad still had a long way to go in convincing Iraqis that the state alone (without American support) has the capacity to impose its will on recalcitrant and belligerent sub-state groups. And in the final analysis, only uncontested state power would seduce individuals from their ethnosectarian comfort zone.

A Faltering Democracy

The growing distance separating the country's various communities might have been the reason for the insistence by all parties in the post-2003 era on a national unity government. It was as though an apportionment of ministerial responsibilities would somehow give lie to the existential conditions of dislocation the country was living through, or that the mere representation of all parties and groups in government would in and of itself create a national consensus not just in Cabinet deliberations, but also in National Assembly debates.

Associated with that was the denigration of "party politics" as somehow divisive; a system that by definition would lead to conflict. Thus, after the Shi'ite United Iraqi Alliance (UIA) won a majority in the general elections of December 2005, a member of the alliance would earnestly and proudly declare: "We will not allow ourselves to descend into party politics."[18] It was as though putting forth and openly defending a party program or ideology was somehow a grave offense against ethical political conduct. This kind of thinking showed a flawed understanding of democracy. Indeed such dismissal of the role of parties in democracies is one symptom of the tortuous development of democratic ideals and practices in Iraq. After all, only in authoritarian states is there an undifferentiated perception of the national interest. Democratic societies allow for pluralism in defining the national interest, and this pluralism manifests itself in multiple party affiliations. Democracies expect political parties to stand ready not only to govern, but also to take up the mantle of the opposition. In fact, it could be legitimately argued that national unity governments, while good for the occasional emergency, tend to be associated with pliant parliaments where everyone is part of the consensus and little space exists for opposition. This could indeed lead to a kind of "consensual authoritarianism."

The problem with the faltering democratic experiment in post-2003 Iraq did not lie with parties per se; it lay with the conception of parties as instruments of ethnosectarian advocacy. Again, a comparison with the monarchical era is instructive. At the end of World War II, Iraq's governing elite decided it was time to liberalize the political system. What followed was a relatively liberal era in which a number of political parties were licensed, and indeed operated for the best part of a decade. What defined these parties was their national reach and programs. They differed on matters of principle and policy; some like *al-Istiqlal* and *al-Watani al-Dimuqrati* were virulently anti-British and advocated a radical redistribution of wealth, others like *al-Ittihad al-Destouri* and *al-Umma al-Ishtiraki* were upholders of the status quo. The point here is that regardless of their differences, not one of them advertised, or indeed saw, itself as ethnically, sectarianally, or regionally bounded. These parties had offices throughout the country, and their membership spanned all of Iraq's communities. Even *al-Umma al-Ishtiraki*, which was led by the Shi'ite Saleh Jabr, and much of whose membership tended to come from the tribal and Shi'ite south, never claimed to be anything but a national party, with an agenda that dealt with national issues, and indeed it had Sunnis, Kurds, and Christians as members, even of its constituent committee.[19] In fact, when denigrated by the opposition, the Party would be labeled *iqta'i* (feudalist), but hardly ever *ta'ifi* (sectarian).

What happened in the post-2003 period was that ethnosectarian identities were reified into fixed political cleavages. Politics and identities were fused into the concept of parties, so that national issues were now viewed from an ethnosectarian prism, with the consequence that particularistic concerns would generally define national policy. Thus, the only party that had an eclectic membership of Shi'ites, Sunnis, Kurds, and Christians was the secular Iraqi List of Ayad 'Allawi, and in the December 2005 general elections it ended up with a paltry twenty-five seats in the 275-seat national assembly. The other 250 seats were distributed among parties and coalitions that were all defined by ethnic and religious/sectarian identities. Indeed the party with the largest number of seats, the Shi'ite United Iraqi Alliance (UIA) was formed at the urging of, and had as its mentor, Grand Ayatollah 'Ali al-Sistani. Regionally bounded and lacking national memberships, these parties were bound to evaluate national issues and policies from perspectives that reflected their own particularistic interests and concerns, thus contributing not only to the progressive fragmentation of the political culture, but also to a policy-making process that would be disjointed, incoherent, and more often than not hopelessly deadlocked.

This would be especially discernible in the stale deliberations of the National Assembly that reflected deeply entrenched ethnosectarian cleavages. Legislative achievements were notable for their stunning mediocrity. While clichéd speeches and unbridled recriminations abounded, members seemed particularly allergic to any bill or initiative of consequence for the country. Consequently, important national policy issues necessitating urgent attention were stymied by the rigidity of the various groups' fixed ethnosectarian positions. Only in January and February 2008, more than two years after the general elections, was Iraq's Parliament finally able to pass laws dealing with de-Ba'thification and provincial elections. Other sorely needed issues such as constitutional reform, the distribution of petroleum resources, and provincial elections would remain buried under the weight of polar ethnosectarian interests. Compounding the problem has been an absence of functional solidarities that could cut across such cleavages. The most disappointing of these has been the lack of gender solidarity in the Assembly. The electoral law had specified that women would constitute no less than 25 percent of the assembly's membership, raising hopes of putting women's issues at the forefront of the Assembly's concerns. Such hopes would turn into huge disappointments as parties nominated pliant women who would obligingly follow the lead of their ethnosectarian-oriented male colleagues. Eventually even attendance of Assembly meetings would suffer as concern over the lack of security and perhaps a realization of their own futility would diminish the status of Parliament in the country.

Could it be that the primary error was the precipitant introduction of democracy? Did Iraq have the essential social requisites for a successful transition to fully functioning national democratic institutions? In a seminal work published half a century ago Seymour Martin Lipset argued that the higher the levels of industrialization, urbanization, wealth, and education, which are concomitant with the development of a vibrant, entrepreneurial middle class, the higher the chances of a successful transition to democracy.[20] While Lipset's thesis has been challenged and modified by others,[21] it still offers compelling avenues of analysis in the case of Iraq.

The fractured development of Iraq, both as a state and society, particularly after the demise of the monarchy, with the intrusion of the military in politics, followed by the suffocating barbarity of the Saddam era, did clearly arrest, or at a minimum retard, the development of Lipset's requisites. Industrialization moved at a snail's pace, and, particularly in the petrochemical field, would be devastated by Saddam's wars against Iran and over Kuwait. Urbanization and education did expand throughout the development of the state. Yet urbanization on the whole simply meant the growth of shanty towns of illiterate, economically and socially disadvantaged people whose culture was hardly different from their rural counterparts. The expansion of education was one of the more impressive achievements of Iraq's successive regimes, but it too would suffer the impact of Saddam's wars and the sanctions regime.

A middle class continued to gain in strength reaching a pinnacle in material prosperity in the 1970s. But with the Iraq-Iran War, followed by the first Gulf War and the crippling United Nations sanctions, the middle class was literally decimated by the time of the 2003 invasion of Iraq. And in any case, much of Iraq's middle class was directly dependent on the state, primarily through employment in the vast bureaucracy, in state-owned industries, in military and security agencies, and during the thirty-five years of Ba'thist rule in the Party's countless political, social, and security bureaus. Moreover, thanks to the country's immense oil wealth, government revenues came mainly from oil sales and not taxation, which further added to middle-class docility. All this hardly would add up to the notion of an independent, entrepreneurial, and self-sustaining middle class which democratic theory holds to be the basis for democratic civil life.

Political culture is another requisite that impacts the successful transition to democracy. The concept refers to peoples' national historical experience and belief system, and the way these tend to influence political behavior.[22] The question that was asked about Iraq was whether the country had a political culture that was conducive to the growth of democracy. In fact, there could not be a definitive, cut and dry answer to this question. Initially, analysts seemed almost unanimous in concluding that the chances for democracy to be implanted in the political and psychological fabric of Iraqi society were too dim to warrant even trying. The culprit was the country's political culture; the lack of a democratic tradition and the absence of previous experience with democracy.[23] Indeed, even as administration officials talked ebulliently about exporting democracy to Iraq and from there to the Middle East, governmental analyses were far less sanguine.[24] But there was also a countervailing point of view that stressed the many instances and periods of democratic practices in the history of the Iraqi state, particularly during the monarchical era.[25]

It is important to note here that historical recollection is neither linear nor cumulative. For instance in the treatment of the "frontier" in U.S. history, particular narratives that at one time had been forcefully asserted were then forgotten and later rediscovered.[26] In the realm of politics, historical memory is often the subject of reinterpretation by those searching for a "usable past" to legitimize public policy.[27] So while undoubtedly much of Iraq's history was authoritarian, there also were rays of democratic hope that those in charge of the new Iraqi project could hold on to in their effort to build democratic structures. And this complexity was reflected in the response of Iraqi citizens during the two elections of 2005. On the one hand, there was great enthusiasm among people to exercise rights that had been denied them for almost half a century, and amid pervasive violence they flocked to the voting booths. However, once inside the booth, they reverted to primordial ethnosectarian loyalties, seemingly using democracy as one of a number of means (not all peaceful) simply to advance the cause of their own group, and hopefully give it dominion over the other groups. What transpired was a complex and somewhat undetermined conclusion in which the existence and functioning of democratic institutions would inspire hope, but the narrow interests and partisanship that came to pervade the workings of these institutions could only engender consternation.

WHAT KIND OF FEDERALISM?

It is argued that the creeping institutionalization of ethnosectarian solidarities, and the antagonisms that this was bound to provoke would more than likely lead to one of two unpalatable eventualities: political disintegration at one extreme, or some variant of authoritarian rule on the other. Yet a contrary argument has also been made that the innate interest of each community to limit the power of the others could provide the political checks and balances that would lead to the promotion of democracy at the expense of rigid communal particularisms. From the very beginning of the effort to build a democratic Iraq, there was almost universal consensus that transforming Iraq's communal diversity from a dislocative force to an agent of positive change would be achieved best through a federal political structure. Federalism is ideal for fractured societies as it cuts across cleavages and conflicts, reduces inequalities among groups, and gives all parties a stake in the system.[28] But the question was: what kind of federalism? It was argued that a federal system that is decentralized on the basis of territory, not ethnicity or sect, where local governments have responsibility for all citizens in their areas, not just for ethnic or sectarian co-nationals, would be the best alternative for sustaining democracy in Iraq.[29]

The recommendation was to maintain Iraq's administrative structure under Saddam, in which the country was divided into eighteen units, but to give these units far greater powers vis-à-vis the center. Keeping these provincial boundaries would serve the interests of Iraq's various communities, while avoiding inordinate emphasis on conflict-inducing ethnic and sectarian concerns. Such an arrangement would also increase healthy political competition for resources among the various units—even among those that reside within specific ethnic or sectarian areas.

A few years into the post-2003 era, it would become evident that while this formulation might have been the most appropriate for the development of a stable and democratic Iraq, it actually had little chance of being implemented given the reality of the country's historical experiences and its sociopolitical condition. In terms of political development, the history of the Iraqi state is one of muscular central governance, where the various parts were tied umbilically to Baghdad. Throughout the state's existence, it was the center that possessed power and controlled resources, and provincial government had little role beyond facilitating central jurisdiction. More than eighty years of hegemony by the central government left its imprint on peoples' psyche, making devolution of power to the provinces seem irrelevant, even fraudulent.

If one historical experience could break the mold of power centralization, it would probably be the post-1991 period of a devouring central government that threw all pretense of secularism and meritocracy to the wind, pursuing instead, with untold savagery, blatant ethnosectarian assaults on Kurds and Shi'ites. In such circumstance, it should not have come as a surprise that the only federal form that the long-suffering Shi'ite and Kurdish communities would accept would be the one embracing ethnosectarian lines. Territoriality thus fell into the crack between the two political structures that people, through their past experiences, understood and were willing to accept: a centralized system on the one hand or devolution based on ethnosectarianism on the other.

What ensued was a tug of war between the adherents of these two ideational and political models. Almost all Sunnis and some Shi'ites clung to the idea of a centralized and unified Iraq, while the Kurds and other Shi'ites advocated an ethnosectarian federal, even confederal, state. Interestingly, the Sunnis, the most adamant on preserving the oneness of Iraq, seem to have grudgingly accepted the notion of a Kurdish region, constitutive of the three Kurdish provinces of Irbil, Sulaymaniya, and Duhok. But the Sunnis have been especially allergic to a similar arrangement for the Shi'ites. Polar positions in such combustible conditions as they pertained in Iraq ultimately degenerated into violence, the most horrifying manifestation of which was the determined ethnic cleansing that with every passing day created a de-facto separation of the three main communities.

Considerable resources were invested to dissuade Iraqis from eviscerating their country. Yet the yawning lacerations incurred on the way to seeming national destruction would not heal lightly. Can Iraq survive these powerful centrifugal forces? It must be said that the increasing physical and psychological distance among the country's various communities makes it difficult to visualize the future Iraq as a truly unified political entity. Even a constitutionally sanctioned federalism, itself based on ethnosectarian cleavages, deepened by willful and terrible acts of violence, would only serve to cement, rather than alleviate, communal mistrust and the penchant for exclusiveness. Admittedly this process need not necessarily be irreversible. Visible improvements in the security situation in 2008 raised hope that some kind of national reconciliation may follow and result in a peaceful compromise. Still what remains uncertain is whether the future Iraq would much resemble the unified political and geographic entity that the British sowed together in 1921 and which survived more or less intact under various monarchical and republican rulers until 2003.

NOTES

Chapter One: Introduction

1. Two excellent studies of Iraq's political history are Phebe Marr, *The Modern History of Iraq*, 2nd edition (Boulder, Colorado: Westview Press, 2004) and Charles Tripp, *A History of Iraq*, 2nd edition (Cambridge, England: Cambridge University Press, 2000).

2. Many books have been written on the failures of that crucial initial period. Among the best are Rajiv Chanrasekaran, *Imperial Life in the Emerald City: Inside Iraq's Green Zone* (New York: Random House, 2006); George Packer, *The Assassins' Gate: America in Iraq* (New York: Farrar, Straus, and Giroux, 2005); Larry Diamond, *Squandered Victory: The American Occupation and the Bungled Efforts to Bring Democracy to Iraq* (New York: Times Books, 2005); and Peter W. Galbraith, *The End of Iraq: How American Incompetence Created a War Without End* (New York: Simon and Schuster, 2006).

3. The following data is taken from the UN Assistance Mission for Iraq, *Human Rights Report, 1 January–31 March 2007*, p. 21, and UN Assistance Mission for Iraq, *Humanitarian Briefing on the Crisis in Iraq, May 2007, pp. 1–3*.

4. Max Weber, *From Max Weber: Essays in Sociology* (London: Oxford University Press, 1946), p. 78.

5. The idea of a radical decentralization of Iraq, based on ethnosectarian lines, was first articulated by Joseph Biden and Leslie Gelb in "Unity Through Autonomy in Iraq," *New York Times*, May 1, 2006. For a representative sample of articles skeptical of democratic viability in Iraq, see Adeed Dawisha, "Democratic Attitudes and Practices in Iraq, 1921–1958," *Middle East Journal*, vol. 59, no. 1, pp. 11–12.

6. See Elizabeth Monroe, *Britain's Moment in the Middle East, 1914–1956* (Baltimore, Maryland: The Johns Hopkins University Press, 1963); and Elie Kedourie, *England and the Middle East: The Destruction of the Ottoman Empire, 1914–1921* (London: Bowes and Bowes, 1956).

Chapter Two: Consolidating the Monarchical State

1. Harold Lasswell, *Politics: Who Gets What, When and How* (New York: McGraw Hill, 1936).

2. Charles Tilly, "War Making and State Making as Organized Crime," in Peter Evans, Dietrich Reuschemeyer, and Theda Skocpol, *Bringing the State Back* (London: Cambridge University Press, 1985), p. 174.

3. Charles Tilly, *Coercion, Capital and European States, A.D. 990–1992* (Cambridge, Massachusetts: Blackwell, 1990), p. 63; quoted in Jeffrey Herbst, *States and Power in Africa: Comparative Lessons in Authority and Control* (Princeton, New Jersey: Princeton University Press, 2000), p. 14.

4. See Michael Mann, "The Autonomous Power of the State: Its Origins, Mechanisms and Results," in Michael Mann, ed., *States, War and Capitalism: Studies in Political Sociology* (Oxford, England: Blackwell, 1988), p. 4.

5. Max Weber, *From Max Weber: Essays in Sociology* (London: Oxford University Press, 1946), p. 78. Tilly, *Coercion, Capital and European States, A.D. 990–1992* , p. 63; quoted in Herbst, *States and Power in Africa: Comparative Lessons in Authority and Control,* p. 14.

6. Stephen H. Longrigg, *Iraq, 1900 to 1950: A Political, Social and Economic History* (London: Oxford University Press, 1953), p. 121.

7. Janet Wallach, *The Desert Queen: The Extraordinary Life of Gertrude Bell* (New York: Doubleday, 1995), p. 336.

8. Ibid., pp. 244–245.

9. Ibid., p. 244.

10. Toby Dodge, *Inventing Iraq: The Failure of Nation-Building and a History Denied* (New York: Columbia University Press, 2003), p. 17.

11. Wallach, *Desert Queen,* p. 280.

12. Longrigg, *Iraq: 1900–1950, A Political, Social and Economic History,* pp. 224–225.

13. 'Abd al-Razak Muhammad Aswad, *Mawsu'at al'Iraq al-Siyasiya, al-Mujalad al-Thani* (Political encyclopedia of Iraq, volume two) (Beirut, Lebanon: al-Dar al-'Arabiya li al-Mausu'at, 1986), p. 436.

14. The most charismatic and conniving of these was the Basra notable, Sayyid Talib. Gertrude Bell, who despised him, conceded that "he was seen by many Arabs and even some British as the most logical candidate to rule the country." See Wallach, *Desert Queen,* p. 251; see also Charles Tripp, *A History of Iraq* (Cambridge, England: Cambridge University Press, 2000), pp. 24–27.

15. Wallach, *Desert Queen,* p. 297.

16. The eminent Iraqi sociologist and historian, the late 'Ali al-Wardi, attributes the unevenness of Faysal's reception to the machinations of a few British officials, especially John Philby, who were not particularly enamored with the Hejazi Emir. See 'Ali al-Wardi, *Lamahat Ijtima'iya min Tarikh al 'Iraq al-Hadith, al-Jusi' al-Sadis, min 'Am 1920 ila 'Am 1924* (Sociological aspects of modern Iraqi

history, part six, 1920–1924) (London: Dar Kofan li al-Nashr, 1992), pp. 85–90; this is confirmed in a standard work on British policies and early Iraqi politics. See Philip Ireland, *Iraq: A Study in Political Development* (New York: Macmillan, 1938), pp. 326–329.

17. Wardi, *Lamahat Ijtima'iya min Tarikh al-'Iraq al-Hadith, al-Jusi' al-Sadis,* p. 115.

18. See Tawfiq al-Suwaydi, *Mudhakarati: Nisf Qarn min Tarikh al-'Iraq wa al-Qadhiya al-'Arabiya* (My memoirs: half a century of the history of Iraq and the Arab undertaking) (London: Dar al-Hikma, 1999), p. 102.

19. Majid Khadduri, *Independent Iraq, 1932–1958: A Study in Iraqi Politics* (London: Oxford University Press, 1960), pp. 19–20.

20. 'Abdul Wahab Hamid Rashid, *al-'Iraq al-Mu'asir* (Contemporary Iraq) (Damascus, Syria: Dar al-Mada li al-Thaqafa wa al-Nashr, 2002), p. 114.

21. Quoted in Hanna Batatu, *The Old Social Classes and the Revolutionary Movements of Iraq: A Study of Iraq's Old Landed and Commercial Classes and of Its Communists, Ba'thists, and Free Officers* (Princeton, New Jersey: Princeton University Press, 1978), p. 336.

22. Ireland, *Iraq: A Study in Political Development,* p. 373.

23. Dodge, *Inventing Iraq,* p. 19.

24. Majid Khadduri, *Nidham al-Hukm fi al-'Iraq* (The system of governance in Iraq) (Baghdad: Matba'at al-Ma'arif, 1946), pp. 14–15.

25. Wardi, *Lamahat Ijtima'iya min Tarikh al-'Iraq al-Hadith, al-Jusi' al-Sadis,* p. 117; Khadduri, *Nidham al-Hukm fi al-'Iraq,* pp. 334–335.

26. Wardi, *Lamahat min Tarikh al-"Iraq al-Hadith,* volume 6, pp. 123–124.

27. 'Abd al-Majid Kamel al-Tikriti, *Al-Malik Faysal al-Awal wa Dawruhu fi Ta'sis al-Dawla al-'Iraqiya al-Haditha, 1921–1933* (King Faysal I and his role in establishing the modern Iraqi state, 1921–1933) (Baghdad: Dar al Shu'un al-Thaqafiya al-'Amma, 1991), p. 366.

28. Wardi, *Lamahat Ijtima'iya min Tarikh al-'Iraq al-Hadith, al-Jusi' al-Sadis,* p. 184.

29. Elie Kedouri, *The Chatham House Version and Other Middle Eastern Studies* (London: Weidenfeld and Nicolson, 1970), p. 243.

30. See Wardi, *Lamahat Ijtima'iya min Tarikh al-'Iraq al-Hadith, al-Jusi' al-Sadis,* pp. 187–195.

31. Ireland, *Iraq: A Study in Political Development,* p. 361.

32. Batatu, *The Old Social Classes and the Revolutionary Movements of Iraq,* p. 100.

33. Ibid., p. 335.

34. Al-Tikriti, *Al-Malik Faysal al-Awal wa Dawruhu fi Ta'sis al-Dawla al-'Iraqiya al-Haditha*, pp. 126–127.

35. Wardi, *Lamahat Ijtima'iya min Tarikh al'Iraq al-Hadith, al-Jusi' al-Sadis*, p. 216.

36. Ibid., p. 312.

37. 'Abd al-Razzak al-Hasani, *Tarikh al-Wizarat al-'Iraqiya, al-Jusi' al-Awal* (The history of Iraqi cabinets, volume 1) (Baghdad: Dar al-Shu'un al Thaqafiya al-'Amma, 1988), p. 173.

38. Wardi, *Lamahat Ijtima'iya min Tarikh al-'Iraq al-Hadith, al-Jusi' al-Sadis*, pp. 261–262.

39. Rashid, *al-'Iraq al'Mu'asir*, p. 281; al-Wardi, *Lamahat min Tarikh al-'Iraq al-Hadith*, volume 6, p. 305.

40. Al-Tikriti, *al-Malik Faysal al-Awal wa Dawruhu fi Ta'sis al-Dawla al-'Iraqiya al-Haditha*, pp. 304–305.

41. Muhammad Mahdi Kubba, *Mudhakirati fi Samim al-Ahdath, 1918–1958* (My memoirs in the midst of events, 1918–1958) (Beirut, Lebanon: Dar al-Tali'ah, 1965), pp. 34–44.

42. 'Abd al-Rahman al-Bazzaz, *al-'Iraq min al-Ihtilal hatta al-Istiqlal* (Iraq: from occupation to independence) (Baghdad: Matba'at al-'Ani, 1967), p. 203.

43. 'Abd al-Ghani al-Mallah, *Tarikh al-Haraka al-Dimuqratiya fi al-'Iraq* (The history of the democratic movement in Iraq) (Baghdad: Wizarat al-I'lam, 1975), p. 135.

44. See Kerim Yildiz, *The Kurds in Iraq: The Past, Present and Future* (London: Pluto Press, 2004), p. 12.

45. See C. J. Edmonds, *Kurds, Turks and Arabs: Politics, Travel and Research in North-Eastern Iraq, 1919–1925* (London: Oxford University Press, 1957), p. 265.

46. Michael Gunter, *The Kurds of Iraq: Tragedy and Hope* (New York: St. Martin's Press, 1992), p. 3.

47. Yildiz, *The Kurds in Iraq*, pp. 13–14.

48. Phebe Marr, *The Modern History of Iraq* (Boulder, Colorado: Westview Press, 1985), p. 41.

49. Longrigg, *Iraq, 1900–1950: A Political, Social and Economic History*, p. 196.

50. Tripp, *A History of Iraq*, p. 68. Adding to Arab concern was the Treaty of Sevres, concluded in August 1920, which provided for Kurdish independence and admittance into the League of Nations. While the treaty was never implemented, it did point to international support for the idea of Kurdish independence.

51. Longrigg, *Iraq, 1900–1950: A Political, Social and Economic History*, pp. 196, 328. See also Gunter, *The Kurds of Iraq: Tragedy and Hope*, pp. 2–3.

52. Phebe Marr, *The Modern History of Iraq*, 2nd edition (Boulder, Colorado: Westview Press, 2004), p. 23.

53. For a critique, see Dodge, *Inventing Iraq*, pp. 92–100.

54. Wardi, *Lamahat min Tarikh al-'Iraq al-Hadith*, volume 6, pp. 130–131.

55. Ibid., pp. 146–152.

56. Hassan al-'Alwi, *al-Shi'a wa al-Dawla al-Qawmiya fi al-'Iraq, 1914–1990* (The Shi'ites and the national state in Iraq, 1914–1990) (n.p., 1990), p. 198.

57. Ireland, *Iraq: A Study in Political Development*, pp. 297–298; al-Wardi, *Lamahat Ijtima'iya min Tarikh al-'Iraq al-Hadith, al-Jusi' al-Sadis*, pp. 30–31.

58. Al-Suwaydi, *Mudhakarati*, pp. 76–77.

59. Wardi, *Lamahat min Tarikh al-'Iraq al-Hadith, al-Jusi' al-Sadis*, p. 128.

60. Quoted in Liona Lukitz, *Iraq: The Search for National Identity* (London: Frank Cass, 1995), p. 65; see also Yitzhak Nakash, *The Shi'is of Iraq* (Princeton, New Jersey: Princeton University Press, 1994), pp. 116–117.

61. Batatu, *The Old Social Classes and the Revolutionary Movements of Iraq*, pp. 24–25.

62. Ibid., p. 26.

63. 'Abd al-Razzak al-Hasani, *Tarikh al-Wizarat al-'Iraqiya, al-Jusi' al-Rabi'* (The history of Iraq cabinets, volume 4) (Baghdad: Dar al-Shu'un al-Thaqafiya al-'Amma, 1988), pp. 165–166.

64. These meetings are cited in the memoirs of one of the most powerful tribal leaders in Iraq at the time, Muhsin Abu Tibikh, who speaks of a number of these clandestine meetings. See Muhsin Abu Tibikh, *al-Mabadi' wa al-Rijal: Bawader al-Inhiyar al-Siyasi fi al-'Iraq* (Principles and men: symptoms of political collapse in Iraq) (Beirut: al-Mu'asasa al-'Arabiya li al-Dirasat wa al-Nashr, 2003), pp. 80–81.

65. Al-Hasani, *Tarikh al-Wizarat al-'Iraqiya, al-Jusi' al-Rabi'*, pp. 66–68.

66. Al-Suwaydi, *Mudhakarati*, p. 263; Tripp, *A History of Iraq*, p. 83.

67. For the details of the 1935–1936 tribal rebellions see al-Hasani, *Tarikh al-Wizarat al-'Iraqiya, al-Jusi' al-Rabi'*, pp. 101–129, 167–190; 'Abd al-Razak Muhammad Aswad, *Mausu'at al-'Iraq al-Siyasiya, al-Mujalad al-Thalith* (Political encyclopedia of Iraq, volume 3) (Beirut, al-Dar al-'Arabiya li al-Mausa'at, 1986), pp. 126–170; Yitzhak Nakash, *The Shi'is of Iraq* (Princeton, New Jersey: Princeton University Press, 1994, pp. 120–125; Marr, *The Modern History of Iraq*, pp. 40–44; Longrigg, *Iraq, 1900 to 1950*, pp. 240–244.

68. See Fadhil al-Barak, *Dawr al-Jaysh al'Iraqi fi Hukumat al-Difa' al-Watani wa al-Harb ma'a Britania Sanat 1941* (The role of the Iraqi army in the national

defense government and the war with Britain in 1941) (Baghdad: al-Dar al-'Arabiya li al-Tiba'a, 1979), pp. 55–56.

69. 'Aqeel al-Nasiri, *al-Jaysh wa al-Sulta fi al-'Iraq al-Malaki, 1921–1958* (The army and political authority in monarchical Iraq, 1921–1958) (Damascus, Syria: Dar al-Hassad li al-Nashr wa al-Tiba'a, wa al-Tawzi', 2000), p. 85.

70. Ibid., p. 76.

71. Longrigg, *Iraq, 1900 to 1950*, p. 166.

72. Thirty Iraqi soldiers were killed and forty were wounded, with Assyrian casualties numbering about half those of the Iraqis. For details of the "Assyrian affair," see Marr, *The Modern History of Iraq*, pp. 38–39; Tripp, *A History of Iraq*, pp. 74–80; Longrigg, *Iraq, 1900 to 1950*, pp. 231–237.

73. Longrigg, pp. 233–234.

74. Al-Suwaydi, *Mudhakarati*, p. 259.

75. One of the main tribal leaders, Muhsin Abu Tibikh, chronicles with some bitterness the military preponderance of the army and the heavy tribal losses in his *al-Mabadi' wa al-Rijal*, pp. 145–146.

CHAPTER THREE: FRAMING DEMOCRACY WITH A CERTAIN INDIFFERENCE

1. Aristotle, "On Democracy and Tyranny," in Bernard E. Brown and Roy C. Macridis, eds., *Comparative Politics: Notes and Readings*, 8th edition (New York: Harcourt, Brace and Company, 1996), p. 126.

2. Ibid., p. 127.

3. Joseph A. Schumpeter, *Capitalism, Socialism and Democracy*, 2nd edition (New York: Harper, 1947), p. 269.

4. See Samuel P. Huntington, *The Third Wave: Democratization in the Late Twentieth Century* (Norman, Oklahoma: University of Oklahoma Press, 1991), pp. 5–13.

5. Robert A. Dahl, *Polyarchy: Participation and Opposition* (New Haven, Connecticut: Yale University Press, 1971), p. 3.

6. Lawrence Whitehead, *Democratization: Theory and Experience* (Oxford, England: Oxford University Press, 2002), p. 7.

7. See Seymour Martin Lipset, *Political Man: The Social Bases of Politics*, 3rd edition (Baltimore, Maryland: The Johns Hopkins University Press, 1981), p. 31.

8. See Dietrich Rueschemeyer, Evelyne Huber Stephens, and John D. Stephens, *Capitalist Development and Democracy* (Chicago: University of Chicago Press, 1992), pp. 49–50; see also Adeed Dawisha and Karen Dawisha, "How to Build a Democratic Iraq," *Foreign Affairs*, vol. 82, no. 3, May/June 2003.

9. Lipset, *Political Man: The Social Bases of Politics*, pp. 74–75.

10. Seymour Martin Lipset, "Some Social Requisites of Democracy: Economic Development and Political Legitimacy," *The American Political Science Review*, vol. 53, no. 1, March 1959, p. 79.

11. Tawfiq al-Suwaydi, *Mudhakarati: Nisf Qarn min Tarikh al-'Iraq wa al-Qadhiya al-'Arabiya* (My memoirs: half a century of Iraqi history and the Arab undertaking) (London: Dar al-Hikma, 1999), p. 100.

12. 'Ali al-Wardi, *Lamahat Ijtima'iya min Tarikh al-'Iraq al-Hadith, al-Jusi' al-Sadis, 1920–1924* (Sociological aspects of modern Iraqi history, volume six, 1920–1924) (London: Dar Kufan li alNashr, 1992), p. 301.

13. Ibid., p. 302.

14. 'Ali al-Wardi, *Lamahat Ijtima'iya min Tarikh al-'Iraq al-Hadith, al-Jusi' al-Thalith*, (Sociological aspects of modern Iraqi history, volume three) (London: Dar Kufan li al-Nashr, 1992), p. 167.

15. Ibid., p. 190.

16. Ibid., p. 168.

17. 'Abdallah al-Fayadh, *al-Thawra al-'Iraqiya al-Kubra Sanat 1920* (The 1920 great Iraqi revolution) (Baghdad: Matba 'at al-Irshad, 1971), pp. 99–100; al-Wardi, *Lamahat Ijtima'iya min Tarikh al-'Iraq al-Hadith, al-Jusi' al Thalith*, pp. 120–121.

18. Al-Wardi, *Lamahat Ijtima'iya min Tarikh al-'Iraq all-Hadith, al-Jusi' al-Thalith*, pp. 179–181, 249–250.

19. al-Wardi, *Lamahat min Tarikh al-'Iraq al-Hadith*, volume six, p. 309.

20. Philip Ireland, *Iraq: A Study in Political Development* (New York: The Macmillan Company, 1938), p.166.

21. Ibid., p. 169.

22. 'Abd al-Ghani al-Mallah, *Tarikh al-Haraka al-Dimuqratiya fi al-'Iraq* (The history of the democratic movement in Iraq) (Baghdad: Kitab al-Jamahir, 1975), pp. 16–17.

23. Ibid., pp. 17–18.

24. Toby Dodge, *Inventing Iraq: The Failure of Nation-Building and a History Denied* (New York: Columbia University Press, 2003), p. 16.

25. Ireland, *Iraq: A Study in Political Development*, p. 173.

26. See Hadi Hassan 'Ulaywi, *al-Ahzab al-Siyasiya fi al-'Iraq: al-Siriya wa al-'Alaniya* (Political parties in Iraq: secret and public) (Beirut: Riad al-Rayyes li al-Kutub wa al-Nashr, 2001), pp. 46–47.

27. 'Abd al-Wahab Hamid Rashid, *al-'Iraq al-Mu'asir* (Contemporary Iraq) (Damascus: al-Mada Publishing Company, 2002), p. 300.

28. 'Ulyawi, *al-Ahzab al Siyasiya fi al'Iraq*, pp. 42 and 48.

29. Quoted in Ireland, *Iraq: A Study in Political Development*, p. 195.

30. Dodge, *Inventing Iraq*, pp. 15–16; Ireland, *Iraq: A Study in Political Development*, p. 219.

31. Over 400 British officers and soldiers were killed, and the rebellion cost the British treasury a staggering 40 million pound sterling. Phebe Marr, *The Modern History of Iraq*, 2nd edition (Boulder, Colorado: Westview Press, 2004), p. 24.

32. Al-Wardi, *Lamahat Ijtima'iya min Tarikh al-'Iraq al-Hadith, al-Jusi' al-Thalith*, p. 310.

33. Jamil Abu Tibikh, *Mudhakarat al-Sayyid Muhsin Abu Tibikh, 1910–1960: Khamsum 'Amman min Tarikh al-'Iraq al-Siyassi al-Hadith* (Memoirs of Sayyid Muhsin Abu Tibikh, 1910–1960: fifty years of Iraq's modern political history) (Beirut: al-Mu'asasa al-'Arabiya li al-Dirasat wa al-Nashr, 2001), pp. 159–161; Muhamed Mahdi al-Basir, *Tarikh al-Qadhiya al-'Iraqiya* (History of the Iraqi case) (Baghdad: Matba'at al-Fallah, 1924), pp. 245–249; al-Fayadh, *al-Thawra al-'Iraqiya al-Kubra*, pp. 275–277; 'Ali al-Wardi, *Lamahat Ijtima'iya min Tarikh al-'Iraq al-hadith, al-Jusi' al-Khamis, al-Qism al-Awal: Hawla Thwrat al-'Ishrin* (Sociological aspects of modern Iraqi history, volume five, part one: On the Revolution of 1920) (London: Dar Kufan li al-Nashr, 1992), pp. 294–295, 300–303.

34. Abu Tibikh, *Mudhakarat al-Sayyid Muhsin Abu Tibikh*, p. 159.

35. Muhamed 'Ali Kamal al-Din, *Thawrat al-'Ishrin fi Dhikraha al-Khamsin: Ma'lumat wa Mushahadat* (The 1920 revolution on its fiftieth anniversary: information and testimony) (Baghdad: Dar al-Bayan, 1971), pp. 87–88; see also 'Ali al-Wardi, *Lamahat Ijtima'iya min Tarikh al-'Iraq al-hadith, al-Jusi' al-Khamis, al-Qism al-Awal: Hawla Thwrat al-'Ishrin*, p. 306.

36. Al-Wardi, *Lamahat Ijtima'iya min Tarikh al-'Iraq al-Hadith, al-Jusi' al-Thalith*, p. 112.

37. 'Abd al-Razzaq al-Hasani, *Tarikh al-Wizarat al-'Iraqiya, al-Jusi' al-Awal* (History of Iraqi cabinets, volume one) (Baghdad: Dr al-Shu'un al-Thaqafiya al-'Amma, 1988), p. 59.

38. Al-Wardi, *Lamahat Ijtima'iya min Tarikh al-'Iraq al-Hadith, al-Jusi' al-Sadis*, p. 114.

39. Al-Hasani, *Tarikh al-Wizarat al-'Iraqiya, al-Jusi' al-Awal*, p.122; see also Ulaywi, *al-Ahzab al-Siyasiya fi al-'Iraq: al-Siriya wa al-'Alaniya*, pp. 54–58.

40. 'Abd al-Majid Kamil al-Tikriti, *al-Malik Faysal al-Awal wa Dawruhu fi Ta'sis al-Dawla al-'Iraqiya al-Haditha* (King Faysal I and his role in establishing the modern Iraqi state) (Baghdad: Dar al-Shu'un al-Thaqafiya, 1991), p. 110.

41. Hasan al-'Alawi, *al-Shi'a wa al-Dawla al-Qawmiyya, 1914–1990* (The Shi'a and the national state, 1914–1990) (Baghdad: n.p., 1990), pp. 330–340;

Yitzhak Nakash, *Reaching for Power: The Shi'a in the Modern Arab World* (Princeton, New Jersey: Princeton University Press, 2006), p. 79.

42. Al-Hasani, *Tarikh al-Wizarat al-'Iraqiya, al-Jusi' al-Awal*, p. 149.

43. Al-Tikriti, *al-Malik Faysal al-Awal wa Dawruhu fi Ta'sis al-Dawla al-'Iraqiya al-Haditha*, p. 113.

44. Dodge, *Inventing Iraq*, p. 18.

45. Al-Hasani, *Tarikh al-Wizarat al-Iraqiya, al-Jusi' al-Awal*, p. 215.

46. Ireland, *Iraq: A Study in Political Development*, p. 394.

47. Mohammed Modhafar Hashim al-Adhami, *Political Aspects of the Iraqi Parliament and Election Processes, 1920–1932*, Ph.D. Thesis, University of London, 1978, p. 92.

48. Elie Kedouri, *The Chatham House Version and Other Middle Eastern Studies* (London: Weidenfeld and Nicolson, 1970), p. 265.

49. Al-Hukuma al-'Iraqiya, *Majmu'at Mudhkarat al-Majlis al-Ta'sisi al-'Iraqi li Sanat 1924, al-Jusi' al-Awal* (Collection of Memoirs of the Iraqi Constituent Assembly, 1924, volume one) (Baghdad: Matba'at Dar al-Salam, 1924), p. 33 (Hereafter cited as *Majmu'at Mudhakarat al Majlis al-Ta'sisi*).

50. *Majmu'at Mudhakarat al-Majlis al-Ta'sisi*, pp. 329–331.

51. *Majmu'at Mudhakarat al-Majlis al-Ta'sisi*, p. 320.

52. Al-Wardi, *Lamahat Ijtima'iya min Tarikh al-'Iraq al-Hadith, al-Jusi' al-Sadis*, p. 286.

53. Ibid., p. 287.

54. Al-Hasani, *Tarikh al-Wizarat al-'Iraqiya, al-Jusi' al-Awal*, pp. 226–227; al-Wardi, *Lamahat Ijtima'iya min Tarikh al-'Iraq al-Hadith , al-Jusi' al-Sadis*, pp. 288–292.

55. *Majmu'at Mudhakarat al-Majlis al-Ta'sisi*, pp. 333–335.

56. Fahad Muslim al-Fajr, *Muzahim al-Pachachi wa Dawrahu fi al-Siyasa al-'Iraqiya, 1890–1933* (Muzahim al-Pachachi and his role in Iraqi politics, 1890–1933) (Beirut: Dar al-'Arabiya li al-Mausu'at, 2004), p. 74.

57. Dodge, *Inventing Iraq*, p. 91.

58. *Majmou'at Mudhakaraat al-Majlis al-Ta'sisi*, p. 445; Rashid, *al-'Iraq al-Mu'asir*, p. 82; al-Wardi, *Lamahat min Tarikh al-'Iraq al-Hadith, vol.6*, pp. 295–296; Ireland, *Iraq: A Study in Political Development*, pp. 401–404.

59. Al-A'dhami, *Political Aspects of the Iraqi Parliament and Election Processes, 1920–1932*, pp. 221–222.

60. 'Abd al-Rahman al-Bazzaz, *al-'Iraq min al-ihtilal ala al-Istiqlal* (Iraq from occupation to independence) (Baghdad: Matba'at al-'Ani, 1967), p. 156.

61. Ireland, *Iraq: A Study in Political Development*, p. 385.

62. Al-Tikriti, *al-Malik Faysal al-Awal wa Dawruhu fi Tai'sis al-Dawla al-'Iraqiya al-Haditha*, p. 283.

63. See Faiz al As'ad, *Inhiraf al-Nidham al-Birlimani fi al-'Iraq* (The deviation of the parliamentary system in Iraq) (Baghdad: Maktabat al-Sindibad, 1984), footnote 10, pp. 32–33.

64. Majid Khadduri, *Nidham al-Hukum fi al-'Iraq* (The System of Governance in Iraq) (Baghdad: Matba'at al-Ma'arif, 1946), p. 93.

65. See Ireland, *Iraq: A Study in Political Development*, p. 431.

66. Ibid., p. 432; A secret letter from the Administrative Inspector of Baghdad to the British Advisor of the Interior Ministry confirms the advisability of allowing a small number of opposition candidates to win in the elections of 1930. See al-Adhami, *Political Aspects of the Iraqi Parliament and Election Processes, 1920–1932*, p. 295.

67. Stephen Hemsley Longrigg, *Iraq, 1900–1950: A Political, Social and Economic History* (London: Oxford University Press, 1953), p. 224. See also al-Suwaydi, *Mudhakarati: Nisf Qarn min Tarikh al-'Iraq wa al-Qadhiya al-'Arabiya*, pp. 104–105.

68. Rashid, *al-'Iraq al-Mu'asir*, p. 84.

69. Khadduri, *Nidham al-Hkum fi al-'Iraq*, p. 90.

70. Ibid., p. 90.

71. Adeed Dawisha, "Democratic Attitudes and Practices in Iraq, 1921–1958," *Middle East Journal*, vol. 59, no. 1, Winter 2005, pp. 21–22.

72. Al-Suwaydi, *Mudhakarati: Nisf Qarn min Tarikh al-Iraq wa al-Qadhiya al-'Arabiya*, p. 104.

73. Ireland, *Iraq: A Study in Political Development*, p. 433.

74. Dawlat al-'Iraq, *Mahadhir Majlis al-Nuwab, 1930* (Debates of the Chamber of Deputies, 1930), pp. 71–90. (Henceforth cited as Mahadhir, various years).

75. *Mahadhir, 1930*, pp. 73–78.

76. Ireland, *Iraq: A Study in Political Development*, footnote 2, p. 42.

77. Longrigg, *Iraq 1900–1950*, p. 225.

78. Khadduri, *Nidham al-Hukum fi al-'Iraq*, pp. 97–98.

79. Al-Wardi, *Lamahat Ijtima'iya min Tarikh al-'Iraq al-Hadith, al-Jusi' al-Thalith*, pp. 185–186; Rashid, *al-'Iraq al-Mu'asir*, p. 301.

80. Ahlam Husayn Jamil, *al-Afkar al-Siyasiya li al-Ahzab al-'Iraqiya fi 'Ahd al-Intidab* (Political ideas of the Iraqi parties in the mandate period) (Baghdad: Maktabat al-Muthana, 1985), p. 21.

81. Rufai'il Butti, *al-Sahafa al-'Iraqiya* (the press in Iraq) (Matba'at al-Hana', 1955), pp. 101–119; see also al-Mallah, *Tarikh al-Haraka al-Dimuqratiya fi al-'Iraq*, p. 107.

82. Khadduri, *Nidham al-Hukum fi al-'Iraq*, pp. 106–107; see also Ireland, *Iraq: A Study in Political Development*, pp. 409–412.

83. Majid Khadduri, *Independent Iraq, 1932–1958: A Study in Iraqi Politics*, 2nd edition (London: Oxford University Press, 1960), pp. 29–30.

84. Muhamed Mahdi Kubba, *Mudhakarati fi Samim al-Ahdath, 1918–1958* (My memoirs in the midst of events) (Beirut: Dar al-Tali'ah, 1965), p. 33.

85. Jamil, *al-Afkar al-Siyasiya li al-Ahzab al-'Iraqiya fi 'Ahd al-Intidab*, p. 24.

86. Al-Wardi, *Lamahat Ijtima'iya min Tarikh al-'Iraq al-Hadith, al-Jusi' al-Thalith*, p. 248.

87. 'Abd al-Razzak al-Hasani, *Tarikh al-Sahafa al-'Iraqiya* (History of Iraqi journalism) (Sayda, Lebanon: Matba'at al-'Irfan, 1971), p. 2.

88. Al-Fayadh, *al-Thawra al-'Iraqiya al-Kubra Sanat 1920*, p. 59.

89. Quoted in Ireland, *Iraq: A Study in Political Development*, p. 230.

90. Butti, *al-Sahafa fi al'Iraq*, p. 60.

91. Al-Wardi, *Lamahat Ijtima'iya min Tarikh al-'Iraq al-Hadith, al-Jusi' al-Sadis*, p. 75.

92. Charles Tripp, *A History of Iraq* (Cambridge, England: Cambridge University Press, 2000), p. 65.

93. Quoted in Ireland, *Iraq: A Study in Political Development*, p. 352.

94. Ibid., p. 416.

95. Kamel al-Chaderji, *Mudhakarat Kamel al-Chaderji wa Tarikh al-Hizb al-Watani al-Dimuqrati* (Memoirs of Kamel al-Chaderji and the history of the National Democratic Party) (Cologne, Germany: Manshurat al-Jamal, 2002), pp. 92–96.

96. Ibid., p. 87.

97. Mudhafar 'Abd Allah al-Amin, *Jama'at al-Ahali: Manshu'ha, 'Aqidatihu, wa Dawruha fi al-Siyasa al-'Iraqiya, 1932–1946* (al-Ahali group: its origin, ideology, and role in Iraqi politics, 1932–1946) (Beirut, Lebanon: al-Mu'sasa al'Arabiya li al-Dirasat wa al-Nashr, 2001), pp. 124–125.

98. Ibid., also Muhammad al-Dulaimi, *Kamel al-Chaderji wa Dawruhu fi al-Siyasa al-'Iraqiya* (Kamel al-Chaderji and his role in Iraqi politics) (Beirut, Lebanon: al-Mu'asasa al-'Arabiya li al-Dirasat wa al-Nashr, 1999), pp. 66–68.

99. 'Abd al-Razzaq al-Hasani, *Tarikh al-Sahafa al-'Iraqiya, al-Jusi' al-Awal*, p. 2.

100. For a detailed discussion of the newspapers of the political parties and their political orientations in this period, see 'Abd al-Jabbar Hasan al-Jubburi, *al-Ahzab wa al-Jim'iyat al-Siyasiyya fi al-Qitr al-Iraqi, 1908–1958* (Political parties and organizations in the Iraqi region, 1908–1958) (Baghdad: Dar al-Huriya li al-Tiba'a, 1977), pp. 58–82; see also Butti, *al-Sahafa fi al-Iraq*, pp. 93–119.

CHAPTER FOUR: THE UNCERTAIN NATION

1. Janet Wallach, *Desert Queen: The Extraordinary Life of Gertrude Bell* (New York: Doubleday, 1996), pp. 297–298.

2. Hugh Seton Watson, *Nations and States: An Inquiry into the Origins of Nations and the Politics of Nationalism* (Boulder, Colorado: Westview Press, 1977), p. 5.

3. Liah Greenfield, *Nationalism: Five Roads to Modernity* (Cambridge, Massachusetts: Harvard University Press, 1992), pp. 4–9.

4. See Rogers Brubaker, *Citizenship and Nationhood in France and Germany* (Cambridge, Massachusetts: Harvard University Press, 1992); Hans Kohn, *Prelude to Nation-States: The French and German Experience, 1789–1815* (London: D. Van Nostrand Company, 1967).

5. A detailed analysis of the two intellectual strands can be found in Adeed Dawisha, "Nation and Nationalism: Historical Antecedents to Contemporary Debates," *International Studies Review*, vol. 4, no.1, Spring 2002.

6. Ernest Gellner, *Nations and Nationalism* (Ithaca, New York: Cornell University Press, 1983), p. 48.

7. Ernest Renan, "What Is a Nation?", in Homi K. Bhabha, ed., *Nation and Narration*, (London: Routledge, 1990), p. 11.

8. Selim Matar, *al-Dhat al-Jariha: Ishkalat al-Hawiya fi al-'Iraq wa al-'Alem al-'Arabi "al-Shirqani* (Wounded essence: problems of identity in Iraq and the "Eastern" Arab world) (Beirut: al-Mu'asasa al-'Arabiya li al-Dirasat wa al-Nashr, 1997), p. 415.

9. David McDowall, *A Modern History of the Kurds* (London: I. B. Tauris, 1996), pp. 450–451.

10. Edmund Ghareeb, *The Kurdish Question in Iraq* (Syracuse, New York: Syracuse University Press, 1981), p. 4.

11. Najdat Fathi Safwat, *al-'Iraq fi Mudhakarat al-Diblomasiyeen al-Ajanib* (Iraq in the memoirs of foreign diplomats) (Baghdad: Maktabat Dar al-Tarbiya, 1984), p. 117.

12. Bernard Lewis, *The Middle East: A Brief History of the Last 2,000 Years* (New York: Scribner, 1995), p. 226.

13. Phebe Marr, *The Modern History of Iraq*, 2nd edition (Boulder, Colorado: Westview Press, 2004), pp. 13–14.

14. Quoted in 'Ali al-Wardi, *Lamahat Ijtima'iya min Tarikh al-'Iraq al-Hadith, al-Jusi' al-Thalith* (Sociological aspects of modern Iraqi history, volume three) (London: Dar Kufan li-al-Nashr, 1992), p. 263.

15. Yitzhak Nakash, *The Shi'is of Iraq* (Princeton, New Jersey: Princeton University Press, 1994), p. 122.

16. See Hassan Al-'Alawi, *al-Shi'a wa al-Dawla al-Qawmiya fi al-'Iraq, 1914–1990* (The Shi'ites and the nationalist state in Iraq, 1914–1990) (n.p., 1990).

17. 'Ali al-Wardi, *Lamahat Ijtima'iya min Tarikh al-'Iraq al-hadith, al-Jusi' al-Sadis, min 'Am 1920 ila 'Am 1924* (Sociological aspects of modern Iraqi history, part six, 1920–1924) (London: Dar Kufan li al-Nashr, 1992), pp. 128–129.

18. Hanna Batatu, *The Old Social Classes and the Revolutionary Movements in Iraq: A Study of Iraq's Old Landed and Commercial Classes and of Its Communists, Ba'thists and Free Officers* (Princeton, New Jersey: Princeton University Press, 1978), pp. 27–28.

19. Bassam Tibi, "The Simultaneity of the Unsimultaneous: Old Tribes and Imposed Nation-States in the Modern Middle East," in Philip S. Khoury and Joseph Kostiner, eds., *Tribes and State Formation in the Middle East* (Berkeley: University of California Press), p. 127.

20. 'Ali al-Wardi, *Lamahat Ijtima'iya min Tarikh al-'Iraq al-Hadith, al-Jusi' al-Rabi', min 'Amm 1914 ila 'Amm 1918* (Sociological aspects of modern Iraqi history, volume four, 1914–1918) (London: Dar Kufan li al-Nashr, 1992), pp. 402–403. See also Fadhil al-Barak, *Dawr al-Jaysh al-'Iraqi fi Hukumat al-Difa' al-Watani wa al-Harb ma'a Britania Sanat 1941* (The role of the Iraqi army in the National Defense Government and the war with Britain, 1941) (Baghdad: al-Dar al-'Arabiya li al-Tiba'a, 1979), p. 54.

21. 'Abd al-Razzak al-Hasani, *Tarikh al-Wizarat al-'Iraqiya, al-Jusi' al-Thalith, 1930–1933* (The history of Iraqi cabinets, volume 3, 1930–1933) (Baghdad: Dar al-Shu'un al-Thaqafiya al-'Amma, 1988), p. 243; see also Nakash, *The Shi'is of Iraq*, p. 114; and Marr, *The Modern History of Iraq*, 2nd edition, p. 42.

22. Quoted in Liona Lukitz, *Iraq: The Search for National Identity* (London: Frank Cass, 1995), p. 65.

23. Quoted in Nakash, *The Shi'is of Iraq*, p. 117.

24. Naji Shawkat, *Sira wa Dhikrayat thamaneena 'Aman, 1894–1974* (Biography and memoirs of eighty years, 1894–1974) (Baghdad: Maktabat al-Yaqdha al-'Arabiya, 1990), pp. 623–626.

25. Philip Ireland, *Iraq: A Study in Political Development* (New York: The Macmillan Company, 1938), pp. 234–235.

26. Al-Wardi, *Lamahat Ijtima'iya min Tarikh al'Iraq al-Hadith, al-Jusi' al-Thalith*, p. 216.

27. Charles Tripp, *A History of Iraq* (Cambridge, England: Cambridge University Press, 2000), p. 27.

28. Ireland, *Iraq: A Study in Political Development*, p. 457.

29. Majid Khadduri, *Nidham al-Hukm fi al-'Iraq* (The system of governance in Iraq) (Baghdad: Matba'at al-Ma'arif, 1946), pp. 6–7.

30. 'Abd al-Wahab Hamid Rashid, *al-'Iraq al-Mu'asir* (Contemporary Iraq) (Damascus, Syria: Dar al-Mada li al-Thaqafa wa al-Nashr, 2002), p. 279.

31. Marr, *The Modern History of Iraq*, 2nd edition, p. 23.

32. 'Ali al-Wardi, *Lamahat Ijtima'iya min Tarikh al-'Iraq al-Hadith, al-Jusi' al Khamis, Hawla Thawrat al-'Ishrin* (Sociological aspects of modern Iraqi history, volume 5, about the 1920 revolution) (London: Dar Kufan li al-Nashr, 1992), pp. 191–192.

33. Quoted in ibid., p. 195.

34. 'Abd al-Rahman al-Bazzaz, *al-'Iraq min al-Ihtilal hatta al-Istiqlal* (Iraq from occupation to independence) (Baghdad: Matba'at al-'Ani, 1967), pp. 105–107.

35. Al-Wardi, *Lamahat Ijtima'iya min Tarikh al-'Iraq al-Hadith, al-Jusi' al-Sadis*, pp. 140–146.

36. For detailed analyses of Husri's life and ideas, see William L. Cleveland, *The Making of an Arab Nationalist: Ottomanism and Arabism in the Life and Thought of Sati' al-Husri* (Princeton, New Jersey: Princeton University Press, 1971); also Bassam Tibi, *Arab Nationalism: A Critical Enquiry* (New York: St. Martin's Press, 1981), parts III and IV; and Adeed Dawisha, *Arab Nationalism in the Twentieth Century: From Triumph to Despair* (Princeton, New Jersey: Princeton University Press, 2003), especially chapter three. For an assessment of Husri written by an Iraqi political scientist, himself an avowed Arab nationalist, see Wamidh Jamal 'Umar Nadhmi, "Fikr Sati' al-Husri al Qawmi," (The nationalist thought of Sati' al-Husri), *al-Mustaqbal al-'Arabi*, no. 81 (November 1985).

37. For the pivotal role of language in national consolidation, the prominent German nationalist writer, Johann Gotlieb Fichte, argues that language ties members of a nation together making them "one indivisible whole." Quoted in K. R. Minogue, *Nationalism* (New York: Basic Books, 1967), p. 64; see also Fichte's "Addresses to the German Nation," in *The Nationalism Reader*, Omar Dahbour and Micheline R. Ishay, eds., (New York: Humanity Books, 1999), p. 69. On the way the reformation facilitated the spread of German as the literary medium, see Benedict Anderson, *Imagined Communities: Reflections on the Origins and Spread of Nationalism* (New York: Verso, 1990), pp. 38–42. On the impact of the "English" Bible in fostering nationalism in England, see Adrian Hastings, *The Construction of Nationhood: Ethnicity, Religion and Nationalism* (Cambridge, England: Cambridge University Press, 1997), pp. 19–25.

38. Albert Hourani, *Arabic Thought in the Liberal Age, 1798–1939* (London: Oxford University Press), p. 315.

39. As already mentioned, a book written by a Syrian Sunni author in 1933, which insinuated that Shi'ite teachers in Iraq were more loyal to Iran than to Iraq, was a pretty close representation of views held by many Iraqi Sunnis. For a description of the incident and its political ramifications, see 'Abd al-Razzak al-Hasani, *Tarikh al-Wizarat al-'Iraqiya, al-Jusi' al-Thalith*, p. 243.

40. See Yitzhak Nakash, *Reaching for Power: The Shi'a in the Modern Arab World* (Princeton, New Jersey: Princeton University Press, 2006), p. 81.

41. 'Aqeel al-Nasiri, *al-Jaysh wa al-Sulta fi al-'Iraq al-Malaki, 1921–1958* (The Army and the political authority in monarchical Iraq, 1921–1958) (Damascus, Syria: Dar al-Hassad li al-Nashr wa al-Tiba'a was al-Tawzi', 2000), p. 71.

42. 'Abd al-Majid Hassan Wali and 'Ala' al-Din al-Rayyas, *Ahwal al-'Iraq al-Ijtima'iya wa al-Iqtisadiya* (Social and economic affairs of Iraq) (Baghdad: Mataba'at al-Rashid, 1946), p. 131.

43. Quoted in Malik Mufti, *Sovereign Creations: Pan Arabism and Political Order in Syria and Iraq* (Ithaca, New York: Cornell University Press, 1996), p. 29.

44. Quoted in Michael Howard, *The Lessons of History* (New Haven, Connecticut: Yale University Press, 1991), p. 145; see also Minogue, *Nationalism*, p. 41.

45. See Eugene Weber, *Peasants into Frenchmen: The Modernization of Rural France, 1870–1914* (London: Chatto and Windus, 1979).

46. Hans Kohn, *Nationalism: Its Meaning and History* (Princeton, New Jersey: D. Van Nostrand Company, Inc., 1955), p. 26.

47. Gellner, *Nations and Nationalism*, p. 34.

48. Al-Wardi, *Lamahat Ijtima'iya min Tarikh al-'Iraq al-Hadith, al-Jusi' al-Thalith*, pp. 260–261.

49. Quoted in Lahouari Addi, "The Failure of Third World Nationalism," *Journal of Democracy,* vol. 8, (October 1997), p. 119.

50. Abu Khaldun Sati' al-Husri, *Ara' wa Ahadith fi al-Wataniya wa al-Qawmiya* (Views and discussions on patriotism and nationalism) (Beirut, Lebanon: Markaz Dirasat al-Wuhda al-'Arabiya, 1984), pp. 95–96.

51. Phebe Marr, "The Development of Nationalist Ideology in Iraq, 1920–1941," *The Muslim World*, vol. LXXV, no.2, April 1985, pp. 96–97.

52. Quoted in Cleveland, *The Making of an Arab Nationalist*, p. 147.

53. See Marr, "The Development of Nationalist Ideology in Iraq, 1920–1941," pp. 92–94; see also Reeva Spector Simon, *Iraq Between the Two World Wars: The Militarist Origins of Tyranny* (New York: Columbia University Press, 2004), p. 85.

54. See Muhammad Mahdi al-Jawahiri, *Dhikrayati* (My memoirs) (Damascus: Dar al-Rafidayn, 1988), p. 163.

55. 'Abd al-Majid Kamel al-Tikriti, *al-Malik Faysal al-Awal wa Dawruhu fi Ta'sis al-Dawla al-'Iraqiya al-Haditha, 1921–1933* (King Faysal I and his role in establishing the modern Iraqi state, 1921–1933) (Baghdad: Dar al-Shu'un al-Thaqafiya al-'Amma, 1991), pp. 277–279.

56. Phebe Marr, *The Modern History of Iraq* (Boulder, Colorado: Westview Press, 1985), p. 138.

57. Ireland, *Iraq: A Study in Political Development*, p. 447.

58. Marr, "The Development of a Nationalist Ideology in Iraq, 1920–1941," p. 98.

59. See Simon, *Iraq Between the Two World Wars*, p. 86; Marr, "The Development of Nationalist Ideology in Iraq," p. 99.

60. Batatu, *The Old Social Classes and the Revolutionary Movements of Iraq*, p. 34, and Marr, "The Development of Nationalist Ideology," p. 99.

61. C. J. Edmonds, *Kurds, Turks and Arabs* (London: Oxford University Press, 1957), pp. 392–394.

62. Kerim Yildiz, *The Kurds in Iraq: The Past, Present and Future* (London: Pluto Press, 2004), pp. 13–14.

63. Tripp, *A History of Iraq*, pp. 67–68.

64. Majid Khadduri, *Independent Iraq, 1932–1958: A Study in Iraqi Politics* (London: Oxford University Pres, 1960), p. 61.

65. Batatu, *The Old Social Classes and the Revolutionary Movements of Iraq*, p. 467.

66. Al-Nasiri, *al-Jaysh wa al-Sulta fi al-'Iraq al-Malaki, 1921–1958*, p. 77.

67. Ibid., pp. 74–78.

68. 'Abd al-Karim al-Uzri, *Tarikh fi Dhikrayat al-'Iraq, 1930–1958* (History in the memoirs of Iraq, 1930–1958) (Beirut, Lebanon: Markaz al-Abjadiya, 1982), p. 145.

Chapter Five: Turbulence in Governance

1. 'Abd al-Razzaq al-Hasani, *Tarikh al-Wizarat al-'Iraqiya, al-Jusi' al-Rabi'* (History of Iraqi Cabinets, volume four) (Baghdad: Dar al-Shu'un al-Thaqafiya al-'Amma, 1988, p. 208.

2. Muhammad al-Dulaymi, *Kamel al-Chaderji wa Dawruhu fi al-Siyasa al-'Iraqiya* (Kamel al-Chaderji and his role in Iraqi politics) (Beirut, al-Mu'asasa al-'Arabiya li al-Dirasat wa al-Nashr, 1999), pp. 71–72.

3. Kamel al-Chaderji, *Mudhakarat Kamel-Chaderji wa Tarikh al-Hizb al-Watani al-Dimuqrati* (The memoirs of Kamel al-Chaderji and the history of the

National Democratic Party) (Cologne, Germany: al-Jamal Publications, 2002), pp. 88–89.

4. Mudhafar 'Abd Allah al-Amin, *Jama'at al-Ahali: Mansha'uha, 'Aqidatuha, wa Dawruha fi al-Siyasa al-'Iraqiya, 1932–1946* (The Ahali group: its origins, belief and role in Iraqi politics, 1932–1946) (Beirut: al-Mu'sasa al-'Arabiya li al-Dirasat wa al-Nashr, 2001), p. 115; see also al-Hasani, *Tarikh al-Wizarat al-'Iraqiya, al-Jusi' al-Rabi'*, p. 216.

5. Tawfiq al-Suwaydi, *Mudhakarati: Nisf Qarn min Tarikh al-'Iraq wa al-Qadhiya al-'Arabiya* (My memoirs: half a century of the history of Iraq and the Arab undertaking) (London: Dar al-Hikma, 1999), pp. 270–271; see al-Hasani, *Tarikh al-Wizarat al-'Iraqiya, al-Jusi' al-Rabi'*, p. 208.

6. Al-Dulaymi, *Kamel al-Chaderji wa Dawruhu fi al-Siyasa al-'Iraqiya,* pp. 75–76.

7. Phebe Marr, *The Modern History of Iraq,* 2nd edition (Boulder, Colorado: Westview Press, 2004), p. 47.

8. Najda Fathi Safwat, *al-'Iraq fi Mudhakarat al-Diblomasiyeen al-Ajanib* (Iraq in the memoirs of foreign diplomats) (Baghdad: Maktabat Dar al-Tarbiya, 1984), pp. 117–118.

9. Al-Hasani, *Tarikh al-Wizarat al-'Iraqiya, al-Jusi' al-Rabi'*, pp. 306–318.

10. Al-Amin, *Jama'at al-Ahali: Mansha'uha, 'Aqidatuha, wa Dawruha fi al-Siyasa al-'Iraqiya, 1932–1946,* p. 132.

11. Muhsin Abu Tibikh, *al-Mabadi'wa al-Rijal: Bawader al-Inhiyar al-Siyasi fi al-'Iraq* (Principles and men: symptoms of political collapse in Iraq) (Beirut: al-Mu'asasa al-'Arabiya li al-Dirasat wa al-Nashr, 2002), p. 328.

12. Taha al-Hashemi, *Mudhakarat Taha al-Hashimi, 1919–1943* (Memoirs of Taha al-Hashimi, 1919–1943) (Beirut: Dar al-Tali'a, 1967), p. 230.

13. Al-Hasani, *Tarikh al-Wizarat al-'Iraqiya, al-Jusi' al-Rabi'*, p. 318.

14. See Abu Tibikh, *al-Mabadi' wa al Rijal,* p. 262.

15. Majid Khadduri, *Independent Iraq, 1932–1958: A Study in Iraqi Politics* (London: Oxford University Press, 1960), pp. 115–116.

16. Taleb Mushtaq, *Awraq Ayami, al-Jusi' al-Awal, 1900–1958* (Papers from my days, volume one, 1900–1958) (Beirut: Dar al-Tali'a, 1968), pp. 247–249.

17. Al-Hasani, *Tarikh al-Wizarat al-'Iraqiya, al-Jusi' al-Rabi'*, p. 46.

18. Al-Suwaydi, *Mudhakarati: Nisf Qarn min Tarikh al-'Iraq wa al-Qadhiya al-'Arabiya,* p. 306.

19. 'Abd al-Razzaq Muhamed al-Aswad, *Mawsu'at al-'Iraq al-Siyasiya, al-Mujaled al-Thalith: al-Intifadhat al-Sha'biya, al-Thwrat fi Mantaqat al-Furat, al-Inqilabat* (Political encyclopedia of Iraq, volume three: popular insurrections, revolutions in the Euphrates region, coups d'etat) (Beirut, Lebanon: al-Dar al-

'Arabiya li al-Mawsu'at, 1986), p. 250; see also al-Suwaydi, *Mudhakarati: Nisf Qarn min Tarikh al-'Iraq wa al-Qadhiya al-'Arabiya*, pp. 47–48.

20. Salah al-Din al-Sabagh, *Fursan al-'Uruba fi al-'Iraq* (The knights of Arabism in Iraq) (Damascus: n.p., 1956), p. 95.

21. Ibid., pp. 122–124.

22. Khadduri, *Independent Iraq*, p. 189.

23. Al-Suwaydi, *Mudhakarati: Nisf Qarn min Tarikh al-'Iraq wa al-Qadhiya al-'Arabiya*, pp. 313–315.

24. 'Aqeel al-Nasiri, *al-Jaysh wa al-Sulta fi al-'Iraq al-Malaki, 1921–1958* (The army and political authority in monarchical Iraq, 1921–1958) (Damascus, Syria: Dar al-Hassad li al-Nashr wa al-Tawzi' wa al-Tiba'a, 2000), p. 85.

25. Walid al-A'dhami, *Intifadhat Rashid 'Ali al-Gaylani wa al-Harb al-'Iraqiya-al-Britaniya, 1941* (The insurrection of Rashid 'Ali al-Gaylani and the 1941 Iraqi-British war) (Baghdad: Dar Wasit, 1986), p. 129.

26. Quoted in Hanna Batatu, *The Old Social Classes and the Revolutionary Movements of Iraq* (Princeton, New Jersey: Princeton University Press, 1978), p. 30.

27. Al-A'dhami, *Intifadhat Rashid 'Ali al-Gaylani wa al-Harb al-'Iraqiya-al-Britaniya, 1941*, pp. 128–129.

28. Batatu, *The Old Social Classes and the Revolutionary Movements in Iraq*, p. 360.

29. al-Hashemi, *Mudhakarat Taha al-Hashemi, 1919–1943*, pp. 432–433.

30. Al-Amin, *Jama'at al-Ahali: Mansha'uha, 'Aqidatuha, wa Dawruha fi al-Siyasa al-'Iraqiya, 1932–1946*, p. 147; see also al-Suwaydi, *Mudhakarati: Nisf Qarn min Tarikh al-'Iraq wa al-Qadhiya al-'Arabiya*, pp. 394–397.

31. Al-Amin, *Jama'at al-Ahali: Mansha'uha, 'Aqidatuha, wa Dawruha fi al-Siyasa al-'Iraqiya, 1932–1946*, p. 148.

32. Michael Eppel, *Iraq from Monarchy to Tyranny: From the Hashemites to the Rise of Saddam* (Gainesville, Florida: University Press of Florida, 2004), p. 61.

33. Phebe Marr, *The Modern History of Iraq* (Boulder Colorado: Westview Press, 1985), pp. 59–60.

34. Al-Amin, *Jama'at al-Ahali: Mansha'uha, 'Aqidatuha, wa Dawruha fi al-Siyasa al-'Iraqiya, 1932–1946*, p. 152.

35. 'Abd al-Razzaq al-Hasani, *Tarikh al-Wizarat al-'Iraqiya, al-Jusi' al-Sadis* (History of Iraqi Cabinets, volume six) (Baghdad: Dar al-Shu'un al-Thaqafiya al-'Amma, 1988), p. 82.

36. Marr, *The Modern History of Iraq*, 2nd edition, p. 59.

37. Al-Amin, *Jama'at al-Ahali: Mansha'uha, 'Aqidatuha, wa Dawruha fi al-Siyasa al-'Iraqiya, 1932–1946*, p. 150.

38. *United Nations Statistical Yearbook 1963* (New York: United Nations, Department of Economic and Social Affairs, 1963), p. 349.

39. Marr, *The Modern History of Iraq*, 2nd ed., p. 60.

40. See 'Abd al-Razzaq al-Hasani, *Tarikh al-Wizarat al-'Iraqiya, al-Jusi'al-Sadis*, pp. 234–237.

41. Ibid., pp. 312–316.

42. Dawlat al-'Iraq, *Mahadhir Majlis al-Nuwab, 1945–1946* (Proceedings of the Chamber of Deputies, 1945–1946), p. 90.

43. Hadi Husayn 'Ulaywi, *al-Ahzab al-Siyasiya fi al-'Iraq: al-Sirriya wa al-'Alaniya* (Political parties in Iraq: secret and open) (Beirut: Riad al-Rayyes Books, 2001), pp. 119, 121.

44. Kadhim al-Musawi, *Al-'Iraq: Safahat min al-Tarikh al-Siyasi, 1945–1958* (Iraq: pages from political history, 1945–1958) (Damascus, Syria: Dar 'Ala' al-Din, 1998), pp. 34–37.

45. Al-Suwaydi, *Mudhakarati: Nisf Qarn min Tarikh al-'Iraq wa al-Qadhiya al-'Arabiya*, p. 417.

46. From Foreign Office documents quoted in al-Amin, *Jama'at al-Ahali: Mansha'uha, 'Aqidatuha, wa Dawruha fi al-Siyasa al-'Iraqiya, 1932–1946*, p. 166.

47. 'Abd al-Razzaq al-Hasani, *Tarikh al-Wizarat al-'Iraqiya, al-Jusi' al-Sabi'* (History of Iraqi Cabinets, volume seven) (Baghdad: Dar al-Shu'un al-Thaqafiya al-'Amma, 1988), pp. 115–121.

48. Ibid., p. 122; also Khadduri, *Independent Iraq, 1932–1958: A Study in Iraqi Politics*, pp. 256–257.

49. Tawfiq al-Suwaydi, *Mudhakarati: Nisf Qarn min Tarikh al-'Iraq wa al-Qadhiya al-'Arabiya*, p. 450; al-Hasani, *Tarikh al-Wizarat al-'Iraqiya, al-Jusi' al-Sabi'*, 127.

50. Al-Amin, *Jama'at al-Ahali: Mansha'uha, 'Aqidatuha, wa Dawruha fi al-Siyasa al-'Iraqiya, 1932–1946*, p. 166.

51. Al-Hasani, *Tarikh al-Wizarat al-'Iraqiya, al-Jusi' al-Sabi'*, pp. 214–222.

52. See Khadduri, *Independent Iraq, 1932–1958: A Study in Iraqi Politics*, p. 272.

53. Al-Hasani, *Tarikh al-Wizarat al-'Iraqiya, al-Jusi' al-Sabi'*, pp. 318–323.

54. 'Abd al-Razzaq al-Hasani, *Tarikh al-Wizarat al-'Iraqiya, al-Jusi' al-Thamin* (History of Iraqi Cabinets, volume eight) (Baghdad: Dar al-Shu'un al-Thaqafiya al-'Amma, 1988), p. 325; Khadduri, *Independent Iraq, 1932–1958: A Study in Iraqi Politics*, p. 282.

55. See Al-Hasani, *Tarikh al-Wizarat al-'Iraqiya, al-Jusi' al-Thamin*, p. 335.

56. Al-Suwaydi, *Mudhakarati: Nisf Qarn min Tarikh al-'Iraq wa al-Qadhiya al-'Arabiya*, p. 519.

57. Al-Hasani, *Tarikh al-Wizarat al-ʻIraqiya, al-Jusi' al-Thamin*, pp. 344–345.

58. George Grassmuck, "The Electoral Process in Iraq, 1952–1958," *Middle East Journal*, vol. 14, no. 4, Autumn 1960, pp. 401–403.

59. For a vivid, yet succinct, eyewitness account told to the newly arrived American Ambassador in Iraq, see Waldemar J. Gallman, *Iraq Under General Nuri: My Recollections of Nuri al-Said, 1954–1958* (Baltimore, Maryland: The Johns Hopkins University Press, 1964), pp. 3–4.

60. Muhammad Tawfiq Husayn, *ʻIndama Yathur al-ʻIraq* (When Iraq rebels) (Beirut, Lebanon: Dar al-ʻIlm li al-Malayeen, 1959), p. 217.

61. ʻAbd al-Razzaq al-Hasani, *Tarikh al-Wizarat al-ʻIraqiya, al Jusi' al-Tasiʻ* (History of Iraqi Cabinets, volume nine) (Baghdad: Dar al-Shu'un al-Thaqafiya al-ʻAmma, 1988), pp. 180–181.

62. Gallman, *Iraq Under General Nuri: My Recollections of Nuri al-Said, 1954–1958*, p. 6; also Grassmuck, "The Electoral Process in Iraq, 1952–1958," pp. 410–411.

63. Al-Hasani, *Tarikh al-Wizarat al-ʻIraqiya, al Jusi' al-Tasiʻ*, pp. 5–6.

64. ʻAbd al-Rahman al-Bayati, *Saʻid Qazzaz wa Dawruhu fi Siyasat al-ʻIraq hatta ʻAmm 1959* (Saʻid Qazzaz and his role in Iraqi politics till 1959) (Beirut, Lebanon: al-Mu'asasa al-ʻArabiya li al-Dirasat wa al-Nashr, 2001), p. 134.

65. Ibid., p. 137.

66. Ahmad Fawzi, *al-Muthir min Ahdath al-ʻIraq al-Siyasiya* (The sensational in Iraqi political events) (Baghdad: Dar al-Huriya li al-Tibaʻa, 1988), p. 222–223; al-Bayati, *Saʻid Qazzaz wa Dawruhu fi Siyasat al-ʻIraq hatta ʻAmm 1959*, pp. 136–138.

67. Grassmuck, "The Electoral Process in Iraq, 1952–1958," p. 414.

68. Nasir's interview with *The Sunday Times* (London), June 24, 1962.

69. Quoted in Robert Stephens, *Nasser: A Political Biography* (London: Allen Lane/Penguin Press, 1971), p. 149.

70. ʻAbd al-Latif al-Baghdadi, *Mudhakarat ʻAbd al-Latif al-Baghdadi, al-Jusi' al-Awal* (Memoirs of ʻAbd al-Latif al-Baghdadi, volume one) (Cairo: al-Maktab al-Musri al-Hadith, 1977), p. 200.

71. The "Voice of the Arabs" mounted virulent attacks on the Iraqi leadership almost on a daily basis during the months of February and March. Full reports of the broadcasts of the Egyptian station are documented in the daily editions of The British Broadcasting Corporation, *Summary of World Broadcasts, Part IV: The Arab World, Israel, Greece, Turkey, Iran*.

72. See al-Hasani, *Tarikh al-Wizarat al-ʻIraqiya, al-Jusi' al Tasiʻ*, footnote 3, pp. 219–220; Gallman, *Iraq Under General Nuri*, p. 49.

73. Al-Suwaydi, *Mudhakarati: Nisf Qarn min Tarikh al-'Iraq wa al-Qadhiya al-'Arabiya*, p. 552.

74. Naji Shawkat, *Sira wa Dhikrayat Thamaneena 'Aman, 1894–1974* (Biography and memoirs of eighty years, 1894–1974) (Baghdad: Maktabat al-Yaqdha al-'Arabiya, 1974), p. 586.

75. See 'Abd al-Jabbar 'Abd Mustafa, *Tajribat al-'Amal al-Jabhawi fi al-'Iraq beina 1921 wa 1958* (The experiment of oppositional work in Iraq between 1921 and 1958) (Baghdad: Manshurat Wizarat al-Thaqafa wa al-Funoon, 1978), pp. 245–246. On the same subject, see also Naji Shawkat, *Sira wa Dhikrayat Thamaneena 'Aman, 1894–1974*, p. 587.

76. Halim Ahmad, *Mujaz Tarikh al-'Iraq al-Hadith, 1920–1958* (A synoptic history of modern Iraq, 1920–158) (Beirut: Dar Ibn Khaldun, 1978), pp. 108–109.

77. 'Abd al-Razzaq al-Hasani, *Tarikh al-Wizarat al-'Iraqiya, al-Jusi' al-'Ashir* (History of Iraqi Cabinets, volume ten) (Baghdad: Dar al-Shu'un al-Thaqafiya al-'Amma, 1988), pp. 113–114. Talib Shabib, Iraq's foreign minister during the first Ba'thist government, February–November, 1963 claims that the battalion's commander, 'Abd al-Wahab al-Shawwaf (who himself was executed in a counter coup against the revolutionary government in March 1959) treated the Najaf population kindly, placing himself as an arbiter between police and citizens. See 'Ali Karim Sa'id 'Abdallah, *Iraq 8 Shibat, 1963: Min Hiwar al-Mafahim ila Hiwar al-Damm, Muraja'at fi Dhakirat Taleb Shabib* (Iraq of 8 February 1963: from a dialogue over norms to a dialogue of blood, reviews of the memory of Taleb Shabib) (Beirut, Lebanon: Dar al-Kunuz al-'Arabiya, 1999), pp. 307–314.

78. Mustafa, *Tajribat al-'Amal al-Jabhawi fi al-'Iraq*, p. 246; al-Hasani, *Tarikh al-Wizarat al-'Iraqiya, al-Jusi' al-Ashir*, p. 113.

79. Elie Podeh, *The Quest for Hegemony in the Arab World: The Struggle Over the Baghdad Pact* (Leiden: E. J. Brill, 1995), p. 212.

80. Ibid., p. 216.

81. 'Ali Jawdat, *Dhikrayat, 1900–1958* (Memoirs, 1900–1958) (Beirut: Matabi 'al-Wafa', 1967), pp. 290–291.

82. Batatu, *The Old Social Classes and the Revolutionary Movements of Iraq*, p. 477.

83. M. E. Yapp, *The Near East Since the First World War: A History to 1995*, 2nd edition (London: Longman, 1996), p. 81.

84. Marr, *The Modern History of Iraq*, p. 141.

85. *United Nations Statistical Yearbook, 1970* (New York: United Nations, Department of Economic and Social Affairs, 1970), p. 145.

86. Eppel, *Iraq from Monarchy to Tyranny: From the Hashemites to the Rise of Saddam*, pp. 93–95.

87. Marr, *The Modern History of Iraq*, p. 130.

88. Quoted in Gallman, *Iraq Under General Nuri*, p. 106.

89. Eppel, *Iraq from Monarchy to Tyranny: From the Hashemites to the Rise of Saddam*, p. 97.

90. *United Nations Statistical Yearbook, 1963* (New York: United Nations, Department of Economic and Social Affairs, 1963), p. 280.

91. Marr, *The Modern History of Iraq*, p. 135; see also Yapp, *The Near East Since the First World War: A History to 1995*, 2nd edition, pp. 75–76.

92. Eppel, *Iraq from Monarchy to Tyranny: From the Hashemites to the Rise of Saddam*, p. 98.

CHAPTER SIX: POTHOLES IN THE DEMOCRATIC ROAD

1. Quoted in Muhammad al-Dulaymi, *Kamel al-Chaderji wa Dawruhu fi al-Siyasa al-'Iraqiya* (Kamel al-Chaderji and his role in Iraqi politics) (Beirut, al-Mu'asasa al-'Arabiya li al-Dirasat wa al-Nashr, 1999), p. 95.

2. Muhsin Abu Tibikh, *al-Mabadi'wa al-Rijal: Bawader al-Inhiyar al-Siyasi fi al-'Iraq* (Principles and men: symptoms of political collapse in Iraq) (Beirut: al-Mu'asasa al-'Arabiya li al-Dirasat wa al-Nashr, 2002), pp. 231–241.

3. Quoted in 'Abd al-Rahman al-Bazzaz, *al'Iraq min al-Ihtilal hatta al-Istiqlal* (Iraq from occupation to independence) (Baghdad: Matba'at al-'Ani, 1967), p. 253.

4. Majid Khadduri, *Independent Iraq, 1932–1958: A Study in Iraqi Politics* (London: Oxford University Press), 1960, p. 136.

5. Mudhafar 'Abd Allah al-Amin, *Jama'at al-Ahali: Mansha'uha, 'Aqidatuha, wa Dawruha fi al-Siyasa al-'Iraqiya, 1932–1946* (The Ahali group: its origins, belief and role in Iraqi politics, 1932–1946) (Beirut: al-Mu'sasa al-'Arabiya li al-Dirasat wa al-Nashr, 2001), p. 146.

6. Khalid Habib al-Rawi, *Min Tarikh al-Sahafa al-'Iraqiya* (From the history of the Iraqi press) (Baghdad: Wizarat al-Thaqafa wa al-Funun, 1978), p. 37.

7. 'Abd al-Razzaq al-Hasani, *Tarikh al-Wizarat al-'Iraqiya, al Jusi' al-Khamis* (History of Iraqi Cabinets, volume five) (Baghdad: Dar al-Shu'un al-Thaqafiya la-'Amma, 1988), pp. 203–204.

8. See al-Rawi, *Min Tarikh al-Sahafa al-'Iraqiya*, pp. 41–52.

9. See 'Abd al-Majid Hassan al-Wali and 'Ala' al-Din al-Rayyes, *Ahwal al-'Iraq al-Ijtima'iya wa al-Iqtisadiya* (Iraq's social and economic conditions) (Baghdad: Matba'at al-Rashid, 1946), pp. 127–129.

10. 'Abd al-'Aziz al-Qassab, *Min Dhikrayati, 1888–1960* (From my memories, 1888–1960) (Beirut: 'Uwaidat Publications, 1962), p. 316; also Muhammed Mahdi Kubba, *Mudkarati fi Samim al-Ahdath, 1918–1958* (My memoirs in the midst of events, 1918–1958) (Beirut: Dar al-Tali'ah, 1965), p. 229.

11. 'Abd al-Amir Hadi al-'Akam, *Tarikh Hizb al-Istiqlal al-Iraqi, 1946–1958* (History of the Iraqi Independence Party, 1946–1958) (Baghdad: Dar al-Shu'un al-Thaqafiya al-'Amma, 1986), p. 219.

12. 'Abd al-Razzaq al-Hasani, *Tarikh al-Wizarat al-'Iraqiya, al-Jusi' al-Sabi'* (History of Iraqi Cabinets, volume seven) (Baghdad: Dar al-Shu'un al-Thaqafiya al-'Amma, 1988), pp. 248–250; Kamel al-Chaderji, *Mudhakarat Kamel al-Chaderji wa Tarikh al-Hizb al-Watani al-Dimuqrati* (Memoirs of Kamel al-Chaderji and history of the national democratic party) (Cologne: al-Jamal Publications, 2002), p. 193.

13. Hadi Husayn 'Ulaywi, *al-Ahzab al-Siyasiya fi al-'Iraq: al-Sirriya wa al-'Alaniya* (Political parties in Iraq: secret and open) (Beirut: Riad al-Rayyes Books, 2001), p. 111; al-'Akam, *Tarikh Hizb al-Istiqlal al-'Iraqi, 1946–1958*, p. 219.

14. The most comprehensive account of the meeting can be found in the memoirs of 'Abd al-Razzaq al-Hilali, who then was the Chamberlain of the Royal Court, and who acted as note-taker during the meeting. See 'Abd al-Razzaq al-Hilali, *Min Hadith al-Dhikrayat* (From the elaboration of reminiscences) (Baghdad: Dar al-Shu'un al-Thaqafiya al-'Amma, 2002), pp. 67–98.

15. Ibid., p. 77.

16. Ibid., p. 72.

17. Stephen Hemsley Longrigg, *Iraq, 1900–1950: A Political, Social, and Economic History* (London: Oxford University Press, 1953), p. 346; see also al-Hasani, *Tarikh al-Wizarat al-'Iraqiya, al-Jusi' al-Sabi'*, p. 256.

18. Al-Hilali, *Min Hadith al-Dhikrayat*, p. 100.

19. Al-Hasani, *Tarikh al-Wizarat al-'Iraqiya, al-Jusi' al-Sabi'*, p. 265.

20. Ibid., p. 272.

21. Chaderji, *Mudhakarat Kamel al-Chaderji*, p. 197; al-'Akam, *Tarikh Hizb al-Istiqlal*, pp. 223–225; Jeanie Singleton, *Al-Hizb al-Watani al-Dimuqrati fi al-'Ahd al-Malaki* (The national democratic party in the monarchical era) (Beirut: al-Mu'asasa al-'Arabiya li al-Dirasat wa al-Nashr, 1999), pp. 104–110.

22. Al-Qassab, *Min Dhikrayati, 1888–1960*, pp. 320–321.

23. The cable is reproduced in al-Hasani, *Tarikh al-Wizarat al-'Iraqiya, al-Jusi' al-Sabi'*, pp. 277–278.

24. In the general elections that followed the two main opposition parties, *al-Watani al-Dimuqrati* and *al-Istiqlal*, rather than unifying their efforts in fact competed against each other in a number of constituencies. There were also incidents of clashes between the supporters of the two parties. See al-Chaderji, *Mudhakarat Kamel al-Chaderji*, p. 243; see also Khadduri, *Independent Iraq, 1932–1958: A Study in Iraqi Politics*, pp. 270, 278.

25. 'Adil Ghaffouri Khalil, *Ahzab al-Mu'aradha al-'Alaniya fi al-'Iraq, 1946–1954* (Public opposition parties in Iraq, 1946–1954) (Baghdad: al-Maktaba al-'Alamiya, 1984), p. 168.

26. 'Abd al-Razzaq al-Hasani, *Tarikh al-Wizarat al-'Iraqiya, al-Jusi' al-Thamin* (History of Iraqi Cabinets, volume eight) (Baghdad: Dar al-Shu'un al-Thaqafiya al-'Amma, 1988), p. 295; see also al-'Akam, *Tarikh Hizb al-Istiqlal*, p. 255.

27. Al-Hasani, *Tarikh al-Wizarat al-'Iraqiya, al-Jusi' al-Thamin*, p. 297.

28. Chaderji, *Mudhakarat Kamel al-Chaderji*, pp. 490–493; al-Hasani, *Tarikh al-Wizarat al-'Iraqiya, al-Jusi' al-Thamin*, pp. 299–302; Fadhil Husayn, *Tarikh al-Hizb al-Watani al-Dimuqrati, 1946–1958* (History of the national democratic party, 1946–1958) (Baghdad: Matba'at al-Sha'ab, 1963), pp. 293–297.

29. Khadduri, *Independent Iraq*, p. 279.

30. See al-Hasani, *Tarikh al-Wizarat al-'Iraqiya, al-Jusi' al-Thamin*, footnote, 1, p. 306.

31. Ibid., p. 306.

32. Fa'iq Butti, *Sahafat al'Iraq: Tarikhiha wa Kifah Ajyaliha* (The Iraqi Press: its history and its generational struggle) (Baghdad: Matba'at al-Adib, 1968), p. 125.

33. Al-'Akam, *Tarikh Hizb al-Istiqlal al-'Iraqi*, p. 198; for the campaign against 'Umari's government, see pp. 191–200; see also Chaderji, *Mudhakarat Kamel al-Chaderji*, pp. 141–151.

34. Fa'iq Butti, *Suhuf Baghdad: Fi Dhikra Ta'sisiha* (Baghdad newspapers: in commemoration of their foundation) (Baghdad: n.p., n.d.), p. 19; see also Butti, *Sahafat al-'Iraq*, p. 123.

35. Of course, after September 1954, with the onset of the new more vigorous authoritarianism under Nuri, the atmosphere of relative tolerance that allowed for a broad measure of judicial independence receded dramatically, and editors, as well as party leaders, were generally convicted and actually imprisoned.

36. Ahmad Fawzi, *al-Muthir min Ahdath al-'Iraq al-Siyasiya* (The sensational in Iraqi political events) (Baghdad: Dar al-Huriya li al-Tiba'a, 1988), p. 246.

37. Butti, *Suhuf Baghdad*, p. 19; Butti, *Sahafat al-'Iraq*, p. 123.

38. See 'Ulaywi, *al-Ahzab al-Siyasiya fi al-'Iraq: al-Siriya wa al-'Alaniya*, pp. 104–105.

39. See al-Chaderji, *Mudhakarat Kamel al-Chaderji*, pp. 493–497; al-Hasani, *Tarikh al-Wizarat al-'Iraqiya, al-Jusi' al-Thamin*, pp. 315–318; al-'Akam, *Tarikh Hizb al-Istiqlal al-'Iraqi*, p. 266.

40. It seems, however, that there was a limit to the Regent's magnanimity, as his apologies were not extended to Taha al-Hashimi and Kamel al-Chaderji. See Chaderji, *Mudhakarat Kamel al-Chaderji*, p. 501.

41. Mir Basri, *A'lam al-Siyasa fi al-'Iraq al-hadith* (Political notables of modern Iraq) (London: Riad al-Rayyis li al-Tiba'a wa al-Nashr, 1987), p. 82.

42. Ibid., p. 83.

43. 'Abd al-Rahman al-Bayati, *Sa'id Qazzaz wa Dawruhu fi Siyasat al-'Iraq hatta 'Amm 1959* (Sa'id Qazzaz and his role in Iraqi politics till 1959) (Beirut, Lebanon: al-Mu'asasa al-'Arabiya li al-Dirasat wa al-Nashr, 2001), pp. 134–137.

Chapter Seven: Nationalism and the Ethnosectarian Divide

1. 'Abd al-Razzaq 'Abd al-Daraji, *Ja'far Abu al-Timman wa Dawruhu fi al-Haraka al-Wataniya fi al-'Iraq, 1908–1945* (Ja'far Abu al-Timman and his role in the national movement in Iraq, 1908–1945) (Baghdad: Wizarat al-Thaqafa wa al-Funoon, 1978), pp. 434–436.

2. Ibid., pp. 437–438.

3. Michael Eppel, *The Palestine Conflict in the History of Modern Iraq: The Dynamics of Involvement, 1928–1948* (London: Frank Cass, 1994), p. 64.

4. See Najda Fathi Safwat, *al-'Iraq fi Mudhakarat al-Diblomasiyeen al-Ajanib* (Iraq in the memoirs of foreign diplomats) (Baghdad: Maktabat Dar al-Tarbiya, 1984), p. 128.

5. Salah al-Din al-Sabagh, *Fursan al-'Uruba fi al-'Iraq* (The knights of Arabism in Iraq) (Damascus: n.p., 1956), p. 123.

6. Salman al-Tikriti, *al-Wasi, 'Abd al-Ilah Yabhath 'an 'Arsh, 1939–1953* (Regent 'Abd al-Ilah searches for a thrown, 1939–1953) (Beirut, Lebanon: al-Dar al-'Arabiya li al-Mausou'at, 1989), pp. 75–76.

7. Anis Sayegh, *al-Hashimiyoun wa Qadhiyat Filasteen* (The Hashemites and the Palestinian issue) (Beirut, Lebanon: Dar al-Tali'a, 1966), p. 308.

8. Su'ad Rauf Muhamed, *Nuri al-Sa'id wa Dawruhu fi al-Siyasa al-'Iraqiya, 1932–1945* (Nuri al-Sa'id and his role in Iraqi politics, 1932–1945) (Baghdad: Maktabat al-Yaqdha al-'Arabiya, 1988), pp. 257–258.

9. For the political maneuverings involved in Iraq's unity schemes, see Majid Khadduri, "The scheme of Fertile Crescent unity: a study in inter-Arab relations,"

in Richard N. Frye, ed., *The Near East and the Great Powers*, (Cambridge, Massachusetts: Harvard University Press, 1951), pp. 137–177.

10. Yiizhak Nakash, *The Shi'is of Iraq* (Princeton, New Jersey: Princeton University press, 1994), pp. 133–134.

11. 'Abd al-Karim al-Uzri, *Tarikh fi Dhikrayat al-'Iraq, 1930–1958* (History in the Memoirs of Iraq) (Beirut, Lebanon: Markaz al-Abjadiya li al-Saf al-Taswiri, 1982), pp. 148–150.

12. Phebe Marr, *The Modern History of Iraq*, 2nd edition (Boulder, Colorado: Westview Press, 2004), p. 145.

13. Phebe Marr, "The Development of a Nationalist Ideology in Iraq, 1920–1941," *The Muslim World*, April 1985, p. 100.

14. See Nakash, *The Shi'is of Iraq*, p. 254.

15. Hanna Batatu, *The Old Social Classes and the Revolutionary Movements of Iraq* (Princeton, New Jersey: Princeton University Press, 1978), p. 47.

16. Ibid., p. 47.

17. See Hassan al-'Alawi, *al-Shi'a wa al-Dawla al-Qawmiyya fi al-'Iraq, 1914–1990* (The Shi'ites and the Nationalist State in Iraq, 1914–1990) (n.p., 1990), pp. 195–197.

18. Al-Uzri, *Tarikh fi Dhikrayat al-'Iraq, 1930–1958, al-Jusi' al-Awal*, pp. 237–243 and 442–443. This is confirmed by Hanna Batatu who maintains that in the army Shi'ites were "very thinly represented in the ranks of staff major and above." See Batatu, *The Old Social Classes and the Revolutionary Movements of Iraq*, p. 765. Brigadier Kadhim al-'Abadi, the Shi'ite Commander of the Air Force during the last years of the monarchy, confirmed to the author the meagerness of the Shi'ite presence in the officer corps. He attributed this to a combination of governmental indifference and a certain detachment among Shi'ite youth.

19. According to Hanna Batatu, from the 1940s onward, coinciding with the Barazani rebellions, "fewer and fewer Kurds were admitted to the [army's] Staff College." Batatu, *The Old Social Classes and the Revolutionary Movements of Iraq*, p. 765.

20. See Marr, *The Modern History of Iraq* (Boulder, Colorado: Westview Press, 1985), p. 146.

21. A succinct account of the origins and structure of the Ba'th Party in Iraq can be found in Batatu, *The Old Social Classes and the Revolutionary Movement of Iraq*, pp.741–748.

22. Ibid., pp.1216–1218.

23. 'Ali Karim Sa'id 'Abdallah, *Iraq 8 Shibat, 1963: Min Hiwar al-Mafahim ila Hiwar al-Damm, Muraja'at fi Dhakirat Taleb Shabib* (Iraq of 8 February 1963:

from a dialogue over norms to a dialogue of blood, reviews of the memory of Taleb Shabib) (Beirut, Lebanon: Dar al-Kunuz al-'Arabiya, 1999), p. 308.

24. Elie Podeh, *The Quest for Hegemony in the Arab World: The Struggle Over the Baghdad Pact* (Leiden: E. J. Brill, 1995), p. 220. See also Adeed Dawisha, *Arab Nationalism in the Twentieth Century: From Triumph to Despair* (Princeton, New Jersey: Princeton University Press, 2003), p. 183.

25. These are the words of 'Abd al-Karim al-Uzri, who had been a cabinet minister in Iraq on a number of occasions. *Al-Uzri, Tarikh fi Dhikrayat al-'Iraq, 1930–1958*, p. 544.

26. Fikrat Namiq 'Abd al-Fattah, *Siyasat al-'Iraq al-Kharijiya fi al-Mantaqa al-'Arabiya, 1953–1958* (Iraq's foreign policy in the Arab region, 1953–1958) (Baghdad: Dar al-Rashid li al-Nashr, 1981), pp. 214–215.

27. Al-Uzri, *Tarikh fi Dhikrayat al-'Iraq, 1930–1958*, p. 550.

28. Malik Mufti, *Sovereign Creations: Pan-Arabism and Political Order in Syria and Iraq* (Ithaca, New York: Cornell University Press, 1996), p. 104.

CHAPTER EIGHT: THE MONARCHY'S POLITICAL SYSTEM

1. See the table detailing the distribution of pivotal Cabinet ministries between 1920 and 1958 in 'Abd al-Wahab Hamid Rashid, *al-'Iraq al-Mu'asir* (Contemporary Iraq) (Damascus, Syria: al-Mada Publishing Company, 2002), pp. 120–121.

2. See the table for the full 59 Cabinets in the monarchical era in 'Aqeel al-Nasiri, *al-Jaysh wa al-Sulta fi al-'Iraq al-Malaki, 1921–1958* (The army and the political authority in monarchical Iraq, 1921–1958) (Damascus, Syria: al-Hassad for Publishing and Distribution, 2000), pp. 214–216.

3. Khalil Kanna, *al-'Iraq: Amsuhu wa Ghadduhu* (Iraq: its yesterday and tomorrow) (Beirut, Lebanon: n.p., 1966), pp. 317–318.

4. Mudhafar 'Abd Allah al-Amin, *Jama'at al-Ahali: Mansha'uha, 'Aqidatuha, wa Dawruha fi al-Siyasa al-'Iraqiya, 1932–1946* (The Ahali group: its origins, its ideology and its role in Iraqi politics, 1932–1946) (Beirut, Lebanon: al-Mu'sasa al-'Arabiya li al-Dirasat wa al-Nashr, 2001), p. 149.

5. Hanna Batatu, *The Old Social Classes and the Revolutionary Movements of Iraq* (Princeton, New Jersey: Princeton University Press, 1978), p. 123.

6. Waldemar J. Gallman, *Iraq Under General Nuri: My Recollections of Nuri al-Said. 1954–1958* (Baltimore, Maryland: The Johns Hopkins University Press, 1964), pp. 115–116.

7. 'Abd al-Khaliq Husayn, *Thawrat 14 Tamuz1958 wa 'Abd al-Karim Qassem* (The 14 July Revolution and 'Abd al-Karim Qassem) (Damascus, Syria: Dar al-Hisad li al-Nashr wa al-Tawzi', 2002), p. 47.

8. Husayn Jamil, *al-'Iraq al-Jadid* (The new Iraq) (Beirut, Lebanon: Dar Munaimana li al-Tiba'a wa al-Nashr, 1958), p. 28.

9. In 1957, migrant peasantry constituted 29 percent of Baghdad's population, and 18 percent of Basra's population. See Batatu, *The Old Social Classes and the Revolutionary Movements of Iraq*, pp. 132–133.

10. Ibid., p. 103. In another authoritative publication, the figure is put considerably higher at 45 percent, perhaps because large landowners who were not necessarily tribal sheikhs were counted. See Phebe Marr, *The Modern History of Iraq*, 2nd edition (Boulder, Colorado: Westview Press, 2004), p. 78.

11. See for example the bitter denunciation of the government of Tawfiq al-Suwaydi in February 1950 by a member of the opposition, deriding it as no different from earlier governments in "believing in feudalism and supporting tribal influence." *Ahmad Fawzi, al-Muthir min Ahdath al-'Iraq al-Siyasiya* (The sensational in Iraqi political events) (Baghdad: Dar al-Huriya li al-Tiba'a, 1988), p. 90.

12. Rashid, *al-'Iraq al-Mu'asir*, p. 127.

13. 'Abd al-Razzaq al-Hasani, *Tarikh al-Wizarat al-'Iraqiya, al-Jusi' al-Thamin* (History of Iraqi Cabinets, volume eight) (Baghdad: Dar al-Shu'un al-Thaqafiya al-'Amma, 1988), footnote 1, p. 331.

14. 'Abd al-Karim al-Uzri, *Tarikh fi Dhikrayat al-Iraq, 1930–1958, al-Jusi' al-Awal* (History in memories of Iraq, 1930–1958, volume one) (Beirut, Lebanon: Markaz al-Abjadiya li al-Saf al-Taswiri, 1982), pp. 454–457.

15. 'Abd al-Hadi al-Khumasi, *al-Amir 'Abd al-Ilah, 1939–1958: Dirasa Tarikhiya Siyasiya* (Prince 'Abd al-Ilah, 1939–1958: a political historical study) (Beirut, Lebanon: al-Mu'asasa al-'Arabiya li al-Dirasat wa al-Nashr, 2001), p. 353.

16. Ismael 'Aref, *Asrar Thawrat 14 Tamuz wa Ta'sees al-Jumhuriya fi al-'Iraq* (The secrets of the July 14 revolution and the creation of the republic in Iraq) (London: Lana Publications, 1986), p. 215; Jamil, *al-'Iraq al-Jadid*, p. 25.

17. Kanna, *al-'Iraq: Amsuhu wa Ghaduhu*, p. 77.

18. For the details of this maneuver, see Tawfiq al-Suwaydi, *Mudhakarati: Nisf Qarn min Tarikh al-'Iraq wa al-Qadhiya al-'Arabiya* (My memoirs: half a century of Iraqi history and the Arab undertaking) (London: Dar al-Tiba'a wa al-Nashr, 1999), pp. 438–447. See also Majid Khadduri, *Independent Iraq, 1932–1958: A Study in Iraqi Politics*, 2nd edition (London: Oxford University Press, 1960), pp. 255–256.

19. Muhamed Mahdi Kubba, *Mudhakarat fi Samim al-Ahdath, 1918–1958* (Memoirs in the heart of events, 1918–1958) (Beirut, Lebanon: Dar al-Tali'a, 1965), p. 11.

20. On the National Union Front, see 'Abd al-Amir Hadi al-'Akam, *Tarikh Hizb al-Istiqlal al-'Iraqi, 1946–1958* (The history of the Iraqi Istiqlal Party, 1946–1958) (Baghdad: Dar al-Shu'un al-Thaqafiya al-'Amma, 1986), pp. 323–339.

21. Al-Nasiri, *al-Jaysh wa al-Sulta fi al-'Iraq al-Malaki, 1921–1958*, pp. 155–156.

22. Ibid., p. 154.

23. Hassan Shibr, *al-'Amal al-Hizbi fi al-'Iraq, 1908–1958* (The activities of political parties in Iraq, 1908–1958) (Beirut, Lebanon: Dar al-Turath al-'Arabi, 1989), pp. 266–267.

24. Marr, *The Modern History of Iraq*, 2nd edition, p. 46. To the British, any opposition was the work of "rebel rousers." See Toby Dodge, *Inventing Iraq: The Failure of Nation-Building and a History Denied* (New York: Columbia University Press, 2003), p. 91.

25. 'Abd al-Rahman al-Bazzaz, *al-'Iraq: min al-Ihtilal ila al-Istiqlal* (Iraq: from occupation to independence) (London: Dar al-Baraq, 1997), p. 119.

26. 'Abd al-Razzaq al-Hasani, *Tarikh al-Wizarat al-'Iraqiya, al-Jusi' al-Awal* (History of Iraqi Cabinets, volume one) (Baghdad: Dar al-Shu'un al-Thaqafiya al-'Amma, 1988), p. 232.

27. 'Ali al-Wardi, *Lamahat Ijtima'iya min Tarikh al-'Iraq al-Hadith, al-Jusi' al-Sadis* (Social aspects from the modern history of Iraq, volume six) (Baghdad: n.p., 1972), p. 296.

28. Muhamed al-A'dhami, *Political Aspects of the Iraqi Parliament and Election Processes, 1920–1932* (London: unpublished London University thesis, 1978), pp. 221–222.

29. Kamel al-Chaderji, *Mudhakarat Kamel al-Chaderji wa Tarikh al-Hizb al-Watani al-Dimuqrati* (The memoirs of Kamel al-Chaderji and the history of the National Democratic Party) (Cologne, Germany: al-Jamal Publications, 2002), pp. 561–562.

30. These were the words of Philip Ireland, a senior American diplomat as confided to 'Abd al-Karim al-Uzri. See al-Uzri, *Tarikh fi Dhikrayat al-Iraq, 1930–1958, al-Jusi' al-Awal*, pp. 520–521.

31. Al-Uzri, *Tarikh fi Dhikrayat al-Iraq, 1930–1958, al-Jusi' al-Awal*, p. 426.

32. Salman al-Tikriti, *al-Wassi 'Abd al-Ilah bin 'Ali Yabhath 'Ann 'Arsh, 1939–1953* (The regent 'Abd al-Ilah bin 'Ali searches for a crown, 1939–1953) (Beirut, Lebanon: al-Dar al-'Arabiya li al-Mausu'at, 1989), pp. 177–179.

33. Taghrid 'Abd al-Zahra Rashid, *al-Bilat al-Malaki al-'Iraqi fi al-Sanawat al-Multahiba, 1953–1958* (The Iraqi Royal Palace in the flammable years) (Beirut, Lebanon: Dar Sader, 2004), p. 54.

34. Kanna, *al-'Iraq: Amsuhu wa Ghadduhu*, p. 262.

35. For the details of the meeting in Paris, see Kamal Mudhhir Ahmad, *Mudhakarat Ahmad Mukhtar Baban, Akhir Ra'is le al-Wizara' fi al-'Ahd al-Malaki fi al-'Iraq* (The memoirs of Ahmad Mukhtar Baban, the last prime minister in the monarchical era in Iraq) (Beirut, Lebanon: al-Mu'asasa al-'Arabiya li al-Dirasat wa al-Nashr, 1999), pp. 63–71.

36. Stephen Hemsley Longrigg, *Iraq, 1900–1950: A Political, Social and Economic History* (London: Oxford University Press, 1953), p. 395.

37. Al-Amin, *Jama'at al-Ahali: Mansha'uha, 'Aqidatuha, wa Dawruha fi al-Siyasa al-'Iraqiya, 1932–1946*, p. 144.

38. 'Abd al-Razzaq al-Hasani, *Tarikh al-Wizarat al-'Iraqiya, al-Jusi' al-Rabi'* (The history of Iraqi Cabinets, volume four) (Baghdad: Dar al-Shu'un al-Thaqafiya al-'Amma, 1988), p. 208.

39. Muhsin Abu Tibikh, *al-Mabadi' wa al-Rijal: Bawader al-Inhiyar al-Siyasi fi al-'Iraq* (Principles and men: symptoms of political collapse in Iraq) (Beirut, Lebanon: al-Mu'asasa al-'Arabiya li al-Dirasat wa al-Nashr, 2003), pp. 80–81.

40. Khalid al-Timmimi, *Ja'far Abu al-Timman: Dirasa fi al-Za'ama al-Siyasiya al-'Iraqiya* (Ja'far Abu al-Timman: a study in Iraqi political leadership) (Damascus, Syria: Dar al-Waraq li al-Dirasat wa al-Nashr, 1996), pp. 330–347.

41. Salah al-Din al-Sabagh, *Fursan al-'Aruba* (Knights of Arabism) (Damascus, Syria: n.p., 1956), pp. 122–124.

42. See Ismael al-'Arif, *Asrar Thawrat 14 Tamuz wa Ta'sis al-Jumhuriya fi al-'Iraq* (The secrets of the 14 July revolution and the establishment of the republic in Iraq) (London: Al-Majid, 1986), p. 33.

43. Al-Uzri, *Tarikh fi Dhikrayat al-Iraq, 1930–1958*, pp. 375–376.

44. Patrick Seale, *The Struggle for Syria: A Study in Post-War Arab Politics, 1945–1958* (London: Oxford University press, 1965), p. 203.

45. His Majesty, King Hussein I of Jordan, *Uneasy Lies the Head: The Autobiography of His Majesty King Hussein I of the Hashemite Kingdom of Jordan* (New York: Random House, 1962), p. 195.

46. Philip Willard Ireland, *Iraq: A Study in Political Development* (New York: The Macmillan Company, 1938), p. 422.

47. Walid al-A'dhami, *Intifadhat Rashid 'Ali al-Gaylani wa al-Harb al-'Iraqiya al-Biritaniya, 1941* (The insurrection of Rashid 'Ali al-Gaylani and the Iraqi-British War, 1941) (Baghdad: Dar Wasit, 1986), p. 128.

48. Khadduri, *Independent Iraq, 1932–1958: A Study in Iraqi Politics*, 2nd edition, p. 293.

49. Al-Suwaydi, *Mudhakarati: Nisf Qarn min Tarikh al-'Iraq wa al-Qadhiya al-'Arabiya*, p. 102.

50. Quoted in Fa'iz As'ad, *Inhiraf al-Nidham al-Birlamani fi al-'Iraq* (Deviation of the parliamentary system in Iraq) (Baghdad: Maktabat al-Sindabad, 1984), pp. 32–33.

51. Ireland, *Iraq: A Study in Political Development*, p. 424.

52. Al-Nasiri, *al-Jaysh wa al-Sulta fi al-'Iraq al-Malaki, 1921–1958*, p. 128; see also al-Suwaydi, *Mudhakarati: Nisf Qarn min Tarikh al-'Iraq wa al-Qadhiya al-'Arabiya*, p. 453.

53. Al-Uzri, *Tarikh fi Dhikrayat al-'Iraq, 1930–1958*, p. 160.

54. Abd al-Razzaq al-Hilali, *Min Hadith al-Dhikrayat, Sabi' Sanawat fi al-Tashrifat al-Malakiya fi al-'Iraq: Ahadith, wa Suwar wa Dhikrayat wa Watha'iq min al-'Iraq, 1947–1954* (From the discourse of memoirs, seven years at the Royal Court: conversations, memories, pictures and documents on Iraq, 1947–1954) (Baghdad: Dar al-Shu'un al-Thaqafiya al-'Amma, 2002), pp. 169–170.

55. Kanna, *al-'Iraq: Amsuhsu wa Ghaduhu*, pp. 289–290.

56. Muhamed Hamdi al-Ja'fari, *Inqilab al-Wassi fi al-'Iraq* (The Regent's coup in Iraq) (Cairo, Egypt: Maktabat Madbouli, 2000), pp. 115–116. The most flagrant example was the September 1954 elections which were so controlled by Nuri al-Sa'id that only 25 out of the 135 seats were contested. See George Grassmuck, "The Electoral Process in Iraq, 1952–1958," *Middle East Journal*, vol. 14, no. 4, Autumn 1960, pp. 410–412.

57. Quoted in 'Abd al-Karim Farhan, *Thawrat 14 Tamuz fi al-'Iraq, al-Jusi' al-Awal* (The July 14 revolution in Iraq, volume one) (Paris: Mu'asasat al-Kitab al-'Arabi li al-Dirasat wa al-Tarjuma wa al-Nashr, 1986), p. 41.

58. For such instances, see Jamil Abu Tibikh, *Mudhakarat al-Sayyid Muhsin Abu Tibikh, 1910–1960: Khamsun 'Aman min Tarikh al-'Iraq al-Siyasi al-Hadith* (Memoirs of Sayyid Muhsin Abu Tibikh: fifty years of Iraq's modern political history) (Beirut, Lebanon: al-Mu'asasa al-'Arabiya li al-Dirasat wa al-Nashr, 2001), pp. 306–307; 'Abd al-Majid Kamil al-Tikriti, *Majlis al-Umma al-'Iraqi: al-Barlaman, al-A'yan wa al-Nuwab, 1945–1953* (The National Assembly of Iraq: Parliament, senators and deputies, 1945–1953) (Baghdad: Dar al-Shu'un al-Thaqafiya al-'Amma), p. 53; 'Abd al-Razzaq al-Hasani, *Tarikh al-Wizarat al-'Iraqiya, al-Jusi' al-Sadis* (History of Iraqi Cabinets, volume six) (Baghdad: Dar al-Shu'un al-Thaqafiya al-'Amma, 1988), p. 316; al-'Akam, *Tarikh Hizb al-Istiqlal al-'Iraqi, 1946–1958*, pp. 224–225; al-Hasani, *Tarikh al-Wizarat al-'Iraqiya, al-Jusi' al-Thamin*, p. 56; Khadduri, *Independent Iraq, 1932–1958: A Study in Iraqi Politics*,

pp. 37, 51–53, 255–256, 269; Ireland, *Iraq: A Study in Political Development,* pp. 428–429; al-Suwaydi, *Mudhakarati: Nisf Qarn min Tarikh al-'Iraq wa al-Qadhiya al-'Arabiya,* p. 532; al-Khumasi, *al-Amir 'Abd al-Ilah, 1939–1958: Dirasa Tarikhiya Siyasiya,* p. 354.

59. See, for example, 'Abd al-Razzaq al-Hasani, *Tarikh al-Wizarat al-'Iraqiya, al-Jusi' al-Tasi'* (History of Iraqi Cabinets, volume nine) (Baghdad: Dar al-Shu'un al-Thaqafiya al-'Amma, 1988), p. 77; also Majid Khadduri, *Nidham al-Hukm fi al-'Iraq* (The system of governance in Iraq) (Baghdad: Matba'at al-Ma'arif, 1946), pp. 167–168.

60. Dawlat al-'Iraq, *Mahadhir Majlis al-Nuwab, 1954* (Debates of the Chamber of Deputies, 1954), p. 643 (henceforth cited as *Mahadhir*). See also Adeed Dawisha, "Democratic Attitudes and Practices in Iraq, 1921–1958," *Middle East Journal,* vol. 59, no. 1, Winter 2005, p. 25.

61. *Mahadhir* (1950), p. 196; see also al-Uzri, *Tarikh fi Dhikrayat al-'Iraq, 1930–1958,* p. 370; Dawisha, "Democratic Attitudes and Practices in Iraq, 1921–1958," p. 25.

62. *Mahadhir* (1956), p. 462. The same is true of another pliant Parliament, see *Mahadhir* (1953), pp. 135–141.

63. 'Abd al-Razzaq al-Hasani, *Tarikh al-Wizarat al-'Iraqiya, al-Jusi' al-'Ashir* (History of Iraqi Cabinets, volume ten) (Baghdad: Dar al-Shu'un al-Thaqafiya al-'Amma, 1988), p. 140.

64. Khalid Habib al-Rawi, *Min Tarikh al-Sahafa al-'Iraqiya* (From the history of the Iraqi press) (Baghdad: Wizarat al-Thaqafa wa al-Funun, 1978), pp. 37–38.

65. 'Abd al-Rahman al-Bayati, *Sa'id Qazzaz wa Dawruhu fi Siyasat al-'Iraq hatta 'Amm 1959* (Sa'id Qazzaz and his role in Iraqi politics until 1959) (Beirut, Lebanon: al-Mu'sasa al-'Arabiya li al-Dirasat wa al-Nashr, 2001), p. 18.

66. Muhamed Mahdi Kubba, *Mudhakarati fi Samim al-Ahdath, 1918–1958* (My memoirs in the midst of events, 1918–1958) (Beirut, Lebanon: Dar al-Tali'a, 1965), p. 227.

67. Fa'iq Butti, *Sahafat al-'Iraq: Tarikhuha wa Kifah Ajyaliha* (The Iraqi press: its history and the struggle of its generations) (Baghdad: Matba'at al-Adib, 1968), p. 122.

68. See Malik Mufti, *Sovereign Creations: Pan-Arabism and Political Order in Syria and Iraq* (Ithaca, New York: Cornell University Press, 1996), p. 29.

69. Elie Podeh, *The Quest for Hegemony in the Arab World: The Struggle Over the Baghdad Pact* (Leiden: E. J. Brill, 1995), p. 220.

70. See Robert Stephens, *Nasser: A Political Biography* (London: Allen Lane/ Penguin Press, 1971), p. 149.

71. Al-Uzri, *Tarikh fi Dhikrayat al-'Iraq,* volume one, p. 609.

72. Farhan, *Thawrat 14 Tamuz fi al-'Iraq, al-Jusi' al-Awal*, footnote 1, p. 54.

73. One example is an Egyptian radio broadcast that reminded its Iraqi listeners that their Prime Minister "has no right to speak on any of the affairs of Iraq, because he speaks on behalf of imperialism." Quoted in A. I. Dawisha, *Egypt in the Arab World: The Elements of Foreign Policy* (London: Macmillan, 1976), p. 166.

74. Al-Uzri, *Tarikh fi Dhikrayat al-Iraq, 1930–1958*, pp. 442–443, 588–589.

75. Yitzhak Nakash, *Reaching for Power: The Shi'a in the Modern Arab World* (Princeton, New Jersey: Princeton University Press, 2006), p. 93.

76. See al-Nasiri, *al-Jaysh wa al-Sulta fi al-'Iraq al-Malaki, 1921–1958*, pp. 218–220; see also Hassan al-'Alawi, *al-Shi'a wa al-Dawla al-Qawmiya fi al-Iraq, 1914–1990* (The Shi'ites and the nationalist state in Iraq, 1914–1990) (n.p., 1990), pp. 198–199. It is worth noting that the three Kurdish prime ministers fall into the category of what Hanna Batatu calls "Arabized Kurds." See Batatu, *The Old Social Classes and the Revolutionary Movements of Iraq*, pp. 180–183.

77. Al-Nasiri, *al-Jaysh wa al-Sulta fi al-'Iraq al-Malaki, 1921–1958*, pp. 219–220.

CHAPTER NINE: THE AUTHORITARIAN REPUBLIC

1. The gruesome events mirrored those that occurred on the same date (July 14) in 1789 during the storming of the Bastille in the French Revolution, which has been explained by reference to the phenomenon of mass hysteria. In Iraq, the total number of those on whom the wrath of the people was exacted was around thirty. See Laith 'Abd al-Hassan al-Zubaydi, *Thawrat 14 Tamuz 1958* (The July 14 Revolution) (Baghdad: Dar al-Rashid li al-Nashr, 1979), p. 233.

2. 'Abd al-Karim Farhan, *Thawrat 14 Tamuz fi al-'Iraq al-Jusi' al-Awal* (The July 14 revolution in Iraq, volume one) (Paris: Mu'asasat al-Kitab al-'Arabi li al-Dirasat wa al-Tarjuma wa al-Nashr, 1986), p. 125.

3. 'Abd al-Razzaq Muhammad al-Aswad, *Mausu'at al-'Iraq al-Siyasiya, al-Mujalad al-Rabi'* (Political encyclopedia of Iraq, volume 4) (Beirut, Lebanon: al-Dar al-'Arabiya li al-Mausa'at, 1986), p. 357.

4. Majid Khadduri, *Republican Iraq: A Study in Iraqi Politics Since the Revolution of 1958* (London: Oxford University Press), p. 87; Phebe Marr, *The Modern History of Iraq* (Boulder, Colorado: Westview Press, 1985), p. 159.

5. 'Ali Karim Sa'id, *Iraq 8 Shibat, 1963: Min Hiwar al-Mafahim ila Hiwar al-Damm, Muraj'at fi Dhakirat Taleb Shabib* (Iraq of 8 February, 1963: from a dia-

logue over norms to a dialogue of blood, reviewing the memory of Taleb Shabib) (Beirut, Lebanon: Dar al-Kunuz al-'Adabiya, 1999), footnote 2, pp. 282–283.

6. British Broadcasting Corporation, *Summary of World Broadcasts, Part IV, the Arab World, Israel, Greece, Turkey, Iran,* July 22, 1958, pp. 7–9; July 25, 1958, p. 6 (hereafter referred to as *SWB*).

7. Benjamin Shwadran, *The Power Struggle in Iraq* (New York: Council for Middle Eastern Affairs Press, 1960), p. 35.

8. See for example, Salah Nasr, *'Abd al-Nasir wa Tajribat al-Wuhda* ('Abd al-Nasir and the unity experiment) (Beirut, Lebanon: al-Watan al-'Arabi, 1976), pp. 171–172, 175; Uriel Dann, *Iraq Under Qassem: A Political History, 1958–1963* (New York: Praeger, 1969), p. 78.

9. *SWB*, November 6, 1958, p. 8.

10. *SWB*, February 9, 1959, p. 9.

11. The UAR had transferred arms and ammunition to Mosul, and had a radio station on the border broadcasting the progress of the coup and inciting people to revolt. UAR officials had also held talks with the sheikhs of the powerful Shammar tribe to initiate a tribal insurrection to coincide with the Shawaf revolt. See A. I. Dawisha, *Egypt in the Arab World: The Elements of Foreign Policy* (London: Macmillan, 1976), p. 27.

12. United Arab Republic, *President Gamal Abd al-Nasser's Speeches and Press Interviews* (Cairo, Egypt: Information Department, 1959), pp. 126–133.

13. Ibid., p. 149; also *SWB*, March 19, 1959, p. 10.

14. *SWB*, March 11, 1959, p. 11; *SWB*, March 12, 1959, p. 12; *SWB*, March 18, 1959, p. 9.

15. Shwadran, *The Power Struggle in Iraq*, p. 50.

16. During this period, the communists were able to maintain their control of professional organizations, disregarding even appeals at inclusiveness from Qasim himself. See, for example, his address to the communist-controlled teachers union on February 6, 1959 in United States Foreign Broadcast Information Service, *Daily Report, Foreign Radio Broadcasts*, February 6, 1959, pp. C 2–3. (Hereafter cited as FBIS, *Daily Reports*.)

17. 'Abd al-Khaliq Husayn, *Thawrat 14 Tamuz 1958 al-'Iraqiya wa 'Abd al-Karim Qassim* (The Iraqi Revolution of 1958 and 'Abd al-Karim Qasim) (Damascus, Syria: Dar al-Hisad li al-Nashr wa al-Tawzi', 2003), p. 121.

18. By 1961, there were only 500 communist officers out of over 5,000. See Sa'id, *Iraq 8 Shibat, 1963: Min Hiwar al-Mafahim ila Hiwar al-Damm, Muraj'at fi Dhakirat Taleb Shabib*, footnote 1, p. 175.

19. Uriel Dann, *Iraq Under Qassem: A Political History, 1958–1963* (New York: Praeger, 1969), p. 205–207.

20. The partisans would repeat these rhythmic chants that would become part of the folklore of the period. See Husayn, *Thawrat 14 Tamuz 1958 al-'Iraqiya wa 'Abd al-Karim Qasim*, p. 117.

21. Hassan al-'Alawi, *al-Shi'a wa al-Dawla al-Qawmiya fi al-'Iraq, 1914–1990* (The Shi'ites and the nationalist state in Iraq, 1914–1990) (n.p., 1990), p. 212–213.

22. See for example, FBIS, *Daily Report*, July 22, 1959, pp. C 3–4; FBIS, *Daily Report*, July 29, 1959, p. C 7.

23. Hanna Batatu, *The Old Social Classes and the Revolutionary Movements of Iraq* (Princeton, New Jersey: Princeton University Press, 1978), p. 913.

24. FBIS, *Daily Report*, July 20, 1959, pp. C 2–5.

25. FBIS, *Daily Report*, July 30, 1959, pp. C 1–7.

26. Dann, *Iraq Under Qassem: A Political History, 1958–1963*, pp. 226–227.

27. Conversations with the author's father, the late Air Force Colonel Isam Dawisha.

28. Michael Eppel, *Iraq from Monarchy to Tyranny: From the Hashemites to the Rise of Saddam* (Gainesville, Florida: University Press of Florida, 2004), p. 157.

29. Batatu, *The Old Social Classes and the Revolutionary Movements of Iraq*, p. 837.

30. Doreen Warriner, *Land Reform in Principle and Practice* (Oxford, England: Clarendon Press, 1969), p. 91.

31. FBIS, *Daily Report*, July 15, 1960, p. C 10.

32. Muhammad Amin Doughan, *al-Haqiqa kama Ra'ytuha fi al-'Iraq* (The truth as I saw it in Iraq) (Beirut, Lebanon: Dar al-Sha'ab, 1962), p. 145.

33. Ismail al-'Aref, *Asrar Thawrat 14 Tamuz wa Ta'sees al-Jumhuriya fi al-'Iraq* (The secrets of the July 14 revolution and the establishment of the republic of Iraq) (London: Lana Publications, 1986), p. 216.

34. Muhammad Mahdi al-Jawahiri, *Dhikrayati* (My memoirs) (Damascus, Syria: Dar al-Rafidayn, 1988), p. 202.

35. For all they are worth, since they are taken from national statistics, United Nations figures show surprisingly low unemployment rates for the Qasim period, which on the whole were under 2 percent. United Nations, Department of Economic and Social Affairs, *United Nations Statistical Yearbook, 1970*, , p. 106.

36. Eppel, *Iraq from Monarchy to Tyranny: From the Hashemites to the Rise of Saddam*, p. 158.

37. Phebe Marr, *The Modern History of Iraq*, 2nd edition (Boulder, Colorado: Westview Press, 2004), p. 101.

38. Eppel, *Iraq from Monarchy to Tyranny: From the Hashemites to the Rise of Saddam*, p. 162.

39. Al-'Aref, *Asrar Thawrat 14 Tamuz wa Ta'sees al-Jumhuriya fi al-'Iraq*, pp. 403–407.

40. J. N. D. Anderson, "A Law of Personal Status for Iraq," in *International and Comparative Law Quarterly*, vol. 9, October 1960, p. 544.

41. Imam al-Sayyid Muhammad al-Husayni al-Shirazi, *Tilka al-Ayyam: Safahat min Tarikh al-'Iraq al-Siyasi* (Those days: pages from Iraq's political history) (Beirut, Lebanon: Bisan li al Nashr wa al-Tawzi' wa al-I'lam, 2000), pp. 186–188; Yitzhak Nakash, *The Shi'is of Iraq* (Princeton, New Jersey: Princeton University Press, 1994), p. 135.

42. Dann, *Iraq Under Qassem: A Political History, 1958–1963*, p. 247.

43. Sa'id, *Iraq 8 Shibat, 1963: Min Hiwar al-Mafahim ila Hiwar al-Damm, Muraj'at fi Dhakirat Taleb Shabib*, pp. 45–47.

44. Ibid., p. 62.

45. Hani al-Fekayki, *Awkar al-Hazeema: Tajribati fi Hizb al-Ba'th fi al-'Iraq* (The nests of defeat: my experience with the Ba'th party in Iraq) (London: Dar al-Rayyas li al-Nashr, 1993), p. 108.

46. Batatu, *The Old Social Classes and the Revolutionary Movements of Iraq*, pp. 1011–1012.

47. Sa'id, *Iraq 8 Shibat, 1963: Min Hiwar al-Mafahim ila Hiwar al-Damm, Muraj'at fi Dhakirat Taleb Shabib*, p. 141.

48. From an internal Party document quoted in Batatu, *The Old Social Classes and the Revolutionary Movements of Iraq*, p. 1012.

49. Ibid., p. 1018.

50. Ibid., p. 988.

51. Sa'id, *Iraq 8 Shibat, 1963: Min Hiwar al-Mafahim ila Hiwar al-Damm, Muraj'at fi Dhakirat Taleb Shabib*, pp. 176–177.

52. Farhan, *Thawrat 14 Tamuz fi al-'Iraq al-Jusi' al-Awal*, p. 125; Dann, *Iraq Under Qassem: A Political History, 1958–1963*, pp. 43–44.

53. Husayn, *Thawrat 14 Tamuz 1958 al-'Iraqiya wa 'Abd al-Karim Qassim*, p. 160.

54. Sa'id, *Iraq 8 Shibat, 1963: Min Hiwar al-Mafahim ila Hiwar al-Damm, Muraj'at fi Dhakirat Taleb Shabib*, p. 102.

55. 'Abd al-Karim Farhan, *Hisad Thawra: Tajribat al-Sulta fi al-'Iraq, 1958–1968* (Harvest of a revolution: the experiment of political rule in Iraq, 1958–1968) (Damascus, Syria: Dar al-Baraq, 1994), pp. 132–134.

56. al-Shirazi, *Tilka al-Ayyam: Safahat min Tarikh al-'Iraq al-Siyasi*, p. 193.

57. Muhammad Karim al-Mashhadani, *'Abd al-Rahman al-Bazzaz wa Dawruhu al-Fikri wa al-Siyasi fi al-'Iraq hatta Thawrat 17 Tamuz 1968* ('Abd al-Rah-

man al-Bazzaz and his ideational and political role in Iraq until the revolution of July 17, 1968) (Baghdad: Maktabat al-Yaqdha al-'Arabiya, 2002), p. 189.

58. Muhammad Jamal Baroot, *Harakat al-Qawmiyeen al-'Arab* (The Arab nationalists movement) (Damascus, Syria: al-Markaz al-'Arabi li al-Dirasat al-Strategiya, 1997), p. 245.

59. Batatu, *The Old Social Classes and the Revolutionary Movements of Iraq*, p. 1033.

60. United Nations, Department of Economic and Social Affairs, *United Nations Statistical Yearbook, 1970*, p. 408.

61. Sa'id, *Iraq 8 Shibat, 1963: Min Hiwar al-Mafahim ila Hiwar al-Damm, Muraj'at fi Dhakirat Taleb Shabib*, fn.1, p. 161; also Khadduri, *Republican Iraq: A Study in Iraqi Politics Since the Revolution of 1958*, p. 236.

62. Farhan, *Hisad Thawra: Tajribat al-Sulta fi al-'Iraq, 1958–1968*, pp. 187–188.

63. This is attested to even by Qasim's own enemies. See among others Jawad Hashim, *Mudhakarat Wazir Iraqi ma'a al-Bakr wa Saddam: Dhikrayat fi al-Siyasa al-'Iraqiya, 1967–2000* (Memoirs of an Iraqi Cabinet Minister with Bakr and Saddam: memories of Iraqi politics, 1967–2000) (Beirut, Lebanon: Dar al-Saqi, 2003), p. 52; Hassan al-'Alawi, *'Abd al-Karim Qasim: Rou'ya ba'd al-'Ishrayn* ('Abd al-Karim Qasim: An assessment after two decades) (London: Dar al-Zawra', 1983), pp. 83–84, 88, 94–95; Husayn, *Thawrat 14 Tamuz 1958 al-'Iraqiya wa 'Abd al-Karim Qasim*, pp. 185–186.

64. See Batatu, *The Old Social Classes and the Revolutionary Movements of Iraq*, pp. 835–836.

65. Husayn, *Thawrat 14 Tamuz 1958 al-'Iraqiya wa 'Abd al-Karim Qasim*, p. 61.

66. Muhammad al-Dulaymi, *Kamel al-Chaderji wa Dawruhu fi al-Siyasa al-'Iraqiya* (Kamel al-Chaderji and his role in Iraqi politics) (Beirut, Lebanon: al-Mu'asasa al-'Arabiya li al-Dirasat wa al-Nashr, 1999), p. 247.

67. Quoted in Batatu, *The Old Social Classes and the Revolutionary Movements of Iraq*, p. 836.

68. Husayn Jamil, *al-'Iraq al-Jadid* (The new Iraq) (Beirut, Lebanon: Dar Munaimana li al-Tiba'a wa al-Nashr, 1958), p. 61.

69. Gabriel Almond, et al., *Comparative Politics Today: A World View*, 7th edition (New York: Longman, 2003), pp. 87–100.

70. Bahjat 'Abbas, "min Dhikrayat Thawrat 14 Tamuz 1958," (from the memories of July 14, 1958 revolution), *Sawt al-'Iraq* (Baghdad), July 16, 2006; Doughan, *al-Haqiqa kama Ra'ytuha fi al-'Iraq*, p. 41.

71. Batatu, *The Old Social Classes and the Revolutionary Movements of Iraq*, pp. 946–949; Dann, *Iraq Under Qassem: A Political History, 1958–1963*, pp. 282–285.

72. Quoted in al-Dulaymi, *Kamel al-Chaderji wa Dawruhu fi al-Siyasa al-'Iraqiya*, p. 265.

73. Al-Aref, *Asrar Thwrat 14 Tamuz wa Ta'sees al-Jumhuriya fi al-'Iraq*, pp. 396–397.

74. Raymond A. Hinnebusch, *Authoritarian Power and State Formation in Ba'thist Syria: Army, Party and Peasant* (Boulder, Colorado: Westview Press, 1990), p. 89. On the inherent contradiction in Ba'thist doctrine between "democracy" and "revolution," see Elie Kedouri, *Democracy and Arab Political Culture* (Washington D.C.: The Washington Institute for Near East Policy, 1992), p. 90.

75. FBIS, *Daily Report*, May 5, 1964, pp. C 1–12.

76. Ibid., p. C 6.

77. Ibid., p. C 12.

78. Farhan, *Hisad Thawra: Tajribat al-Sulta fi al-'Iraq, 1958–1968*, pp. 143–144.

79. Al-Dulaymi, *Kamel al-Chaderji wa Dawruhu fi al-Siyasa al-'Iraqiya*, pp. 256–257.

80. P. J. Vatikiotis, "Dilemmas of Political Leadership in the Arab Middle East: The Case of the United Arab Republic," *American Political Science Review*, vol. 55, no. 1, March 1961, p. 106.

81. Even writers who are generally sympathetic to 'Aref's rule, would admit that a primary motivation for the provisional constitution was 'Aref's determination not to allow any encroachments on his powers. See, for example, Haitham Ghaleb al-Nahi, *Khiyanat al-Nasr fi al-Kharita al-Siyasiya li al-Mu'aradha al-'Iraqiya* (The betrayal of victory in the political roadmap of Iraqi opposition) (London: al-Dar al-Andulusiya, 2002), p. 199.

82. *Al-Ahram* (Cairo), July 2, 1959 and June 3, 1960.

83. Leonard Binder, "Political Recruitment and Participation in Egypt," in J. La Palombara and Myron Wiener, eds., *Political Parties and Political Development* (Princeton, New Jersey: Princeton University Press, 1966), p. 227.

84. This is confirmed by the ASU's first secretary-general, 'Abd al-Karim Farhan. See Farhan, *Hisad Thawra: Tajribat al-Sulta fi al-'Iraq, 1958–1968*, p. 142. See also Hadi Hassan 'Ulaywi, *al-Ahzab al-Siyasia fi al-'Iraq: al-Siriya wa al-'Alaniya* (Political parties in Iraq: clandestine and public) (Beirut, Lebanon: Riad al-Rayyes li al-Kutub wa al-Nashr, 2001), p. 217.

85. Khadduri, *Republican Iraq: A Study in Iraqi Politics Since the Revolution of 1958*, pp. 253–254.

86. Al-Mashhadani, *'Abd al-Rahman al-Bazzaz wa Dawruhu al-Fikri wa al-Siyasi fi al-'Iraq hatta Thawrat 17 Tamuz 1968*, p. 160.

87. Ibid., p. 185.

88. From the Ba'th Party Constitution. An English translation of this Constitution can be found in Sylvia Haim, ed., *Arab Nationalism: An Anthology* (Berkeley, California: California University Press, 1962), pp. 233–241.

89. Abu Khaldun Sati' al-Husri, *Mahiya al-Qawmiya?: Abhath wa Dirasat 'ala Dhaw'i al-Ahdath wa al-Nadhariyat* (What is nationalism?: enquiries and studies in light of events and theories) (Beirut, Lebanon: Dar al-'Ilm li al-Malayeen, 1963), p. 57.

90. FBIS, *Daily Report*, July 15, 1960, p. C 5.

91. Amatzia Baram, "Mesopotamian Identity in Ba'thi Iraq," *Middle Eastern Studies*, vol. 19, October 1983, p. 427.

92. Al-'Aref, *Asrar Thawrat 14 Tamuz wa Ta'sees al-Jumhuriya fi al-'Iraq*, pp. 394–395; Husayn, *Thawrat 14 Tamuz 1958 al-'Iraqiya wa 'Abd al-Karim Qasim*, p. 102.

93. Dann, *Iraq Under Qassem: A Political History, 1958–1963*, p. 138.

94. *Al-Rafidayn* (Baghdad), September 9, 2006.

95. Husayn, *Thawrat 14 Tamuz 1958 al-'Iraqiya wa 'Abd al-Karim Qasim*, pp. 103–104.

96. Ibid., pp. 105–106.

97. Edmund Ghareeb, *The Kurdish Question in Iraq* (Syracuse, New York: Syracuse University Press, 1981), p. 39.

98. David McDowall, *A Modern History of the Kurds* (London: I. B. Tauris, 1996), p. 308.

99. Hanna Batatu in his effort to characterize the resistance to the Ba'thist coup as ideologically, rather than Shi'ite-based, argues that poor Sunnis also joined in the effort to support Qasim. Be that as it may, the indisputable fact, admitted by Batatu himself, was that the heart of the resistance was situated in the Shi'ite areas, and that, in Batatu's own words, "no Sunni neighborhood stood in the face of the Ba'thi coup. . . ." Batatu, *The Old Social Classes and the Revolutionary Movements of Iraq*, p. 983.

100. The full text of the communiqué can be found in Sa'id, *Iraq 8 Shibat, 1963: Min Hiwar al-Mafahim ila Hiwar al-Damm, Muraj'at fi Dhakirat Taleb Shabib*, footnote 1, pp. 67–68.

101. For a concise exposition of Aflaq's ideas, see Leonard Binder, *The Ideological Revolution in the Middle East* (New York: John Wiley and Sons, Inc., 1964), pp. 154–197.

102. This trend began in Syria in the early 1950s, when the Ba'th Party established extensive contacts inside the Syrian armed forces. See Nasr, *'Abd al-Nasir wa Tajribat al-Wuhda*, p. 51.

103. Yunis Bahri, *Thawat Ramadhan al-Mubaraka* (The blessed Ramadhan revolution) (Beirut, Lebanon: Dar al-Andalus, 1963), p. 118.

104. The proceedings of the talks were published in Cairo immediately after their failure. For relevant excerpts, see Adeed Dawisha, *Arab Nationalism in the Twentieth Century: From Triumph to Despair* (Princeton, New Jersey: Princeton University Press, 2003, pp. 237–240, and Khadduri, *Republican Iraq: A Study in Iraqi Politics Since the Revolution of 1958*, pp. 205–206.

105. Al-'Alawi, *'Abd al-Karim Qasim: Rou'ya ba'd al-'Ishrayn*, p. 96.

106. Khadduri, *Republican Iraq: A Study in Iraqi Politics Since the Revolution of 1958*, pp. 232–233.

107. Farhan, *Hisad Thawra: Tajribat al-Sulta fi al-'Iraq, 1958–1968*, pp. 148–149.

108. Ibid., p. 169.

109. Selim Matar, *Al-Dhat al-Jariha: Ishkaliyat al-Hawiya fi al-'Iraq wa al-'Alam al-'Arabi "al-Shirqani"* (Wounded essence: problems of identity in Iraq and the "Eastern" Arab world) (Beirut, Lebanon: al-Mu'asasa al-'Arabiya li al-Dirasat wa al-Nashr), p. 172.

110. Husayn, *Thawrat 14 Tamuz 1958 al-'Iraqiya wa 'Abd al-Karim Qasim*, p. 96; Matar, *Al-Dhat al-Jariha: Ishkaliyat al-Hawiya fi al-'Iraq wa al-'Alam al-'Arabi "al-Shirqani,"* p. 172.

111. Farhan, *Hisad Thawra: Tajribat al-Sulta fi al-'Iraq, 1958–1968*, p. 137.

112. Baroot, *Harakat al-Qawmiyeen al-'Arab*, p. 248.

113. This is detailed in Farhan, *Hisad Thawra: Tajribat al-Sulta fi al-'Iraq, 1958–1968*, pp. 134–135, 261–262.

114. See for example, Matar, *Al-Dhat al-Jariha: Ishkaliyat al-Hawiya fi al-'Iraq wa al-'Alam al-'Arabi "al-Shirqani,"* p. 172.

115. Husayn, *Thawrat 14 Tamuz 1958 al-'Iraqiya wa 'Abd al-Karim Qasim*, pp. 155–156.

116. Khadduri, *Republican Iraq: A Study in Iraqi Politics Since the Revolution of 1958*, p. 229.

117. FBIS, *Daily Report*, January 17, 1967, pp. C 1–4

118. Charles Tripp, *A History of Iraq*, 2nd edition (Cambridge, England: Cambridge University Press, 2000), p. 149. Tripp agrees that the new leaders "exercised a power greater than any enjoyed by the politicians under the monarchy."

Chapter Ten: The State Rules without Rules

1. Amir Eskander, Saddam Husayn: Munadhilan, wa Mufakiran wa Insanan (Saddam Husayn: struggler, thinker and human being) (Paris: Hachette, 1980), p. 110.

2. Ayad 'Allawi, Prime Minister of Iraq from June 2004 to April 2005, told me in early 1978 shortly before he was attacked by an assassin wielding an axe in his home in England, that once in the early 1970s he had met with Saddam Husayn, and during the course of a cordial conversation, Saddam had expressed his admiration for Stalin's use of the "psychology of mass coercion," which the then Vice President thought was the only viable policy for a fractious country like Iraq.

3. *The Guardian* (London), May 14, 1981.

4. Quoted in Efraim Karsh and Inari Rautsi, *Saddam Hussein: A Political Biography* (New York: The Free Press, 1991), pp. 38–39.

5. *The Guardian* (London), November 26, 1971.

6. Salam 'Aboud, *Thaqafat al-'unf fi al-'Iraq* (The culture of violence in Iraq) (Cologne, Germany: Manshurat al-Jamal, 2002), pp. 138–139.

7. It appears that as early as 1974 Bakr had ceded much of his responsibilities to his young and dynamic deputy. See 'Ali Karim Sa'id, *'Iraq 8 Shibat, 1963: Min Hiwar al-Mafahim ila Hiwar al-Damm, Muraja'at fi Dhakirat Taleb Shabib* (Iraq of 8 February, 1963: from a dialogue over norms to a dialogue of blood, reviewing the memory of Taleb Shabib) (Beirut, Lebanon: Dar al-Kunuz al-Adabiya, 1999), p. 345.

8. Said K. Aburish, *Saddam Hussein: The Politics of Revenge* (New York: Bloomsbury, 2000), pp. 100–101.

9. *Al-Thawra* (Baghdad), December 28, 1982.

10. Quoted in Karsh and Rautsi, *Saddam Hussein: A Political Biography*, p. 112.

11. Patrick Seale, *Asad of Syria: The Struggle for the Middle East* (Berkeley, California: University of California Press, 1988), p. 355.

12. Michel 'Aflaq, *Fi Sabil al Ba'th* (For the sake of the Ba'th [resurrection]) (Beirut, Lebanon: Dar al-Tali'ah, 1963), pp. 161–162; see also Kanan Makiya,

Republic of Fear: The Politics of Modern Iraq, updated edition (Berkeley, California: California University Press, 1998), p. 206.

13. Makiya, *Republic of Fear: The Politics of Modern Iraq*, updated edition, p. 38. This of course includes conscripts to the army who probably were there for no other reason but to inflate the size of the army. The goal was to score political points by impressing upon the Arabs and Iraq's neighbors the newly found power of Iraq and its leader.

14. The scientist Husayn al-Shahristani, later a minister of petroleum in the post-Saddam era, spent twelve years in prison (1979–1991) in which he endured all kinds of maltreatment because he had counseled caution on the issue of nuclear weapons. See his *al-Hurub ila al-Huriya: Awraq min Ayam al-Mihna fi Sujun Saddam* (Flight to freedom: papers from the days of the ordeal in Saddam's prisons) (Tehran, Iran: Dar Muhibi al-Husayn, 2000).

15. *Al-Thawra* (Baghdad), June 29, 1982.

16. Tariq Ibrahim Braysem, *al-'Abqariya al-'Arabiya bayn al-Farouk 'Umar wa Saddam Husayn* (Arab genius from the [khalifa] Umar to Saddam Husayn) (Baghdad: Dar al-Shu'un al-Thaqafiya al-'Amma, 1991), p. 145.

17. The best and earliest analyses of the efforts to revive Mesopotamia in the consciousness of Iraqis can be found in Amazia Baram's two articles, "Culture in the Service of *Wataniya*: The Treatment of Mesopotamia-Inspired Art in Ba'thi Iraq," *Asian and African Studies*, vol. 17, Fall 1983; and "Mesopotamian Identity in Ba'thi Iraq," *Middle Eastern Studies*, vol. 19, November 1983.

18. Eric Davis, *Memories of State: Politics, History, and Collective Identity in Modern Iraq* (Berkeley, California: University of California Press, 2005), footnote 53, p. 323.

19. The Foreign Broadcast Information Service, *Daily Report: Near East and South Asia* (Hereafter, FBIS, *Daily Report*), August 25, 1995, p. 41.

20. *Al-Thawra* (Baghdad), May 9, 1980.

21. FBIS, *Daily Report*, September 1, 1995, p. 37.

22. Hani Ibrahim 'Ashour, *Saddam Husayn wa al-Numudhaj al-Hidhari al-'Arabi* (Saddam Husayn and the Arab civilizational model) (Baghdad: Dar al-Huriya li al-Tiba'a, 1994), p. 10.

23. Ibid. Dedication page.

24. Marion Farouk-Sluglett and Peter Sluglett, *Iraq Since 1958: From Revolution to Dictatorship* (London: Routledge and Kegan Paul, 1987), p. 232. The figures in the Sluglett book are in Iraqi dinars. I have changed them to dollars using the average 3.3 exchange rate, which can be found in the annual publication *The Middle East and North Africa, 1976–1977* (London: Europa Publications Limited, 1976), p. 386.

25. United Nations, Department of Economic and Social Affairs, *United Nations Statistical Abstract, 1982*, p. 959.

26. See among others, Phebe Marr, *The Modern History of Iraq*, 2nd edition. (Boulder, Colorado: Westview Press, 2004), pp. 166–168; Adeed Dawisha, "Iraq: The West's Opportunity," *Foreign Policy*, no. 41, Winter 1980–1981, pp. 142–143; Karsh and Rautsi, *Saddam Hussein: A Political Biography*, pp. 90–91; Aburish, *Saddam Hussein: The Politics of Revenge*, pp. 109–111.

27. These figures are taken from Table A.4 in Marr, *The Modern History of Iraq*, 2nd edition, p. 312.

28. Makiya, *Republic of Fear: The Politics of Modern Iraq*, updated edition, p. 88.

29. Saddam Husayn, *al-'Iraq wa al-Siyasa al-Duwaliya* (Iraq and international politics) (Baghdad: Dar al-Huriya li al-Tiba'a, 1981), p. 196.

30. Aburish, *Saddam Hussein, The Politics of Revenge*, p. 198; Karsh and Rautsi, *Saddam Husayn: A Political Biography*, pp. 147–149; Makiya, *Republic of Fear: The Politics of Modern Iraq*, updated edition, pp. 258, 270–276.

31. Frederick Axelgard, "War and Oil: Implications for Iraq's Postwar Role in Gulf Security," in Frederick Axelgard, ed., *Iraq in Transition: A Political, Economic and Strategic Perspective* (Boulder, Colorado: Westview Press, 1986), p. 9.

32. See Marr, *The Modern History of Iraq*, 2nd edition, pp. 225–228.

33. On January 20, Saddam issued a statement aimed at bolstering the morale of his population, which had been subjected to savage daily bombardment from the air, promising ultimate victory, since "our ground forces have not entered the battle so far." When that would happen, "the deaths on the allied side will be increased with God's help. When the deaths and dead mount on them, the infidels will leave and the flag of Allahu Akbar will fly over the mother of all battles." Quoted from Iraqi radio in Karsh and Rautsi, *Saddam Hussein: A Political Biography*, p. 252.

34. Marr, *The Modern History of Iraq*, 2nd edition, p. 251.

35. United Nations, Department of Economic and Social Affairs, *United Nations Statistical Yearbook, 2000*, p. 142.

36. For example, there were still over 4 million Iraqis who were illiterate by the year 2000. See Marlita A. Reddy, editor, *Statistical Abstract of the World*, 2nd edition (Detroit, Gale Research, 1996), p. 441.

37. John F. Devlin, *The Ba'th Party: A History from its Origins to 1966* (Stanford, California: Hoover Institution Press, 1976), p. 31.

38. Aflaq, *Fi Sabil al-Ba'th*, p. 189.

39. Saddam Husayn, *Nidhaluna wa al-Siyasa al-Duwaliya* (Our struggle and international politics) (Beirut, Lebanon: Dar al-Tali'ah, 1978), pp. 56–57.

40. *The Guardian*, May 22, 1972.

41. Such as his treatise on the need to emphasize patriotism to Iraq seemingly at the expense of Ba'thist absolute insistence on the primacy of the Arab nation. See Saddam Husayn, *Hawla Kitabat al-Tarikh* (On the writing of history) (Baghdad: Dar la-Huriya li al-Tiba'a, 1979), pp. 15–17.

42. Husayn, *Nidhaluna wa al-Siyasa al-Duwaliya*, p. 89.

43. Quoted in Dawisha, "Iraq: The West's Opportunity," p. 141.

44. Amatzia Baram, "The June 1980 Elections to the National Assembly in Iraq: An Experience in Controlled Democracy," *Orient*, September 1981, pp. 391–412, quoted in Christine Moss Helms, *Iraq: Eastern Flank of the Arab World* (Washington D.C.: The Brookings Institution, 1984), p. 101; and Karsh and Rautsi, *Saddam Hussein: A Political Biography*, p. 120.

45. Ofra Bengio, *Saddam's Word: Political Discourse in Iraq* (Oxford, England: Oxford University Press, 1998), p. 64.

46. Aflaq, *Fi Sabil al-Ba'th*, p. 181.

47. Saddam Husayn, *al-Thawra wa al-Tarbiya al-Wataniya* (The revolution and national education) (Baghdad: Dar al-Huriya li al-Tiba'a, 1977), pp. 62–63.

48. The following information is taken from Baram, "Mesopotamian Identity in Ba'thi Iraq," pp. 426–455.

49. Ibid., p. 428.

50. Sa'id, *'Iraq 8 Shibat, 1963: Min Hiwar al-Mafahim ila Hiwar al-Damm, Muraja'at fi Dhakirat Taleb Shabib*, footnote 1, p. 208.

51. See for example The British Broadcasting Corporation, *Summary of World Broadcasts*, ME/7079/A/10–11, July 16, 1982.

52. Selim Mattar, *al-Dhat al-Jariha: Ishkalat al-Hawiya fi al-'Iraq wa al-'alam al-'Arabi "al-Shirqani"* (Wounded essence: Problems of identity in Iraq and the "eastern" Arab world) (Beirut, Lebanon: al-Mu'asasa al-'Arabiya li al-Dirasat wa al-Nashr, 1997), p. 120.

53. Quoted in Dawisha, "Iraq: The West's Opportunity," p. 142.

54. *Al-Thawra* (Baghdad), March 3, 1981.

55. See Andrew T. Parasiliti, *Iraq's War Decisions* (unpublished doctoral dissertation, The Johns Hopkins University, 1998), p. 126.

56. Amatzia Baram, *Culture, History and Ideology in the Formation of Ba'thist Iraq, 1968–89* (New York: St. Martin's Press, 1991), pp. 101–109.

57. *Al-Thawra* (Baghdad), January 16, 1982.

58. *Middle East Economic Digest* (London), March 30, 1990 (hereafter cited as MEED); see also FBIS, *Daily Report*, June 17, 1994, p. 22.

59. Amatzia Baram, "Neo-Tribalism in Iraq: Saddam Hussein's Tribal Policies, 1991–1996," *International Journal of Middle East Studies*, vol. 29, no. 1, February 1997, p. 1.

60. Ibid., pp. 8–10.

61. FBIS, *Daily Report*, September 3, 1992, p. 17.

62. FBIS, *Daily Report*, April 25, 1994, p. 42.

63. FBIS, *Daily Report*, March 4, 1993, p. 27.

64. FBIS, *Daily Report*, December 3, 1992, p. 21.

65. For example, FBIS, *Daily Report*, September 1, 1992, p. 22; FBIS, *Daily Report*, August 28, 1992, p. 21; FBIS, *Daily Report*, August 27, 1993, p. 22; FBIS, *Daily Report*, June 14, 1995, p. 36.

66. FBIS, *Daily Report*, September 3, 1992, p. 18.

67. *MEED*, May 22, 1992, p. 22; FBIS, *Daily Report*, May 12, 1992, p. 18.

68. FBIS, *Daily Report*, July 8, 1994, p. 27.

69. *MEED*, June 17, 1994, p. 22; *MEED*, June 24, 1994, p. 2; FBIS, *Daily Report*, June 7, 1994, p. 47.

70. *Al-Thawra* (Baghdad), September 9, 1994.

71. As'ad al-'Ali, "Muhnat al-Ustadh al-Jami'i Dakhil al-Watan wa fi al-Ghurba," (The crisis of the university professor inside the country and abroad) in *Qadhaya 'Iraqiya* (Washington D.C.), vol. 3, January 1999, p. 17.

72. Davis, *Memories of State: Memories of State: Politics, History, and Collective Identity in Modern Iraq*, p. 264.

73. *Al-Thawra* (Baghdad), February 23, 1996.

74. FBIS, *Daily Report*, March 26, 1996, pp. 29–32.

75. Davis, *Memories of State: Memories of State: Politics, History, and Collective Identity in Modern Iraq*, pp. 262–264.

76. Not that this was a new phenomenon. Even in the 1970s, the political leadership was imbued with anti-Shi'ite impulses. In the testimony of an ex-Ba'thist Minister during the 1970s, Shi'ite Party members were looked upon as lacking true loyalty to the ideas of the party and somehow "not from us" (meaning the Sunni membership). Indeed, when a Shi'ite was appointed Director of the National Oil Company, the majority Sunni Ba'thists took to calling the company a "Husayniya" (a Shi'ite religious congregation). On a broader scale, RCC member and Defense Minister, Hamad Shihab al-Tikriti, would refer to the Shi'ite population of the south of Iraq as *'Ajam* (Persians) "who need to be disposed of in order to purify the Arab blood of Iraq." See Jawad Hashem, *Mudhakarat Wazir 'Iraqi Ma'a al-Bakr wa Saddam: Dhikrayat fi al-Siyasa al-'Iraqiya, 1967–2000*

(Memoirs of an Iraqi minister with al-Bakr and Saddam: recollections in Iraqi politics, 1967–2000) (Beirut, Lebanon: Dar al-Saqi, 2002), pp. 94–96.

77. Frederick Starr, "A Usable Past," *The New Republic*, May 5, 1989.

CHAPTER ELEVEN: POLITICS IN THE NEW ERA

1. *New York Times*, February 6, 2003.

2. CBS, *60 Minutes*, January 11, 2004.

3. *New York Times*, September 26, 2003.

4. One Iraqi ally of the American project would lament that there was "widespread consternation in Iraq regarding the coalition forces, most of whom treat the Iraqi people harshly and with contempt." *Al-Quds al-ʿArabi* (London), September 16, 2003.

5. Larry Diamond, *Squandered Victory: The American Occupation and the Bungled Effort to Bring Democracy to Iraq* (New York: Henry Holt, 2006), pp. 290–291.

6. Ibid., p.15.

7. *Al-Rafidayn* (Baghdad), October 13, 2005.

8. See *al-Rafidayn* (Baghdad*)*, October 30, 2005; *USA Today*, November 2, 2005; *Economist*, December 10, 2005.

9. *Al-Sharq al-Awsat* (London), December 9, 2005; *al-Rafidayn* (Baghdad), December 17, 2005.

10. *Al-Rafidayn* (Baghdad), November 29, 2005; *al-Sharq al-Awsat* (London), December 9, 2005.

11. *Al-Sharq al-Awsat* (London), December 9, 2005; *Al-Ahali* (Baghdad), December 7, 2005.

12. *Al-Sharq al-Awsat* (London), December 11, 2005.

13. *Al-Ahali* (Baghdad), December 7, 2005; *al-Sharq l-Awsat* (London), December 9, 2005.

14. *Al-Sharq al-Awsat* (London), November 30, 2005.

15. *New York Times*, December 4, 2005.

16. *New York Times*, December 11, 2005.

17. *Al-Sharq al-Awsat* (London), December 11, 2005.

18. *Al-Sharq al-Awsat* (London), December 9, 2005.

19. *Al- Sharq al-Awsat* (London), December 11, 2005.

20. *Al-ʿArabiya Television*, December 12, 2005.

21. *Al-Ahali* (Baghdad), January 4, 2006.

22. For example, *Al-Rafidayn* (Baghdad), October 26, 2005; *al-Sharq al-Awsat* (London), December 13, 2005; *al-Ahali* (London), October 19, 2005; *al-Hayat* (Beirut), November 24, 2005; *al-Sharq al-Awsat* (London), December 11, 2005; *al-Rafidayn* (Baghdad), December 11, 2005.

23. For instance, *Al-Sabah* (Baghdad), December 13, 2005; *al-Ahali* (Baghdad), December 7, 2005; *al-'Arabiya Television*, October 28, 2005; *al-Zaman* (Baghdad), October 29, 2005.

24. Prime Minister Ibrahim al-Ja'fari of the UIA defended the practice by saying that "a party has the right to put in its posters the picture of someone it respects, be that someone a cleric, an intellectual or an athlete." *Al-Sharq al-Awsat* (London), December 13, 2005.

25. *Al-Sabah* (Baghdad), January 14, 2006; *al-Arabiya Television*, January 14, 2006.

26. *Al-Zaman* (Baghdad), June 19, 2006.

27. *Al-Zaman* (Baghdad), August 10, 2006; *al-Ahali* (Baghdad), August 12, 2006.

28. United Nations Assistance Mission for Iraq, *Human Rights Report, 1 January–31 March 2007*, p. 19.

29. United States Government Accounting Office (GAO), *Securing, Stabilizing and Rebuilding Iraq*, GAO-07–1195, September 2007.

30. Conversation with a young, highly-placed Kurdish official, March 17, 2006.

31. *Al-Rafidayn* (Baghdad), August 17, 2006. Such was the persistence of Shi'ite parliamentarians that a prominent Sunni member of the institution was moved to remark: "I regret to say that it is unlikely we will be able to prevent the partition of Iraq. I think it is going to be the way they (the Shi'ites) want" *Al-Jazeera Television*, August 18, 2006.

32. Max Weber, *From Max Weber: Essays in Sociology* (London: Oxford University Press, 1946), p. 78.

33. *Al-Ahali* (Baghdad), August 5, 2006. The American military in Iraq complained repeatedly throughout 2006 and 2007 about the brazen infiltration by Shi'ite militia of the Ministry of Interior, and of the partiality of Ministry officials toward the militia. An American general, for example, pointed to the release of more than 24 armed men who had been captured fighting American and Iraqi security forces in the Shi'ite southern city of Hilla. See *al-Zaman* (Baghdad), June 10, 2007.

34. *Al-Rafidayn* (Baghdad), August 8, 2006.

35. *Al-Rafidayn* (Baghdad), December 2, 2005.

36. *Al-Hayat* (Beirut), January 6, 2006.

37. *Al-Ahali* (Baghdad), January 4, 2006.

38. In measuring governmental corruption, one study ranked Iraq 160th among 163 states. See Transparency International, *Corruption Percentage Index, 2006*, pp. 5–7.

39. See Diamond, *Squandered Victory: The American Occupation and the Bungled Effort to Bring Democracy to Iraq*, pp. 103–139; 179–210; see also Adeed Dawisha, "Iraq: Setbacks, Advances, Prospects," *Journal of Democracy*, January 2004, pp. 13–14.

40. The following data is taken from the UN Assistance Mission for Iraq, *Human Rights Report, 1 January–31 March 2007*, p. 21, and UN Assistance Mission for Iraq, *Humanitarian Briefing on the Crisis in Iraq*, May 2007, pp. 1–3.

41. *BBC World Service*, June 24, 2006, October 23, 2006; *al-Rafidayn* (Baghdad), August 30, 2007.

42. *CNN International*, May 1, 2007.

43. *Al-Zaman* (Baghdad), June 11, 2007.

44. *Economist*, September 8, 2007; *CNN*, November 14, 2007.

45. *Economist*, October 20, 2007.

46. *CNN*, March 1, 2007.

47. *Al-Rafidayn* (Baghdad), November 7, 2007.

48. *CNN*, February 8, 2008.

49. *New York Times*, April 2, 2008.

50. *Al-Arabiya Television*, April 20, 2008.

51. *Al-Hayat* (Beirut), February 13, 2008.

Chapter Twelve: W(h)ither Iraq?

1. Peter Sluglett, *Britain in Iraq, 1914–1932* (London: Ithaca Press, 1976), pp. 36–45.

2. Naji Shawkat, *Sira wa Dhikrayat Thamaneena 'Aman, 1894–1974* (Biography and memoirs of eighty years, 1894–1974) (Baghdad: Maktabat al-Yaqdha al-'Arabiya, 1990), pp. 623–626.

3. Of course, Faysal's government did pursue policies, such as granting the tribes separate legal structures that might seem contrary to the goal of nation building. But in its formative years, when its ability to project power effectively was limited, such policies allowed the state to secure a hold over all of its national territory.

4. 'Aqeel al-Nasiri, *al-Jaysh wa al-Sulta fi al-'Iraq al-Malaki, 1921–1958* (The army and the political authority in monarchical Iraq, 1921–1958) (Damascus, Syria: Dar al-Hassad li al-Nashr wa al-Tiba'a was al-Tawzi', 2000), p. 71.

5. 'Abd al-Majid Hassan Wali and 'Ala' al-Din al-Rayyas, *Ahwal al-'Iraq al-Ijtima'iya wa al-Iqtisadiya* (The social and economic affairs of Iraq) (Baghdad: Mataba'at al-Rashid, 1946), p. 131.

6. See Muhammad Mahdi al-Jawahiri, *Dhikrayati* (My memoirs) (Damascus: Dar al-Rafidayn, 1988), p. 163.

7. Phebe Marr, "The Development of Nationalist Ideology in Iraq, 1920–1941," *The Muslim World*, vol. LXXV, no.2, April 1985.

8. Selim Matar, *Al-Dhat al-Jariha: Ishkaliyat al-Hawiya fi al-'Iraq wa al-'Alam al-'Arabi "al-Shirqani"* (Wounded essence: problems of identity in Iraq and the "eastern" Arab world) (Beirut, Lebanon: al-Mu'asasa al-'Arabiya li al-Dirasat wa al-Nashr), p. 172; 'Abd al-Karim Farhan, *Hisad Thawra: Tajribat al-Sulta fi al-'Iraq, 1958–1968* (Harvest of a revolution: the experiment of political rule in Iraq, 1958–1968) (Damascus, Syria: Dar al-Baraq, 1994). p. 137; 'Abd al-Khaliq Husayn, *Thawrat 14 Tamuz 1958 al-'Iraqiya wa 'Abd al-Karim Qassim* (The Iraqi revolution of 1958 and 'Abd al-Karim Qasim) (Damascus, Syria: Dar al-Hisad li al-Nashr wa al-Tawzi', 2003), p. 96.

9. Matar, *Al-Dhat al-Jariha: Ishkaliyat al-Hawiya fi al-'Iraq wa al-'Alam al-'Arabi "al-Shirqani,"* p. 397.

10. Max Weber, *From Max Weber: Essays in Sociology* (London: Oxford University Press, 1946), p. 78.

11. Hanna Batatu, *The Old Social Classes and the Revolutionary Movements of Iraq* (Princeton, New Jersey: Princeton University Press, 1978), pp. 63–152; see also Waldemar J. Gallman, *Iraq Under General Nuri: My Recollections of Nuri al-Said. 1954–1958* (Baltimore, Maryland: The Johns Hopkins University Press, 1964), pp. 113–119.

12. Muhsin Abu Tibikh, *al-Mabadi' wa al-Rijal: Bawader al-Inhiyar al-Siyasi fi al-'Iraq* (Principles and men: symptoms of political collapse in Iraq) (Beirut: al-Mu'asasa al-'Arabiya li al-Dirasat wa al-Nashr, 2003), pp. 145–146.

13. For the transformation of the Shi'ite condition during the monarchy, see Phebe Marr, *The Modern History of Iraq*, 2nd edition (Boulder, Colorado: Westview Press, 2004), p. 145; Phebe Marr, "The Development of a Nationalist Ideology in Iraq, 1920–1941," *The Muslim World*, April 1985, p. 100; Yitzhak Nakash, *The Shi'is of Iraq* (Princeton, New Jersey: Princeton University Press, 1994), p. 254; and Batatu, *The Old Social Classes and the Revolutionary Movements of Iraq*, p. 47.

14. United States Foreign Broadcast Information Service, *Daily Report, Foreign Radio Broadcasts*, July 15, 1960, p. C 10; see also Muhammad Amin Doughan, *al-Haqiqa Kama Ra'ytuha fi al-'Iraq* (The truth as I saw it in Iraq) (Beirut, Lebanon: Dar al-Sha'ab, 1962), p. 145; Ismail al-'Aref, *Asrar Thawrat 14 Tamuz wa Ta'sees al-Jumhuriya fi al-'Iraq* (The secrets of the July 14 revolution and the establishment of the Republic of Iraq) (London: Lana Publications, 1986), p. 216; Muhammad Mahdi al-Jawahiri, *Dhikrayati* (my memoirs) (Damascus, Syria: Dar al-Rafidayn, 1988), p. 202.

15. Kanan Makiya, *Republic of Fear: The Politics of Modern Iraq* (Berkeley, California: University of California Press, 1998), pp. 93–94; Phebe Marr, *The Modern History of Iraq*, 2nd edition, pp. 163–164.

16. *Al-Ahali* (Baghdad), July 3, 2005; *al-Rafidayn* (Baghdad), March 4, 2006.

17. *Al-Zaman* (Baghdad), June 19, 2007.

18. As one Shi'ite politician would proudly declare, "We shall not descend into party politics." *Al-Sabah* (Baghdad), March 24,2006; see also *al-Zaman* (Baghdad), April 14, 2006.

19. Hadi Hassan 'Ulaywi, *al-Ahzab al-Siyasiyafi al-'Iraq: al-Siriya wa al-'Alaniya* (Political parties in Iraq: secret and public) (Beirut, Lebanon: Riad al-Rayyes li al-Kutub wa al-Nashr, 2001), pp. 132–133.

20. Seymour Martin Lipset, "Some Social Requisites of Democracy: Economic Development and Political Legitimacy," *American Political Science Review*, March 1959, pp. 69–105.

21. See among others Adam Przeworski, et al., *Democracy and Development: Political Institutions and Well-Being in the World, 1950–2000* (Cambridge, England: Cambridge University Press, 2000); Adam Przeworski and Fernando Limongi, "Modernization: Theories and Facts," *World Politics*, vol. 49, no. 2, January 1997; Dankwart Rustow, "Transitions to Democracy: Toward a Dynamic Model," *Comparative Politics*, vol. 2, no. 3, 1970.

22. The classic statement can be found in Gabriel Almond and Sidney Verba, *The Civic Culture: Political Attitudes and Democracy in Five Nations* (Princeton, New Jersey: Princeton University Press, 1963).

23. A representative sample of such opinions and conclusions are to be found in Adeed Dawisha, "Democratic Attitudes and Practices in Iraq, 1921–1958," *Middle East Journal*, vol. 59, no. 1, Winter 2005, pp. 1 1–12.

24. The General Accounting Office in a report to Congress in 2003 was hardly upbeat about the chances of democracy in Iraq. See GAO-03-792R, *Rebuilding Iraq*, pp. 2, 26.

25. See Dawisha, "Democratic Attitudes and Practices in Iraq, 1921–1958," pp. 11–30.

26. See Frances FitzGerald, *America Revised: History School Books in the Twentieth Century* (New York: Vintage Books, 1980), pp. 76–77, 90–91, 132–133.

27. Frederick Starr, "A Usable Past," *The New Republic*, May 15, 1989.

28. See Donald L. Horowitz, *Ethnic Groups in Conflict* (Berkeley, California: University of California Press, 1985), especially pp. 601–628; see also Seymour Martin Lipset, "The Social Requisites of Democracy Revisited," *American Sociological Review*, vol. 59, no. 1, February 1994, p. 10.

29. For the argument for territoriality, see Donald L. Horowitz, "Democracy in Divided Societies," in Larry Diamond and Marc F. Plattner, eds., *Nationalism, Ethnic Conflict and Democracy* (Baltimore, Maryland: The Johns Hopkins University Press, 1994), p. 53. For its relevance to Iraq, see Adeed Dawisha and Karen Dawisha, "How to Build a Democratic Iraq," *Foreign Affairs*, vol. 82, no. 3, May/June 2003, pp. 37–39.

BIBLIOGRAPHY

BOOKS AND ARTICLES

Fikrat Namiq 'Abd al-Fattah, *Siyasat al-'Iraq al-Kharijiya fi al-Mantaqa al-'Arabiya, 1953–1958* (Iraq's foreign policy in the Arab region, 1953–1958) (Baghdad: Dar al-Rashid li al-Nashr, 1981.

'Ali Karim Sa'id 'Abdallah, *Iraq 8 Shibat, 1963: Min Hiwar al-Mafahim ila Hiwar al-Damm, Muraja'at fi Dhakirat Taleb Shabib* (Iraq of 8 February 1963: from a dialogue over norms to a dialogue of blood, reviews of the memory of Taleb Shabib) (Beirut, Lebanon: Dar al-Kunuz al-'Arabiya, 1999).

Salam 'Aboud, *Thaqafat al-'unf fi al-'Iraq* (The culture of violence in Iraq) (Cologne, Germany: Manshurat al-Jamal, 2002).

Said K. Aburish, *Saddam Hussein: The Politics of Revenge* (New York: Bloomsbury, 2000).

Jamil Abu Tibikh, *Mudhakarat al-Sayyid Muhsin Abu Tibikh, 1910–1960: Khamsum 'Amman min Tarikh al-'Iraq al-Siyassi al-Hadith* (Memoirs of Sayyid Muhsin Abu Tibikh, 1910–1960: fifty years of Iraq's modern political history) (Beirut: al-Mu'asasa al-'Arabiya li al-Dirasat wa al-Nashr, 2001).

Muhsin Abu Tibikh, *al-Mabadi' wa al-Rijal: Bawader al-Inhiyar al-Siyasi fi al-'Iraq* (Principles and men: symptoms of political collapse in Iraq) (Beirut: al-Mu'asasa al-'Arabiya li al-Dirasat wa al-Nashr, 2003).

Lahouari Addi, "The Failure of Third World Nationalism," *Journal of Democracy*, vol. 8, (October 1997).

Mohammed Modhafar Hashim al-A'dhami, *Political Aspects of the Iraqi Parliament and Election Processes, 1920–1932*, Ph.D. Thesis, University of London, 1978.

Walid al-A'dhami, *Intifadhat Rashid 'Ali al-Gaylani wa al-Harb al-'Iraqiya al-Biritaniya, 1941* (The insurrection of Rashid 'Ali al-Gaylani and the Iraqi-British War, 1941) (Baghdad: Dar Wasit, 1986).

Michel 'Aflaq, *Fi Sabil al Ba'th* (For the sake of the Ba'th [resurrection]) (Beirut, Lebanon: Dar al-Tali'ah, 1963).

Halim Ahmad, *Mujaz Tarikh al-'Iraq al-Hadith, 1920–1958* (A synoptic history of modern Iraq, 1920–1958) (Beirut: Dar Ibn Khaldun, 1978).

Kamal Mudhhir Ahmad, *Mudhakarat Ahmad Mukhtar Baban, Akhir Ra'is le al-Wizara' fi al-'Ahd al-Malaki fi al-'Iraq* (The memoirs of Ahmad Mukhtar Baban, the last prime minister in the monarchical era in Iraq) (Beirut, Lebanon: al-Mu'asasa al-'Arabiya li al-Dirasat wa al-Nashr, 1999).

'Abd al-Amir Hadi al-'Akam, *Tarikh Hizb al-Istiqlal al-Iraqi, 1946–1958* (History of the Iraqi Independence Party, 1946–1958) (Baghdad: Dar al-Shu'un al-Thaqafiya al-'Amma, 1986).

Hassan al-'Alawi, *'Abd al-Karim Qasim: Rou'ya ba'd al-'Ishrayn* ('Abd al-Karim Qasim: an assessment after two decades) (London: Dar al-Zawra', 1983).

Gabriel Almond, et al., *Comparative Politics Today: A World View*, 7th edition (New York: Longman, 2003).

———— and Sidney Verba, *The Civic Culture: Political Attitudes and Democracy in Five Nations* (Princeton, New Jersey: Princeton University Press, 1963).

Hassan al-'Alwi, *al-Shi'a wa al-Dawla al-Qawmiya fi al-'Iraq, 1914–1990* (The Shi'ites and the national state in Iraq, 1914–1990) (n.p., 1990).

Mudhafar 'Abd Allah al-Amin, *Jama'at al-Ahali: Manshu'ha, 'Aqidatihu, wa Dawruha fi al-Siyasa al-'Iraqiya, 1932–1946* (al-Ahali group: its origin, ideology, and role in Iraqi politics, 1932–1946) (Beirut, Lebanon: al-Mu'sasa al'Arabiya li al-Dirasat wa al-Nashr, 2001).

Benedict Anderson, *Imagined Communities: Reflections on the Origins and Spread of Nationalism* (New York: Verso, 1990).

J.N.D. Anderson, "A Law of Personal Status for Iraq," in *International and Comparative Law Quarterly*, vol. 9, October 1960.

Ismael 'Aref, *Asrar Thawrat 14 Tamuz wa Ta'sees al-Jumhuriya fi al-'Iraq* (The secrets of the July 14 revolution and the creation of the republic in Iraq) (London: Lana Publications, 1986).

Faiz al As'ad, *Inhiraf al-Nidham al-Birlimani fi al-'Iraq* (The deviation of the parliamentary system in Iraq) (Baghdad: Maktabat al-Sindibad, 1984).

Hani Ibrahim 'Ashour, *Saddam Husayn wa al-Numudhaj al-Hidhari al-'Arabi* (Saddam Husayn and the Arab civilizational model) (Baghdad: Dar al-Huriya li al-Tiba'a, 1994).

'Abd al-Razak Muhammad Aswad, *Mawsu'at al'Iraq al-Siyasiya*, (Political encyclopedia of Iraq), seven volumes, (Beirut, Lebanon: al-Dar al-'Arabiya li al-Mausu'at, 1986).

Frederick Axelgard, "War and Oil: Implications for Iraq's Postwar Role in Gulf Security," in Frederick Axelgard, ed., *Iraq in Transition: A Political, Economic and Strategic Perspective* (Boulder, Colorado: Westview Press, 1986).

'Abd al-Latif al-Baghdadi, *Mudhakarat 'Abd al-Latif al-Baghdadi, al-Jusi' al-Awal* (Memoirs of 'Abd al-Latif al-Baghdadi, volume one) (Cairo: al-Maktab al-Musri al-Hadith, 1977).

Yunis Bahri, *Thawrat Ramadhan al-Mubaraka* (The blessed Ramadhan revolution) (Beirut, Lebanon: Dar al-Andalus, 1963).

Fadhil al-Barak, *Dawr al-Jaysh al'Iraqi fi Hukumat al-Difa' al-Watani wa al-Harb ma'a Britania Sanat 1941* (The role of the Iraqi army in the national defense government and the war with Britain in 1941) (Baghdad: al-Dar al-'Arabiya li al-Tiba'a, 1979).

Amatzia Baram, *Culture, History and Ideology in the Formation of Ba'thist Iraq, 1968–89* (New York: St. Martin's Press, 1991).

———, "Culture in the Service of *Wataniya*: The Treatment of Mesopotamia-Inspired Art in Ba'thi Iraq," *Asian and African Studies*, vol. 17, Fall 1983.

———, "Mesopotamian Identity in Ba'thi Iraq," *Middle Eastern Studies*, vol. 19, October 1983.

———, "Neo-Tribalism in Iraq: Saddam Hussein's Tribal Policies, 1991–1996," *International Journal of Middle East Studies*, vol. 29, no. 1, February 1997.

———, "The June 1980 Elections to the National Assembly in Iraq: An Experience in Controlled Democracy," *Orient*, September 1981.

Muhammad Jamal Baroot, *Harakat al-Qawmiyeen al-'Arab* (The Arab nationalists movement) (Damascus, Syria: al-Markaz al-'Arabi li al-Dirasat al-Strategiya, 1997).

Muhammad Mahdi al-Basir, *Tarikh al-Qadhiya al-'Iraqiya* (History of the Iraqi case) (Baghdad: Matba'at al-Fallah, 1924).

Mir Basri, *A'lam al-Siyasa fi al-'Iraq al-hadith* (Political notables of modern Iraq) (London: Riad al-Rayyis li al-Tiba'a wa al-Nashr, 1987).

Hanna Batatu, *The Old Social Classes and the Revolutionary Movements of Iraq: A Study of Iraq's Old Landed and Commercial Classes and of Its Communists, Ba'thists, and Free Officers* (Princeton, New Jersey: Princeton University Press, 1978).

'Abd al-Rahman al-Bazzaz, *al-'Iraq min al-Ihtilal hatta al-Istiqlal* (Iraq: from occupation to independence) (Baghdad: Matba'at al-'Ani, 1967).

'Abd al-Rahman al-Bayati, *Sa'id Qazzaz wa Dawruhu fi Siyasat al-'Iraq hatta 'Amm 1959* (Sa'id Qazzaz and his role in Iraqi politics till 1959) (Beirut, Lebanon: al-Mu'asasa al-'Arabiya li al-Dirasat wa al-Nashr, 2001).

Ofra Bengio, *Saddam's Word: Political Discourse in Iraq* (Oxford, England: Oxford University Press, 1998).

Leonard Binder, *The Ideological Revolution in the Middle East* (New York: John Wiley and Sons, Inc., 1964).

Leonard Binder, "Political Recruitment and Participation in Egypt," in J. La Palombara and Myron Wiener, eds., *Political Parties and Political Development* (Princeton, New Jersey: Princeton University Press, 1966).

Tariq Ibrahim Braysem, *al-'Abqariya al-'Arabiya bayn al-Farouk 'Umar wa Saddam Husayn* (Arab genius from the [khalifa] Umar to Saddam Husayn) (Baghdad: Dar al-Shu'un al-Thaqafiya al-'Amma, 1991).

Bernard E. Brown and Roy C. Macridis, eds., *Comparative Politics: Notes and Readings*, 8th edition (New York: Harcourt, Brace and Company, 1996).

Rogers Brubaker, *Citizenship and Nationhood in France and Germany* (Cambridge, Massachusetts: Harvard University Press, 1992).

Fa'iq Butti, *Sahafat al-'Iraq: Tarikhiha wa Kifah Ajjaliha* (The Iraqi Press: its history and its generational struggle) (Baghdad: Matba'at al-Adib, 1968).

————, *Suhuf Baghdad: Fi Dhikra Ta'sisiha* (Baghdad newspapers: in commemoration of their foundation) (Baghdad: n.p., n.d.).

Rufai'il Butti, *al-Sahafa al-'Iraqiya* (the press in Iraq) (Matba'at al-Hana', 1955).

Kamel al-Chaderji, *Mudhakarat Kamel al-Chaderji wa Tarikh al-Hizb al-Watani al-Dimuqrati* (Memoirs of Kamel al-Chaderji and the history of the National Democratic Party) (Cologne, Germany: Manshurat al-Jamal, 2002).

Rajiv Chanrasekaran, *Imperial Life in the Emerald City: Inside Iraq's Green Zone* (New York: Random House, 2006).

William L. Cleveland, *The Making of an Arab Nationalist: Ottomanism and Arabism in the Life and Thought of Sati' al-Husri* (Princeton, New Jersey: Princeton University Press, 1971).

Robert A. Dahl, *Polyarchy: Participation and Opposition* (New Haven, Connecticut: Yale University Press, 1971).

Uriel Dann, *Iraq Under Qassem: A Political History, 1958–1963* (New York: Praeger, 1969).

'Abd al-Razzaq 'Abd al-Daraji, *Ja'far Abu al-Timman wa Dawruhu fi al-Haraka al-Wataniya fi al-'Iraq, 1908–1945* (Ja'far Abu al-Timman and his role in the national movement in Iraq, 1908–1945) (Baghdad: Wizarat al-Thaqafa wa al-Funoon, 1978).

Eric Davis, *Memories of State: Politics, History, and Collective Identity in Modern Iraq* (Berkeley, California: University of California Press, 2005).

Adeed Dawisha, *Arab Nationalism in the Twentieth Century: From Triumph to Despair* (Princeton, New Jersey: Princeton University Press, 2003).

————, "Democratic Attitudes and Practices in Iraq, 1921–1958," *Middle East Journal*, vol. 59, no. 1, Winter 2005.

————, "Iraq: Setbacks, Advances, Prospects," *Journal of Democracy*, vol. 15, no. 1, January 2004.

————, "Nation and Nationalism: Historical Antecedents to Contemporary Debates," *International Studies Review,* vol. 4, no.1, Spring 2002.

———— and Karen Dawisha, "How to Build a Democratic Iraq," *Foreign Affairs,* vol. 82, no. 3, May/June 2003.

———— and Larry Diamond, "Iraq's Year of Voting Dangerously," *Journal of Democracy,* vol. 17, no. 2, April 2006.

John F. Devlin, *The Ba'th Party: A History from Its Origins to 1966* (Stanford, California: Hoover Institution Press, 1976).

Larry Diamond, *Squandered Victory: The American Occupation and the Bungled Efforts to Bring Democracy to Iraq* (New York: Times Books, 2005).

Toby Dodge, *Inventing Iraq: The Failure of Nation-Building and a History Denied* (New York: Columbia University Press, 2003).

Muhammad Amin Doughan, *al-Haqiqa kama Ra'ytuha fi al-'Iraq* (The truth as I saw it in Iraq) (Beirut, Lebanon: Dar al-Sha'ab, 1962).

Muhammad al-Dulaymi, *Kamel al-Chaderji wa Dawruhu fi al-Siyasa al-'Iraqiya* (Kamel al-Chaderji and his role in Iraqi politics) (Beirut, Lebanon: al-Mu'asasa al-'Arabiya li al-Dirasat wa al-Nashr, 1999).

C. J. Edmonds, *Kurds, Turks and Arabs: Politics, Travel and Research in North-Eastern Iraq, 1919–1925* (London: Oxford University Press, 1957).

Michael Eppel, *Iraq from Monarchy to Tyranny: From the Hashemites to the Rise of Saddam* (Gainesville, Florida: University Press of Florida, 2004).

Amir Eskander, *Saddam Husayn: Munadhilan, wa Mufakiran wa Insan* (Saddam Husayn: struggler, thinker and human being) (Paris: Hachette, 1980).

Fahad Muslim al-Fajr, *Muzahim al-Pachachi wa Dawrahu fi al-Siyasa al-'Iraqiya, 1890–1933* (Muzahim al-Pachachi and his role in Iraqi politics, 1890–1933) (Beirut: Dar al-'Arabiya li al-Mausu'at, 2004).

'Abd al-Karim Farhan, *Thawrat 14 Tamuz fi al-'Iraq, al-Jusi' al-Awal* (The July 14 revolution in Iraq, volume one) (Paris: Mu'asasat al-Kitab al-'Arabi li al-Dirasat wa al-Tarjuma wa al-Nashr, 1986).

Marion Farouk-Sluglett and Peter Sluglett, *Iraq Since 1958: From Revolution to Dictatorship* (London: Routledge and Kegan Paul, 1987).

Ahmad Fawzi, *al-Muthir min Ahdath al-'Iraq al-Siyasiya* (The sensational in Iraqi political events) (Baghdad: Dar al-Huriya li al-Tiba'a, 1988).

'Abdallah al-Fayadh, *al-Thawra al-'Iraqiya al-Kubra Sanat 1920* (The 1920 great Iraqi revolution) (Baghdad: Matba 'at al-Irshad, 1971).

Hani al-Fekayki, *Awkar al-Hazeema: Tajribati fi Hizb al-Ba'th fi al-'Iraq* (The nests of defeat: my experience with the Ba'th party in Iraq) (London: Dar al-Rayyas li al-Nashr, 1993).

Johan Gotlieb Fichte "Addresses to the German Nation," in Omar Dahbour and Micheline R. Ishay, eds., *The Nationalism Reader* (New York: Humanity Books, 1999).

Frances FitzGerald, *America Revised: History School Books in the Twentieth Century* (New York: Vintage Books, 1980).

Peter W. Galbraith, *The End of Iraq: How American Incompetence Created a War Without End* (New York: Simon and Schuster, 2006).

Waldemar J. Gallman, *Iraq Under General Nuri: My Recollections of Nuri al-Said, 1954–1958* (Baltimore, Maryland: The Johns Hopkins University Press, 1964).

Ernest Gellner, *Nations and Nationalism* (Ithaca, New York: Cornell University Press, 1983).

Edmund Ghareeb, *The Kurdish Question in Iraq* (Syracuse, New York: Syracuse University Press, 1981).

George Grassmuck, "The Electoral Process in Iraq, 1952–1958," *Middle East Journal*, vol. 14, no. 4, Autumn 1960.

Liah Greenfield, *Nationalism: Five Roads to Modernity* (Cambridge, Massachusetts: Harvard University Press, 1992).

Michael Gunter, *The Kurds of Iraq: Tragedy and Hope* (New York: St. Martin's Press, 1992).

Sylvia Haim, ed., *Arab Nationalism: An Anthology* (Berkeley, California: California University Press, 1962).

'Abd al-Razzak al-Hasani, *Tarikh al-Sahafa al-'Iraqiya* (History of Iraqi journalism) (Sayda, Lebanon: Matba'at al-'Irfan, 1971).

———, *Tarikh al-Wizarat al-'Iraqiya* (The history of Iraqi cabinets), ten volumes, (Baghdad: Dar al-Shu'un al Thaqafiya al-'Amma, 1988).

Taha al-Hashemi, *Mudhakarat Taha al-Hashimi, 1919–1943* (Memoirs of Taha al-Hashimi, 1919–1943) (Beirut: Dar al-Tali'a, 1967).

Jawad Hashim, *Mudhakarat Wazir Iraqi ma'a al-Bakr wa Saddam: Dhikrayat fi al-Siyasa al-'Iraqiya, 1967–2000* (Memoirs of an Iraqi cabinet minister with Bakr and Saddam: memories of Iraqi politics, 1967–2000) (Beirut, Lebanon: Dar al-Saqi, 2003).

Adrian Hastings, *The Construction of Nationhood: Ethnicity, Religion and Nationalism* (Cambridge, England: Cambridge University Press, 1997).

Christine Moss Helms, *Iraq: Eastern Flank of the Arab World* (Washington D.C.: The Brookings Institution, 1984).

Jeffrey Herbst, *States and Power in Africa: Comparative Lessons in Authority and Control* (Princeton, New Jersey: Princeton University Press, 2000).

'Abd al-Razzaq al-Hilali, *Min Hadith al-Dhikrayat* (From the elaboration of reminiscences) (Baghdad: Dar al-Shu'un al-Thaqafiya al-'Amma, 2002).

Raymond A. Hinnebusch, *Authoritarian Power and State Formation in Ba'thist Syria: Army, Party and Peasant* (Boulder, Colorado: Westview Press, 1990).

Donald L. Horowitz, "Democracy in Divided Societies," in Larry Diamond and Marc F. Plattner, eds., *Nationalism, Ethnic Conflict and Democracy* (Baltimore, Maryland: The Johns Hopkins University Press, 1994).

———, *Ethnic Groups in Conflict* (Berkeley, California: University of California Press, 1985).

Albert Hourani, *Arabic Thought in the Liberal Age, 1798–1939* (London: Oxford University Press).

Michael Howard, *The Lessons of History* (New Haven, Connecticut: Yale University Press, 1991).

Samuel P. Huntington, *The Third Wave: Democratization in the Late Twentieth Century* (Norman, Oklahoma: University of Oklahoma Press, 1991).

His Majesty, King Hussein I of Jordan, *Uneasy Lies the Head: The Autobiography of His Majesty King Hussein I of the Hashemite Kingdom of Jordan* (New York: Random House, 1962).

'Abd al-Khaliq Husayn, *Thawrat 14 Tamuz 1958 wa 'Abd al-Karim Qassem* (The 14 July Revolution and 'Abd al-Karim Qassem) (Damascus, Syria: Dar al-Hisad li al-Nashr wa al-Tawzi', 2002).

Muhammad Tawfiq Husayn, *'Indama Yathur al-'Iraq* (When Iraq rebels) (Beirut, Lebanon: Dar al-'Ilm li al-Malayeen, 1959).

Saddam Husayn, *Hawla Kitabat al-Tarikh* (On the writing of history) (Baghdad: Dar la-Huriya li al-Tiba'a, 1979).

———, *al-'Iraq wa al-Siyasa al-Duwaliya* (Iraq and international politics) (Baghdad: Dar al-Huriya li al-Tiba'a, 1981).

———, *Nidhaluna wa al-Siyasa al-Duwaliya* (Our struggle and international politics) (Beirut, Lebanon: Dar al-Tali'ah, 1978), pp. 56–57.

———, *al-Thawra wa al-Tarbiya al-Wataniya* (The revolution and national education) (Baghdad: Dar al-Huriya li al-Tiba'a, 1977).

Abu Khaldun Sati' al-Husri, *Ara' wa Ahadith fi al-Wataniya wa al-Qawmiya* (Views and discussions on patriotism and nationalism) (Beirut, Lebanon: Markaz Dirasat al-Wuhda al-'Arabiya, 1984).

———, *Mahiya al-Qawmiya?: Abhath wa Dirasat 'ala Dhaw'i al-Ahdath wa al-Nadhariyat* (What is nationalism?: enquiries and studies in light of events and theories) (Beirut, Lebanon: Dar al-'Ilm li al-Malayeen, 1963).

Philip Willard Ireland, *Iraq: A Study in Political Development* (New York: Macmillan, 1938).

Muhamed Hamdi al-Ja'fari, *Inqilab al-Wassi fi al-'Iraq* (The Regent's coup in Iraq) (Cairo, Egypt: Maktabat Madbouli, 2000).

Ahlam Husayn Jamil, *al-Afkar al-Siyasiya li al-Ahzab al-'Iraqiya fi 'Ahd al-Intidab* (Political ideas of the Iraqi parties in the mandate period) (Baghdad: Maktabat al-Muthana, 1985).

Husayn Jamil, *al-'Iraq al-Jadid* (The new Iraq) (Beirut, Lebanon: Dar Munaimana li al-Tiba'a wa al-Nashr, 1958).

Muhammad Mahdi al-Jawahiri, *Dhikrayati* (My memoirs) (Damascus: Dar al-Rafidayn, 1988).

'Ali Jawdat, *Dhikrayat, 1900–1958* (Memoirs, 1900–1958) (Beirut: Matabi' al-Wafa', 1967).

'Abd al-Jabbar Hasan al-Jubburi, *al-Ahzab wa al-Jim'iyat al-Siyasiyya fi al-Qitr al-Iraqi, 1908–1958* (Political parties and political societies in the Iraqi region, 1908–1958) (Baghdad: Dar al-Huriya li al-Tiba'a, 1977).

Muhamed 'Ali Kamal al-Din, *Thawrat al-'Ishrin fi Dhikraha al-Khamsin: Ma'lumat wa Mushahadat* (The 1920 revolution on its fiftieth anniversary: information and testimony) (Baghdad: Dar al-Bayan, 1971).

Khalil Kanna, *al-'Iraq: Amsuhu wa Ghadduhu* (Iraq: its yesterday and tomorrow) (Beirut, Lebanon: n.p., 1966).

Efraim Karsh and Inari Rautsi, *Saddam Hussein: A Political Biography* (New York: The Free Press, 1991).

Elie Kedouri, *The Chatham House Version and Other Middle Eastern Studies* (London: Weidenfeld and Nicolson, 1970).

———, *Democracy and Arab Political Culture* (Washington D.C.: The Washington Institute for Near East Policy, 1992).

———, *England and the Middle East: The Destruction of the Ottoman Empire, 1914–1921* (London: Bowes and Bowes, 1956).

Majid Khadduri, *Independent Iraq, 193–1958: A Study in Iraqi Politics* (London: Oxford University Press, 1960).

———, *Nidham al-Hukm fi al-'Iraq* (The system of governance in Iraq) (Baghdad: Matba'at al-Ma'arif, 1946).

Majid Khadduri, *Republican Iraq: A Study in Iraqi Politics Since the Revolution of 1958* (London: Oxford University Press, 1969).

———, "The Scheme of Fertile Crescent Unity: A Study in Inter-Arab Relations," in the *Near East and the Great Powers*, Richard N. Frye, ed., (Cambridge, Massachusetts: Harvard University Press, 1951).

'Adil Ghaffouri Khalil, *Ahzab al-Mu'aradha al-'Alaniya fi al-'Iraq, 1946–1954* (Public opposition parties in Iraq, 1946–1954) (Baghdad: al-Maktaba al-'Alamiya, 1984).

'Abd al-Hadi al-Khumasi, *al-Amir 'Abd al-Ilah, 1939–1958: Dirasa Tarikhiya Siyasiya* (Prince 'Abd al-Ilah, 1939–1958: a political historical study) (Beirut, Lebanon: al-Mu'asasa al-'Arabiya li al-Dirasat wa al-Nashr, 2001).

Hans Kohn, *Nationalism: Its Meaning and History* (Princeton, New Jersey: D. Van Nostrand Company, Inc., 1955).

———, *Prelude to Nation-States: The French and German Experience, 1789–1815* (London: D. Van Nostrand Company, 1967).

Muhammad Mahdi Kubba, *Mudhakirati fi Samim al-Ahdath, 1918–1958* (My memoirs in the midst of events, 1918–1958) (Beirut, Lebanon: Dar al-Tali'ah, 1965).

Harold Lasswell, *Politics: Who Gets What, When and How* (New York: McGraw-Hill, 1936).

Bernard Lewis, *The Middle East: A Brief History of the Last 2,000 Years* (New York: Scribner, 1995).

Seymour Martin Lipset, *Political Man: The Social Bases of Politics*, 3rd edition (Baltimore, Maryland: The Johns Hopkins University Press, 1981).

———, "Some Social Requisites of Democracy: Economic Development and Political Legitimacy," *The American Political Science Review*, vol. 53, no. 1, March 1959.

Stephen Hemsley Longrigg, *Iraq, 1900 to 1950: A Political, Social and Economic History* (London: Oxford University Press, 1953).

Liona Lukitz, *Iraq: The Search for National Identity* (London: Frank Cass, 1995).

Kanan Makiya, *Republic of Fear: The Politics of Modern Iraq*, updated edition (Berkeley, California: California University Press, 1998).

'Abd al-Ghani al-Mallah, *Tarikh al-Haraka al-Dimuqratiya fi al-'Iraq* (The history of the democratic movement in Iraq) (Baghdad: Wizarat al-I'lam, 1975).

Michael Mann, "The Autonomous Power of the State: Its Origins, Mechanisms and Results," in Michael Mann, ed., *States, War and Capitalism: Studies in Political Sociology* (Oxford, England: Blackwell, 1988).

David McDowall, *A Modern History of the Kurds* (London: I. B. Tauris, 1996).

Phebe Marr, "The Development of Nationalist Ideology in Iraq, 1920–1941," *The Muslim World*, vol. LXXV, no.2, April 1985.

———, *The Modern History of Iraq*, 2nd edition (Boulder, Colorado: Westview Press, 2004).

Muhammad Karim al-Mashhadani, *'Abd al-Rahman al-Bazzaz wa Dawruhu al-Fikri wa al-Siyasi fi al-'Iraq hatta Thawrat 17 Tamuz 1968* ('Abd al-Rahman al-Bazzaz and his ideational and political role in Iraq until the revolution of July 17, 1968) (Baghdad: Maktabat al-Yaqdha al-'Arabiya, 2002.

Selim Matar, *al-Dhat al-Jariha: Ishkalat al-Hawiya fi al-'Iraq wa al-'Alem al-'Arabi "al-Shirqani"* (Wounded essence: problems of identity in Iraq and the "Eastern" Arab world) (Beirut: al-Mu'asasa al-'Arabiya li al-Dirasat wa al-Nashr, 1997).

K. R. Minogue, *Nationalism* (New York: Basic Books, 1967).

Elizabeth Monroe, *Britain's Moment in the Middle East, 1914–1956* (Baltimore, Maryland: The Johns Hopkins University Press, 1963).

Malik Mufti, *Sovereign Creations: Pan Arabism and Political Order in Syria and Iraq* (Ithaca, New York: Cornell University Press, 1996).

Su'ad Rauf Muhamed, *Nuri al-Sa'id wa Dawruhu fi al-Siyasa al-'Iraqiya, 1932–1945* (Nuri al-Sa'id and his role in Iraqi politics, 1932–1945) (Baghdad: Maktabat al-Yaqdha al-'Arabiya, 1988).

'Abd al-Jabbar 'Abd Mustafa, *Tajribat al-'Amal al-Jabhawi fi al-'Iraq beina 1921 wa 1958* (The experiment of oppositional work in Iraq between 1921 and 1958) (Baghdad: Manshurat Wizarat al-Thaqafa wa al-Funoon, 1978).

Kadhim al-Musawi, *Al-'Iraq: Safahat min al-Tarikh al-Siyasi, 1945–1958* (Iraq: pages from political history, 1945–1958) (Damascus, Syria: Dar 'Ala' al-Din, 1998).

Taleb Mushtaq, *Awraq Ayami, al-Jusi' al-Awal, 1900–1958* (Papers from my days, volume one, 1900–1958) (Beirut: Dar al-Tali'a, 1968).

Wamidh Jamal 'Umar Nadhmi, "Fikr Sati' al-Husri al Qawmi," (The nationalist thought of Sati' al-Husri), *al-Mustaqbal al-'Arabi*, no. 81 (November 1985).

Haitham Ghaleb al-Nahi, *Khiyanat al-Nasr fi al-Kharita al-Siyasiya li al-Mu'aradha al-'Iraqiya* (The betrayal of victory in the political roadmap of Iraqi opposition) (London: al-Dar al-Andulusiya, 2002).

Yitzhak Nakash, *Reaching for Power: The Shi'a in the Modern Arab World* (Princeton, New Jersey: Princeton University Press, 2006).

———, *The Shi'is of Iraq* (Princeton, New Jersey: Princeton University Press, 1994).

'Aqeel al-Nasiri, *al-Jaysh wa al-Sullta fi al-'Iraq al-Malaki, 1921–1958* (The army and political authority in monarchical Iraq, 1921–1958) (Damascus, Syria: Dar al-Hassad li al-Nashr wa al-Tiba'a, wa al-Tawzi', 2000).

Salah Nasr, *'Abd al-Nasir wa Tajribat al-Wuhda* ('Abd al-Nasir and the unity experiment) (Beirut, Lebanon: al-Watan al-'Arabi, 1976).

George Packer, *The Assassins' Gate: America in Iraq* (New York: Farrar, Straus, and Giroux, 2005).

Andrew T. Parasiliti, *Iraq's War Decisions* (unpublished doctoral dissertation, The Johns Hopkins University, 1998).

Elie Podeh, *The Quest for Hegemony in the Arab World: The Struggle Over the Baghdad Pact* (Leiden: E. J. Brill, 1995).

Adam Przeworski, et al., *Democracy and Development: Political Institutions and Well-Being in the World, 1950–2000* (Cambridge, England: Cambridge University Press, 2000).

Adam Przeworski and Fernando Limongi, "Modernization: Theories and Facts," *World Politics*, vol. 49, no. 2, January 1997.

'Abd al-'Aziz al-Qassab, *Min Dhikrayati, 1888–1960* (From my memories, 1888–1960) (Beirut: 'Uwaidat Publications, 1962).

'Abdul Wahab Hamid Rashid, *al-'Iraq al-Mu'asir* (Contemporary Iraq) (Damascus, Syria: Dar al-Mada li al-Thaqafa wa al-Nashr, 2002).

Taghrid 'Abd al-Zahra Rashid, *al-Bilat al-Malaki al-'Iraqi fi al-Sanawat al-Multahiba, 1953–1958* (The Iraqi Royal Palace in the flammable years, 1953–1958) (Beirut, Lebanon: Dar Sader, 2004).

Khalid Habib al-Rawi, *Min Tarikh al-Sahafa al-'Iraqiya* (From the history of the Iraqi press) (Baghdad: Wizarat al-Thaqafa wa al-Funun, 1978).

Ernest Renan, "What is a Nation?," in Homi K. Bhabha, ed., *Nation and Narration* (London: Routledge, 1990).

Dietrich Rueschemeyer, Evelyne Huber Stephens, and John D. Stephens, *Capitalist Development and Democracy* (Chicago: University of Chicago Press, 1992).

Dankwart Rustow, "Transitions to Democracy: Toward a Dynamic Model," *Comparative Politics*, vol. 2, no, 3, 1970.

Salah al-Din al-Sabagh, *Fursan al-'Uruba fi al-'Iraq* (The knights of Arabism in Iraq) (Damascus: n.p., 1956).

Najdat Fathi Safwat, *al-'Iraq fi Mudhakarat al-Diblomasiyeen al-Ajanib* (Iraq in the memoirs of foreign diplomats) (Baghdad: Maktabat Dar al-Tarbiya, 1984).

Anis Sayegh, *al-Hashimiyoun wa Qadhiyat Filasteen* (The Hashemites and the Palestinian issue) (Beirut, Lebanon: Dar al-Tali'a, 1966).

Joseph A. Schumpeter, *Capitalism, Socialism and Democracy*, 2nd edition (New York: Harper, 1947).

Patrick Seale, *Asad of Syria: The Struggle for the Middle East* (Berkeley, California: University of California Press, 1988).

———, *The Struggle for Syria: A Study in Post-War Arab Politics, 1945–1958* (London: Oxford University Press, 1965).

Husayn al-Shahristani, *al-Hurub ila al-Huriya: Awraq min Ayam al-Mihna fi Sujun Saddam* (Flight to freedom: papers from the days of the ordeal in Saddam's prisons) (Tehran, Iran: Dar Muhibi al-Husayn, 2000).

Naji Shawkat, *Sira wa Dhikrayat thamaneena 'Aman, 1894–1974* (Biography and memoirs of eighty years, 1894–1974) (Baghdad: Maktabat al-Yaqdha al-'Arabiya, 1990).

Hassan Shibr, *al-'Amal al-Hizbi fi al-'Iraq, 1908–1958* (The activities of political parties in Iraq, 1908–1958) (Beirut, Lebanon: Dar al-Turath al-'Arabi, 1989).

Imam al-Sayyid Muhammad al-Husayni al-Shirazi, *Tilka al-Ayyam: Safahat min Tarikh al-'Iraq al-Siyasi* (Those days: pages from Iraq's political history) (Beirut, Lebanon: Misan li al Nashr wa al-Tawzi' wa al-I'lam, 2000).

Benjamin Shwadran, *The Power Struggle in Iraq* (New York: Council for Middle Eastern Affairs Press, 1960).

Reeva Spector Simon, *Iraq Between the Two World Wars: The Militarist Origins of Tyranny* (New York: Columbia University Press, 2004).

Jeanie Singleton, *Al-Hizb al-Watani al-Dimuqrati fi al-'Ahd al-Malaki* (The national democratic party in the monarchical era) (Beirut: al-Mu'asasa al-'Arabiya li al-Dirasat wa al-Nashr, 1999).

Peter Sluglett, *Britain in Iraq, 1914–1932* (London: Ithaca Press, 1976).

Robert Stephens, *Nasser: A Political Biography* (London: Allen Lane/Penguin Press, 1971).

Tawfiq al-Suwaydi, *Mudhakarati: Nisf Qarn min Tarikh al-'Iraq wa al-Qadhiya al-'Arabiya* (My memoirs: half a century of the history of Iraq and the Arab undertaking) (London: Dar al-Hikma, 1999).

Bassam Tibi, *Arab Nationalism: A Critical Enquiry* (New York: St. Martin's Press, 1981).

———, "The Simultaneity of the Unsimultaneous: Old Tribes and Imposed Nation-States in the Modern Middle East," in Philip S. Khoury and Joseph Kostiner, eds., *Tribes and State Formation in the Middle East* (Berkeley: University of California Press).

Charles Tilly, *Coercion, Capital and European States, A.D. 990–1992* (Cambridge, Massachusetts: Blackwell, 1990).

———, "War Making and State Making as Organized Crime," in Peter Evans, Dietrich Reuschemeyer, and Theda Skocpol, *Bringing the State Back* (London: Cambridge University Press, 1985).

'Abd al-Majid Kamel al-Tikriti, *Al-Malik Faysal al-Awal wa Dawruhu fi Ta'sis al-Dawla al-'Iraqiya al-Haditha, 1921–1933* (King Faysal I and his role in establishing the modern Iraqi state, 1921–1933) (Baghdad: Dar al Shu'un al-Thaqafiya al-'Amma, 1991).

————, *Majlis al-Umma al-'Iraqi: al-Barlaman, al-A'yan wa al-Nuwab, 1945–1953* (The National Assembly of Iraq: Parliament, senators and deputies, 1945–1953) (Baghdad: Dar al-Shu'un al-Thaqafiya al-'Amma, 2001).

Salman al-Tikriti, *al-Wasi 'Abd al-Ilah Yabhath 'an 'Arsh, 1939–1953* (Regent 'Abd al-Ilah searches for a thrown, 1939–1953) (Beirut, Lebanon: al-Dar al-'Arabiya li al-Mausou'at, 1989).

Khalid al-Timmimi, *Ja'far Abu al-Timman: Dirasa fi al-Za'ama al-Siyasiya al-'Iraqiya* (Ja'far Abu al-Timman: a study in Iraqi political leadership) (Damascus, Syria: Dar al-Waraq li al-Dirasat wa al-Nashr, 1996).

Charles Tripp, *A History of Iraq*, 2nd edition (Cambridge, England: Cambridge University Press, 2000).

Hadi Hassan 'Ulaywi, *al-Ahzab al-Siyasiya fi al-'Iraq: al-Siriya wa al-'Alaniya* (Political parties in Iraq: secret and public) (Beirut: Riad al-Rayyes li al-Kutub wa al-Nashr, 2001).

'Abd al-Karim al-Uzri, *Tarikh fi Dhikrayat al-'Iraq, 1930–1958* (History in the memoirs of Iraq, 1930–1958) (Beirut, Lebanon: Markaz al-Abjadiya, 1982).

P. J. Vatikiotis, "Dilemmas of Political Leadership in the Arab Middle East: The Case of the United Arab Republic," *American Political Science Review*, vol. 55, no. 1, March 1961.

'Abd al-Majid Hassan Wali and 'Ala' al-Din al-Rayyas, *Ahwal al-'Iraq al-Ijtima'iya wa al-Iqtisadiya* (Social and economic affairs of Iraq) (Baghdad: Mataba'at al-Rashid, 1946).

Janet Wallach, *The Desert Queen: The Extraordinary Life of Gertrude Bell* (New York: Doubleday, 1995).

'Ali al-Wardi, *Lamahat Ijtima'iya min Tarikh al 'Iraq al-Hadith* (Sociological aspects of the modern history of Iraq) six volumes, (London: Dar Kofan li al-Nashr, 1992).

Doreen Warriner, *Land Reform in Principle and Practice* (Oxford, England: Clarendon Press, 1969).

Hugh Seton Watson, *Nations and States: An Inquiry into the Origins of Nations and the Politics of Nationalism* (Boulder, Colorado: Westview Press, 1977).

Eugene Weber, *Peasants into Frenchmen: The Modernization of Rural France, 1870–1914* (London: Chatto and Windus, 1979).

Max Weber, *From Max Weber: Essays in Sociology* (London: Oxford University Press, 1946).

Lawrence Whitehead, *Democratization: Theory and Experience* (Oxford, England: Oxford University Press, 2002).

M. E. Yapp, *The Near East Since the First World War: A History to 1995*, 2nd edition (London: Longman, 1996).

Kerim Yildiz, *The Kurds in Iraq: The Past, Present and Future* (London: Pluto Press, 2004).

Laith 'Abd al-Hassan al-Zubaydi, *Thawrat 14 Tamuz 1958* (The July 14 Revolution) (Baghdad: Dar al-Rashid li al-Nashr, 1979).

DOCUMENTS AND NEWSPAPERS

Al-Ahali (Baghdad)

Al-Ahram (Cairo)

Al-'Arabiya Television

British Broadcasting Corporation, *Summary of World Broadcasts, Part IV: The Arab World, Israel, Greece, Turkey, Iran*

CNN International

Dawlat al-'Iraq, *Mahadhir Majlis al-Nuwab, 1930* (Debates of the Chamber of Deputies)

Dawlat al-'Iraq, *Mahadhir Majlis al-Nuwab, 1945–1946*

Dawlat al-'Iraq, *Mahadhir Majlis al-Nuwab, 1954*

The Economist (London)

The Guardian (London)

Al-Hayat (Beirut)

Al-Hukuma al-'Iraqiya, *Majmu'at Mudhkarat al-Majlis al-Ta'sisi al-'Iraqi li Sanat 1924, al-Jusi' al-Awal* (Collection of Memoirs of the Iraqi Constituent Assembly, 1924, volume one) (Baghdad: Matba'at Dar al-Salam, 1924)

Al-Jazeera Television

Middle East Economic Digest (London)

The New Republic

New York Times

Al-Quds al-'Arabi (London)

Al-Rafidayn (Baghdad),

Al-Sabah (Baghdad),

Sawt al-'Iraq (Baghdad)

Al-Sharq al-Awsat (London)

Statistical Abstract of the World, 2nd ed.

The Sunday Times (London)

Al-Thawra (Baghdad)

Transparency International, *Corruption Percentage Index, 2006*

United Arab Republic, *President Gamal Abd al-Nasser's Speeches and Press Interviews* (Cairo, Egypt: Information Department, 1959)

United Nations Assistance Mission for Iraq, *Humanitarian Briefing on the Crisis in Iraq, May 2007*

United Nations Assistance Mission for Iraq, *Human Rights Report*, various issues

United Nations, Department of Economic and Social Affairs, *Statistical Yearbook*, various years

United States Foreign Broadcast Information Service, *Daily Report, Foreign Radio Broadcasts*

United States Government Accounting Office (GAO), *Securing, Stabilizing and Rebuilding Iraq*, GAO-07–1195, September 2007

Al-Zaman (Baghdad)

INDEX